# Lecture Notes in Computer Scie

Commenced Publication in 1973
Founding and Former Series Editors:
Gerhard Goos, Juris Hartmanis, and Jan van Leeuwen

T0237804

## Editorial Board

Aditya Bagchi   Vijayalakshmi Atluri (Eds.)

# Information
# Systems
# Security

Second International Conference, ICISS 2006
Kolkata, India, December 19-21, 2006
Proceedings

 Springer

Volume Editors

Aditya Bagchi
Indian Statistical Institute
Computer and Statistical Service Center
203, B.T. Road, Kolkata, 700108, India
E-mail: aditya@isical.ac.in

Vijayalakshmi Atluri
Rutgers University
Department of Management Science and Information Systems
180 University Avenue, Newark, NJ 07102, USA
E-mail: atluri@cimic.rutgers.edu

Library of Congress Control Number: 2006938424

CR Subject Classification (1998): C.2.0, D.4.6, E.3, H.2.0, K.4.4, K.6.5

LNCS Sublibrary: SL 4 – Security and Cryptology

| ISSN | 0302-9743 |
| ISBN-10 | 3-540-68962-1 Springer Berlin Heidelberg New York |
| ISBN-13 | 978-3-540-68962-1 Springer Berlin Heidelberg New York |

Springer is a part of Springer Science+Business Media

springer.com

© Springer-Verlag Berlin Heidelberg 2006
Printed in Germany

Typesetting: Camera-ready by author, data conversion by Scientific Publishing Services, Chennai, India
Printed on acid-free paper     SPIN: 11961635     06/3142     5 4 3 2 1 0

# Preface

The 2nd International Conference on Information Systems Security (ICISS 2006) was held during December 19-21, 2006 at the Indian Statistical Institute, Kolkata, India. Following the success of the first conference also held at Kolkata, this conference attracted submissions from different parts of the globe. Besides India, the accepted papers are from Australia, Austria, France, Germany, Iran, Italy, Korea, New Zealand, Spain and USA. Out of the 20 full papers accepted for presentation, only 9 are from India. It shows that wihin two years, this conference has earned good acceptance among the research communities around the world.

The refereed papers, which were selected from 79 submissions, were rigorously reviewed by the Program Committee members. They did a wonderful job in selecting the best papers. The acceptance rate is 25%. Besides the 20 full papers, this volume also contains 4 invited papers, 5 short papers and 3 ongoing project summaries. The volume provides researchers with a broad perspective of recent developments in information systems security.

We are particularly grateful to Pierangela Samarati, Patrick McDaniel, Vipin Swarup and Nasir Memon for accepting our invitation to deliver invited talks at the conference. The conference was preceeded by four tutorials during December 17-18, 2006. We are thankful to Partha Pal, Ravi Mukkamala, Nasir Memon and Subhamoy Maitra for delivering the tutorial lectures. We are grateful to Birla Institute of Technology, Mesra, Ranchi for hosting the tutorials at their Kolkata Center. We are also grateful to Malay Kundu and Chandan Majumdar for serving as the General Chairs. We are indebted to the Director of the Indian Statistical Institute for hosting the conference this year as a part of the Platinum Jubilee Celebration of the institute.

Last, but certainly not least, our thanks go to all members of the Program Committee, volunteers and students of the Indian Statistical Institute and Rutgers University whose efforts made this conference a success.

December 2006

Aditya Bagchi
Vijayalakshmi Atluri
Program Chairs

# General Chairs' Message

After the success of the 1st International Conference on Information Systems Security (ICISS 2005), it was our pleasure to organize the 2nd Conference, ICISS 2006, at the Indian Statistical Institute, Kolkata, India during December 19-21, 2006. We are grateful to the Director of the institute for allowing us to organize the conference as part of the Platinum Jubilee Celebration of the institute.

This is the only conference organized in this part of the globe which is totally dedicated to information systems security. The basic aim of this conference is to provide a forum for interaction among researchers working in areas of information and system security both in India and abroad. We are very happy to note that within the short span of two years, the conference has drawn the attention of the international research community. As a result, we received a good number of submissions from many countries.

The Program Chairs, V. Atluri and A. Bagchi, along with a very committed and dedicated Program Committee did a wonderful job and maintained the high academic standard achieved in the first conference. We are very grateful to all members of the Program Committee. We are thankful to the tutorial speakers for offering interesting tutorials. We are also very grateful to the keynote speakers for accepting our invitations and for delivering highly thought-provoking lectures covering the current state of research and practice in different areas of information systems security.

The Organizing Committee under the leadership of S.C. Kundu also did a wonderful job. Organizing a conference needs money. We are particularly grateful to the Indian Statistical Institute for sponsoring this conference from the Platinum Jubilee Celebration fund. We are also grateful to all other sponsors for their generous help. In this connection, we take the opportunity to also thank Mandar Maitra, the Finance Chair of the conference.

December 2006

Malay K. Kundu
Chandan Mazumdar

# Organization

| | |
|---|---|
| Advisory Committee Chair | S.K. Pal |
| | Director |
| |     Indian Statistical Institute, Kolkata, India |
| General Chairs | Malay K. Kundu |
| | Indian Statistical Institute, Kolkata, India |
| | Chandan Mazumdar |
| | Jadavpur University, Kolkata, India |
| Program Chairs | Aditya Bagchi |
| | Indian Statistical Institute, Kolkata, India |
| | Vijayalakshmi Atluri |
| | Rutgers University, USA |
| Organizing Chair | S.C. Kundu |
| | Indian Statistical Institute, Kolkata, India |
| Tutorial Chair | Indrajit Ray |
| | Colorado State University, USA |
| Tutorial Coordinators | R.T. Goswami |
| | Birla Institute of Technology, Mesra, Ranchi, India |
| | Pinakpani Pal |
| | Indian Statistical Institute, Kolkata, India |
| Finance Chair | Mandar Mitra |
| | Indian Statistical Institute, Kolkata, India |
| Publicity Chair | B.B. Pant |
| | Birla Institute of Technology, Mesra, Ranchi, India |
| Industrial Track Chair | Kushal Banerjee |
| | Tata Consultancy Services, Kolkata, India |

## Steering Committee

| | |
|---|---|
| Sushil Jajodia | George Mason University, USA, Chair |
| Arun K. Majumdar | Indian Institute of Technology, Kharagpur, India |
| Aditya Bagchi | Indian Statistical Institute, Kolkata, India |
| Chandan Mazumdar | Jadavpur University, Kolkata, India |
| Vijay Varadharajan | Macquarie University, Australia |
| Pieranjela Samarati | University of Milan, Italy |
| R. Sekar | Stony Brook University, USA |
| A.K. Chakrabarti | Adviser, Dept. of IT, Govt. of India |
| N. Sitaram | Director, CAIR, India |
| Prem Chand | V.P., Mahindra British Telecom, India |

# Program Committee

| | |
|---|---|
| Mridul S. Barik | Jadavpur University, Kolkata, India |
| Rana Barua | Indian Statistical Institute, Kolkata, India |
| Joachim Biskup | University of Dortmund, Germany |
| B. Bruhadeshwar | IIIT, Hyderabad, India |
| Frdric Cuppens | ENST, France |
| Ernesto Damiani | University of Milan, Italy |
| Deborah Frincke | PNNL and University of Idaho, USA |
| K. Gopinath | Indian Institute of Science, India |
| Qijun Gu | Texas State University, USA |
| S.K. Gupta | Indian Institute of Technology, Delhi, India |
| Sushil Jajodia | George Mason University, USA |
| Christopher Kruegel | TU Vienna, Austria |
| Michiharu Kudo | IBM Tokyo Research Laboratory, Japan |
| Yingjiu Li | Singapore Management University, Singapore |
| Subhamoy Maitra | Indian Statistical Institute, Kolkata, India |
| A.K. Majumdar | Indian Institute of Technology, Kharagpur, India |
| Fabio Massacci | University of Trento, Italy |
| Patrick McDaniel | Pennsylvania State University, USA |
| Sharad Mehrotra | University of California, Irvine, USA |
| Ravi Mukkamala | Old Dominion University, USA |
| Sukumar Nandi | Indian Institute of Technology, Guwahati, India |
| Brajendra Panda | University of Arkansas, USA |
| Arun K. Pujari | University of Hyderabad, India |
| Indrajit Ray | Colorado State University, USA |
| Indrakshi Ray | Colorado State University, USA |
| Bimal Roy | Indian Statistical Institute, India |
| Pierangela Samarati | University of Milan, Italy |
| A.K. Sarje | Indian Institute of Technology, Roorkee, India |
| R. Sekar | Stony Brook University, USA |
| Indranil Sengupta | Indian Institute of Technology, Kharagpur, India |
| Basit Shafiq | Purdue University, USA |
| Shamik Sural | Indian Institute of Technology, Kharagpur, India |
| Kian-Lee Tan | National University of Singapore, Singapore |
| Patrick Traynor | Pennsylvania State University, USA |
| Jaideep Vaidya | Rutgers University, USA |
| Vijay Varadharajan | Macquarie University, Australia |
| Alec Yasinsac | Florida State University, USA |
| Meng Yu | Monmouth University, USA |
| Bill Yurcik | University of Illinois, USA |

# Advisory Committee

| | |
|---|---|
| S.K. Pal | Director, Indian Statistical Institute |
| S.K. Sanyal | Vice Chancellor, Jadavpur University |

A.R. Thakur                    Vice Chancellor, West Bengal University of
                               Technology
S.K. Mukherjee                 Vice Chancellor, Birla Institute of Technology,
                               Mesra, Ranchi
D. Dutta Mazumdar              Professor Emeritus, Indian Statistical Institute
B.B. Bhattacharya              Professor, Indian Statistical Institute
B. Chanda                      Professor In-Charge, Computer and Communica
                               tion Sciences Division, Indian Statistical
                               Institute
P.K. Das                       Chairman, IEEE Computer Chapter, Kolkata
                               Section

## Collaborating Institutions

Center for Secure Information Systems, George Mason University, USA
Center for Distributed Computing, Jadavpur University, India
Birla Institute of Technology, Mesra, Ranchi, India
IEEE Computer Chapter, Kolkata Section

# Table of Contents

## Invited Papers

## Data and Application Security

## Access Control

## Key Management and Security in Wireless Networks

## Threat Analysis, Detection and Recovery

## Cryptography and Encryption

## Short Papers and Research Reports

# Privacy in the Electronic Society

Sabrina De Capitani di Vimercati and Pierangela Samarati

Dipartimento di Tecnologie dell'Informazione
Università degli Studi di Milano
26013 Crema - Italy
samarati@dti.unimi.it

**Abstract.** Internet provides unprecedented opportunities for the collection and sharing of privacy-sensitive information from and about users. Information about users is collected every day, as they join associations or groups, shop for groceries, or execute most of their common daily activities. Such information is subsequently processed, exchanged and shared between different parties; with users often having users have often little control over their personal information once it has been disclosed to third parties. Privacy is then becoming an increasing concern. In this paper we discuss some problems to be addressed in the protection of information in our electronic society, surveying ongoing work and open issues to be investigated.

## 1  Introduction

We live today in a global information infrastructure connecting remote parties worldwide through the use of large scale networks, relying on application level protocols and services such as the World Wide Web. Human activities are increasingly based on the use of remote resources and services, and on the interaction between different, remotely located, and unknown parties. The vast amounts of personal information thus available has led to growing concerns about the privacy of users: effective information sharing and dissemination can take place only if there is assurance that, while releasing information, disclosure of sensitive information is not a risk.

Unfortunately, users' privacy is often poorly managed. For instance, personal information is often disclosed to third parties without the consent of legitimate data owners or that there are professional services specialized on gathering and correlating data from heterogeneous repositories, which permit to build user profiles and possibly to disclose sensitive information not voluntarily released by their owners. Ensuring proper privacy protection requires the investigation of different aspects. Among them, there we look at the following:

- *data protection requirements composition* to take into consideration requirements coming from the data owner, the data holder, and possible privacy law. These multiple authorities scenario should be supported from the administration point of view providing solutions for modular, large-scale, scalable policy composition and interaction.

A. Bagchi and V. Atluri (Eds.): ICISS 2006, LNCS 4332, pp. 1–21, 2006.

- *security and privacy specifications and secondary usage control* to identify
  under which conditions a party can trust others for their security and privacy.
  Trust models are one of the techniques be evaluated. In particular, *digital
  certificates* (statements certified by given entities) can be used to establish
  properties of their holder (such as identity, accreditation, or authorizations.
  Users should be given the ability to constraint possible secondary uses of
  their information.
- *inference and linking attacks protection* to ensure that released (sanitized)
  information is not open to channels allowing attackers to infer sensitive (not
  released, but related) information.

In this paper, we discuss these problems and illustrate some current approaches and ongoing research. The remainder of this paper is organized as follows. Section 2 addresses the problem of combining authorization specifications that may be independently stated. We describe the characteristics that a policy composition framework should have and illustrate some current approaches and open issues. Section 3 addresses the problem of defining policies in open environments such as the Internet. We then describe current approaches and open issues. Section 4 addresses the problem of protecting released data against inference and linking attacks. We describe the $k$-anonymity concept and illustrate some related current approaches and open issues. Finally, Section 5 concludes the paper.

## 2   Policy Composition

Traditionally, authorization policies have been expressed and managed in a centralized manner: one party administers and enforces the access control requirements. In many cases however, access control needs to combine restrictions independently stated that should be enforced as one, while retaining their independence and administrative autonomy. For instance, the global policy of a large organization can be the combination of the policies of its independent and geographically distributed departments. Each of these departments is responsible for defining access control rules to protect resources and each brings its own set of constraints. To address these issues, a *policy composition framework* by which different component policies can be integrated while retaining their independence should be designed. The framework should be flexible to support different kinds of composition, yet remain simple so to keep control over complex compound policies. It should be based on a solid formal framework and a clear semantics to avoid ambiguities and enable correctness proofs.

Some of the main requirements that a policy composition framework should have can be summarized as follows [11].

- *Heterogeneous policy support.* The composition framework should be able to
  combine policies expressed in arbitrary languages and possibly enforced by
  different mechanisms. For instance, a datawarehouse may collect data from
  different data sources where the security restrictions autonomously stated by

the sources and associated with the data are stated with different specification languages, or refer to different paradigms (e.g., open vs closed policy).

- *Support of unknown policies.* It should be possible to account for policies that may be not completely known or even be specified and enforced in external systems. These policies are like "black-boxes" for which no (complete) specification is provided, but that can be queried at access control time. Think, for instance, of a situation where given accesses are subject, in addition to other policies, to a policy $P$ enforcing "central administration approval". Neither the description of $P$, nor the specific accesses that it allows might be available; whereas $P$ can respond yes or no to each specific request. Runtime evaluation is therefore the only possible option for $P$. In the context of a more complex and complete policy including $P$ as a component, the specification could be partially compiled, leaving only $P$ (and its possible consequences) to be evaluated at run time.

- *Controlled interference.* Policies cannot always be combined by simply merging their specifications (even if they are formulated in the same language), as this could have undesired side effects. The accesses granted/denied might not correctly reflect the specifications anymore. As a simple example, consider the combination of two systems $P_{closed}$, which applies a closed policy, based on rules of the form "*grant access if $(s, o, +a)$*", and $P_{open}$ which applies an open policy, based on rules of the form "*grant access if $\neg(s, o, -a)$*". Merging the two specifications would cause the latter decision rule to derive all authorizations not blocked by $P_{open}$, regardless of the contents of $P_{closed}$. Similar problems may arise from uncontrolled interaction of the derivation rules of the two specifications. Besides, if the adopted language is a logic language with negation, the merged program might not be stratified (which may lead to ambiguous or undefined semantics).

- *Expressiveness.* The language should be able to conveniently express a wide range of combinations (spanning from minimum privileges to maximum privileges, encompassing priority levels, overriding, confinement, refinement etc.) in a uniform language. The different kinds of combinations must be expressed without changing the input specifications (as it would be necessary even in most recent and flexible approaches) and without ad-hoc extensions to authorizations (like those introduced to support priorities). For instance, consider a policy $P_1$ regulating access to given documents and the central administration policy $P_2$. Assume that access to administrative documents can be granted only if authorized by both $P_1$ and $P_2$. This requisite can be expressed in existing approaches only by explicitly extending all the rules possibly referred to administrative documents to include the additional conditions specified by $P_2$. Among the drawbacks of this approach is the rule explosion that it would cause and the complex structure and loss of controls of two specifications; which, in particular, cannot be maintained and managed autonomously anymore.

- *Support of different abstraction levels.* The composition language should highlight the different components and their interplay at different levels of abstraction. This is important to: *i)* facilitate specification analysis and design; *ii)* facilitate cooperative administration and agreement on global policies; *iii)* support incremental specification by refinement.

- *Support for dynamic expressions and controlled modifications.* Mobile policies that follow (*stick with*) the data and can be enriched, subject to constraints, as the data move.
- *Formal semantics.* The composition language should be declarative, implementation independent, and based on a solid formal framework. The need of an underlying formal framework is widely recognized and in particular it is important to *i)* ensure non-ambiguous behavior, and *ii)* reason about and prove specifications properties and correctness. In our framework this is particular important in the presence of *incomplete* specifications.

Various models have been proposed to reason about security policies [1,21,24,33,31]. In [1,24] the authors focused on the secure behavior of program modules. McLean [33] proposed a formal approach including combination operators: he introduced an algebra of security which enables to reason about the problem of policy conflict that can arise when different policies are combined. However, even though this approach permits to detect conflicts between policies, it did not propose a method to resolve the conflicts and to construct a security policy from inconsistent sub-policies. Hosmer [21] introduced the notion of meta-policies (i.e., policies about policies), an informal framework for combining security policies. Subsequently, Bell [8] formalized the combination of two policies with a function, called *policy combiner*, and introduced the notion of *policy attenuation* to allow the composition of conflicting security policies. Other approaches are targeted to the development of a uniform framework to express possibly heterogeneous policies [25,42]. Recently, Bonatti et al. [11] proposed an algebra for combining security policies together with its formal semantics. Following Bonatti et al.'s work, Jajodia et al. [41] presented a propositional algebra for policies with a syntax consisting of abstract symbols for atomic policy expressions and composition operators. The basic idea of these proposals is to define a set of policy operators used for combining different policies. In particular, in [11] a policy is defined as a set of triples of the form $(s,o,a)$, where $s$ is a constant in (or a variable over) the set of subjects S, $o$ is a constant in (or a variable over) the set of objects O, and $a$ is a constant in (or a variable over) the set of actions A. Here, complex policies can then be obtained by combining policy identifiers, denoted $P_i$, through the following *algebra operators*.

- *Addition* (+) merges two policies by returning their set union. For instance, in an organization composed of different divisions, access to the main gate can be authorized by any of the administrator of the divisions (each of them knows users who needs the access to get to their division). The totality of the accesses through the main gate to be authorized would then be the union of the statements of each single division. Intuitively, additions can be applied in any situation where accesses can be authorized if allowed by any of the component (operand) policies.
- *Conjunction* (&) merges two policies by returning their intersection. For instance, consider an organization in which divisions share certain documents

(e.g., clinical folders of patients). Access to the documents is to be allowed only if all the authorities that have a say on the document agree on it. Intuitively, while addition enforces maximum privilege, conjunction enforces minimum privilege.

- *Subtraction* (−) restricts a policy by eliminating all the accesses in the second policy. Intuitively, subtraction specifies exceptions to statements made by a policy and it encompasses the functionality of negative authorizations in existing approaches, while probably providing a clearer view of the combination of positive and negative statements. The advantages of subtraction over explicit denials include a simplification of the conflict resolution policies and a clearer semantics. In particular, the scoping of a difference operation allows to clearly and unambiguously express the two different uses of negative authorizations, namely *exceptions to positive statements* and *explicit prohibitions*, which are often confused in the models or requires explicit ad-hoc extension to the authorization form. The use of subtraction provides extensible as the policy can be enriched to include different overriding/conflict resolution criteria as needed in each specific context, without affecting the form of the authorizations.
- *Closure* (∗) closes a policy under a set of inference (derivation) rules. Intuitively, derivation rules can be thought of as logic rules whose head is the authorization to be derived and whose body is the condition under which the authorization can be derived. Examples of derivation rules can be found in essentially all logic based authorization languages proposed in the literature, where derivation rules are used, for example, to enforce propagation of authorizations along hierarchies in the data system, or to enforce more general forms of implication, related to the presence or absence of other authorizations, or depending on properties of the authorizations [25].
- *Scoping restriction* (ˆ) restricts the application of a policy to a given set of subjects, objects, and actions. Scoping is particularly useful to "limit" the statements that can be established by a policy and, in some way, enforcing authority confinement. Intuitively, all authorizations in the policy which do not satisfy the scoping restriction are ignored, and therefore ineffective. For instance, the global policy of an organization can identify several component policies which need to be merged together; each component policy may be restricted in terms of properties of the subjects, objects and actions occurring in its authorizations.[1]
- *Overriding* (o) replaces part of a policy with a corresponding fragment of the second policy. The portion to be replaced is specified by means of a third policy. For instance, consider the case where users of a library who have passed the due date for returning a book cannot borrow the same book anymore *unless* the responsible librarian vouchers for (authorizes) the loan. While the accesses otherwise granted by the library are stated as a policy $P_{lib}$, black-list of accesses, meaning triples (user, book, loan) are stated as a

---

[1] A simple example of scoping constraint is the limitation of authorizations that can be stated by a policy to a specific portion of the data system hierarchy [25].

policy $P_{block}$. In the absence of the *unless* portion of the policy, the accesses to be allowed would simply be $P_{lib} - P_{block}$. By allowing the librarian discretion for "overriding" the black list, calling $P_{vouch}$ the triples authorized by the librarians, we can express the overall policy as $o(P_{lib}, P_{vouch}, P_{block})$.

- *Template* ($\tau$) defines a partially specified policy that can be completed by supplying the parameters. Templates are useful for representing partially specified policies, where some component $X$ is to be specified at a later stage. For instance, $X$ might be the result of further policy refinement, or it might be specified by a different authority.

To fix ideas and make concrete examples, consider a drug-effects warehouse that might draw information from many hospitals. We assume that the warehouse receives information from three hospitals, denoted $h_1$, $h_2$, and $h_3$, respectively. These hospitals are responsible for granting access to information under their (possibly overlapping) authority domains, where domains are specified by a scoping function. The statements made by the hospitals are then unioned meaning that an access is authorized if any of the hospital policy states so. In term of the algebra, the warehouse policy can be represented as an expression of the form $P_1\hat{}[o \leq \mathsf{O}_{\mathsf{h}_1}] + P_2\hat{}[o \leq \mathsf{O}_{\mathsf{h}_2}] + P_3\hat{}[o \leq \mathsf{O}_{\mathsf{h}_3}]$, where $P_i$ denotes the policy defined by hospital $h_i$, and the scope restriction $\hat{}[o \leq \mathsf{O}_{\mathsf{h}_i}]$ selects the authorizations referred to objects released by hospital $h_i$.[2] Each policy $P_i$ can then be further refined. For instance, consider policy $P_1$. Suppose that hospital $h_1$ defines a policy $P_{drug}$ regulating the access to drug-effects information. Assume also that the drug-effects information can be released only if the hospital's researchers obtain a patient's consent; $P_{consents}$ reports accesses to drug-effects information that the patients agree to release. We can then express $P_1$ as $P_{drug}\&P_{consents}$.

## 2.1 Open Issues

We briefly describe some open issues that need to be taken into consideration in the future development of a policy composition framework.

- Investigate different *algebra operators and formal languages* for enforcing the algebra and proving properties. The proposed policy composition frameworks can be enriched by adding new operators. Also, the influence of different rule languages on the expressiveness of the algebra has to be investigated.
- *Administrative policies and language* with support for multiple authorities. The proposed approaches could be enriched by adding administrative policies that define who can specify authorizations/rules (i.e., who can define a component policy) governing access control.
- *Policy enforcement*. The resolution of the algebraic expression defining a policy $P$ determines a set of ground authorization terms, which define exactly the accesses to be granted according to $P$. Different strategies can be

---

[2] We assume that the information collected from the hospitals can be organized in abstractions defining groups of objects that can be collectively referred to with a given name. Objects and groups thereof define a partial order that naturally introduces a hierarchy, where $\mathsf{O}_{\mathsf{h}_i}$ contains objects obtained from hospital $h_i$.

used to evaluate the algebraic expression for enforcing access control: materialization, run-time evaluation, and partial evaluation. The first one allows a one-time compilation of the policy against which all accesses can be efficiently evaluated and which will then need to be updated only if the policy changes. The second strategy consists in enforcing a run-time evaluation of each request (access triple) against the policy expression to determine whether the access should be allowed. Between these two extremes, possibly combining the advantages of them, there are partial evaluation approaches, which can enforce different degrees of computation/materialization.

- Incremental approaches to enforce *changes to component policies*. When a materialization approach is used to evaluate the algebraic expression for enforcing access control, incremental approaches can be applied to minimize the recomputation of the policy [25].

- *Mobile policies*. Intuitively, a *mobile policy* is the policy associated with an object and that follows the object when it is passed to another site. Because different and possibly independent authorities can define different parts of the mobile policy in different time instants, the policy can be expressed as a policy expression. In such a context, there is the problem on how ensure the obedience of policies when the associated objects move around. Within the context of mobile policies we can also classify the problem of providing support for handling "sticky" policies [13], that is, policies that remain attached to data as they move between entities and are needed to enforce secondary use constraints (see Section 3). Mobile policies encompass also the problem of digital right management (DRM) as they also require constraints of the owner to remain attached to the data.

## 3   Access Control in Open Systems

Open environments are characterized by a number of systems offering different resources/services. In such a scenario, interoperability is a very important issue and traditional assumptions for establishing and enforcing policies do not hold anymore. A server may receive requests not just from the local community of users, but also from remote, previously unknown users. The server may not be able to authenticate these users or to specify authorizations for them (with respect to their identity). Early approaches that attempt to solve these issues, PolicyMaker [10] and KeyNote [9], basically use credentials to describe specific delegation of trusts among keys and to bind public keys to authorizations. Although early trust management systems do provide an interesting framework for reasoning about trust between unknown parties, assigning authorizations to keys may result limiting and make authorization specifications difficult to manage.

A promising direction to overcome such a disadvantage is represented by *digital certificates*. A digital certificate is basically the on-line counterparts of paper credentials (e.g., drivers licenses). Digital certificates can be used to determine whether or not a party may execute an access on the basis properties that the requesting party may have. These properties can be proven by presenting one or

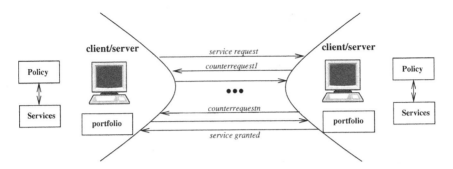

**Fig. 1.** Client/server interaction

more certificates [22,29,35,48]. The development and effective use of credential-based models require tackling several problems related to credential management and disclosure strategies, delegation and revocation of credentials, and establishment of credential chains [19,30,39,40,47].

Figure 1 depicts the basic scenario we consider. We are given different parties that interact with each other to offer services. A party can act both as a server and a client and each party has *i)* a set of services it provides and *ii)* a *portfolio* of properties (attributes) that the party enjoys. Access restrictions to the services are expressed by policies that specified the properties that a requester should enjoy to gain access to the services. The services are meant to offer certain functionalities that depend on the input parameters supplied by its users. Often input parameters must fulfill certain conditions to assure correct behavior of a service. We identified the following requirements for specifying credential-based access control.

- *Attribute interchange.* A server should be able to communicate to the client the requirements it need to satisfy to get access. Also, a client should be able to prove its eligibility for a service. This communication interchange could be performed in different ways (e.g., the involved parties can apply different strategies with respect to which properties are submitted).
- *Support for fine-grained reference to attributes within a credential.* The system should allow the selective disclosure of credentials which is a requirement that is not usually supported because users attributes are defined according to functional needs, making it easier to collect all credentials in a row instead of iteratively asking for the ones strictly necessary for a given service only.
- *Support for hierarchical relationships and abstractions on services and portfolio.* Attribute-based access control policies should be able to specify accesses to collection of services based upon collection of attributes processed by the requester.
- *Expressiveness and flexibility.* The system must support the specification of complex access control requirements. For instance, consider a service that offers telephone contracts and requires that the customer is at least 18 years of age. The telephone selling service has two input parameters, namely

`homeAddress` and `noticePeriod`. The `homeAddress` must be a valid address in Italy and `noticePeriod` must be either one or three months. Further, the service's access control policy requires that contracts with one month notice period and home address outside a particular geographical region are closed only with users who can prove their AAA membership. Hence, we see that the access control requirements of a service may require more than one interaction between a client and a server.

– *Purpose specific permission.* The permission to release data should relate to the purpose for which data are being used or distributed. The model should prevent information collected for one purpose from being used for other purposes.

– *Support for meta-policies.* The system should provide meta-policies for protecting the policy when communication requisites. This happens when a list of alternatives (policies) that must be fulfilled to gain the access to the data/service is returned to the counterpart. For instance, suppose that the policy returned by the system is "citizenship=EU". The party can decide to return to the client either the policy as it is or a modified policy simply requesting the user to prove its nationality (then protecting the information that access is restricted to EU citizens).

– *Support for secondary use specifications and control.* The information owner should be able to control further dissemination and use of personal information. This represents a novel feature that is no simply concerned with authorizing the access to data and resources but also with defining and enforcing the way data and resources are subsequently managed.

### 3.1 Overview of Ongoing Work

The first proposals investigating the application of credential-based access control regulating access to a server were made by Winslett et al. [39]. Here, access control rules are expressed in a logic language and rules applicable to an access can be communicated by the server to clients. In [47] the authors investigated trust negotiation issues and strategies that a party can apply to select credentials to submit to the opponent party in a negotiation. In [12] the authors proposed a uniform framework for regulating service access and information disclosure in an open, distributed network system like the Web. Like in previous proposals, access regulations are specified as logical rules, where some predicates are explicitly identified. Certificates are modeled as *credential expressions* of the form "credential_name(attribute_list)", where credential_name is the attribute credential name and attribute_list is a possibly empty list of elements of the form "attribute_name=value_term", where value_term is either a ground value or a variable. Besides credentials, the proposal also allows to reason about declarations (i.e., unsigned statements) and user-profiles that the server can maintain and exploit for taking the access decision. Communication of requisites to be satisfied by the requester is based on a filtering and renaming process applied on the server's policy, which exploits partial evaluation techniques in logic programs. Yu et al. [47,48] developed a service negotiation framework for requesters and providers to gradually expose their attributes. The *PRUdent NEgotiation Strategy* (PRUNES) in [47] has been presented ensures that the client communicates its credentials to the server only if the access will be granted and the set of certificates communicated to the server is the minimal necessary for granting it. Each party defines a set of *credential policies* that regulates how and under what conditions the party releases its credentials. The negotiation consists of a series of requests for credentials and counter-requests on the basis of the parties' credential policies. The credential policies established can be graphically represented through a tree, called *negotiation search tree*, composed of two kinds of nodes: *credential nodes*, representing the need for a specific credential, and *disjunctive nodes*, representing the logic operators connecting the conditions for credential release. The root of a tree node is a service (i.e., the resource the client wants to access). The negotiation can therefore be seen as a backtracking operation on the tree. The backtracking can be executed according to different strategies. For instance, a *brute-force* backtracking is complete and correct, but is too expensive to be used in a real scenario. The authors therefore proposed the PRUNES method that prunes the search tree without compromising completeness or correctness of the negotiation process. The basic idea is that if a credential $C$ has just been evaluated and the state of the system is not changed too much, than it is useless to evaluate again the same credential, as the result will be exactly as the result previously computed. The same research group proposed also a method for allowing parties adopting different negotiation strategies to interoperate through the definition of a *Disclosure Tree Strategy* (DTS) family [48]. The authors show that if two parties use different strategies from the DST family, they are able to establish a negotiation process. The DTS family is a closed set, that is, if a negotiation strategy can interoperate with any DST strategy, it must also be a member of the DST family.

In [46] a *Unified Schema for Resource Protection* (UniPro) has been proposed. This mechanism is used to protect the information in policies. UniPro gives (opaque) names to policies and allows any named policy $P_1$ to have its own policy $P_2$ meaning that the contents of $P_1$ can only be disclosed to parties who have shown that they satisfy $P_2$. Another approach for implementing access control based on credentials is the *Adaptive Trust Negotiation and Access Control* (ATNAC) [36]. This method grants or denies access to a resource on the basis of a *suspicion level* associated with subjects. The suspicion level is not fixed but may vary on the basis of the probability that the user has malicious intents. In [48] the authors presented a negotiation architecture, called *TrustBuilder*, that is independent from the language used for policy definition and from the strategies adopted by the two parties for policy enforcement. Other logic-based access control languages based on credentials have been introduced. For instance, D1LP and RT [28], the SD3 language [26], and Binder [17]. In [25,42] logic languages are adopted to specify access restrictions in a certificate-based access control model.

Some proposals have instead addressed the problem of how to regulate the use of personal information in secondary applications. In [5], the authors proposed an XML-based privacy preference expression language, called *PReference Expression for Privacy* (PREP), for storing the user's privacy preferences with Liberty Alliance. PREP allows users to specify, for each attribute, a *privacy label* that is characterized by a purpose, type of access, recipient, data retention, remedies, and disputes. The *Platform for Privacy Preferences Project* (P3P) [44] is another XML-based language that allows service providers and users to reach an agreement on the release of personal data. Basically, a service provider can define a P3P policy, which is an XML document, where it is possible to define the recipient of the data, desired data, consequence of data release, purpose of data collection, data retention policy, and dispute resolution mechanisms. Users specify their privacy preferences in term of a policy language, called APPEL [43], and enforce privacy protection through a user agent: the user agent compares the users' privacy policy with the service provider P3P policy and checks whether the P3P policy conforms to the user privacy preferences. Although P3P is a good starting point, it is not widely adopted by the service providers and presents some limitations on the user side [4]. The main limitation is that the definition of simple privacy preferences is a complex task and writing APPEL preferences is error prone. For this reason, Agrawal et al. [4] proposed a new language, called XPref, for user preferences. However, both APPEL and XPref are not sufficiently expressive because, for example, they do not support negotiation and contextual information, and they do not allow the definition of attribute-based conditions. Another important disadvantage of these approaches is that users have a passive role: a service provider defines a privacy policy that users can only accept or reject. In [6] a new type of privacy policy, called *data handling policy*, that regulates the secondary use of a user's personal data has been discussed. A data handling policy regulates how Personal Identifiable Information (PII) will be used (e.g., information collected through a service will be combined with information collected from other services and used in aggregation for market research purposes), how long PII will be retained (e.g., information will be retained as long as necessary to perform the service), and so on. Users can therefore use these policies to define how their information will be used and processed by the counterpart.

## 3.2  Open Issues

Although current approaches supporting attribute-based policies are technically mature enough to be used in practical scenarios, there are still some issues that need to be investigated in more detail to enable more complex applications. We summarize these issues as follows [12].

- *Ontologies.* Due to the openness of the scenario and the richness and variety of security requirements and attributes that may need to be considered, it is important to provide parties with a means to understand each other with respect to the properties they enjoy (or request the counterpart to enjoy). Therefore, common languages, dictionaries, and ontologies must be developed.

- *Access control evaluation and outcome.* Users may be occasional and they may not know under what conditions a service can be accessed. Therefore, to make a service "usable", access control mechanisms cannot simply return "yes" or "no" answers. It may be necessary to explain why authorizations are denied, or - better - how to obtain the desired permissions.
- *Privacy-enhanced policy communication.* Since access control does not return only a "yes" or "no" access decision, but it returns the information about which conditions need to be satisfied for the access to be granted ("undefined" decision), the problem of communicating such conditions to the counterpart arises. To fix the ideas, let us see the problem from the point of view of the server (the client's point of view is symmetrical). A naive solution consists in giving the client a list with all the possible sets of credentials that would enable the service. This solution is however not feasible due to the large number of possible alternatives. Also, the communication process should not disclose "too much" of the underlying security policy, which might also be regarded as sensitive information.
- *Negotiation strategy.* Credentials grant parties different choices with respect to what release (or ask) the counterpart and when to do it, thus allowing for multiple trust negotiation strategies [48]. For instance, an *eager* strategy, requires parties to turn over all their credentials if the release policy for them is satisfied, without waiting for the credentials to be requested. By contrast, a *parsimonious* strategy requires that parties only release credentials upon explicit request by the server (avoiding unnecessary releases).
- *Composite services.* In case of a composite service (i.e., a service that is decomposable into other services called component services) there must be a semi-automatic mechanism to calculate the policy of a composite service from the policies of its component services.
- *Semantics-aware rules.* Although attribute-based policies allow the specifications of restrictions based on generic attributes or properties of the requestor and the resources, they do not fully exploit the semantic power and reasoning capabilities of emerging web applications. It is therefore important to be able to specify access control rules about subjects accessing the information and about resources to be accessed in terms of rich ontology-based metadata (e.g., Semantic Web-style ones) increasingly available in advanced e-services applications [16].

## 4    Privacy Issues in Data Collection and Disclosure

Inference and linking attacks are becoming today easier and easier because of the increased information availability and ease of access as well as the increased computational power provided by today's technology. Released data too often open up privacy vulnerabilities through, for example, data mining techniques and record linkage. Indeed, the restricted access to information and its expensive processing, which represented a form of protection in the past do not hold anymore. In addition, while in the past data were principally released in tabular form (macrodata) and through statistical databases, many situations require today that the specific stored data themselves, called microdata, be released. The advantage of releasing microdata instead of specific pre-computed statistics is an increased flexibility and availability of information for the users. At the same time however microdata, releasing more specific information, are subject to a greater risk of privacy breaches. To this purpose, the main requirements that must be taken into account are the following.

- *Identity disclosure protection.* Identity disclosure occurs whenever it is possible to identify a subject, called *respondent*, from the released data. It should therefore be adopted techniques for limiting the possibility of identifying respondents.
- *Attribute disclosure protection.* Identity disclosure protection alone do not guarantee privacy of sensitive information because all the respondents in a group could have the same sensitive information. To overcome this issue, mechanisms that protect sensitive information about respondents should be adopted.
- *Inference channel.* Given the possibly enormous amount of data to be considered, and the possible inter-relationships between data, it is important that the security specification and enforcement mechanisms provide automatic support for complex security requirements, such as those due to inference and data association channels.

To protect the anonymity of the respondents to whom the released data refer, data holders often remove, encrypt, or code identity information. Identity information removed or encoded to produce anonymous data includes names, telephone numbers, and Social Security Numbers. Although apparently anonymous, however, the de-identified data may contain other quasi-identifying attributes such as race, date of birth, sex, and geographical location. By linking such attributes to publicly available databases associating them with the individual's identity, data recipients can determine to which individual each piece of released data belongs, or restrict their uncertainty to a specific subset of individuals. This problem has raised particular concerns in the medical and financial fields, where microdata, which are increasingly released for circulation or research, can be or have been subject to abuses, compromising the privacy of individuals.

To better illustrate the problem, consider the microdata table in Figure 2(a) and the non de-identified public available table in Figure 2(b). In the microdata table, which we refer to as private table (PT), data have been de-identified by suppressing names and Social Security Numbers (SSNs) so not to explicitly disclose the identities of respondents. However, the released attributes Race, Date of birth, Sex, ZIP, and Marital status can be linked to the public tuples in Figure 2(b) and reveal information on Name, Address, and City. In the private table, for example, there is only one single female (F) born on 71/07/05 and living in the 20222 area. This combination, if unique in the external world as well, uniquely identifies the corresponding tuple as pertaining to "Susan Doe, 20222 Eye Street, Washington DC", thus revealing that she has reported hypertension. While this example demonstrates an exact match, in some cases,

| SSN | Name | Race | Date of birth | Sex | ZIP | Marital status | Disease |
|-----|------|------|---------------|-----|-----|----------------|---------|
| | | asian | 71/07/05 | F | 20222 | Single | hypertension |
| | | asian | 74/04/13 | F | 20223 | Divorced | Flu |
| | | asian | 74/04/15 | F | 20239 | Married | chest pain |
| | | asian | 73/03/13 | M | 20239 | Married | Obesity |
| | | asian | 73/03/18 | M | 20239 | Married | hypertension |
| | | black | 74/11/22 | F | 20238 | Single | short breath |
| | | black | 74/11/22 | F | 20239 | Single | Obesity |
| | | white | 74/11/22 | F | 20239 | Single | Flu |
| | | white | 74/11/22 | F | 20223 | Widow | chest pain |

(a)

| Name | Address | City | ZIP | DOB | Sex | Status |
|------|---------|------|-----|-----|-----|--------|
| ............ | ............. | ............. | ...... | ...... | ...... | ............. |
| Susan Doe | Eye street | Washington DC | 20222 | 71/07/05 | F | single |
| ............ | ............. | ............. | ...... | ...... | ...... | ............. |

(b)

**Fig. 2.** An example of private table PT (a) and non de-identified public available table

linking allows one to detect a restricted set of individuals among whom there is the actual data respondent.

## 4.1 Overview of Ongoing Work

Among the microdata protection techniques used to protect de-identified microdata from linking attacks, there are the commonly used approaches like sampling, swapping values, and adding noise to the data while maintaining some overall statistical properties of the resulting table. For a comprehensive review of these approaches see [15]. However, many uses require the release and explicit management of microdata while needing truthful information within each tuple. This "data quality" requirement makes inappropriate those techniques that disturb data and therefore, although preserving statistical properties, compromise the correctness of single tuples [15]. $k$-anonymity, together with its enforcement via *generalization* and *suppression*, has been proposed as an approach to protect respondents' identities while releasing truthful information [38,37].

The concept of $k$-anonymity tries to capture, on the private table to be released, one of the main requirements that has been followed by the statistical community and by agencies releasing the data, and according to which the *released data should be indistinguishably related to no less than a certain number of respondents*.

The set of attributes included in the private table, also externally available and therefore exploitable for linking, is called *quasi-identifier*. The requirement above-mentioned is then translated in the $k$-anonymity requirement [37]: *each release of data must be such that every combination of values of quasi-identifiers can be indistinctly matched to at least $k$ respondents*. Since it seems impossible, or highly impractical and limiting, to make assumptions on the datasets available for linking to external attackers or curious data recipients, essentially $k$-anonymity takes a safe approach requiring that, in the released table itself, the respondents be indistinguishable (within a given set) with respect to a set of attributes. To guarantee the $k$-anonymity requirement, $k$-anonymity requires each quasi-identifier value in the released table to have at least $k$ occurrences. This is clearly a sufficient condition for the $k$-anonymity requirement: if a set of attributes of external tables appears in the quasi-identifier associated with the private table PT, and the table satisfies this condition, the combination of the released data with the external data will never allow the recipient to associate each released tuple with less than $k$ respondents. For instance, with respect to the microdata table in Figure 1 and the quasi-identifier Race, Date of birth, Sex, ZIP, Marital status, the table satisfies $k$-anonymity with $k = 1$ only, since there are single occurrences of values over the quasi-identified (e.g., "asian, 71/07/05, F, 20222, single").

$k$-anonymity proposals focus on *generalization* and *suppression* techniques. Generalization consists in representing the values of a given attribute by using more general values. This technique is based on the definition of a *generalization hierarchy*, where the most general value is at the root of the hierarchy and the leaves correspond to the most specific values. Formally, the notion of *domain* (i.e., the set of values that an attribute can assume) is extended by assuming the existence of a set of *generalized domains*. The set of original domains together with their generalizations is referred to as Dom. Each generalized domain contains generalized values and there exists a mapping between each domain and its generalizations. This mapping is stated by means of a *generalization relationship* $\leq_D$. Given two domains $D_i$ and $D_j \in$ Dom, $D_i \leq_D D_j$ states that values in domain $D_j$ are generalizations of values in $D_i$. The generalization relationship $\leq_D$ defines a partial order on the set Dom of domains, where each $D_i$ has at most *one* direct generalization domain $D_j$, and all values in each domain can always be generalized to a single value. The definition of a generalization relationship implies the existence, for each domain $D \in$ Dom, of a totally ordered hierarchy, called *domain generalization hierarchy*, denoted $DGH_D$. As an example, consider attribute ZIP code and suppose that a step in the corresponding generalization hierarchy consists in suppressing the least significant digit in the ZIP code. Figure 3 illustrates the corresponding domain generalization hierarchy. In this case, for example, if we choose to apply one generalization step, values 20222, 20223, 20238, and 20239 are generalized to 2022* and 2023*. A generalization process therefore proceeds by replacing the values represented by the leaf nodes with one of their ancestor nodes at a higher level. Different generalized microdata tables can be built, depending on the amount of generalization applied on the considered attribute.

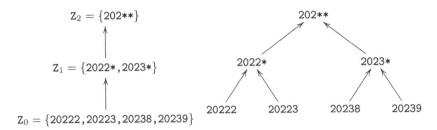

**Fig. 3.** An example of domain generalization hierarchy for attribute ZIP

Suppression is a well-known technique that consists in protecting sensitive information by removing it. The introduction of suppression can reduce the amount of generalization necessary to satisfy the $k$-anonymity constraint.

Generalization and suppression can be applied at different levels of granularity. Generalization can be applied at the level of single column (i.e., a generalization step generalizes all the values in the column) or single cell (i.e., for a specific column, the table may contain values at different generalization levels). Suppression can be applied at the level of row (i.e., a suppression operation removes a whole tuple), column (i.e., a suppression operation obscures all the values of a column), or single cells (i.e., a $k$-anonymized table may wipe out only certain cells of a given tuple/attribute). The possible combinations of the different choices for generalization and suppression (including also the choice of not applying one of the two techniques) result in different $k$-anonymity proposals and different algorithms for $k$-anonymity.

Note that the algorithms for solving $k$-anonymity aim at finding a $k$-minimal table, that is, one that does not generalize (or suppress) more than it is needed to reach the threshold $k$. As an example, consider the microdata table in Figure 2(a) and suppose that the quasi-identifier is {Race, Date of birth, Sex, ZIP}.

Figure 4 illustrates an example of 2-anonymous table obtained by applying the algorithm described in [37], where generalization is applied at the column level and suppression is applied at the row level. Note that the first tuple in the original table has been suppressed and attribute Date of birth has been generalized by removing the day and attribute ZIP has been generalized by applying two generalization steps along the domain generalization hierarchy in Figure 3.

In [14] we defined a possible taxonomy for $k$-anonymity and discussed the main proposals existing in the literature for solving the $k$-anonymity problems. Basically, the algorithms for enforcing $k$-anonymity can be partitioned into three main classes: *exact*, *heuristic*, and *approximation* algorithms, respectively. While exact and heuristic algorithms produce $k$-anonymous tables by applying attribute generalization and tuple suppression and are exponential in the size of the quasi-identifier [7,20,27,37,23], approximation algorithms produce $k$-anonymous tables by applying cell suppression without generalization or cell generalization without suppression [2,3,34]. In these case, exact algorithms are not applicable because the computational time could be exponential in the number of tuples in the table.

| SSN | Name | Race | Date of birth | Sex | ZIP | Marital status | Disease |
|---|---|---|---|---|---|---|---|
| | | asian | 74/04/ | F | 202** | divorced | Flu |
| | | asian | 74/04/ | F | 202** | married | chest pain |
| | | asian | 73/03/ | M | 202** | married | obesity |
| | | asian | 73/03/ | M | 202** | married | hypertension |
| | | black | 74/11/ | F | 202** | single | short breath |
| | | black | 74/11/ | F | 202** | single | obesity |
| | | white | 74/11/ | F | 202** | single | flu |
| | | white | 74/11/ | F | 202** | Widow | chest pain |

**Fig. 4.** An example of a 2-anonymized table for the private table PT in Figure 2(a)

Samarati [37] presented an algorithm that exploits a binary search on the domain generalization hierarchy to avoid an exhaustive visit of the whole generalization space. Since the $k$-anonymity definition is based on a quasi-identifier, the algorithm works only on this set of attributes and on tables with more than $k$ tuples (this last constraint being clearly a necessary condition for a table to satisfy $k$-anonymity). Bayardo and Agrawal [7] presented an optimal algorithm, called $k$-*Optimize*, that starts from a fully generalized table (with all tuples equal) and specializes the dataset in a minimal $k$-anonymous table, exploiting ad-hoc pruning techniques. LeFevre, DeWitt, and Ramakrishnan [27] described an algorithm that uses a bottom-up technique and a priori computation.

Iyengar [23] presented genetic heuristic algorithms and solves the $k$-anonymity problem using an incomplete stochastic search method. The method does not assure the quality of the solution proposed, but experimental results show the validity of the approach. Fung, Wang and Yu [20] presented a top-down heuristic to make a table to be released $k$-anonymous. The algorithm starts from the most general solution, and iteratively specializes some values of the current solution until the $k$-anonymity requirement is violated. Each step of specialization increases the information and decreases the anonymity.

Meyerson and Williams [34] presented an algorithm for $k$-anonymity, which guarantees a $O(k \log(k))$-approximation. Aggarwal et al. [2,3] illustrated two approximation algorithms that guarantee a $O(k)$-approximation solution. Note that although both heuristics and approximation algorithms do not guarantee the minimality of their solution, and we cannot perform any evaluation on the result of a heuristic, an approximation algorithm guarantees near-optimum solutions.

$k$-anonymity is also currently the subject of many interesting studies. In particular, these studies aim at: studying efficient algorithms for $k$-anonymity enforcement; using $k$-anonymity as a measure on information disclosure due to a set of views [45]; extending its definition to protect the released data against attribute, in contrast to identity, disclosure ($\ell$-diversity) [32]; supporting fine-grained application of generalization and suppression; and investigating additional techniques for $k$-anonymity enforcement [18].

## 4.2 Open Issues

We now summarize the main open issues in developing a $k$-anonymity solution.

- *Extensions and enrichment of the definition.* $k$-anonymity captures only the defence against identity disclosure attacks, while remaining exposed to attribute disclosure attacks [37]. Some researchers have just started proposing extensions to $k$-anonymity [32] to capture also attribute disclosure, however research is still to be done.
- *Protection against utility measures.* As we can imagine the more the protection, the less precise or complete the data will be. Research is needed to develop measures to allow users to assess, besides the protection offered by the data, the utility of the released data. Clearly, utility may be different depending on the data recipients and the use intended for the information. Approaches should be therefore devised that maximize information utility with respect to intended uses, while properly guaranteeing privacy
- *Efficient algorithms.* Computing a table that satisfies $k$-anonymity guaranteeing minimality (i.e., minimal information loss or, in other words, maximal utility) is an NP-hard problem and therefore computationally expensive. Efficient heuristic algorithms have been designed, but still research in needed to improve the performance. Indexing techniques could be exploited in this respect.
- *New techniques.* The original k-anonymity proposal assumed the use of generalization as suppression since, unlike others, they preserve truthfulness of the data. The $k$-anonymity property is however not tied to a specific technique and alternative techniques could be investigated.
- *Merging of different tables and views.* The original $k$-anonymity proposal as well as most subsequent work assume the existence of a single table to be released with the further constraints that the table contains at most one tuple for each respondents. Work is needed to release these two constraints. In particular, the problem of releasing different tables providing anonymity even in presence of join that can allow inferring new information needs to be investigated.
- *External knowledge.* $k$-anonymity assumes the data recipient has access to external database linking identities with quasi identifiers; it did not however model external knowledge that can be further exploited for inference and expose the data to identity or attribute disclosure. Work is needed to allow modeling external knowledge and taking it into account in the process of computing the table to be released.

# 5   Conclusions

This paper discussed aspect related to the protection of information in today's globally networked society. We outlined the needs for providing means to: combine security specifications to enforce security (and privacy) in the dynamic interactions among different, possibly unknown, parties; protect privacy in the dissemination of data. For these contexts, we discussed ongoing researches and open challenges.

## Acknowledgements

This work was supported in part by the European Union within the PRIME Project in the FP6/IST Programme under contract IST-2002-507591 and by the Italian MIUR within the KIWI and MAPS projects.

## References

1. M. Abadi and L. Lamport. Composing specifications. *ACM Transactions on Programming Languages*, 14(4):1–60, October 1992.
2. G. Aggarwal, T. Feder, K. Kenthapadi, R. Motwani, R. Panigrahy, D. Thomas, and A. Zhu. Anonymizing tables. In *Proc. of the 10th International Conference on Database Theory (ICDT'05)*, pages 246–258, Edinburgh, Scotland, January 2005.
3. G. Aggarwal, T. Feder, K. Kenthapadi, R. Motwani, R. Panigrahy, D. Thomas, and A. Zhu. Approximation algorithms for $k$-anonymity. *Journal of Privacy Technology*, paper number 20051120001, 2005.
4. R. Agrawal, J. Kiernan, R. Srikant, and Y. Xu. An xpath based preference language for P3P. In *Proc. of the 12th International World Wide Web Conference*, Budapest, Hungary, May 2003.
5. Gail-J. Ahn and J. Lam. Managing privacy preferences in federated identity management. In *Proc. of the ACM Workshop on Digital Identity Management*, Fairfax, VA, USA, November 2005.
6. C.A. Ardagna, S. De Capitani di Vimercati, and P. Samarati. Enhancing user privacy through data handling policies. In *Proc. of the 20th IFIP WG 11.3 Conference on Data and Applications Security*, Sophia Antipolis, France, August 2006.
7. R.J. Bayardo and R. Agrawal. Data privacy through optimal $k$-anonymization. In *Proc. of the 21st International Conference on Data Engineering (ICDE'05)*, pages 217–228, Tokyo, Japan, April 2005.
8. D.E. Bell. Modeling the multipolicy machine. In *Proc. of the New Security Paradigm Workshop*, August 1994.
9. M. Blaze, J. Feigenbaum, J. Ioannidis, and A.D. Keromytis. *The KeyNote Trust Management System (Version 2)*, internet rfc 2704 edition, 1999.
10. M. Blaze, J. Feigenbaum, and J. Lacy. Decentralized trust management. In *Proc. of the 17th IEEE Symp. on Security and Privacy*, Oakland, CA, May 1996.
11. P. Bonatti, S. De Capitani di Vimercati, and P. Samarati. An algebra for composing access control policies. *ACM Transactions on Information and System Security*, 5(1):1–35, February 2002.
12. P. Bonatti and P. Samarati. A unified framework for regulating access and information release on the web. *Journal of Computer Security*, 10(3):241–272, 2002.
13. M. Casassa Mont, S. Pearson, and P. Bramhall. Towards accountable management of identity and privacy: Sticky policies and enforceable tracing services. In *Proc. of the 14th International Workshop on Database and Expert Systems Applications*, Prague, Czech, September 2003.

14. V. Ciriani, S. De Capitani di Vimercati, S. Foresti, and P. Samarati. $k$-anonymity. In *Security in Decentralized Data Management*. Springer, 2006.
15. V. Ciriani, S. De Capitani di Vimercati, S. Foresti, and P. Samarati. Microdata protection. In *Security in Decentralized Data Management*. Springer, 2006.
16. E. Damiani, S. De Capitani di Vimercati, C. Fugazza, and P. Samarati. Extending policy languages to the semantic web. In *Proc. of the International Conference on Web Engineering*, Munich, Germany, July 2004.
17. J. DeTreville. Binder, a logic-based security language. In *Proc. of the 2001 IEEE Symposium on Security and Privacy*, Oakland, CA, USA, May 2002.
18. J. Domingo-Ferrer and J.M. Mateo-Sanz. Practical data-oriented microaggregation for statistical disclosure control. *IEEE Transactions on Knowledge and Data Engineering*, 14(1):189–201, 2002.
19. C.M. Ellison, B. Frantz, B. Lampson, R.L. Rivest, B.M. Thomas, and T. Ylonen. SPKI certificate theory. RFC2693, September 1999.
20. B. Fung, K. Wang, and P. Yu. Top-down specialization for information and privacy preservation. In *Proc. of the 21st International Conference on Data Engineering (ICDE'05)*, Tokyo, Japan, April 2005.
21. H. Hosmer. Metapolicies II. In *Proc. of the 15th National Computer Security Conference*, 1992.
22. K. Irwin and T. Yu. Preventing attribute information leakage in automated trust negotiation. In *Proc. of the 12th ACM Conference on Computer and Communications Security*, Alexandria, VA, USA, November 2005.
23. V. Iyengar. Transforming data to satisfy privacy constraints. In *Proc. of the Eigth ACM SIGKDD International Conference on Knowledge Discovery and Data Mining*, pages 279–288, Edmonton, Alberta, Canada, 2002.
24. T. Jaeger. Access control in configurable systems. *Lecture Notes in Computer Science*, 1603:289–316, 2001.
25. S. Jajodia, P. Samarati, M. Sapino, and V. Subrahmanian. Flexible support for multiple access control policies. *ACM Transactions on Database Systems*, 26(2):18–28, June 2001.
26. T. Jim. SD3: A trust management system with certified evaluation. In *Proc. of the 2001 IEEE Symposium on Security and Privacy*, Oakland, CA, USA, May 2001.
27. K. LeFevre, D.J. DeWitt., and R. Ramakrishnan. Incognito: Efficient full-domain $k$-anonymity. In *Proc. of the 24th ACM SIGMOD International Conference on Management of Data*, pages 49–60, Baltimore, Maryland, USA, June 2005.
28. N. Li, B. Grosof, and Feigenbaum. Delegation logic: A logic-based approach to distributed authorization. *ACM Transactions on Information and System Security*, 6(1):128–171, February 2003.
29. N. Li, J.C. Mitchell, and W.H. Winsborough. Beyond proof-of-compliance: Security analysis in trust management. *Journal of the ACM*, 52(3):474–514, May 2005.
30. N. Li, W.H. Winsborough, and J.C. Mitchell. Distributed credential chain discovery in trust management. *Journal of Computer Security*, 11(1):35–86, 2003.
31. P. Liu, P. Mitra, C. Pan, and V. Atluri. Privacy-preserving semantic interoperation and access control of heterogeneous databases. In *ACM Symposium on InformAtion, Computer and Communications Security*, Taipei, Taiwan, March 2006.
32. A. Machanavajjhala, J. Gehrke, and D. Kifer. $\ell$-diversity: Privacy beyond $k$-anonymity. In *Proc. of the ICDE'06*, Atlanta, GA, USA, April 2006.
33. J. McLean. The algebra of security. In *Proc. of the 1988 IEEE Computer Society Symposium on Security and Privacy*, Oakland, CA, USA, April 1988.
34. A. Meyerson and R. Williams. On the complexity of optimal $k$-anonymity. In *Proc. of the 23rd ACM PODS*, pages 223–228, Paris, France, 2004.

35. J. Ni, N. Li, and W.H. Winsborough. Automated trust negotiation using cryptographic credentials. In *Proc. of the 12th ACM Conference on Computer and Communications Security*, Alexandria, VA, USA, November 2005.

36. T. Ryutov, L. Zhou, C. Neuman, T. Leithead, and K.E. Seamons. Adaptive trust negotiation and access control. In *Proc. of the 10th ACM Symposium on Access Control Models and Technologies*, Stockholm, Sweden, June 2005.

37. P. Samarati. Protecting respondents' identities in microdata release. *IEEE Transactions on Knowledge and Data Engineering*, 13(6):1010–1027, November 2001.

38. P. Samarati and L. Sweeney. Generalizing data to provide anonymity when disclosing information. In *Proc. of the 17th ACM PODS*, Seattle, WA, 1998.

39. K. E. Seamons, W. Winsborough, and M. Winslett. Internet credential acceptance policies. In *Proc. of the Workshop on Logic Programming for Internet Applications*, Leuven, Belgium, July 1997.

40. L. Wang, D. Wijesekera, and S. Jajodia. A logic-based framework for attribute based access control. In *Proc. of the 2004 ACM Workshop on Formal Methods in Security Engineering*, Washington DC, USA, October 2004.

41. D. Wijesekera and S. Jajodia. A propositional policy algebra for access control. *ACM Transactions on Information and System Security*, 6(2):286–325, May 2003.

42. T.Y.C. Woo and S.S. Lam. Authorizations in distributed systems: A new approach. *Journal of Computer Security*, 2(2,3):107–136, 1993.

43. World Wide Web Consortium. *A P3P Preference Exchange Language 1.0 (APPEL1.0)*, April 2002. http://www.w3.org/TR/P3P-preferences/.

44. World Wide Web Consortium. *The Platform for Privacy Preferences 1.1 (P3P1.1) Specification*, July 2005. http://www.w3.org/TR/2005/WD-P3P11-20050701.

45. C. Yao, X.S. Wang, and S. Jajodia. Checking for *k*-anonymity violation by views. In *Proc. of the 31st International Conference on Very Large Data Bases (VLDB'05)*, Trondheim, Norway, August 2005.

46. T. Yu and M. Winslett. A unified scheme for resource protection in automated trust negotiation. In *Proc. of the IEEE Symp. on Security and Privacy*, Oakland, CA, May 2003.

47. T. Yu, M. Winslett, and K.E. Seamons. Prunes: An efficient and complete strategy for automated trust negotiation over the internet. In *Proc. of the 7th ACM Conf. on Computer and Communications Security*, Athens, Greece, November 2000.

48. T. Yu, M. Winslett, and K.E. Seamons. Supporting structured credentials and sensitive policies trough interoperable strategies for automated trust. *ACM Transactions on Information and System Security (TISSEC)*, 6(1):1–42, February 2003.

# A Data Sharing Agreement Framework

Vipin Swarup, Len Seligman, and Arnon Rosenthal

The MITRE Corporation
7515 Colshire Drive
McLean, VA 22102
{swarup,seligman,arnie}@mitre.org

**Abstract.** When consumers build value-added services on top of data resources they do not control, they need to manage their information supply chains to ensure that their data suppliers produce and supply required data as needed. Producers also need to manage their information supply chains to ensure that their data is disseminated and protected appropriately. In this paper, we present a framework for data sharing agreements (DSA) that supports a wide variety of data sharing policies. A DSA is modeled as a set of obligation constraints expressed over a dataflow graph whose nodes are principals with local stores and whose edges are (typed) channels along which data flows. We present a specification language for DSAs in which obligations are expressed as distributed temporal logic (DTL) predicates over data resources, dataflow events, and datastore events. We illustrate the use of our framework via a case study based on a real-world data sharing agreement and discuss issues related to the analysis and compliance of agreements.

## 1 Introduction

Data sharing refers to the act of letting another party use data. It has become prevalent with the spread of Internet technologies such as email, websites, and P2P systems. Computer users routinely share ideas, documents, multimedia files, etc. while organizational entities share large-scale data sets, e.g., scientific datasets, counter-terrorism information, etc. Four critical capabilities that are essential to any data sharing system are: a means for providers and consumers to discover each other; a means for consumers to access data; a means for consumers to understand data; and a means to manage sharing policies. In this paper, we will focus on issues regarding cross-boundary sharing policies.

In organizations, sharing provides value by improving the ability of information recipients to achieve mission objectives. However, sharing requires information to cross various kinds of boundaries and this carries risks, e.g., risks of disclosure of the information to adversaries, and risks of compromise of the sources and methods used to collect the information. In addition to these mission benefits and risks of sharing, information providers also have incentives and disincentives to share. Possible incentives include prestige, satisfying legal requirements or organizational directives, rewards, and altruism, while disincentives include fear that consumers might misuse or fail to protect the data or not give due credit to the data's creator or provider.

A. Bagchi and V. Atluri (Eds.): ICISS 2006, LNCS 4332, pp. 22–36, 2006.

The decision to share involves a trade-off between the risks of sharing and the risks of not sharing information. These risks can change dramatically when providers and consumers have confidence that certain obligations will be met by their sharing partners. This is greatly facilitated by policy management, which provides a mechanism to express and realize desired behavior of a data sharing arrangement (e.g., access controls, constraints on usage and subsequent sharing, guarantees about data quality and availability, compensation, penalties for violating agreements).

At the sharing transaction level, sharing policies have typically focused on meeting protection goals, e.g., usage control policies that are enforced using techniques such as digital rights management (DRM) engines and trusted computing platforms. At the organizational level, data sharing policies are expressed in documents called Memoranda of Understanding (MOUs) or Memoranda of Agreement (MOAs) that document the obligations and expectations of parties to the agreement. Current practice is to use textual memoranda, an approach with several disadvantages. First, there is little help for the writers, so important sharing issues are often omitted. Second, the documents are typically filed away in a drawer and seldom used thereafter. Third, it is hard to provide automated support for reasoning about the contents of textual memoranda.

Service Level Agreements (SLAs) have emerged as the paradigm used by organizations to express policies regarding service-level parameters. For instance, for network provider services, SLAs describe obligations over parameters such as availability, latency, throughput, packet loss, etc. Similarly, for data sharing services that focus on the sharing of information, SLAs can describe a variety of obligations over a similar set of parameters. However, there are several key aspects of data sharing services that are not addressed by traditional SLAs that focus on functional business services. First, data sharing obligations may require a provider to actively engage in actions that result in wider sharing of its data. These obligations may include parameters such as data freshness and quality, regular update dissemination, etc. Second, data sharing obligations may require a data recipient to engage in certain actions, e.g., further share the data, share derivatives of the data, share audit records of actions that it invoked on the data, notify the provider when the data is shared with a third party, etc. Third, obligations may restrict what the recipient may do with the data, e.g., whether the recipient can print a document. Finally, data objects subsume other data objects and this property can be exploited—e.g., an agreement about European Union persons' data is relevant to a demand for German persons' data.

Obligation policies are a key component of SLAs. An *obligation* is a constraint that a principal commits to satisfy in the future. Obligations are distinct from provisions (i.e., actions that a principal takes in order to gain access to a resource) and expectations (i.e., actions that one principal expects another to satisfy). Unlike access control rules which must always be satisfied, obligations may be violated. Hence, obligations are typically associated with penalty clauses that describe the consequences of violating the obligations. Obligation platforms provide support for obligation policies, maintain representations of obligations, enforce the satisfaction of (some) obligations, monitor and detect violations of obligations, and manage penalties associated with obligation violations.

In prior work, we have proposed the notion of a *data sharing agreement* (DSA) [19] as a variant of SLAs, and we have proposed an initial model for DSAs [20]. In this paper, we elaborate on our model for *data sharing agreements* (DSAs) that encode data sharing obligations. We focus on obligations about data stores and data flows, although the model can be extended to express obligations about the collection and processing of data, the use of data by parties, etc. We represent data stores as collections of typed values, dataflows as data streams between principals, and obligations as temporal constraints on data store and data stream events. Our model was developed by studying several real-world Memoranda of Agreements (MOAs) that are used by large U.S. government organizations to capture data sharing obligations. We present a specification language based on the model, as well as an example specification of a DSA that is motivated by a real-world MOA. We sketch a variety of analyses that are enabled by our approach and discuss technical challenges related to compliance. We conclude with a comparison with related work and future directions enabled by this work.

## 2   Data Sharing Agreements (DSAs)

DSAs share many aspects of SLAs, for instance, descriptions of the parties to the agreements, availability constraints, and temporal constraints like agreement lifetimes [14]. They also inherit from the general notion of agreements, that a party may incur obligations in return for benefits. For example, a consumer may promise to pay cash, to refrain from certain activities (e.g., non-compete agreements), or even to supply the consumer's own information to competitors. However, the primary purpose of DSAs is to capture data sharing clauses including descriptions of the data being shared, and obligations that constrain both the providers and consumers of the data and the data flows among them. The data may be described using standard techniques such as relational schema, XML schemas or DTDs, or object classes.

Obligations on data providers can concern both the need to send certain data (which the provider must then produce or acquire) and the quality of what is sent. They include recency constraints (data will reflect real world events, or data updates will be forwarded, with specified promptness or periodicity); visibility constraints (access will be provided to specified data views); and quality constraints (shared data will be of specified freshness, accuracy, precision, etc.).

Obligations on data consumers include protection constraints (e.g., data will not be copied, data will be deleted after 3 days, etc.); dissemination or sharing constraints (e.g., original source will be credited, subsequent research products based on the data will be shared back with the data providers; data will be shared with certain other consumers; providers will be notified of who has accessed the data); and generic security constraints (e.g., providers will be notified of security breaches in consumer networks). Note that parties may be data consumers in one

DSA, and providers (e.g., of derived products) in another. Parties may even be both data consumers and providers in the same DSA (e.g., providers of logistical data and consumers of end-user audit data).

All obligations may be conditional on events (e.g., receipt of a data object, detection of attack or compromise, etc.) and state predicates (e.g., declaration of local emergency, system failures, relationship among data values). Further, data sharing agreements may include obligations whose fulfillment depends on other DSAs or SLAs. For instance, suppose that B is obliged to ensure that C receives fresh and accurate data at regular intervals. In order to meet this obligation, B might rely on DSAs with data suppliers and SLAs with network providers. Finally, parties to a DSA may agree to inherit obligations from other DSAs.

A DSA's obligations impose global constraints on access control policies of various parties, even in future states. The exact nature depends on how the parties meet the obligations. For instance, suppose that a data recipient B is obligated to share data updates back with the provider A. Then either A must be given access rights to the data, or B must allow release and create a process that pushes the update notifications to A.

## 3   DSA Model

A DSA pertains to specific data schemas and data instance sets. Data may be represented in any *data model* that provides constructs to represent data, and operations over those constructs (e.g., query, update). Three prevalent data models are the relational data model, the XML data model, and the object data model. Our language is based on the data model of the $C\omega$ research programming language [6] which integrates the above three models into a single succinct framework. It provides a uniform model for representing relational data (e.g., database tables), semi-structured data (e.g., XML documents), object data (e.g., Java objects), and data streams (e.g., sequences). It also provides a uniform means for expressing queries over data. We shall use the syntax of $C\omega$ in our examples and will provide informal descriptions of the semantics [6,1,2].

A DSA is an agreement between a set of principals regarding the sharing of data among themselves. In this context, data sharing refers to the explicit flow of data from one principal to another, and not to the subtler notions of information flow or data inference. Hence, we model a DSA as a set of sharing obligations expressed over a dataflow graph whose nodes are principals with local stores, and whose edges are (typed) channels along which data flows.

*Principals* can be specified in well-understood ways and include both simple principals (e.g., named individuals or organizations) and compound principals (e.g., groups, roles, etc.). Each principal is associated with a local data store. A *data store* is a function that maps (location) names to data values. The data values may be data relations, data streams, documents, objects, etc. as mentioned above.

*Data resources* describe the data to which a data sharing agreement pertains. A data resource is a tuple $\langle rn, p, DV \rangle$, where $rn$ is a globally unique data resource name, $p$ is the principal offering the data resource, and $DV$ (i.e., a data view) is a set of tuples $\langle q, T \rangle$, where $q$ is a query language expression over $p$'s local data store and $T$ is the type of the query's result. A data resource might describe both the data content that is being shared, and metadata such as the sharing context and attributes of principals.

A *dataflow* [15] $F$ is a tuple $\langle s, d, T \rangle$ where $s$ and $d$ are principals and $T$ is a type. $F$ represents a data stream of values of type $T$ flowing from source $s$ to destination $d$. The source $s$ can place value $o$ of type $T$ into the dataflow stream (which we write as $F.send(o)$), while the destination principal $d$ can read values from the stream ($F.receive(o)$). The state of a dataflow $F$ is a tuple $state(F) = \langle f, r \rangle$ where $f \in T^*$ is the sequence of values that have been placed in the stream, and $r \in T^*$ is the sequence of values that $F$'s destination principal has read from the stream. Data values can include message identifiers to capture which values in the stream have been received.

An *obligation* $O$ is a pair $\langle \psi, p \rangle$ where $\psi$ is a formula in Distributed Temporal Logic (DTL) [9,12] and $p$ is the penalty that is incurred if $\psi$ is not satisfied. Obligation formulae specify properties of traces of dataflow events (sending and receiving data) and data store events (updating data stores). DTL is a generalization of Linear Temporal Logic (LTL) and includes both past-time and future-time temporal operators including **Y** (*previous*), **P** (*sometime in the past*), **H** (*always in the past*), **S** (*since*), **X** (*next*), **G** (*always*), and **U** (*weak until*). A DTL formula can refer to a specific principal's local data space and hence can be true only for that specific principal. Thus, the DTL formula $@_a[\psi]$ asserts that proposition $\psi$ holds in the local context of principal $a$. A *penalty* can be any action imposed on a principal, e.g., the payment of money by one principal to another. In this paper, for simplicity, we assume that each event corresponds to a fixed time step (e.g., 1 hour or 1 day per time step). An alternate approach would be to have explicit clocks (e.g., a local clock per principal) and predicates over the clocks.

Finally, a *data sharing agreement* $DSA$ is a tuple $\langle P, S, DS, DR, DF, O \rangle$ where $P$ is a set of principals (i.e., the parties referenced in the agreement), $S \subseteq P$ is the set of signatories of the agreement, $DS$ is a function that maps each principal in $P$ to a data store (that represents the local data store of the principal), $DR$ is a set of data resources that are views of the data stores in $DS$, $DF$ is a set of dataflows between principals in $P$, and $O$ is a set of obligations of principals in P. Note that only principals in $S$ are signatories of the DSA and hence have agreed to the terms of the obligations that oblige them.

# 4   DSA Specification Language

We now sketch a specification language for DSAs based on the above model. A data sharing agreement specification includes the parties to the DSA, time bounds for validity, a timestep duration (to specify the fixed time duration of each event), a set of statements that specify the data resources referenced in the DSA, and a set of obligations expressed over the data resources, the local data stores of the parties, and dataflows among the parties. Parties and time bounds are expressed in the usual ways (e.g., using X.509 distinguished names, timestamps, etc.). In this section, we will present a language to specify data stores, dataflows, and obligations.

As mentioned earlier, we use the data model of the $C\omega$ research programming language [6]. We shall rely on informal descriptions of $C\omega$ language constructs in this paper. $C\omega$ is a typed language with the usual primitive types (**boolean**, **integer**, **string**, and **void**) and four structured types: streams, which consist of zero or more members; anonymous structs, which are like structs in C but with the possibility of multiple fields with the same name; choice types, which are discriminated unions (i.e., a value of a choice type consists of one of the listed field types and a value of that type); and classes, whose members are objects that encapsulate data values and methods.

A snippet of our DSA language is presented in Figure 1. Informally, the statement "**Channel**(P,Q,T) c" declares c to be a (dataflow) channel from P to Q that carries values of type T. The expressions c.**src** and c.**dest** denote the source and destination of channel c respectively, while **getloc**(Q,x) denotes the value bound to location x in Q's data store. The predicates c.**send**(o) and c.**rcv**(o) are true if object o was just sent and received (respectively) on channel c, while the predicate **setloc**(Q,x,e) holds if Q's data store was just updated to bind location x to value e.

Expressions are typed terms that evaluate to a value of the appropriate type. The $C\omega$ expression language contains usual terms for boolean, integer and string literals, built-in operators, object and structure creation, and method invocation. The power of the language comes from the overloaded "dot" term. If $e$ evaluates to a stream $v$, then $e.\{h\}$ returns the stream created by applying the expression $h$ to each member of $v$. $h$ may contain the special variable $it$ which gets bound to each successive element of $v$. The language does not permit nested streams, and hence if $h$ returns a stream as result, then the resulting stream of streams is "flattened" to a simple stream (see below). If $e$ evaluates to a structure $v$, then $e.f$ returns the values of the fields named $f$ in structure $v$. Since a structure may contain multiple fields with the same name, $e.f$ returns a stream of values. Finally, if $e$ evaluates to a structure $v$, then $e[i]$ returns the value of the i'th field in structure $v$.

For instance, let:

$$x = \{ \text{city} = \text{"Rome"} ; \text{ctry} = \text{"USA"} ; \text{ctry} = \text{"Italy"} ; \}$$
$$y = \{ \text{city} = \text{"Paris"}; \text{ctry} = \text{"USA"} ; \text{ctry} = \text{"France"} ; \}$$
$$z = \{ \text{info} = x; \text{info} = y; \}$$

Then, x.city is the string "Rome", x[2] is the string "USA", while x.ctry is the stream with two values "USA" and "Italy". z.info is the stream of the two structure values (x and y), while z.info.{it.ctry} is the flattened stream with four values ("USA", "Italy", "USA", and "France").

Statement terms include variable declarations and assignments, conditionals, loops, method invocations and returns, and blocks. For streams, the language provides a dot statement $e.h$ that applies the expression $h$ to each element of the stream yielded by evaluating $e$ (again, the variable $it$ is bound to each successive value of the stream); a loop construct ("foreach") for iterating over all elements of a stream; and a "yield" term that returns a member of a stream. For instance, continuing with the above example, x.ctry.{print it;} applies the print method to each member of the x.ctry stream, hence printing out the two country names "USA" and "Italy".

The obligation language (see Figure 1) is based on distributed temporal logic. Formulas are evaluated at a specific temporal and distributed state. An obligation term includes a DTL formula, a predicate that specifies the cancellation policy for the obligation, and the penalty for violating the obligation formula. We use syntactically sugared DTL operators, e.g., ($\phi$ **innext** $t$) specifies that $\phi$ must hold sometime in the next $t$ timesteps, while ($\phi$ **at** $B$) specifies that $\phi$ must hold in the local state of principal $B$.

Finally, a DSA is specified by a name, a set of principals, a sequence of statement and obligation terms, start and end timestamps representing the validity period of the DSA, and a timestep that specifies the time interval between successive states in the temporal model.

## 5   Examples

We now present several examples of sharing obligations that can be expressed in our framework. For brevity, we have taken significant liberty with the syntax here, e.g., by omitting certain clauses such as cancellation and penalty clauses in obligations, and by using time intervals and timestamps rather than time-step counts. In these examples, let $A$, $B$, and $C$ be principals; $c1$ be a channel (of type T) from $A$ to $B$; $c2$ be a channel from $B$ to $C$; and $c3$ be a channel from $B$ to $A$.

**Responsive forwarding:**  $B$ will send $C$ on channel $c2$ each object it receives from $A$ on channel $c1$ within 24 hours of receiving it:

> (**forall** T o) **if** c1.rcv(o) **then**
>   (c2.send(o) **innext** 24 hrs
> **at** B **until** 1/1/2007

**Nondisclosure agreements:**  If B receives object o from A on channel c1, then B will not thereafter send o to any other principal for a year.

> (**forall** T o) **if** c1.rcv(o) **then**
>   (**forall** Channel c) **if** (c.dest $\neq$ A) **then**
>     (**not** c.send(o) **until** 1 year)
> **at** B **until** 1/1/2007

**Usage notification:**  If B receives object o from A on channel c1, then for the next 365 days, B will notify A each time B sends o to another principal. We construct the notification object via an externally defined function called "notify".

```
s     ::= ... Channel(P,Q) c ...
e     ::= c.src | c.dest
        | getloc(Q,x) | ...
p     ::= c.send(e) | c.rcv(e)
        | setloc(Q,x,e) | ...
```

| | | |
|---|---|---|
| ob | ::= obf **cancelif** p | Time-bound obligation |
| | **penalty** penalty | |

| | | |
|---|---|---|
| obf | ::= p | Simple predicate |
| | \| obf **and** obf | Conjunction |
| | \| obf **or** obf | Disjunction |
| | \| **not** p | Negation |
| | \| (**forall** $\tau$ x) obf | Universal quantification |
| | \| (**exists** $\tau$ x) obf | Existential quantification |
| | \| obf **at** Q | obf holds in the local data space of principal Q |
| | \| **if** p **then** obf | Conditional obligation formula |
| | \| ( obf ) | Precedence brackets |
| | \| obf **innext** i | obf holds sometime during the next i states |
| | \| obf **until** i | obf holds for the next i states |
| | \| obf **until** p | obf holds until p holds |
| | \| obf **atnext** i | obf holds at the i'th next state |
| | \| obf **inprev** i | obf held sometime during the previous i states |
| | \| obf **fromprev** i | obf held during all the previous i states |
| | \| obf **fromprev** p | obf held since the last time that p held |
| | \| obf **atprev** i | obf held at the i'th previous state |

| | | |
|---|---|---|
| DSA | ::= **DSA** id **with** | Data sharing agreement |
| | **principals** $\overline{Q}$ | |
| | **statements** $\overline{s}$ | |
| | **obligations** $\overline{ob}$ | |
| | **from** timestamp | |
| | **to** timestamp | |
| | **timestep** duration | |

**Fig. 1.** DSA Language Snippet

```
(forall T o) if c1.rcv(o) then
    (forall Channel c)
        if (c.send(o) and c.dest ≠ A) then
            c3.send(notify(B,c.dest,o)) innext 1 day
    until 365 days
at B until 1/1/2007
```

**Recurrence:**  A will send B the latest update to object o every 24 hours.

> **if** c1.send(o) **then**
>   c1.send(update(o)) **innext** 1 day
> **at A until** 1/1/2007

**Privacy:**  Privacy obligations may arise when a person or an organization shares personal data with another organization. They may also arise when an organization receives data about a human, imposed by government (via laws) rather than the provider.[1] The simple privacy obligation specified below asserts that A must delete all personal information about B from location x within one year of A's storing it.

> **(forall** T e) **if** setloc(A,x,e)
>     **and** (e.subject = B) **then**
>   setloc(A,x,null) **innext** 1 year
> **at A until** 1/1/2007

The above examples can be combined to form complex obligations. For instance, if B receives data O from A, then B will not share O with foreign citizens, and will notify A about US citizens who are shown the data. Furthermore, even for US citizens, B will not reveal that A was the source. Our model is quite powerful and can capture a wide variety of such data sharing policies. To illustrate this, we now describe a sanitized and substantially simplified fragment of a data sharing agreement that is based on a real U.S. government Memorandum of Agreement (MOA). We have changed organization names and altered their missions to facilitate release of this information. The agreement is between the military's fictional Antarctica Command (USANTCOM), which maintains a logistics database we shall call AntLog, and the fictitious Logistics Information Agency (LIA), which consolidates logistics information from many sources into the Logistics InfoMart (LIM) and provides analysis on logistics requirements and feasibility of both hypothetical and actual operations. We have augmented the agreement with additional terms not found in the real MOA in order to illustrate important features of data sharing agreements.

**MOA:**  The DSA in this example addresses data services that permit authorized LIM users to access the AntLog database service via a LIM data brokering service. The brokering service exposes specific data views to LIM users and only permits them to execute specific queries over those data views. The AntLog database service is hosted on AntLog database servers, while the brokering service is hosted on LIM data brokering servers.

USANTCOM must notify LIA whenever the AntLog database schema is changed or a new data feed into AntLog is created; this notification must

---

[1] Some obligations (e.g., those imposed by law) are implicit—they are not part of any explicit DSA even though the parties are obliged to satisfy them. Such implicit obligations may be specified in our model although they are not the focus of this paper.

occur 30 days in advance of the change. AntLog engineers must provide technical assistance to LIA to create and optimize the SQL queries that LIM users are permitted to execute against the AntLog database. USANT-COM must provide the LIA manager of the LIM data brokering service with credentials to access a group account on AntLog.

LIA must ensure that all LIM users of the LIM data brokering service are authenticated, and that only cleared and authorized users can use the provided group credentials to access AntLog via the data brokering service. Further, LIA must audit all such successful transactions. LIA is also responsible for maintaining valid (interim or final) accreditation status for all LIM systems and networks and must ensure that there are no actual or probable security breaches on those systems and networks. Finally, LIA must notify USANT-COM and AntLog administrators of any violation of these assertions, and the penalty will be that USANTCOM may disconnect AntLog from all affected systems/servers.

Figure 2 contains a specification of the data brokering DSA. In this instantiation, dbs is a data view of AntLog and represents a relational table whose rows consist of a resource descriptor ("rsrc"), current location ("curloc"), and destination location ("destloc"). query1 returns the current locations of all resources, while query2 returns all resources which are not yet at their destination. The obligations encode the constraints described above.

# 6   Analysis and Compliance

A formal data sharing model enables us to reason about a range of properties:

1. Is it possible for me to satisfy all my obligations? E.g., we're obliged to share all data with a business partner but we receive product documentation under a stringent nondisclosure agreement; is there a sequence of events that will satisfy my obligations? If we assume that all data types are finite, and if we restrict ourselves to the LTL fragment of our language, then satisfiability is tractable and is answerable by standard model checkers (e.g., NuSMV).
2. Do I need a new DSA, or are my information needs already covered by existing DSAs? This can be formulated as subsumption, i.e., does an obligation entail another? Again, if we assume that all data types are finite, and if we restrict ourselves to the LTL fragment of our language, then entailment is tractable and is answerable by standard model checkers.
3. What actions must I take in order to meet all my obligations? Which customers must I send data to, or notify about potential changes to my data schema or to the frequency of data updates? Can we automatically generate dataflows from a DSA that satisfy the DSA's dataflow obligations? This is largely an unexplored problem since, unlike access control policies, obligations are not always enforceable. In fact, obligation formulae place constraints on future behavior and they may well be violated by parties, e.g.,

**DSA** InfoMart **with**
  **principals** USANTCOM, LIA, AntLog, Broker,
  LIM, LIMusers
  **signatories** USANTCOM, LIA

  **statements**
    Channel(Broker,AntLog) cba;
    Channel(USANTCOM,LIA) cul;
    Channel(LIA,USANTCOM) clu;

    **struct** { String rsrc; String curloc; String destloc } * dbs;
    dbs = **getloc**(AntLog,tracker).{ {rsrc — it.rsrc; curloc = it.cloc;
                                   destloc = it.dloc; } };
    String query1 = dbs.{it.curloc};
    String query2 = dbs.{ **if** it.curloc $\neq$ it.destloc **then** it.rsrc };

  **obligations**
    **if** dbs.update(u) **then**
      cul.send(notify("schema update")) **inprev** 30 days

    **if** clu.rcv("credentials", "AntLog") **then**
      cul.send(credentials("AntLog",uname,passwd))
        **innext** 24 hrs

    **if** cba.send(q) **then**
      (q == query1 **or** q == query2) **and**
      (**exists** Principal Q) (**exists** Channel(Q,Broker) cqb)
        (cqb.rcv(q) **and** cqb.authenticated()) **inprev** 24 hrs
        **and setloc**(Broker,audit,**getloc**(Broker,audit).add(Q,q))

    **if** LIM.system.securitybreach() **then**
      clu.send(notify("breach", "LIM")) **innext** 2 hrs
    **penalty** USANTCOM may disconnect AntLog

  **from** 6 May 2003
  **to** indefinite

**Fig. 2.** USANTCOM–LIA Data Brokering DSA

due to changes in external circumstances. Obligations carry penalties that describe actions to be taken when the obligation formulae are violated. Irwin et al. [13] formulate compliance in terms of accountability, namely whether a given policy can ensure that the system can hold principals accountable for obligation constraint violations.

# 7    Related Work

Several researchers have proposed policy languages for expressing obligations for data protection. Park and Sandhu [18] propose a usage control model that constrains how a data consumer can use data. Bettini et al. [4,5] propose an access control model based on provisions and obligations, where a reference monitor creates obligations while making an authorization decision. In contrast to this body of work, our focus is on data sharing obligations, not on data protection obligations. Thus, for instance, we support obligations that require data consumers to share data further with other consumers; such obligations may not be associated with any authorization decision.

Ponder [8] and PDL [7] use event-condition-action (ECA) rules to express obligations. In those models, obligations are actions that are triggered immediately when certain events occur and certain predicates are satisfied. In contrast, our model is based on a temporal logic that can place temporal constraints on when obligations must be satisfied. For instance, our model can express obligations that are activated when certain events occur (or predicates are satisfied) in the future.

Bettini et al. [3] propose an obligation model in which events are represented as predicates; an event predicate is true in a state iff the corresponding event occurs in that state. We take a similar approach but we also incorporate a general data model and a dataflow model, and our work is motivated by several real-world MOAs.

Gama and Ferreira [11] describe a policy language (xSPL, Extended Security Policy Language) and enforcement platform (Heimdall) for specifying and enforcing complex policies, including history-based and obligation-based policies. Our focus, in this paper, has been on the data specific aspects of such policies.

Several systems use deontic logic [17] to express obligations. Other systems are based on temporal logics that enable the specification of temporally-constrained obligations. We have adopted Hilty et al.'s distributed temporal logic framework [12].

A distinction between our work and prior work is that we distinguish between expectations and obligations. Formulas that express constraints on future actions are expectations; they become obligations only when the obliged parties accept them as obligations, for instance, by signing them. In contrast, most previous work does not require obliged parties to accept (or agree to) the obligations.

Firozabadi et al. [10] address the sharing of scarce resources and they address conflicts between entitlements, obligations, and resource scarcity. Data, on the other hand, may be freely replicated. Thus, it is an opportunity rather than a conflict if many parties want the same data item. Subsumption and derivation of data schemas and queries are well-understood problems (e.g., [16]) and can be exploited in sharing data with multiple parties.

Irwin et al. [13] present an analysis and modeling approach for obligations. They present the notion of accountability as a key goal for obligation mechanisms. In their model, obligations are defined as actions that subjects are obliged to take on a set of objects, within a time window. They provide detailed analyses for determining whether a system will remain accountable, given obligation and authorization policies. Obligations in our model are at a much higher abstraction level, and it would be interesting to map our abstract obligation specifications to low-level action specifications.

## 8    Conclusion

In this paper, we have presented a model for data sharing agreements. The model is based on a dataflow graph whose nodes are principals with local stores, and whose edges are (typed) channels along which data flows. Data sharing constraints are expressed as DTL predicates over data stores and data flows. These constraints can include both *past* events and *future* events, and may hold only at certain principals' local states. We have argued why this approach is central to the problem of secure information sharing, one of the most fundamental problems in information security.

Our work has been motivated by several real-world data sharing agreements (currently expressed as textual Memoranda of Agreement). We illustrated the expressive power of our language by expressing a sanitized fragment of a real MOA. Since our language can be given a precise formal semantics, DSAs specified in our language are amenable to a variety of automated analyses.

This work is an important first step towards our ultimate goal of building a comprehensive technical infrastructure for secure information sharing policies. We are beginning to develop a prototype platform that manages and enforces DSAs. This platform will include wizards to assist in the creation of comprehensive and consistent DSAs; repositories to assist in the lifecycle management of DSAs; distributed agents to monitor and enforce the terms of the DSAs, when possible; and modules to provide automated analysis capabilities.

Note that obligations are binding on the obliged parties and the parties may be subject to penalties for failing to meet their obligations. Hence, obligation systems are subject to a variety of attacks by adversaries. Attacks include creating obligations that are not undertaken by the obliged principals, freeing principals from their obligations, causing principals to violate their obligations, and preventing obligation monitors from detecting violations of obligations. Hence, a secure DSA system must protect against such attacks while managing DSAs and monitoring for potential violations of obligations.

## References

1. Arvind Arasu and Jennifer Widom.   A denotational semantics for continuous queries over streams and relations. *SIGMOD Record*, 33(3):6–12, 2004.
2. Brian Babcock, Shivnath Babu, Mayur Datar, Rajeev Motwani, and Jennifer Widom. Models and issues in data stream systems. In *Proceedings of the ACM SIGACT-SIGMOD Symposium on Principles of Database Systems*, pages 1–16, 2002.

3. Claudio Bettini, Sushil Jajodia, Xiaoyang Sean Wang, and Duminda Wijesekera. Obligation monitoring in policy management. In *3rd IEEE International Workshop on Policies for Distributed Systems and Networks (POLICY 2002)*, pages 2–12, June 2002.

4. Claudio Bettini, Sushil Jajodia, Xiaoyang Sean Wang, and Duminda Wijesekera. Provisions and obligations in policy management and security applications. In *VLDB*, pages 502–513, 2002.

5. Claudio Bettini, Sushil Jajodia, Xiaoyang Sean Wang, and Duminda Wijesekera. Provisions and obligations in policy rule management. *J. Network Syst. Manage.*, 11(3), 2003.

6. Gavin M. Bierman, Erik Meijer, and Wolfram Schulte. The essence of data access in C$\omega$. In *Proceedings of the 19th European Conference on Object-Oriented Programming (ECOOP 2005)*, volume 3586 of *Lecture Notes in Computer Science*, pages 287–311. Springer, 2005.

7. Jan Chomicki, Jorge Lobo, and Shamim A. Naqvi. Conflict resolution using logic programming. *IEEE Trans. Knowl. Data Eng.*, 15(1):244–249, 2003.

8. Nicodemos Damianou, Naranker Dulay, Emil Lupu, and Morris Sloman. The Ponder policy specification language. In *POLICY '01: Proceedings of the International Workshop on Policies for Distributed Systems and Networks*, pages 18–38, London, UK, 2001. Springer-Verlag.

9. Hans-Dieter Ehrich and Carlos Caleiro. Specifying communication in distributed information systems. *Acta Inf.*, 36(8):591–616, 2000.

10. Babak Sadighi Firozabadi, Marek J. Sergot, Anna Cinzia Squicciarini, and Elisa Bertino. A framework for contractual resource sharing in coalitions. In *Proceedings of the 5th IEEE International Workshop on Policies for Distributed Systems and Networks (POLICY 2004)*, pages 117–126, 2004.

11. Pedro Gama and Paulo Ferreira. Obligation policies: An enforcement platform. In *Proceedings of the 6th IEEE International Workshop on Policies for Distributed Systems and Networks (POLICY 2005)*, pages 203–212, 2005.

12. Manuel Hilty, David Basin, and Alexander Pretschner. On obligations. In *10th European Symposium on Research in Computer Security (ESORICS 2005)*, volume 3679 of *Lecture Notes in Computer Science*, pages 98–117. Springer, 2005.

13. Keith Irwin, Ting Yu, and William H. Winsborough. On the modeling and analysis of obligations. In *To appear in Proceedings 13th ACM Conference on Computer and Communications Security*, 2006.

14. Alexander Keller and Heiko Ludwig. The WSLA framework: Specifying and monitoring service level agreements for web services. *Journal of Network and Systems Management, Special Issue on E-Business Management*, 11(1), March 2003.

15. Gary T. Leavens, Tim Wahls, and Albert L. Baker. Formal semantics for SA style data flow diagram specification languages. In *Proceedings of the ACM Symposium on Applied Computing (SAC)*, pages 526–532, 1999.

16. Alon Y. Levy, Alberto O. Mendelzon, Yehoshua Sagiv, and Divesh Srivastava. Answering queries using views. In *Proceedings of the Fourteenth ACM SIGACT-SIGMOD-SIGART Symposium on Principles of Database Systems*, pages 95–104, 1995.

17. John-Jules Ch. Meyer, Roel Wieringa, and Frank Dignum. The role of deontic logic in the specification of information systems. In *Logics for Databases and Information Systems*, pages 71–115. Kluwer, 1998.

18. Jaehong Park and Ravi Sandhu. The UCON$_{ABC}$ usage control model. *ACM Transactions on Information and System Security*, 7(1):128–174, 2004.

19. Len Seligman, Arnon Rosenthal, and James Caverlee. Data service agreements: Toward a data supply chain. In *Workshop on Information Integration on the Web, at VLDB 2004*, 2004.
20. Vipin Swarup, Len Seligman, and Arnon Rosenthal. Specifying data sharing agreements. In *Seventh IEEE International Workshop on Policies for Distributed Systems and Networks (POLICY'06)*, pages 157–162, Los Alamitos, CA, USA, 2006. IEEE Computer Society.

# Password Exhaustion: Predicting the End of Password Usefulness

Luke St. Clair, Lisa Johansen, William Enck, Matthew Pirretti, Patrick Traynor,
Patrick McDaniel, and Trent Jaeger

Systems and Internet Infrastructure Security Laboratory
The Pennsylvania State University, University Park PA 16802
{lstclair,johansen,enck,pirretti,traynor,mcdaniel,
jaeger}@cse.psu.edu

**Abstract.** Passwords are currently the dominant authentication mechanism in computing systems. However, users are unwilling or unable to retain passwords with a large amount of entropy. This reality is exacerbated by the increasing ability of systems to mount offline attacks. In this paper, we evaluate the degree to which the previous statements are true and attempt to ascertain the point at which passwords are no longer sufficient to securely mediate authentication. In order to demonstrate this, we develop an analytical model for computation to understand the time required to recover random passwords. Further, an empirical study suggests the situation is much worse. In fact, we found that past systems vulnerable to offline attacks will be obsolete in 5-15 years, and our study suggests that a large number of these systems are already obsolete. We conclude that we must discard or fundamentally change these systems, and to that effect, we suggest a number of ways to prevent offline attacks.

## 1   Introduction

Password-based authentication mechanisms are the primary means by which users gain legitimate access to computing systems. Because of their central role in the protection of these systems, the vulnerabilities inherent to these methods have long been known throughout the security community. The best known of these vulnerabilities is password choice. A variety of studies [21,25,32] cite the lack of *entropy*, or unpredictability, included in each password as the root of the problem. Because of the chronic under-use of the available key space, as many as 30% of user passwords are recoverable within a period of hours [24].

The common wisdom is that if users can be educated to select "perfect" passwords, offline brute-force attacks to recover such information will remain beyond the computational ability of modern machines [19]. In reality, the current entropy in a perfectly-random 8 character password, the most common password length, is actually less than that of a 56-bit DES key[1]. Thus, the security provided by these passwords is questionable. In order to increase the security provided by passwords, password length increases and password policies are commonly employed. A variety of password policies now request 15 character passwords. In this case, the entropy is comparable to 3DES or AES.

---

[1] DES was effectively broken by a brute-force attack in 1999 [2].

A. Bagchi and V. Atluri (Eds.): ICISS 2006, LNCS 4332, pp. 37–55, 2006.

Password policies for guiding users to select more effective passwords have become more prevalent. As systems continue to rely on passwords to provide authentication security, it is important to investigate the validity of these improvements.

In addition to the future increases in computing power, the viability of password systems is limited by the entropy that humans are actually able to use in practice. Given than human beings are only capable of remembering approximately seven random items [10], an increase in password length does not necessarily mean a commensurate increase in real entropy. As passwords lengths increase, users may develop techniques to use predictable chunks of randomly arranged passwords. Also, users will be tremendously challenged to memorize multiple passwords of such length.

In this paper, we investigate two fundamental claims: (1) near-term increases in available computing power will soon enable offline brute-force cracking of perfectly-random 8 character passwords on a variety of commodity platforms, and (2) the maximum entropy that we can expect from a password is limited to no more than the commonly used 8 characters we have already, thus rendering password systems that permit offline attacks obsolete. First, we use current forecasting of hardware performance to estimate the end of the computational infeasibility for offline password attacks given the entropy of an 8 character password. We find that computing power that should be easily available to a typical user will be sufficient to break a perfectly random 8 character password in May 2016. For more motivated attackers, the time to recover passwords will be insignificant. Secondly, we examine the entropy of real passwords and the impact of password policies upon that entropy. NIST has done an analysis of the entropy present in real-world passwords, and based on this measure and the capabilities of modern password cracking tools, an attacker with only one machine who could search the potential password space in order of increasing randomness would be able to recover even an 8-character password including numbers and symbols in less than 15 hours. We find that in real passwords of the CSE department at Penn State, the entropy is only slightly better than this figure. Further, we find that password policies significantly limit password entropy and do not appreciably improve the protection of passwords. No solution is known to exist that can save password systems susceptible to offline attacks from obsolescence in the near future.

The remainder of this paper is organized as follows: in Section 2, we discuss predictions of future computer performance and their bearing on password vulnerabilities; Section 3 examines the ways in which entropy is actually removed from systems and revisits the above predictions; Section 4 considers solutions to this problem; related works are presented in Section 5; Section 6 offers concluding remarks.

## 2    Future of Password Recovery Power

This section considers how hardware improvements and processor availability impact the security provided by password authentication systems. We begin by introducing a model of computing used to assess the vulnerability of password systems to offline attacks. Using this model, we consider the present and future security of popular password systems.

## 2.1 Forecasting Model for Password Recovery

To assess the viability of current and future password systems, we introduce a model for investigating the impact of increasing processor speeds and parallelism on brute-force attacks. These factors, modeled as functions $s(t)$ and $p(t)$, are based on expert predictions of future computing trends. We also evaluate the effect of the growing availability of large systems of computers on brute-force attack speed.

### Model Definition

Our model is composed of the following components: password space, processor performance, parallelism, and system size.

**Password Space($c$):** The password space is the set of all possible passwords that a system can represent. In terms of password recovery, the password space indicates the average amount of work required to recover a password. Given the limitations of human memory, we shall assume a typical user password is composed of 8 characters, where each character can be any of the 95 characters readily represented with a keyboard. In the best case scenario (from the point of view of system security), user passwords will be uniformly distributed across the password space. Thus, an adversary on average must search half of the password space to recover a password. Based on these parameters, we represent the average number of tries required to recover a password as a constant:

$$c = 95^8/2 \approx 3.3 \times 10^{15}, \tag{1}$$

where each attempt to break a password is termed as *try*.

**Processor Performance($s(t)$):** The processor performance function models the amount of work that can be accomplished by a single processing element[2]. To map this factor to password recovery, we define processor performance as the number of seconds required to perform a single try, denoted as a time varying function $s(t)$. In Section 2.1 we consider several models that predict how processor performance will change with time.

**Parallelism($p(t)$):** The parallelism function models the increasing prevalence of processor replication in contemporary computing systems by measuring the number of processor cores present within a single computer. Password recovery is a highly parallelizable activity; the password space can be subdivided into disjoint components and independently processed by different processor cores. The level of parallelism present in a given machine greatly increases the rate at which the password space is examined. For instance, a machine with 4 processing cores can simultaneously perform 4 tries. We denote the level of parallelism present in a given computer as a time varying function $p(t)$. In Section 2.1 we consider different models that have been used to forecast the number of independent processing cores present within a single computer.

**System Size($z$):** System size models the increasing prevalence of computational devices. For instance, the number of computers in homes is steadily increasing [16]. Further, the number of computers present in computing clusters is quickly growing. Finally, the overwhelming size of botnets is increasing. To capture this trend we represent the number of independent computers present in a system as a variable $z$.

---

[2] To avoid ambiguity, this factor specifically measures the amount of work a single processor core can perform.

**Password Cracking Forecasting Model($T(t)$):** Given our definitions of $c, s(t), p(t)$, and $z$ we can now introduce our model of forecasting how the computing trends of increasing processor performance and increasing parallelism will affect the viability of brute-force password cracking attacks. Our model represents the amount of time required to recover a random 8 character password:

$$T(t) = \frac{(3.3 \times 10^{15}) \cdot s(t)}{p(t) \cdot z}. \tag{2}$$

**Predicting Processor Performance $s(t)$**

This section examines predictions on the growth of future processor performance as made by experts in the field. It then defines the function for this growth, $s(t)$, over time which is used in our model.

Determining future processor performance has been a widely studied problem for more than 50 years. Moore stated in 1965 that chip density will double every 12 to 18 months. Unfortunately, chip density is reaching its limits due to heat and power consumption [14]. Because of these challenges, the industry is looking towards other methods to increase overall computing power instead of focusing on clock speed. Nanotechnologies, compiler optimization and other innovations are being considered as approaches for increasing chip performance [14,20]. However, the industry still looks to Moore's law as a predictor of future computing power [20].

Shown in Figure 1(a), Moore's Law is represented by the function, $s_M(t)$. However, studies have shown that the rate of performance growth proposed in Moore's law is unrealistically fast [18]. One of these studies states that, over the past 7.5 years, the actual rate of computer performance growth has been closer to 41% per year. This more conservative predictor serves as a second function for performance growth, $s_R(t)$.

Because the limits of physics are affecting the application of traditional methods for performance improvement, $s_M(t)$ and $s_R(t)$ may be unrealistic for future predictions. Because chip density reaching its limit, there has been much discussion that Moore's law is no longer valid [17]. Experts are beginning to doubt that processor power is going to continue to grow at rates that we have seen in the past. Taking this into consideration, we define two more functions, $s_{SG}(t)$ and $s_0(t)$, to more conservatively project the growth of processor performance. The first function, $s_{SG}(t)$, is a conservative estimate of 20% processor power growth per year derived from the expert predictions of future computing power. The second function, $s_0(t)$, assumes no growth over the next 15 years. All four of our processor performance growth functions are plotted in Figure 1(a).

**Predicting Parallelism Factor $p(t)$**

Parallel computing is popularly seen as a counterbalance to slowing growth of processor performance. Multi-core technologies, multiple processors and hyper-threading have been proposed to increase performance. Intel and AMD have released estimates for the amount of parallelism that they expect will exist in a single computer in the near future. Intel believes that a processor will have anywhere from tens to hundreds of cores within ten years [14]. AMD projects that processors will contain more than 2 cores by 2007 and more than 8 by 2008 [1].

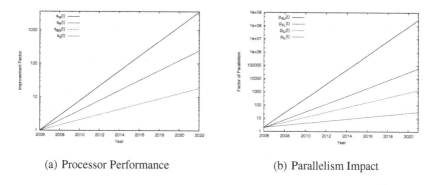

(a) Processor Performance  (b) Parallelism Impact

**Fig. 1.** Future Computing Performance Estimates

Given these estimates, we predict where parallelism will be in the near future. We extrapolate two functions for AMD's estimates and two functions for Intel's estimates. The first function of parallelism growth, $p_{AU}(t)$, is based on AMD's upper estimate of the number of processors available in a single computer while $p_{AL}(t)$ is their lower estimate. Similarly, Intel's upper estimate defines the function $p_{IU}(t)$ and their lower estimate defines $p_{IL}(t)$. From the graph of these four functions shown in Figure 1(b) we see that AMD's estimates, $p_{AU}(t)$ and $p_{AL}(t)$, are the upper approximations for parallelism growth while Intel's estimates, $p_{IU}(t)$ and $p_{IL}(t)$, establish the lower bound.

**System Size $z$**

Another way to gain parallelism in the password recovery computations is to use multiple computers. The more computers that are used, the less time it takes to recover a password. A system of computers can consist of personal computers, clustered nodes, or large networks like botnets. Any personal computer user can own any number of computers. In the case of a computing cluster, the size of these systems can be much larger. Sizes of 20 to 500 nodes are not atypical for today's standard computer clusters. Large networks of computers provide the largest factor of parallelism when executing one task. A botnet, a large number of compromised machines that can be remotely controlled by an attacker, is an example of such a network. Botnets can range in size from thousands to hundreds of thousands of computers. This growing availability of computers directly affects the amount of parallelism available to any user.

**2.2 Future Password Recovery**

This section depicts the extent to which computing performance improvements threaten the security of password authentication systems as determined by our model. We begin by briefly describing the password systems that we attempt to break and the time to recover passwords for each system on today's commodity hardware. The processor performance, $s(t)$, parallelism factor, $p(t)$, and system size, $z$, of the future computing systems used in the experiment are defined. The ability to recover passwords of these future systems is then evaluated in Figure 2 and discussed.

In our experiments, we analyze three password systems: Unix crypt, MD5 crypt and Kerberos. Unix crypt [9] is based on the DES algorithm and, with the increasing processing power available, has become vulnerable to brute force attacks. The MD5 algorithm [30] is also used in Unix-based systems and has been implemented as an upgrade from the DES algorithm. Compared to DES's 56-bit key size, MD5 uses a 128-bit value making brute force attacks comparatively more difficult. Kerberos [23] is a widely-used single-sign-on network authentication system. Tickets in the Kerberos system are encrypted with a key derived from a user's password. These tickets can be attacked in order to recover that password. As explained in the introduction, we chose to analyze these systems due to their current wide spread use. For more information about these password systems see Appendix A. We ran password recovery software on commodity hardware to determine the speed of tries for each password system. The results from these experiments are illustrated in Table 1. These values serve as indicators of current day password recovery ability. Using them as inputs to our models, we can derive the password recovery ability of future computing systems.

**Table 1.** Password Recovery Speeds

| System | Tries/Sec |
|---|---|
| Unix Crypt | 1557890 |
| MD5 Crypt | 17968 |
| Kerberos | 55462 |

For the following analysis, we posit one possible future computer type. Given the fact that chip technologies are reaching the limits of power and heat, the slow growth processor performance function, $s_{SG}(t)$, is used. In order to determine a median parallelism factor, we take the average of the two middle values; AMD's lower estimate and Intel's higher estimate. This results in a function, $p_{AVG}(t)$, that characterizes the average of $p_{AL}(t)$ and $p_{IU}(t)$. We analyze the impact of this computing power as it exists within these systems of the future with the following model:

$$T_z(t) = \frac{(3.3 \times 10^{15}) \cdot s_{SG}(t)}{p_{AVG}(t) \cdot z}. \tag{3}$$

The number of computers within a system, the parameter $z$ in Equation 3, can range anywhere from one to hundreds of thousands. We examine a six different systems in our study: a personal computer system consisting of 2 computers, clusters of 10 and 100 nodes, and botnets of 1000, 10000, and 100000 compromised hosts.

Beginning with the initial values presented in Table 1, we were able to determine, for each password system, what each of the modeled computer systems was capable of recovering over the span of 15 years. The results from these experiments are presented in Figure 2.

The most apparent result is that a botnet with 10,000 or more compromised computers is currently able to recover any password from any password system in under 6 months. In less than five years, any botnet with at least 1,000 compromised computers can recover any password in under a month.

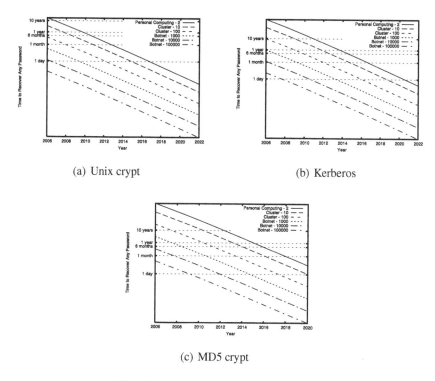

(a) Unix crypt                                    (b) Kerberos

(c) MD5 crypt

**Fig. 2.** Future Password Recovery Analysis

Given a smaller system, like a cluster, we see that password recovery, naturally, takes longer. An average sized cluster is able to recover any Unix crypt password in under 6 months today. However, within only 8 years, a cluster of minimal size will be able to recover any password from our three presented password systems.

Examining the extreme case of personal computing systems, the results are startling. Within three years, any Unix crypt password will be recoverable in under 6 months. Unix crypt is obviously broken. The more devastating result is that any password from any of the other evaluated systems is recoverable in under 6 months by a single personal computing system in 10 years. This means that our trusted authentication systems will be vulnerable to raw computing power from the comfort of your own home before 2017.

## 3  Passwords in Practice

In this section we show that the current state of password security is actually much worse than the theoretical model presented in Section 2.1 suggests. The preceding model examines the effect of improving hardware on password recovery, but does so considering the full password space of $95^8$ possibilities. In reality, the password space is often much smaller, thus an adversary is not required to try every one of the $95^8$ possible passwords. For example, password policies serve to reduce the amount of work an attacker is required to do to recover random passwords by reducing the possible password space. We examine specific password policies and demonstrate the effect that they have on the speed of brute force attacks.

Password systems are further weakened due to the poor choice of passwords. In practice, users choose non-random passwords that contain much less than their maximum allowable entropy. We demonstrate the degree to which this occurs by examining passwords within an actual institution and also by discussing NIST's study of passwords and their actual entropy. The effect of this reduced entropy on the speed of password recovery is examined.

### 3.1 Password Policy Restrictions

Based on the recommendations of the security community [8,31], many password systems have begun to implement password policies restricting the types of passwords that may be chosen. For instance, some sites do not allow users to choose characters outside the alphanumeric set. Others require passwords to be between a minimum and maximum length. Still others make restrictions on the types of characters that must be present in a password. While these rules help to prevent users from choosing dictionary-based passwords, we show that they decrease the total password space and that this is not effective in preventing brute-force attacks. We examine a number of policies and evaluate their effect on the speed of password recovery attacks in comparison with the results presented in Section 2.1.

We first analyze how policy restrictions reduce the number of possible passwords. Let $R_i$ be the set of passwords that do not satisfy a certain policy $i$. For instance, if policy $i$ required users to choose a lower-case letter $|R_i| = (95 - 26)^8$ thus, the password space is $|\neg R_i| = 95^8 - (95 - 26)^8$. We also define $R_i \cap R_j$ to be the intersection of passwords that do not satisfy both policies $i$ and $j$ (i.e. both policies are not satisfied). Now, we apply a variant of the inclusion-exclusion principle[3] to the total password space to get the following formula, which computes how many passwords satisfy all of the policies specified:

$$| \bigcap_{1 \leq i \leq k} \neg R_i| = (95^8)/2 + (-1)^1 ( \sum_{1 \leq i \leq k} |R_i|) + (-1)^2 ( \sum_{1 \leq i_1 \leq i_2 \leq k} |R_{i_1} \cap R_{i_2}|) +$$
$$\dots + (-1)^{k-1} (|R_1 \cap R_2 \cap \dots \cap R_{k-1} \cap R_k|) \tag{4}$$

The first password policy we examine is from a recommendation made by the SANS Institute password policy page [8]. SANS (SysAdmin, Audit, Network, Security) is a large collaborative group of security professionals that provide information security training and certification [7]. Their recommended policy is intended to be used by businesses when they establish password policies for their enterprise networks. SANS recommends that users pick at least one upper and lower case character, 1 digit and 1 special character. Applying the formula in Equation 4, this fairly typical policy reduces the number of valid passwords by more than a factor of 2.

---

[3] The inclusion-exclusion principle is used to determine the cardinality of multiple finite sets without double counting. It over compensates by repeatedly including set intersections, then recompensates by excluding the excess intersections.

The Computer Science and Engineering department at The Pennsylvania State University recently enacted a password policy applying to the password choices of all students and faculty in the department. Following the common wisdom, they used the Sun password policy mechanisms to define a policy requiring all users to have 2 upper case characters, 2 lower case characters, 1 digit, and one special character. Using the previous formula, this reduces the pool of potential passwords by nearly a third.

The last set of potential passwords examined here are those generated with the pwgen utility [6]. pwgen is a Unix utility which generates "memorable" passwords of user-defined size (default is 8 characters). However, until recently, pwgen would only mix alphanumeric characters randomly to form passwords, and would not use symbols. According to the pwgen changelog [5], this was done so that passwords would be "much more usable." Obviously, this greatly restricts the number of potential passwords that can be chosen to the size $62^8$, down from $95^8$. Unfortunately, pwgen is widely used to generate "random" passwords when secure initial or replacement passwords are needed.

We now examine how limiting the password space affects the speed of brute-force attacks. We perform this examination with the same models used in Section 2. Because the previous section already demonstrated that older Unix crypt hashes are too weak to provide practical security, we evaluate the speed of brute-force attacks under the Kerberos system. In this way, we demonstrate the degree to which attacks can be sped up in a system that would otherwise remain somewhat secure for the next few years.

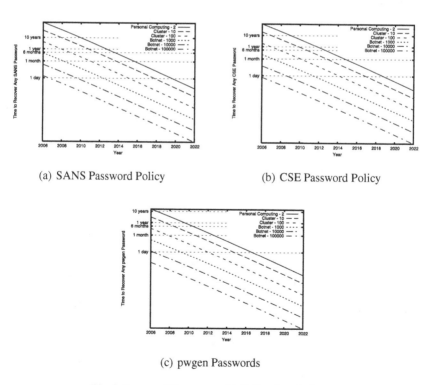

(a) SANS Password Policy          (b) CSE Password Policy

(c) pwgen Passwords

**Fig. 3.** Password Recovery with Policy Restrictions

The new estimates for future brute-force attacks are shown in Figure 3. As a point of reference, under the full password space, a single user will be able to crack a Kerberos password in under a year in October, 2013. We see that, under the restricted password space that SANS defines, this will happen around October, 2012. The Computer Science and Engineering policy restricts that password space such that a personal computer will be able to recover a Kerberos password in one year by around November 2011. And, most devastatingly, pwgen-generated passwords can be recovered approximately 30 times faster than passwords without restrictions. This makes pwgen passwords approximately as weak as older Unix crypt hashes without password restrictions. This policy, the most restrictive of the three, creates a situation in which a single personal computer can crack a Kerberos password in 1 year around June, 2009. This demonstrates how policy decisions can negate benefits accrued through proper algorithm choice

We conclude that password policies, while useful for eliminating the weakest passwords, can severely restrict the pool of passwords attackers must search. Requiring users to pick only a subset of potential passwords can drastically reduce the password space provided by perfectly random passwords in that system. The time to crack a perfect password is reduced by up to a factor of 30, as shown in Figure 3(c). It is important to note that when password policies are enforced, this sizable restriction is applied to each and every password, no matter how random the user's password is.

### 3.2   User Passwords

Despite password policies which try to force users to create more random passwords, users still choose passwords which contain very little entropy. Users often pick words with obvious letter replacements, like "0" for O, dictionary words with numbers or characters appended, and misspellings of common words. Also, by nature, users are much more likely to pick certain characters than others based on elements of a language [27]. In short, they still pick passwords that are not truly random and thus are vulnerable to intelligent password guessing attacks. In response to these tendencies, most password recovery tools today contain fairly sophisticated methods of guessing words with common symbol-for-letter replacements, words with numbers appended, and variations on words out of the dictionary. Some password crackers also have an intelligent brute-force mode which tries all possible passwords, but in order of increasing likelihood. For instance, the string "bgtyae1T" would be tried long before "t,I}&[*v". Then end result of this is that the brute-force times depicted in Figures 2 and 3 are still much too conservative when applied to actual passwords.

In order to evaluate the severity of weakly chosen passwords, a password file for the entire Computer Science and Engineering Department at Penn State University was obtained as described in Appendix A. This recovered the password hashes for 3500 users. The password recovery jobs were then submitted to a cluster of 20 nodes with dual AMD Opteron 250 processors. 16 of the 20 nodes were used for brute-forcing passwords based on character frequencies, and 4 nodes for trying passwords derived from dictionary words. The password recovery tool John the Ripper was used since it is widely available and has good support for both dictionary and brute-force based attacks. This program ran for 5 days, with the number of passwords recovered as a function of time graphed in Figure 4.

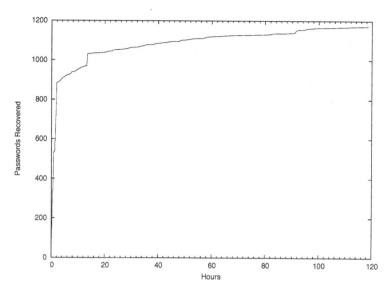

**Fig. 4.** Time to Recover Penn State CSE Passwords

One of the most startling observations from this graph is that approximately 25% of all passwords were cracked within the first 2 hours. It is particularly interesting to note that only 10.1% of the passwords recovered were recovered as a result of guesses based on dictionary words. The remaining 1118 passwords were all recovered by the nodes performing an intelligent brute-force attack. The brute-forcing method found in John the Ripper [3], which we used for these experiments, is clearly able to recover a large number of non-dictionary based passwords. This is a somewhat surprising result, as common lore in the security community is that the biggest problem with passwords is that users choose commonly used or dictionary-based passwords. Instead, this data may reflect both a growing consciousness about the weakness of dictionary passwords and a persistent inability of users to pick passwords uniformly from the potential space of all possible passwords.

### 3.3   Study of User Passwords

Although the results in the preceding section paint a dire picture of password strength in practice, there is evidence that the actual resistance of passwords to attack is much worse. According to the National Institute of Standards and Technology (NIST), passwords in practice are much weaker than the theoretical maximum previously discussed [32]. Based on experimental findings, NIST has given some guidelines as to the practical entropy provided by passwords that users choose. In this section, we evaluate the time to crack an 8 character password using password entropy guidelines from NIST.

NIST measures the amount of randomness within a given password using bits of entropy. Each bit of entropy under a given password policy multiplies the possible password space by 2 (e.g., 5 bits of entropy means there are $2^5$ possible passwords). In a system where a user may chose any 8 character password, NIST specifies that the first character of a password gives 4 bits of entropy, and successive characters give 2 bits apiece. We will call this the *permissive policy*. In many systems, however, users are forced to choose both upper-case and non-alphanumeric characters. This nets a password with an additional 6 bits of entropy, according to NIST. We will refer to this as the *special-character policy*. If passwords are checked against an exhaustive dictionary of at least 50,000 words (a factor of 10 less than the dictionary searched in the preceding results), 6 bits of entropy are added. Two new policies can be constructed, the *dictionary policy* and the *special-character and dictionary policy*, when the dictionary is applied to the permissive and special-character policies, respectively.

Given the previously discussed entropy values and equation for password space as determined by these values, we estimate the amount of time required to recover any password with a single machine and with a 20-node cluster. Table 2 presents the amount of time required to recover these passwords in theory as determined by NIST. Note that all of these measurements assume full 8 character passwords, as the time to compromise with 7 or fewer characters became negligible.

**Table 2.** Time to recover passwords as specified by NIST

| Password Type | Bits of Entropy | Time to recover for single machine | 20-node Cluster |
|---|---|---|---|
| permissive | 18 | < 1 minute | < 1 second |
| special-character | 24 | 14 minutes | 20 seconds |
| dictionary | 24 | 14 minutes | 20 seconds |
| special-character and dictionary | 30 | 15 hours | 22 minutes |

Using the NIST entropy guidelines, our estimates predict faster recovery than our experimental results show, though not by much. As Table 2 shows, the average special-character and dictionary password, the strongest password type that the government identifies, takes 15 hours to recover. However, only a third of the CSE user passwords were recoverable in this time. The discrepancy in these values is likely caused by better passwords chosen within the computer science department as opposed to the general population.

Software may also play a role in explaining the discrepancy between the actual brute-force recovery speed and the theoretical brute-force recovery speed. For example, although John the Ripper is a sophisticated program, it does not do a perfect job of guessing passwords in order of increasing randomness. Thus, even though a user password may not be very random, it may not be quickly recovered due to the imperfect nature of the password recovery software. Our experience has confirmed this, as we have seen many passwords (like "myPword!") take a long time to crack, while possessing little randomness. Software algorithms for guessing passwords have room for improvement, and the recent development of new password recovery methods [3] indicates that these improvements will likely continue to be made. This would decrease the time to recover a password on every system in every configuration for every password.

# 4   Mitigating Password Vulnerability

This section considers ways of mitigating the vulnerabilities of current password systems, now and in the future. We consider two broad approaches to limiting the vulnerabilities associated with passwords: the first is to simply prevent offline attacks from occurring, and the second is to reduce the effectiveness of the offline attack.

## 4.1   Preventing Offline Attacks

In order to mount an offline password attack, recovery material must be obtained, for example, a password file or a TGT. This material normally consists of encrypted or digested versions of passwords. Password material can be obtained actively or passively. Active recovery requires the adversary to perform some observable behavior such as initiating a fake login or reading a password file in order to obtain the necessary material. Passive recovery is a covert action such as eavesdropping a network exchange to acquire the material. Preventing the adversary from obtaining this password material would effectively prevent offline attacks. The mechanism used to prevent the attack is related to the means by which the password material is obtained.

In an attempt to prevent active password material recovery, recent UNIX systems have begun to provide mechanisms to reduce the visibility of password material to all users of the system. Recent versions of Unix introduced the concept of the /etc/shadow file, which stores the password hash in a file readable only by root, instead of by all users. This makes active recovery schemes more difficult, thus making offline attacks more difficult.

Preventing passive recovery of password material involves eliminating the availability of the material on unprotected networks. One option is to not send password material over the network. Password material includes anything that is encrypted with a password or a derivation of a password. Thus, in order to abstain from sending password material, data must be encrypted with something besides the password. The secure remote password protocol (SRP) [33] and similar protocols [11] have created a way for two parties to agree on a symmetric session key with which to encrypt data instead of using passwords. However, authentication is still performed with passwords, as both parties must have knowledge of the password in order to agree on the symmetric key. Thus, these protocols have eliminated the need to send password material over an insecure network in order to support authentication. They are designed such that they effectively prevent brute-force online and offline attacks.

Protecting the network over which passwords are sent is another way to protect password material. This technique is useful in systems that cannot support changes to their protocols. For instance, SRP could be difficult to apply to authentication to financial web services, due to time synchronization restraints, export restrictions, and network latencies. Encrypting the link over which credentials are transmitted is a common method used to prevent cracking material from falling into the wrong hands. This could be done using a virtual private network (VPN) or secure sockets layer (SSL). In this way, a system may continue to use password systems which are vulnerable to brute-force attacks but trust the network to protect against them.

## 4.2  Hardening Password Systems

In many cases, protecting password material can be a complicated or impossible task thus, the security of the system lies in the difficulty of offline brute-force attacks. A number of methods for making password guessing more difficult have been proposed. One proposed solution is simply to make the encryption more complex and computationally expensive, thus reducing the speed of brute-force attacks. However, this presents a few problems. First, this may put a great strain on the server. In the case of Kerberos, if the KDC must hash TGTs 1000 times instead of just once, the computational load on the server would increase considerably. This exposes authentication servers to DoS attacks, since an attacker can repeatedly attempt to authenticate in most systems. Complex encryption would also make it difficult to incorporate legacy systems into new authentication schemes. For example, an older 100MHz Pentium system cannot do 100 billion MD5 hashes very easily. Moreover, low power devices are also much less capable of complex encryption. Other solutions, such as hardware-dependent encryption algorithms [28], result in a hardware-cryptography arms race. As hardware increases in speed, cryptography is deliberately slowed to maintain its security.

Another often proposed solution is to increase the minimum number of characters required for passwords. Unfortunately, this solution is restricted by a fundamental human limitation of remembering no more than 7 random items easily. While some users may be able to memorize random strings of 12 or more characters, many will not be able to, and will be forced to write down passwords or pick passwords will very little randomness. A good password recovery tool will be able to try such non-random combinations quickly, negating most of the benefit to having a longer password.

Implementation restrictions also make this solution practically difficult. Any system that must inter-operate with older crypt() implementations is limited to 8 characters. Many sites today require passwords of no longer than 8 characters because of this. Additionally, since users must remember such a large number of passwords, they often re-use them from site to site. As such, they often pick passwords that will be universally accepted, thus restricting their password choices to 6-8 character passwords conforming to standard password policies.

Pass phrases are an interesting alternative to passwords. In this system, a user would choose a pass phrase of around 7 words. Since there are around 500,000 words in the English language [4], the potential combination of these words can provide a larger password space. However, in practice, informal studies have shown that it may be the case that pass phrases often provide less randomness than passwords [29]. This is conjectured to be the result of users picking common phrases and words, resulting in less total randomness.

Two-factor authentication is another solution that has gained recent prominence with the strong recommendation of the Federal Financial Institutions Examination Council that two-factor authentication should be used by 2006 for all Internet financial transactions [15]. As long as the method of two-factor authentication used includes some type of random number or symmetric key, this information could be combined with the user's password to create a key that falls randomly within the keyspace of the encryption method used. This then eliminates the fundamental restriction of passwords: that they only occupy a very limited subset of the keyspace supported by the encryption used.

# 5   Related Work

Morris and Thompson first addressed the issue of password security in 1979 [26] by describing the challenges faced by the UNIX password system. They observed problems that existed within the system stemming from the availability of the password file and then identified guessing passwords as a general approach that was successful in penetrating the system. However, the time to encrypt each guess and compare the result with the file entries was highlighted as the main challenge in password guessing. They analyzed passwords from 1 to 6 characters long from key spaces of 26 to 128 characters and found that exhaustively searching the key space was beneficial in finding a fraction of a system's passwords given enough time. To simplify the searching task, they also noticed that the users of the system chose short and simple passwords, which greatly reduced the key space.

In order to make cracking user passwords more challenging, Morris and Thompson proposed a list of tips to make stronger passwords. The suggestions were attempts to slow the process of password cracking and included basic ideas like choosing longer passwords, choosing passwords constructed from a larger character set, or having the system create passwords. The authors also proposed password salting, combining the password with extra well-known data, as a technique to make pre-computation impossible and increase the time necessary to crack a password. These defenses became the basis for future password cracking prevention techniques.

Ten years later, a paper was published discussing the claims of Morris and Thompson as well as the progress of password security and cracking [19]. Like its predecessor, the paper examined the performance of key space searches. They looked at the possible times for cracking passwords with the same key space as Morris and Thompson, but examined lengths ranging from 4 to 8 characters. With the addition of password salting, the searches had indeed become more complex. The authors claimed that a large key space of 95 characters "is large enough to resist brute force attacks in software ... It is impossible to use exhaustive search over the large search space..." However, they determined that password cracking was very possible if the search space was limited. This could be done by creating a common password word list to guess passwords from instead of attempting to guess every possible password.

In order to maximize the difficulty of password cracking, [19] discussed execution speed of the hashing mechanism and password entropy. The authors concluded that, because computing speed and power were changing, attacking the problem by increasing the speed of the encryption algorithm was not plausible. They also analyzed other solutions including changing the encryption algorithm and better protecting the cracking material. It was concluded that making passwords less predictable was the principal defense against password cracking.

Dictionary attacks are the fastest, easiest way to crack passwords because passwords are commonly chosen from a small set of words. In order to prevent these fast, simple attacks, systems implemented policies that required passwords contain a certain amount of entropy. The policies include rules on minimal length and required password characters. To enforce these policies, password checking software was developed, which determined if a given password had enough entropy to be considered secure. However, dictionary attacks then evolved by exploiting common non-dictionary choices for passwords. The techniques used by these attacks included searching for random capitalization, permutations of dictionary words and usernames, letter and number manipulations, and foreign language words. These attacks continue to evolve by examining and exploiting common policies. Unfortunately, research has shown that despite password policy advice, users still tend towards dictionary words for passwords [22].

Sophisticated analysis of the English language has aided in password guessing. For example, character frequency, once very successfully used as a spellchecker in UNIX, is now being used in password cracking [3]. Analysis of common passwords has also contributed to faster password cracking. Possible passwords are tried in a certain order based on how common the password is. From these advanced methods, we see that password guessing techniques continue to evolve as long as passwords are still in use. As a result, a variety of solutions have been proposed to combat password guessing.

Twenty five years after Morris and Thompson's paper, modern passwords are still vulnerable to offline cracking attacks. Basic hashes and digests are still used to encrypt these passwords, thus today's cracking material is similar to that available in the 1980s. However, the ability hash passwords, and thus recover passwords, has drastically improved due to developments in software that have quickened the performance of these encryption techniques, sometimes by as much as a factor of 5 [13]. These improvements have impacted the speed at which passwords can be cracked, thus increasing the difficulty of preventing offline password cracking.

## 6  Conclusion

The limited protection passwords provide to authentication systems that allow offline attacks is clearly no longer sufficient to resist serious attacks. Such systems are fundamentally restricted in the amount of protection they can provide, while the resources of the attackers grows exponentially. Due to the ease with which even random passwords will be recoverable in the next 5 years, the security of any system based on passwords will be equivalent to the availability of the cracking material, not how random the passwords are. As such, protocols must be designed to not allow any type of offline attack, and the material that can be used to mount such an attack must be protected with the understanding that its confidentiality is equivalent to the security of the authentication mechanism as a whole.

## References

1. AMD 3-year technology outlook. http://www.amdcompare.com/techoutlook/.
2. EFF DES cracker project. www.eff.org/Privacy/Crypto/Crypto_misc/DESCracker/.
3. John the ripper password cracker. http://www.openwall.com/john/.
4. Number of words in the English language. http://hypertextbook.com/facts/2001/JohnnyLing. shtml.
5. pwgen CVS changelog. http://pwgen.cvs.sourceforge.net/pwgen/src/ChangeLog?revision= 1.8&view=markup.
6. pwgen password generator. http://sourceforge.net/projects/pwgen/.
7. Sans institute. http://www.sans.org/aboutsans.php.

8. SANS password policies. http://www.sans.org/resources/policies/.

9. Unix cyrpt man page. http://bama.ua.edu/cgi-bin/man-cgi?crypt_unix+5.

10. The magical number seven, plus or minus two: Some limits on our capacity for processing information, 1956.

11. Mihir Bellare, David Pointcheval, and Phillip Rogaway. Authenticated key exchange secure against dictionary attacks. *Lecture Notes in Computer Science*, 1807:139–156, 2000.

12. S. M. Bellovin and M. Merritt. Limitations of the kerberos authentication system. *SIGCOMM Comput. Commun. Rev.*, 20(5):119–132, 1990.

13. Eli Biham. A fast new DES implementation in software. *Lecture Notes in Computer Science*, 1267:260–272, 1997.

14. Shekhar Y Borkar, Pardeep Dubey, Kevin C Kahn, David J Kuck, Hans Mulder, Stephen S Pawlowski, Justing R Rattner, R M Ramanathan, and Vince Thomas. Platform 2015: Intel Processor and Platform Evolution for the Next Decade. Technical report, Intel, 2005.

15. Federal Fiancial Institutions Examination Council. Authentication in an internet banking environment. http://federalreserve.gov/boarddocs/srletters/2005/SR0519a1.pdf.

16. Larry Cuban. *Oversold and Underused: Computers in the Classroom*. Harvard University Press, 2001.

17. Manek Dubash. Moore's Law is dead, says Gordon Moore. *http://www.techworld.com/opsys/news/index.cfm?NewsID=3477*, 2005.

18. Magnus Ekman, Fredrik Warg, and Jim Nilsson. An in-depth look at computer performance growth. *SIGARCH Comput. Archit. News*, 33(1):144–147, 2005.

19. David C. Feldmeier and Philip R. Karn. Unix password security - ten years later. In *CRYPTO '89: Proceedings of the 9th Annual International Cryptology Conference on Advances in Cryptology*, pages 44–63, London, UK, 1990. Springer-Verlag.

20. Radhakrishna Hiremane. From Moore's Law to Intel Innovation - Prediction to Reality. *Technology@Intel Magazine*, April 2005.

21. Ian Jermyn, Alain Mayer, Fabian Monrose, Michael Reiter, and Aviel Rubin. The Design and Analysis of Graphic Passwords. In *Proceedings of the 8th Annual USENIX Security Symposium*, 1999.

22. Daniel V. Klein. "foiling the cracker" – A survey of, and improvements to, password security. In *Proceedings of the second USENIX Workshop on Security*, pages 5–14, Summer 1990.

23. J. Kohl and C. Neuman. RFC 1510: The Kerberos Network Authentication Service (V5), September 1993. Status: PROPOSED STANDARD.

24. Rob Lemos. Passwords: The Weakest Link. http://news.com.com/2009-1001-916719.html, 2002.

25. Fabian Monrose and Aviel Rubin. Authentication via Keystroke Dynamics. In *Proceedings of the 4th ACM Conference on Computer and Communication Security*, 1997.

26. Robert Morris and Ken Thompson. Password security: a case history. *Commun. ACM*, 22(11):594–597, 1979.

27. Arvind Narayanan and Vitaly Shmatikov. Fast dictionary attacks on passwords using time-space tradeoff. In *CCS '05: Proceedings of the 12th ACM conference on Computer and communications security*, pages 364–372, New York, NY, USA, 2005. ACM Press.

28. Niels Provos and David Mazières. A Future-Adaptable Password Scheme. In *USENIX Annual Technical Conference, FREENIX Track*, pages 81–91, 1999.

29. Arnold G. Reinhold. Results of a survey on pgp pass phrase usage. http://www.ecst.csuchico.edu/ atman/Crypto/misc/pgp-passphrase-survey.html.

30. R. Rivest. The MD5 Message-Digest Algorithm . RFC 1321 (Informational), April 1992.

31. Wayne C. Summers and Edward Bosworth. Password policy: the good, the bad, and the ugly. In *WISICT '04: Proceedings of the winter international synposium on Information and communication technologies*, pages 1–6. Trinity College Dublin, 2004.

32. W. Timothy Polk William E. Burr, Donna F. Dodson. Electronic authentication guidelines. NIST Special Publication 800-63.
33. Thomas Wu. The secure remote password protocol. In *Proceedings of the 1998 Internet Society Network and Distributed System Security Symposium*, pages 97–111, 1998.
34. Thomas Wu. A real-world analysis of Kerberos password security. In *Internet Society Network and Distributed System Security Symposium*, 1999.

# Appendix

### Unix Crypt

The previous work in this field has examined password cracking primarily as it applies to cracking attempts against the Unix/Linux /etc/passwd, so we start by examining this password storage type to give a sense of how modern techniques and equipment compare to what was previously available. This type of authentication system is used to authenticate users to a Unix/Linux system. In the traditional Unix crypt system, hashes of users' passwords are stored in a password file often named either /etc/password or /etc/shadow, with the 2 letter salt prepended to the hash. A user enters their password, which is then combined with the salt in the password file, and then encrypted using a variation of the DES algorithm. The resulting ciphertext is compared with the hash in the password file, and if the values match, the user is successfully authenticated. Newer systems, such as the one first found in modern crypt function, hash the password with MD5 repeatedly (up to 1000+ times), instead of just once[28].

For this type of authentication system, an attacker must somehow obtain a copy of this password hash file. Unfortunately, this can be made available to an attacker in a variety of ways. The simplest of these is if an attacker has root access on a machine, in which case he can simply copy the /etc/shadow file. If the password hashes have not been moved to /etc/shadow, they will reside in the world-readable /etc/passwd file, in which case an attacker with normal user access to the system can simply copy the file. However, amongst other attacks, there is one attack in particular which allows a large number of attackers access to the password file. The Network Information Services, or NIS, is often used to centralize authentication decisions over a large number of machines. NIS provides a utility, ypcat, which allows users to view portions of information about system users. We found ypcat to be often misconfigured in a way that allows any user on any system connected to NIS to simply ypcat the password hash portion of each user in the system. In this way, an attacker can gain access to the credentials of each user on any system tied to NIS.

The actual process of guessing a user's password is very simple. To recover passwords from this password file, an attacker takes candidate passwords, combines them with the appropriate salt, which is well known, and applies the appropriate hashing technique to this value. The attack then checks to see if the result from hashing his guess matches the hash value in the password file.

### Kerberos

We also evaluate password cracking as it relates to modern versions of Kerberos. Kerberos, a popular single-sign-on protocol, is widely touted today as a solution to "the password problem." It is used to authenticate to a variety of services, including IPsec, Email, Web Services, Directory Services, and many more. Because Kerberos is often used as a single-sign-on service, a compromise of Kerberos credentials is often equivalent to a compromise of the users' credentials to every service in the network. Unfortunately, Kerberos, in every version, is vulnerable to a variety of password-guessing attacks[12,34].

One of the biggest issues with Kerberos as it relates to password cracking is that as opposed to most Unix/Linux systems, where an attacker must have a valid user account (or have compromised one), all the cracking material necessary to mount an offline attack against Kerberos credentials can be obtained either by anyone who asks or anyone who can sniff Kerberos traffic, depending on the restrictions in place. During a client's initial authentication In the Kerberos protocol, a client sends an authentication request to a server in charge of authentication for the Kerberos realm called the KDC. If the client makes a correct request, the KDC will return a token called a ticket granting ticket (TGT). This token can be used to obtain credentials to any Kerberized service the client can access. Unfortunately, when this TGT is given to the client, it is transmitted over the network, encrypted with a key derived from the user's password. While the user's password itself is never sent in any form, this TGT is still vulnerable to password guessing attacks, as described below.

An attacker has a variety of options for obtaining cracking material (the TGT) required for this attack. In Kerberos v4, a KDC will return a TGT to anyone who asks for it. Thus, in this case, an attacker's job is completely trivial, and he can easily obtain a TGT to crack for each user in the system by simply asking. However, Kerberos v5 introduced the idea of preauthentication. With preauthentication, a user must use the key derived from his password (as described above) to encrypt a timestamp, which is included in the client's request for TGT. The server will only return a TGT if the timestamp received by the server decrypts correctly with the client's key. In this way, the server attempts to insure that a TGT is only sent to the user to whom it belongs.

However, an attacker attempting to crack a Kerberos 5 deployment still has a number of options for recovering a TGT. First, many Kerberos deployments do not have preauthentication required for all users. In this situation, an attacker may simply ask for TGTs as he did for Kerberos v4. Many deployments, in order to ensure backwards compatibility, still support Kerberos v4, so an attacker may simply ask for v4 tickets for each user. Finally, in any of these systems, the TGT itself is sent over the network in the clear, so an attacker that can sniff the network can trivially recover the TGT.

In order to compromise Kerberos credentials, an attacker first captures the TGT using one of the aforementioned methods. Then, an attacker generates a password guess. This guess is transformed into a key using the Kerberos "stringToKey" function, which uses both the password guess and information found in the TGT itself, such as the user's name and the name of the Kerberos realm. Then, this key is used to decrypt the captured TGT. Since each TGT, if decrypted correctly, contains the string "krbtgt", it is easy for an attacker to know if the decryption, and therefore the candidate password, was correct.

# Network Monitoring for Security and Forensics

Kulesh Shanmugasundaram and Nasir Memon

Department of Computer and Information Science,
Polytechnic University, Brooklyn, NY 11201
memon@isis.poly.edu
http://isis.poly.edu/memon/

**Abstract.** Networked environment has grown hostile over the years. In order to guarantee the security of networks and the resources attached to networks it is necessary to constantly monitor and analyze network traffic. Increasing network bandwidth, however, prohibits the recording and analysis of raw network traffic. In this paper we discuss some challenges facing network monitoring and present monitoring strategies to alleviate the challenges.

**Keywords:** Network Monitoring, Network Security, Network Forensics, Synopses.

## 1 Introduction

Networked environment has grown hostile over the years. Networks are augmented with multiple layers of perimeter defenses, such as firewalls, Intrusion Detection Systems (IDS), antivirus, antispam, etc., to protect the networks and the resources attached to the networks from adversaries. Unfortunately attacks mounted by adversaries have also evolved with the evolution of perimeter defenses. The attacks will continue to evolve in future. Today most attacks are carried out through a firewall's open ports and in multiple stages to avoid detection by the defense systems. It seems attacks have adapted and are capable of circumventing the defenses in place. Therefore, currently there is a need to constantly monitor network traffic for two reasons. The first is to monitor and collect network traffic for offline analysis to identify potential troublemakers. The second is to collect and retain network traffic to facilitate forensics when the perimeter defenses fail.

Most of state-of-the-art security solutions address a specific problem but what we need is a solution that can address the more general problem of collecting network data for analysis and for supporting postmortems during incident response. Some of the perimeter defenses, such as firewalls and intrusion detection systems, assume a priori knowledge of the modus operandi. The others, especially commercial Network Forensic Analysis Tools (NFATs), take a brute-force approach of recording everything on the network. Note that these solutions either archive *all* evidence for short periods of time or keep *very selective* evidence for long periods of time, either of which makes them less useful for forensics or

A. Bagchi and V. Atluri (Eds.): ICISS 2006, LNCS 4332, pp. 56–70, 2006.
© Springer-Verlag Berlin Heidelberg 2006

for long term correlations of events. There is a need to develop techniques to collect and retain sufficient data for analysis and forensics in a storage efficient manner. In general any such technique must answer two questions:

- What type of data should be collected?
- What is the optimal strategy to collect this data?

We expand on these questions in the following section.

## 2   Major Challenges

In this section we explore two major challenges in collecting network traffic for security analysis and forensics.

### 2.1   What to Collect?

Millions of network events occur every second. Collecting data without prior knowledge on what will be needed for a future postmortem or analysis is a challenging problem for two reasons. First, we cannot selectively collect data like an IDS or a firewall because that would limit the scope of postmortems and analysis. Second, we cannot collect everything because that would impose enormous storage requirements on the system making it infeasible. Therefore, to understand the type of data we can collect on networks we must first understand the types of data that are available.

Suppose we consider a network to be a large finite-state machine which changes its state with the introduction of every packet. In order to support postmortems we should be able to recall the exact state of the networks at any given time in the past. Of course, this is the ideal case but to build a system that is close to the ideal case we need to collect and retain data that fall under the following four categories.

*Link States.* Networks are formed by inter-connecting a multitude of hosts. The hosts establish links or connections via a variety of protocols at different levels of protocol abstractions. These links can last for varying lengths of time, anywhere from a few seconds to many months. The links can also change over time. Old links may disappear and new ones may be established. Therefore, it is useful to keep track of what is linked to what on the Internet and certain properties of these links. A system designed to support forensics should keep track of end-to-end links and hop-by-hop links. End-to-end links are established at transport and upper level protocols that reveal which hosts are connected to which other hosts. This information can be inferred from network protocols such as from a TCP connection or from a UDP "connection." Hop-by-hop links are established at the infrastructure level and can help us determine which networks are connected to which other networks and their physical proximity. These links can be inferred from routing protocols such as BGP and OSPF.

*Link Content.* Links are established between hosts to carry a variety of content. Links may carry anything from audio streams to routing updates. Contents traversing these links are the most useful sources of evidence in a postmortem. Therefore a system designed to support postmortems should keep track of the contents traversing the links in a network. Ideally a forensic system should capture and archive every single packet that traverses a link. However, when keeping raw packets is not feasible the system may instead decide to keep what it perceives at the time as sufficient evidence for a postmortem. For example, instead of keeping raw packets the system may infer the type of an application using a link such as Kazaa or Bittorent or the type of content being transferred over the link such as audio or encrypted streams. In order to collect this data the system may capture raw content, like many NFATs do, create digests, like SPIE, or infer content type from a sample of packets, like Nabs [4].

*Link Aggregates.* As a network state machine changes states many state transitions can generate a lot of aggregate information that can be useful for forensics. Therefore, we also need to keep track of such aggregates. These aggregates can be generated by network devices in the form of SNMP statistics or can be gathered by monitoring network links. The system can keep track of useful statistics about links such as, protocol types, amount of data transferred, number of packets transferred, length of the link (in time), etc.

*Mappings.* The Internet comprises of millions of heterogeneous nodes communicating with each other. In order to make them inter-operate and to make the heterogeneity transparent to end users, protocols and applications use many aliases or protocol mappings. An example of such a mapping is the Domain Name System (DNS) which maps a user friendly domain name like `isis.poly.edu` to a 32-bit IP address like `0x80EE400F`. These mappings often change with time therefore a forensic system must keep track of these mappings to be able to find the correct host at a later time. These mappings usually fall under the following three categories:

- *Protocol Mappings*: These mappings are used by various network protocols to talk to each other or to translate between the mappings from lower layers to upper layers or vice versa. Examples of protocol mappings include MAC addresses and DNS names that map corresponding addresses or names to IP addresses. Other examples include IP multicast mappings where one multicast IP address may map to a group of IP addresses, and Network Address Translation (NAT) where one IP address on one side of a network interface is mapped to one or many IP addresses on the other side.
- *Application Mappings*: These mappings are unique to a particular application and are used by the application to improve scalability, reliability, or efficiency. Examples of application level mappings include VirtualHost of HTTP and various routing protocol mappings in peer-to-peer networks such as KeyId in FreeNet.
- *Administrative Mappings*: These mappings are created and maintained for administrative purposes of networks or hosts and are generally not enforced

by a protocol. An example of administrative mapping is Autonomous System Numbers (ASN) to IP address mappings as assigned by IANA (Internet Assigned Numbers Authority).

## 2.2   How to Collect?

Given the increasing speed of networks it is not trivial to collect data without overwhelming a network's routine operations. Once we decide on what data to collect there must also be a strategy on how to properly collect this data. A collection strategy is partly determined by what type of data is being collected. For example, a centralized collection of network data at a traffic concentration point of a network maximizes the visibility of interactions of the network with rest of the Internet. This is the most popular strategy currently used on many networks for deploying network monitors. This centralized collection strategy, however, has two major flaws.

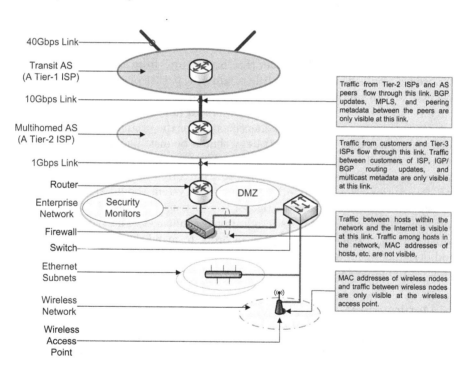

**Fig. 1.** A cross section of the Internet showing the hierarchy of Autonomous Systems (AS), network speeds between various AS, and a typical deployment of security monitors in an enterprise network

*Visibility.* A centralized collection point does not see all the packets traversing a network. Since each subnet of a network is usually a broadcast domain and a switch (or a hub) does not leak packets sent within a domain outside, a collection point outside of a subnet does not see packets shared within the subnet. We call the ability of a collection point to observe events within a domain *event visibility*. A centralized collection strategy lacks *event visibility*. Furthermore, a centralized collection may not see all necessary data. For example, even though a packet sent from a host within a subnet to a host on the Internet is visible to a centralized collection strategy, the MAC address of the host that sent the packet is not visible because a MAC address is visible only at the first hop of a packet. We call the ability of a collection point to observe data *data visibility*. A centralized collection strategy lacks *data visibility*. Postmortems require that a forensic system have both data and event visibility. For example, suppose a disgruntled employee decided to take revenge on the employer by installing a Trojan horse on critical systems. A postmortem of this incident would require elaborate information on network connections established within the organization so that an investigator could reconstruct the modus operandi for evidential as well as recovery purposes. A collection point at the edge of the organization's network would not be useful for this postmortem.

*Correctness.* A centralized collection point sees only one instance of an event and does not see the "big picture." Thanks to lack of integrity checks on Internet protocol suite it is impossible to infer the "big picture" from a single observation. Suppose we would like to identify the origin of a packet on the Internet. In an ideal case we can simply look at its source IP address to identify its origin. Since source IP addresses can easily be spoofed, only a hop-by-hop verification of the packet's passage can yield reliable identification of the origin.

Therefore, a proper collection strategy should be distributed through out the Internet with full event and data visibility. The system should collect data from multiple points so that it can corroborate the correctness of one observation with observations from many other points. The system should also provide the necessary information for an investigator to construct the "big picture." Having a distributed system also brings in additional challenges. The system must co-ordinate its data collection operation in order to avoid duplicate collection. A good design of the system must also include fault tolerance and redundancy to minimize the impacts of failures.

## 3 Deployment and Usage

ForNet is a system designed around the principles described above [5]. At the time of this writing ForNet has been operational at Polytechnic University for well over two years. It has been used for network monitoring, trouble-shooting, and retrospective analysis of incidents, such as a denial of service attack, identifying frequent scanners of the University resources, bandwidth hogs, and service outages. This chapter, however, presents two use cases of ForNet with the most impact on the security of the network. The first use-case demonstrates the usefulness of ForNet in identifying hosts in a network that may have been infected with a 0-day malware. The second use-case demonstrates the usefulness of For-Net in a proactive (or reactive) identification of, possibly malicious, proxies or proxy-nets in and outside of a network and possible "victims" in the network. There are about 2, 700 active IP addresses spread across 14 subnets in the network. The network is linked to the Internet via a 100Mbps Ethernet link and about 1TB of network traffic transits the link daily.

## 3.1 Following the Trails of an Outbreak

We now describe an actual case where we used the Hierarchical Bloom Filters (HBF) [3] to track the propagation of a mass-mailing virus MyDoom in the network. These attributions can be used to identify and quarantine infected machined within the network and to evaluate the threat or risk posed by hosts outside of the network and block them at the firewall. With this method we can find instances of viruses that infected the hosts before signature information was ever available to intrusion detection systems or virus scanners. The synopsis was deployed at SynApp which monitors the Internet link and was setup to monitor all email related traffic (POP, IMAP, SMTP) in and out of the network. Although we were not aware of MyDoom at the time, we were also collecting raw network traffic for experiments from the same vantage point. The raw packet trace was used to determine the "actual attribution rate" of MyDoom.

*MyDoom.* MyDoom is a mass-mailing computer worm affecting Windows operating system. It is also known as Novarg, Mimail.R and Shimgapi. The worm first appeared on the Internet on January $26^{th}$, 2004 and quickly became one of the fastest spreading worms in record. Although the worm primarily relied on e-mail for spreading it also copied itself into shared directories of peer-to-peer service Kazaa. The worm arrives as an email attachment of 22,528 bytes. The attachment has a random file name but the file extension is one of `.cmd`, `.pif`, `.scr`, `.exe`, or `.bat`. Attachments may also arrive as ZIP archives. When executed the worm scans files in the infected host for email addresses which are then used to spread the worm further. In addition, the worm also opens a backdoor on one of the TCP ports in the range of 3127-3198. The worm was programmed to perform a denial of service attack on `www.sco.com` on February $1^{th}$, 2004 and to stop spreading after February $12^{th}$, 2004.

*Payload Processing.* Using the effective false positive rates in [3] we chose 0.1090 as the $FP_o$ of Bloom filter on which the HBF is built. Our implementation of HBF uses MD5 as the hash function for the Bloom filter. Each MD5 operation yields 4 32-bit integers and two of these are used to achieve the required $FP_o$. Using the email traffic statistics of the network we concluded that on average 70, 000 blocks will be inserted into an HBF every minute. For the chosen false positive rate of the Bloom filter we need to commit 5 bits per block ($m = 5$) and the optimal number of elements the filter can contain is 70, 000 ($n = 70,000$) which in turn translates to a filter of size 43.75KB (i.e., $n \times m = 43.75$KB). HBF is flushed to disk when the filter is full (70, 000 blocks are inserted) or 60 seconds have elapsed, whichever comes first. The PAS also maintained a list of *hostIDs* of the form ($SourceIP, DestinationIP$) per HBF so that the system does not rely on other sources for candidate *hostID*s. During the experiments, we noted on average each HBF had about 260 *hostID*s. In summary, the PAS was run on a 3GHz Pentium4 machine with 1*GB* of RAM. The average incoming rate of email traffic was 1MB/minute and the average HBF output, including *hostID*s, was 46KB/minute. Average time to insert a packet into HBF was 28.6$\mu s$.

*Query Processing.* Given the HBFs of the email traffic we now set to look for the presence of the MyDoom virus. To query the HBF we need three parameters, namely: an excerpt, time interval, and candidate *hostID*s. Each copy of the virus comes with a 22KB attachment part of which can be used as the excerpt. Note, however, at the network layer the attachment is MIME-encoded so we MIME-encoded one of the attachments and used the first 96-bytes to 256-bytes as the signatures of MyDoom. In email parlance, these signatures are two to seven line-long excerpts. Time interval and *hostID* were left open in which case the query processor tries to attribute the excerpt using *all* available data over *all hostID*s. For this particular use case, the query processor used data observed over a five day period (more precisely, 138 hours and 13 minutes) over 136,631 unique *hostID*s. For the sole goal of quantifying the accuracy, we used the raw packet trace and the actual attribution rate was obtained by grepping the raw packet trace with **ngrep** for the virus signature.

Figure 2 shows the number of MyDoom instances given full attribution every hour over the five day period whereas Figure 3 zooms in on a 24-hour period. As

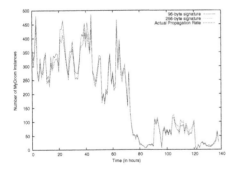
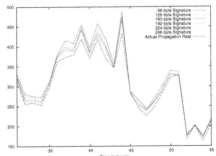

**Fig. 2.** Number of MyDoom attributions in the monitored network for five days

**Fig. 3.** Zooming in on a 24-hour period in Figure 2 with more signatures

we can see from the figures, the actual number of attributions forms the lower bound and the attributions using the smallest excerpt (96-byte signature) forms the upper bound. Figure 3 clearly illustrates how increasing the length of excerpts reduces number of false attributions. When we use a 256-byte excerpt the number of attributions converges to that of actual attributions. More precisely, using the 256-byte signature correctly found all the 25328 actual attributions observed during the five day period–hosts that received at least one copy of the virus– along with 33 incorrect attributions– hosts that did not receive the virus but was identified as if they did because of false positives. The following table lists the number of incorrect attributions found for the whole five days for various lengths of the excerpts.

**Table 1.** For a total number of 25328 actual attributions of MyDoom over the five day period, the table lists number of incorrect attributions for varying lengths of excerpts used for querying the PAS

| Length | 96 | 128 | 160 | 192 | 224 | 256 |
|---|---|---|---|---|---|---|
| Incorrect | 1375 | 932 | 695 | 500 | 293 | 33 |

In conclusion, the system as deployed was quite effective in finding all the instances of the virus in the email traffic during a five day period, with acceptable false positive rate and no false negatives. With the help of the attributions we were also able to obtain the following facts about the outbreak:

- Over the five day period 679 unique source addresses originated at least a copy of the virus.
- 52 machines were from the network monitored by ForNet and rest of the machines were outside the network.
- Of 52 local hosts 24 of them sent more than 50 copies of the virus not including 4 known mail-servers.
- We found one host in the network which sent out more than 5000 copies of the virus!
- The local hosts sent copies of the virus to 2011 unique IP addresses outside the network of which 74 got more than 50 copies of the virus.

These statistics would have helped a network administrator modify the security policies to abate the severity of the infection. For example, network administrator could have blocked the traffic from infected machines. Although we were lucky in collecting the packet traffic during that time period, we only learned about the virus afterwards, and still had all the data needed for our analysis. This is the main advantage of ForNet as opposed to intrusion detection, where we would only have been able to gather the portion of the data after the virus was identified and its signature isolated.

### 3.2 Identifying Proxies in the Network

Traditionally proxies are used to shuttle end-user requests to web servers and/or mail servers. They have been used to improve latency observed by clients or simply used to protect the client/network from outside world. Today proxies are being used for a much wider purposes, some legitimate others malicious. Here we list some uses of proxies:

- **Malicious Proxies.** The attack trend today is to compromise hosts en masse, install backdoors on them, and turn them into zombies that serve a variety of purposes. One such purpose is to use them as proxies or a set of zombies as a proxy network (proxy-net). Malicious proxies are generally used along with malware that configures a victim host to tunnel all or a selected web traffic through the proxy. These proxies are modified to scan the traffic for valuable personal information, such as username/passwords, credit card numbers, email addresses, or even mailing-addresses. When such information is found it is extracted from the traffic and stored at the proxy. An attacker can later retrieve the collected information from the proxies.

- **Spyware & Proxies.** Sometimes even legitimate businesses use the combination of proxies and "spywares" to gain information on the user behavior. These proxies are mostly interested in a user's browsing behavior which can then be used in various surveys or simply to display suitable advertisements.
- **Security & Proxies.** Legitimate use of a proxy is to either enhance performance or to enhance security or both. Large network operators tunnel user web requests through a proxy in order to reduce the exposure of the clients behind a firewall and to control the browsing of the users. Often application proxies are used in the same manner to boost performance or to have a central chocking point to potentially dangerous network traffic.

A network operator would want to know proxies in the networks for two reasons. The first, if the network operator has a web-proxy (or any application proxy) then the operator needs to be sure that the users are in fact using the proxy. The most popular technique to circumvent application proxies is to tunnel the traffic through another proxy outside the network perimeters through an open port. Identifying hosts that use outside proxies is a valuable information because it is a violation of the organization's policy. On the other hand, even when there are no application proxies in a networks, like that of an ISP, identifying proxies can help the operators identify customers who may have fallen victim to a malicious proxy!

**Identifying Proxies.** Observe that a proxy simply receives a web request, for example, from a host and passes it on to a web server and passes the web server's response back to the host. Given access to network traffic we can identify the proxy by comparing the contents of the connection from a host to the proxy with that of the proxy to a web server. Unfortunately, we have no a priori knowledge to distinguish a host from a proxy. This means we need to compare every single connection in a network to each other to determine whether there is a proxy! This clearly is not feasible for networks with a lot of connections. Furthermore, this method assumes that we can observe the connection from a host to a proxy and a proxy to a web server. This, however, is not the case for proxies operating outside of a network.

The following strategy, along with ForNet, is used to identify web-proxies in the network. This strategy, obviously, assumes that proxies do not encrypt their traffic.

1. *Selection of Query Strings.* The first step in the process is to select a set of popular web sites frequented by users, such as google.com, yahoo.com,

cnn.com, and so on. Then for each web site, select a long string from a web page that is frequently visited by users, such as google.com's front page or yahoo.com's login page. Selection of the string must be given some careful consideration as these web sites attach session specific strings in image names and other HTML text. A good rule of thumb in selecting a query string is to choose portion of an embedded javascript, style-sheet, menu items, or copyright notices. Also note that we need choose the string from the HTML source of a web page and not from a browser rendering because to query ForNet we need the network's view of the string.

2. *Querying HBF.* For each query string chosen above we ask ForNet to attribute the string using its payload attribution synopsis. In this particular case we used HBF data from two and a half months of traffic observed by the SynApp monitoring the network's Internet link. This data amounted to about 1.1TB in HBF form and would have been about 30TB raw network traffic.

3. *Domain Name Confirmation.* Now that we have a set of source and destination IP addresses for each query string we need to make sure the query string came from the right source and not from a proxy. For example, a query string from CNN's front page should come from an IP address that was cnn.com. Most of the popular web sites use round-robin DNS for load balancing the web servers. Which means, from the perspective of a host/network the IP address representing a popular web site's name would change frequently. Therefore, for each attribution from the PAS we need to verify that that origin in fact is the right web site. For example, if the PAS attributed a string from Google's front page to IP address 216.239.65.147 then we need to make sure that google.com resolved to the IP address during that time period for that particular host. The DNS records synopsis was used for this reverse DNS lookup.

4. *Prune False Positives.* As you may recall from Chapter 5 HBFs have false positives. Although with larger strings the chances of false positives are lower we can still use data from flow records [4] to corroborate HBF's attributions. Therefore, in Step-1 in addition to a query string we also obtain the size of the web page that contained the string. Then for each attribution from the HBF we can confirm whether flow records in fact observed approximately the same size. This was used to prune false positives from HBF.

This procedure was repeated over many popular web sites. The following Procedure 1 describes the above process in pseudo code. indent=2em

We used Graphviz [1] to visualize some of the results we obtained using the proxy identification process described above and present the results in the following pages. In these graphs yellow nodes denote the original web server, orange nodes denote harmless proxies (though not sanctioned by the network operator, in this case) in the network monitored by ForNet, and red nodes denote (possibly) malicious proxies in and outside of the network. Each directed edge on a graph denotes the path of the respective query string in the network.

---

**Algorithm 1.** *IdentifyProxies(QueryStrings S)*

---

```
 1: for (each QueryString s in S) do
 2:     A ← QueryPAS(s)
 3:     for (each Attribution a in A) do
 4:         if (a.SourceIP == LocalIP) then
 5:             if (S.PageSize == QueryNeoflow(a, GetFlowSize)) then
 6:                 Print "Host a.SourceIP Could be an Internal Proxy!"
 7:             end if
 8:         else if (S.DomainName ! =
                      QueryReverseDNS(a.SourceIP, a.DestinationIP, a.Time)) then
 9:             if (S.PageSize == QueryNeoflow(a, GetFlowSize)) then
10:                 Print "Host a.SourceIP Could be External Proxy!"
11:             end if
12:         end if
13:     end for
14: end for
```

---

From the graphs we can immediately conclude that there are at least two proxies in the network, namely 35.24 and 35.35, the nodes marked in orange. We can also note that these proxies only seem to be serving hosts outside of the network. This is a good illustration of an attacker using a subverted host as a proxy to prey on unsuspecting users beyond the network perimeters. Further investigations in this case revealed that the two hosts are part of an experimental network called Planetlab [2] and were involved in a research project to crawl the web.

Now turn your attention to the red node labeled "9.201" in the graph of Google and Amazon proxies, Figures 4, 5 respectively. This node is part of the network monitored by ForNet and seems to be functioning as a proxy serving up pages from Amazon and Google. Also note that in both cases this proxy serves only one and the same IP address. This is in fact a proxy within the network being used to (possibly) circumvent a web-proxy in another network. This was later confirmed by the network operator.

The third and the final case is the discovery of a proxy-net! In the graph for CNN proxies, Figure 6, observe the node labeled "129.29" (top right corner) is always served by the surrounding red nodes and not by any of the CNN web servers. This is a clear indication of the red nodes being part of a network of proxies. In fact the red nodes are part of a legitimate network of proxies being used by that node.

# 4    Conclusion

In this paper we reasoned constant monitoring of networks is crucial to the security. In addition to perimeter defenses we also need to monitor networks to collect network traffic for offline security analysis and forensics. Furthermore, we presented two major challenges facing the collection of network data and

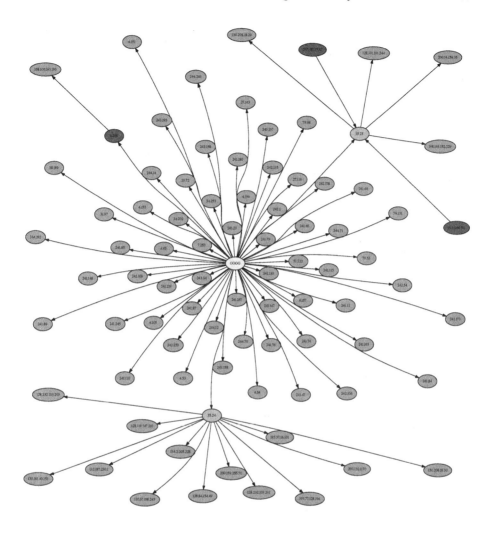

**Fig. 4.** Graphviz visualization of the attributions returned by the HBF for querying a string from the Google web page. Multiple IP addresses resolving to google.com are represented by the node "GOOG".

provided a set of guidelines for data collection and long-term retention. We concluded the paper with two use-cases illustrating the use of collected, synopsized data to follow a virus outbreak post-facto and to proactively identify proxies in a moderately large network.

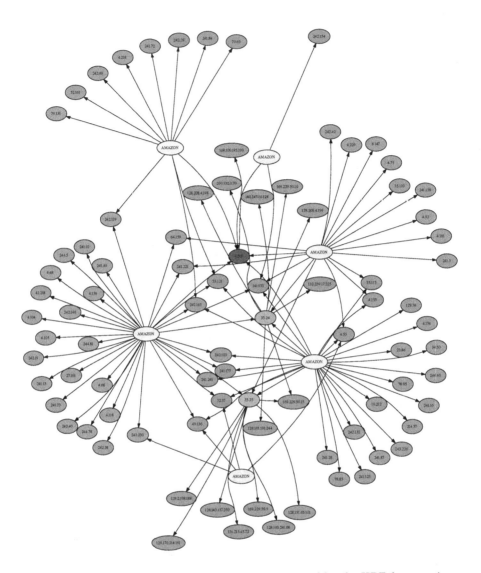

**Fig. 5.** Graphviz visualization of the attributions returned by the HBF for querying a string from the Amazon web page. Multiple Amazon IP addresses are not merged.

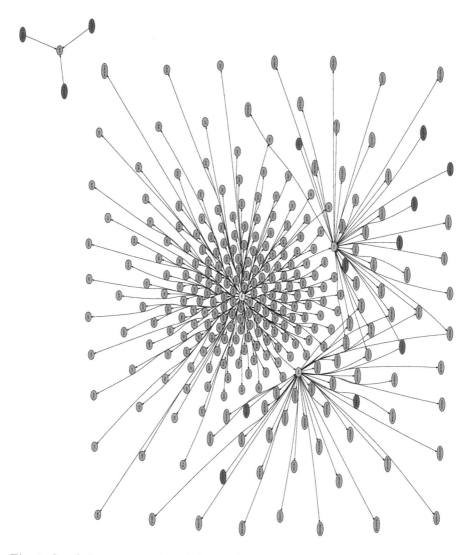

**Fig. 6.** Graphviz representation of the attributions returned by the HBF for querying a string from CNN. Multiple IP addresses resolving to cnn.com are represented by the node "CNN."

# References

1. Graphviz. http://www.graphviz.org/.
2. Planetlab. http://www.planet-lab.org/.
3. K. Shanmugasundaram, H. Brönnimann, and N. Memon. Payload attribution via hierarchical Bloom filters. In *Proceedings of the 11th ACM Conference on Computer and Communications Security*, pages 25–29, Washington, DC, October 2004.

4. K. Shanmugasundaram, M. Kharrazi, and N. Memon. Nabs: A system for detecting resource abuses via characterization of flow content type. In *Annual Computer Security Applications Conference*, pages 316–325, Tucson, AZ, December 2004.
5. K. Shanmugasundaram, A. Savant, H. Brönnimann, and N. Memon. ForNet: A distributed forensics network. In *The Second International Workshop on Mathematical Methods, Models and Architectures for Computer Networks Security*, pages 1–16, St. Petersburg, Russia, October 2003.

# Fairness Strategy for Multilevel Secure Concurrency Control Protocol

Navdeep Kaur, Rajwinder Singh, Manoj Misra, and A.K. Sarje

Department of Electronics and Computer Engineering,
Indian Institute of Technology Roorkee, Roorkee, India
{nrwsingh,rwsingh}@yahoo.com

**Abstract.** The conventional concurrency control protocols cannot be directly used in the multilevel secure database management systems (MLS/DBMS), because they may be exploited to establish covert channels. The stringent non-interference requirements imposed by multilevel security dictate modification of the conventional concurrency control. A number of multilevel secure concurrency control protocols have been proposed in the literature, which address the problem of covert channels. To prevent covert channels, most of these concurrency control protocols give high priority to the operations of low security level transaction when it conflicts with the operations of a high security level transaction. This may lead to the abortion or re-execution of high security level transactions over and over again and making the concurrency control protocols unfair towards high security level transactions. Motivated by fairness concerns, we present a fairness strategy for multilevel secure concurrency control protocol to achieve fair performance across different security levels while guaranteeing Orange security. Our simulation results show that fairness strategy can achieve a significant performance improvement, in terms of fairness.

**Keywords:** Multilevel secure database systems, concurrency control, covert channel, fairness.

## 1 Introduction

In many applications, security is an important requirement since the database system maintains sensitive data with different security levels to be shared by multilevel users with different security levels is called multilevel secure database system (MLS/DBS). Therefore, it is important that all accesses to the database be performed without violating security of the database. The database system that can store and manage data with different security levels in a single system is called multilevel secure database management system (MLS/DBMS) and trusted DBMS. Many of these applications are inherently distributed in nature. An MLS distributed database management system (MLS/DDBMS) can be shared by users at different security (clearance) levels and contains distributed database consisting of data at different security (classification) levels. Most of the multilevel secure database systems are based on the Bell-LaPadula model

A. Bagchi and V. Atluri (Eds.): ICISS 2006, LNCS 4332, pp. 71–85, 2006.

[1], which is described in terms of subjects and objects. Objects are data items and subjects are active processes, i.e., transactions in databases, which request access to objects. Data and transactions are classified into several security levels, (e.g., Top Secret, Secret, Classified, and Unclassified). In the Bell-LaPadula model, two main restrictions are imposed on all data accesses. A transaction can read an object only if the transaction's security level is equal to or higher than the object's security level. A transaction can write an object only if its security level is equal the object's security level. Informally, these access restrictions are called "read-below" and "restricted write" restrictions, respectively. It prevents direct flow of information from high security level to low security levels, but not sufficient to ensure that security is not violated indirectly through covert channels. As a result, all database management system components designed and implemented for use in a traditional database system must be modified to ensure that there is no indirect flow of information through covert channels.

Concurrency control is an integral component of the database systems. It is used to manage the concurrent execution of operations by different transactions on the same data item such that consistency is maintained. Conventional concurrency control protocols such as two phase locking and timestamp ordering protocols are not suitable for multilevel secure database systems, because they can establish the unexpected communication path called covert channel [3]between transactions of different security levels that have shared access to data item in the database. The bandwidth of covert channel must be determined and limited depending upon the degree of assurance [2] required by the system. The higher the covert channel bandwidth, the less secure is the system. The system environment is called Full secure, where the covert channel bandwidth is zero while the Orange Secure where the covert channels bandwidth is bounded to a maximum of 1 bit/second. The objective of multilevel secure concurrency control is to ensure serializability without introducing covert channels. A number of multilevel secure concurrency control protocols for centralized database management system have been proposed in the literature, which address the problem of covert channels. Most of these protocols [4],[5],[6],[7],[8] achieve correctness and security at the cost of declined performance of high security level transactions.

In this paper we propose fairness strategy, using feedback based admission control, to achieve fairness across different security levels while guaranteeing Orange security. The strategies for ensuring fairness can be categorized into static and dynamic strategies. Static strategies for ensuring fairness such as resource reservation can provide fairness while still maintaining full security. However, they may significantly degrade the performance arising out of resource wastage due to their inability to readjust themselves to varying workload conditions. On the other hand, dynamic strategies have the ability to adapt to workload variations depending upon certain performance statistics that are collected by the system. However, providing full security fairness with dynamic mechanisms appears to be hard since changing the parameters that control the performance of low security level transactions on the basis of the observed performance of high security level transaction introduces a covert channel. Therefore, this strategy could be exploited for covert signaling. In this paper, we present and evaluate dynamic fairness strategy while guaranteeing Orange security (i.e. covert channel bandwidth of less than one bit per second). We study our fairness strategy in conjunction with Secure Distributed Two Phase Locking (SD2PL) concurrency control protocol. In this paper, we use two security levels (i.e., High and Low).

In a simulation study, we evaluate the performance of SD2PL concurrency control protocol with or without fairness strategy for a large range of workloads. Results show that our strategy can achieve a significant performance improvement, in terms of fairness. In addition, our strategy shows slightly performance improvement, in terms of overall response time.

The rest of this paper is organized as follows. In Section 2, analyze the unfairness problem against high security level transactions. Section 3 presents the fairness strategy. Section 4 gives the details of the simulation model. The results of simulation experiments have been discussed in Section 5. Section 6 concludes the paper.

## 2   Unfairness Problem Against High Security Level Transaction

Secure Distributed Two Phase Locking (SD2PL) concurrency control protocol exhibits unfairness against high security level transactions. Since, when a low security level transaction requests for a write lock on a low security data item that is currently held by a high security level transaction for its read operation on same data item, the high security level transaction is aborted to release the lock. This modification to the conventional two-phase locking protocol ensures that there are no covert channels between transactions, but it degrades the performance of high security level transactions and may lead to the starvation of high security level transactions. To analyze the unfairness problem under SD2PL, we modeled database and transactions as follows:

1. The MLS database is distributed, in a non-replicated manner, over N sites connected by a trusted network. Thus no communication between two sites is subject to eavesdropping, masquerading, reply or integrity violations.
2. The MLS database is modeled as a collection of D data pages that are uniformly distributed across all the N sites.
3. All transactions and data pages are classified at two security levels.
4. All incoming transactions are equally likely to belong to any security levels (i.e. transaction arrival rate for both security level is same).
5. Transactions (cohorts) can read (write) data pages according the Restricted Write Bell-LaPadula model. The security model allows a transaction to issue read-equal, read-down and write-equal operations. Based upon these permitted operations three types of conflicts may occur: (a) Read-down conflict among different security levels, (b) Read-write conflict at same security level and (c) Write-write conflict at same security level.

6. Upon different security level data conflict (Read-down conflict among different levels), a low security level transaction receives higher priority to prevent covert channels. In case of same security level data conflicts, (Read-write conflict and Write-write conflict at the same level) conflicts are resolved as traditional two phase locking protocol, since there is no security problem within same security level. Note that low security level transaction can only be blocked if the lock is held by another low security level transaction.

7. Both high and low security level transaction have fixed size (i.e. the number of sites at which each distributed transaction executes and the size of cohort is fixed).

8. We consider the database is running on a system with an infinite number of physical resources (CPUs and Disks). There is no queuing for these resources. Thus transaction will never block unless it is waiting for a lock to be released by another transaction.

Let us consider the behavior of Direct Secure system (i.e. which satisfied only Bell-LaPadula conditions, but not covert channel free). In this system, both high and low security level transactions have equal average response time. Since no priority is given to any security level transaction and both the transactions will be equally blocked due to data conflict. The response time of a transaction is the time between when a transaction originates at site until it finally completes successfully, regardless of the number of times it has been aborted and restarted. Now consider the Full Secure System (i.e. which satisfied Bell-LaPadula conditions as well as covert channel free). When a low security level transaction requests for a lock held by a high security level transaction, the high security level transaction is aborted and the lock is granted to the low security level transaction. Thus, from the point of view of a high security level transaction, each lock request made by low security level transactions has the potential to abort its execution if it currently holds the requested lock. In this system, the response time of a high security level transaction depends upon how often it is preempted by low security level transactions. If a high security level transaction is not preempted during its execution, its response time will be equal to the sum of its processing time, the total time it spends waiting for locks held by low security level transactions and message processing time. Thus the response time of high security level transaction depends on probability of lock conflict with low security level transaction and the rate at which low security level transaction request locks. Note that the response time of low security level transaction only depends on number of other low security level transactions in the system. To improve the performance of SD2PL with respect to high security level transactions, it is necessary to keep the probability of lock conflict with low security level transaction and the rate at which low security level transaction request locks as low as possible. In this paper, we control the rate of lock requests to be made by low security level transaction by controlling the admission of low security level transactions in the system.

# 3   Fairness Strategy for Secure Concurrency Control Protocol

Feedback based admission control is well known for its effectiveness to support a specified performance when the system model may include uncertainties[9]. The specified performance can be achieved by dynamically adapting the system behavior considering the current performance error measured in the feedback control loop. Feedback-based approaches [10],[11],[12]have substantially improved the database throughput/response time by applying high-level notions of feedback control. Feedback based admission control has been developed in [13],[14] to control deadline miss ratio while granting partial security in multilevel secure real time database systems. In this method [13], whenever a low security level transaction requests to acquire a write lock on a data item already locked in share mode (read) by a high security level transaction, then the high security level transaction is not automatically aborted. Instead, the concurrency control protocol looks at other system parameters and may decide to delay the low security level transaction or abort the high security level transaction. This decision to delay or abort is to be taken at every data conflict instance.

To the best of our knowledge, unfairness problem of transactions executing at different security levels has not been considered before for MLS/DDBS. In this section, we adapt an admission control policy for centralized MLS/DBs [15] and extend it to feedback based admission control policy for the fairness of transactions executing at different security levels for MLS/DDBs.

## 3.1   Admission Control Strategy

Our fairness strategy, implements a system wide admission control mechanism by controlling entry of low security level transactions into database system. This strategy control unfairness measured in terms of fairness factor for transactions executing at different security levels. The basic idea in the strategy is that based on the imbalance in transaction response time at different security levels, the admission of low security level transactions into system is periodically controlled after every T seconds. The fairness factor (FF) is defined as the ratio of the average transactions response time at high security level to average transactions response time at low security levels, captures the degree of unfairness during the last observation period.

Each site has a local admission control manager (ACM) and global information collector. Global information collector monitors and collects the fairness factor periodically from all participating sites of distributed transaction and itself. Global information collector cooperates with local admission control manager in order to obtain global fairness factor (GFF) and to adapt control parameters. The global fairness factor decides whether the admission of low security level transaction at that site is allowed or rejected. This needs communication between sites. The global fairness factor is calculated by the following formula:

Global Fairness Factor (GFF) = $\beta$[FF of local site] + (1- $\beta$ ) [Avg. of FF of remaining sites involved in distributed transaction].

Where $\beta$ is a smoothing factor, which determines how much weight is given to the FF of remaining sites, involved in distributed transaction.

## 3.2    Covert Channel Bandwidth Measurement

In dynamic admission control strategies, covert channels can establish due to the admission control mechanism. For example, a corrupt high security level transaction can, by modulating the results of the admission control manager computation (increase, decrease or constant the admission of low security level transactions), indirectly flow the information to collaborating low security level transactions. Corresponding to each computation, $\log_2 M = 3.32 \log_{10} 3 = 1.6$ bits of information can be transmitted [16] and since the computation is made once every T seconds, the total channel bandwidth is 1/T bits per second.

## 3.3    Feedback Based Admission Control Model

Feedback based admission control (FBAC) follows the 'observe-predict-react' principle using feedback loop. The system observes the fairness factor by collecting the statistics, of average transaction response times of each security level over an interval of time. The observed value of fairness factor reflects both; how often high security level transaction is aborted and restarted due to data conflict with low security level transaction and its impact on the average response time of transactions at high security level. The fairness factor predicts potential of unfairness. When the value of observed fairness factor exceeds and below the desired value of fairness factor, this is interpreted as a prediction of unfairness, so that correspondingly reaction must be initiated. As shows in Fig. 1 , the fairness factor controller computes the required fairness factor adjustment $\Delta F$ according to the error = DFF-MFF, which is the difference between the desired Fairness Factor and measured Fairness Factor. Whenever the value of measured fairness factor exceeds above the desired value (i.e. $\Delta F < 0$), the number of active transactions at low security level is reduced and when the value of measured fairness factor drops below the desired value (i.e. $\Delta F > 0$), the number of active transactions at low security level is increased again in the system. To reduce the number of active transactions at low security level involves admission control.

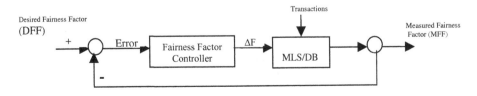

**Fig. 1.** Fairness Factor Controller

The working principle of admission control model is illustrated in Fig. 2. Newly arriving transactions (either originates on that site or cohorts from remote site) are scheduled in one of the two queues according to their security levels. The admission control manager decides whether a newly arriving low security level transaction can be admitted for processing or should wait in the transaction queues at the system entry. Thus, admission control manager serves as a gate-keeper for the system. ACM computes the FF periodically after T seconds. If ACM monitors a significant imbalance (i.e. FF > 1+ $\alpha$ or FF < 1- $\alpha$), the admission of low security level transactions is decreased or increased accordingly. The value $\alpha$ has been set to a nominal 5 percent.

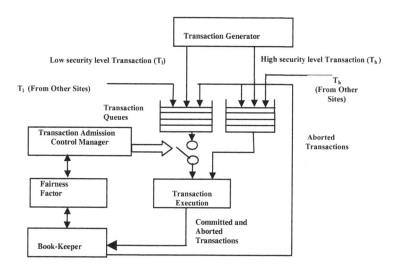

**Fig. 2.** Working Principle of Admission Control

Therefore, admission control becomes operative only when FF > 1.05 or FF< 0.95. The admission control manager checks the value of fairness factor once in every T seconds. The T is set in accordance with the degree of security required. For an orange secure two security level system, the T parameter is set to 1.6 seconds.

## 4   Simulation Model

To evaluate the performance of fairness strategy described in Section 3, we developed a detailed simulation model of MLS distributed database system. Our simulation model is similar in many aspects to the distributed database model presented in [17], which has also been used in several other studies of distributed database system behavior. It consists of an MLS database distributed over N sites connected by a network. There is no replication of data items. Each site in the model has seven components: a transaction generator which generates transaction workload of the system; database which models the data and its organization; a admission control manager which allow or deny the admission of newly arriving low security level transaction; a transaction manager which models the execution behavior of the transaction; a concurrency control manager which implements the concurrency control algorithm; a resource manager which manages the physical resources (CPU and I/O); and a book keeper which collects statistics on the completed transactions of the site. In addition to these per site components, the model also has a network manager, which models the behavior of the communications network. Fig. 3 shows detailed view of these components and their key interaction.

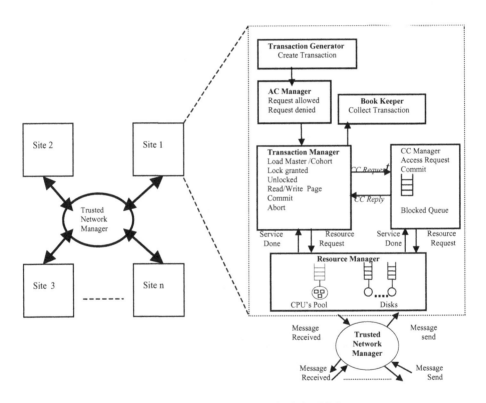

**Fig. 3.** Simulation Model of the DDB

*Transaction Generator:* The transaction generator is responsible for generating the workload for each data site. Transactions are generated as a Poisson stream with mean equal to ArriRate. All sites receive the same workload, i.e. have an identical transaction arrival rate. Each transaction in the system is distinguished by a globally unique transaction id. The id of a transaction is made up of two parts: a transaction number, which is unique at the originating site of the transaction and the id of the originating site, which is unique in the system. The unit of database granularity is the page. Each transaction consists of a sequence of pages to be read and set of pages that are to be written. Each transaction has an associated security clearance level. A transaction is likely to belong to any of ClearLevel security clearance levels. We assume that the clearance level remains constant throughout the life of transaction inside the system.

*Database Model:* The database is modeled as a collection of DBSize pages. These pages have been assigned ClassLevels and are uniformly distributed in a non-replicated fashion across all the NumSites sites, so that each data item is managed by only one site. Accesses to data pages are distributed uniformly over the entire database, i.e. each data page is accessed with equal probability. The database is equally partitioned into ClassLevels security classification levels (e.g. if database has 1000 pages and number of classification is 2, pages 1 through 500 belongs to level 1, pages 501 through to 1000 belongs to level 2). Table 1 summarizes the parameters of simulation model.

**Table 1.** Simulation Model Parameters and Values

| Parameter | Meaning | Value |
|-----------|---------|-------|
| NumSites | Number of sites in the database | 8 |
| DBSize | Number of pages in the database | 4000 |
| ClassLevels | Number of Classification Levels | 2 |
| ArriRate | Mean transaction arrival rate / site | 1-10 |
| ClearLevel | Number of Clearance Levels | 2 |
| TransType | Transaction Type (Sequential or Parallel) | Sequential |
| DistDegree | Degree of Distribution (number of cohorts) | 3 |
| CohortSize | Cohort size (in pages) | 6 |
| WriteProb | Page write probability | 0.5 |
| NumCPUs | Number of processors per site | Infinite |
| NumDisks | Number of disks per site | Infinite |
| PageCPU | CPU page processing time | 5ms |
| PageDisk | Disk page access time | 20ms |
| MsgCPU | Message send / receive time | 5ms |

*Admission Control Manager:* The admission control manager decides whether a newly arriving low security level transaction can be admitted for processing or should better wait in the transaction queue at the system entry.

*Transaction Manager:* Each distributed transaction in the workload has single process, called the master or coordinator that executes at the originating site of the transaction and multiple other processes, called cohort that execute at the various sites where the required data pages reside. The transaction manager at a site is responsible for creation of master process and cohort processes for each transaction submitted to that site. The cohorts are created dynamically as need. There can be at most one cohort of a transaction at each site. If there exists any local data page in the access list of the transaction, one cohort will be executed locally. When a cohort completes its data access and processing requirements, it waits for the master process to initiate commit protocol. The master process provides the coordination of cohort processes; the master process commits a transaction only if all cohorts of the transaction are ready to commit, otherwise it aborts and restarts the transaction after a delay and makes the same data accesses as before. Following the successful commitment of the distributed transaction, the cohorts write into the local database, if any. The number of sites at which each transaction executes is specified by the DistDegree parameter. At each of the execution sites, the number of pages accessed by the transaction's cohort varies uniformly between 0.5 and 1.5 times CohortSize. These pages are chosen randomly from among the database pages located at that site. Transactions in a distributed system can execute in either sequential or parallel fashion. The distinction is that cohorts in a sequential transaction execute one after another, whereas cohorts in a parallel transaction are started together and execute independently until commit processing is initiated. We consider only sequential execution of transactions in our study. TransType specifies whether the transaction execution is sequential or parallel. The WriteProb parameter determines the probability that a transaction operation is a write.

*Resource Manager:* The resource manager manages the physical resources at each site. The physical resources at each site consist of NumCPUs processors and NumDisks disks. There is a single common queue for the processors whereas each of the disks has its own queue. The message processing is given higher priority than data processing at the CPUs. The PageCPU and PageDisk parameters capture the CPU and disk processing times per data page, respectively.

*Concurrency Control Manager:* Each cohort of a transaction performs one or more database operations on specified data pages. Concurrent data access requests of the cohort processes, at a site are controlled by concurrency control manager at that site. It orders the data accesses based on the concurrency control protocol executed. Concurrency Control Manager is responsible for handling concurrency control requests made by the transaction manager, including read and write access requests, requests to get permission to commit or abort a cohort, and several types of master and cohort management requests to initialize and terminate master and cohort processes. Concurrency Control Manager uses SD2PL concurrency control protocol. Concurrency control is implemented at the page granularity.

*Deadlocks:* Since we are using Locking based concurrency control protocol, deadlocks are a possibility, of course. In our simulation implementation, both global and local deadlock detection is immediate, that is, a deadlock is detected as soon as a lock conflict occurs and a cycle is formed. Local deadlocks are detected by maintaining a local Wait-For Graph (WFG) at each site. WFGs contain the 'wait-for' relationships among the transactions. For detection of global deadlocks a global WFG is used which is constructed by merging local WFGs. The choice of a victim in resolving a deadlock is made based on cohort timestamps; the youngest cohort in the cycle to be aborted to resolve the deadlock. The master process of the victim cohort is notified to abort and later restart the whole transaction. In Secure locking based concurrency control protocols, deadlock always occur due data contention at same security level, since at different security levels, high security level cohort never blocks the low security level cohort. We do not explicitly model the overheads for detecting deadlocks.

*Trusted Network Manager:* We assumed a reliable and trusted system, in which no site failures or communication network failures occur and no communication between two sites is subject to eavesdropping, masquerading, reply or integrity violations. The communication network is simply modeled as a switch that routes messages without any delay since we assume a local area network that has high bandwidth. However, the CPU overheads of message transfer, message transfer are taken into account at both sending and receiving sites. This means that there are two classes of CPU requests - local data processing requests and message processing requests, and message processing is given higher priority than data processing. The CPU overheads for message transfers are captured by the MsgCPU parameter.

*BookKeeper:* The bookkeeper module receives both completed and aborted transactions from transaction manager. It collects statistics on these transactions of the site.

## 5    Experiments and Results

In this section, we present the performance results of our simulation experiments. The simulation program is written in C language. For each experiment, we run the simulation with same parameters for four different random number seeds. Each simulation run is continuing up to 2,000 transactions of each security level are committed. The results depicted are the average over the four runs. All the data reported in this paper have 95 percentage confidence intervals.

In our study, the primary performance metric used is the average response times of transactions at each security level for varying arrival rates. This not only is a measure of comparison between different secure concurrency control protocols, but is also one estimate of fairness since a fair concurrency control algorithm must ensure near identical response times across security levels. In addition, we also measure the transaction throughput at different security levels, that is, number of transactions committed at each security level per unit time. Measuring transaction throughput an indication of the optimal arrival rate the system can sustain without severe degradation in the performance, that is, the arrival rate beyond which system starts thrashing resulting in a decrease in the throughput. Since our goal is to address the problem of unfairness of secure concurrency control protocol with respect to high security level transaction performance, we also evaluate fairness factor, is defined as the ratio of the average transactions response time at high security level to average transactions response time at low security levels which captures how evenly the abort transactions are spread across the transactions of the various security levels. With this formulation, a protocol is ideally fair, if the fairness factor value is 1.0 for all security levels. Fairness values greater than one and lesser than one indicate positive bias and negative bias, respectively.

The aim of the experiments is to obtain a measure of fairness for transactions at different security levels in a MLS distributed database system. To evaluate the fairness, in the following experiments, we compare two systems: (1) Full: A full secure MLS/DDBS equipped with S2PL concurrency control manager (2) Orange: An orange secure MLS/SDDBS that is equipped with S2PL concurrency control manager, and the admission control manager.

The parameter settings used for our experiments are shown in Table 1. The value of $\beta$ used in all experiments is 0.6. The performance of fairness strategy depends upon the control parameter $\beta$. We first analyze the effect of $\beta$ on transaction response time at fixed arrival rate (i.e., Arrival rate = 4), where system achieves peak throughput. We observe that by keeping all parameters same as in table 1, the minimum average transaction response time is achieved when $\beta$ is 0.6.

### 5.1   Average Response Time

In the experiments, we evaluate the average response time of transactions at each security level for varying arrival rates. We also consider that there is no contention for physical resources among transactions (i.e., CPUs and disks were made "infinite"). Thus, any increase in transaction response time beyond the execution time and message processing time of transaction is due to data contention. The results of the experiment are shown in figure Fig. 4, Fig. 5, Fig. 6.

In Fig. 4, we present the average transactions response times at each security level of Full and Orange systems as a function of overall transaction arrival rate per site. In Full system, we observe that the response of high security level transactions is significantly higher than that of low security level transactions throughout the arrival rates. This is because higher priority is given to low security level transactions, whenever data conflict occurs between the transactions at different security levels. The high security level transaction is aborted and restarted after some delay whenever a data conflicts occur between a high and

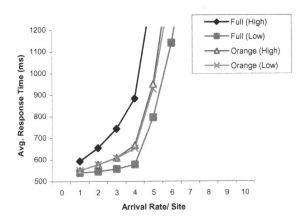

**Fig. 4.** Arrival Rate versus Avg. Response time at each Security Level

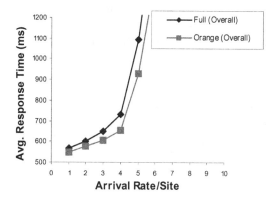

**Fig. 5.** Arrival Rate versus Overall Response time

low security level transactions. This graph clearly shows how the high security level transactions suffer much more than the low security level transactions to satisfy the goal of avoiding covert channels. In this figure we see that Orange system achieves close to ideal fairness. Fig. 5 shows the average overall transactions response times of FULL and Orange systems as a function of transaction arrival rate per site. Over the entire range of arrival rates [1, 7], the performance of Orange is slightly better than that of Full system. This is because, in Orange system the abort ratio of high security level transactions is significantly reduced throughout the arrival rates. This graph shows the slightly performance improvement, in terms of overall response time.

Fig. 6 compares the fairness factor of both Full and Orange systems. The fairness factor is the ratio of average response time of high security level transactions to the average response time of low security level transactions. We observe that the fairness factor of Full system ranges from 1.1 to 2.4 and it increases with the increase in arrival rate, while the fairness factor of Orange system ranges

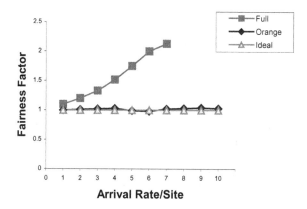

**Fig. 6.** Arrival Rate versus Fairness Factor

from 0.95 to 1.05. From figure, we see that Orange system achieves close to ideal fairness. In summary, our results show that Orange system is successful in improving the significant performance of high security level transactions.

## 5.2  Throughput

The next experiment is conducted to measure of overall throughput as function of overall transaction arrival rate per site. We see from Fig. 7that the peak overall throughput is achieved at an arrival rate of approximately 4 transactions per second for both Full and Orange systems. Moving on to the relative performance of Full and Orange, we observe that the throughput of both systems initially increases with the increase in arrival rates then decreases when arrival rate becomes more than 4. However the overall throughput of Full is always less than Orange system.

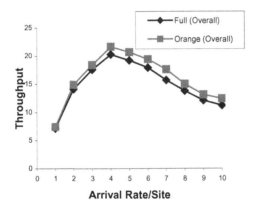

**Fig. 7.**  Arrival Rate versus Overall Throughput

## 6  Conclusion

This paper examines the problem of unfairness against high security level transactions exhibited by SD2PL concurrency control protocol. We proposed fairness strategy for multilevel secure concurrency control for MLS/DDBMS that ensures fairness property for transactions at different security level. We have also presented a simulation model and evaluation of relative performance of secure concurrency control with or without fairness strategy. Results show that our strategy can achieve a significant performance improvement, in terms of fairness. In addition, it shows slightly performance improvement, in terms of overall response time. In this paper, we have restricted ourselves to only two security levels. As a part of future work, we would like to relax this assumption and consider multiple security levels.

# References

1. Bell, D.E., LaPadula, L.J.: Secure Computer Systems: Unified Exposition and Multics Interpretation. The MITRE Corp., 1976.
2. Department of Defense Computer Security Center, Department of Defense Trusted Computer Systems Evaluation Criteria, December 1985.
3. Lampson, B.W.: A Note on the Confinement Problem. Communications of the ACM, Vol. 16, No. 10, ACM Press (1973.) 613-615.
4. McDermott, J., Jajodia, S.: Orange locking: channel-free database concurrency control via locking. Database Security, VI: Status and Prospects(1995) 267-284.
5. Mancini, L.V., Ray I.: Secure Concurrency Control in MLS Databases with Two Versions of Data. Proceedings of Esorics , Italy(1996).
6. Atluri, V., Jajodia, S., Keefe, T. F., McCollum C,. Mukkamala R.: Multilevel Secure Transaction Processing: Status and Prospects" Proceeding WG11.3 Working Group on Database Security, Como, Italy(1996) 79-98.
7. Ammann, P., Jajodia, S.: A Timestamp Ordering Algorithm for Secure, Single version, Multilevel Database. Database Security, V: Status and Prospectus, North Holland (1992) 23-25.
8. Amman, P., Jaeckle, F., Jajodia, S.: A two snapshot algorithm for concurrency control in secure multilevel databases. IEEE Symposium on Security and Privacy, Oakland (1992).
9. Skeen, D.: Nonblocking Commit Protocols. ACM SIGMOD International Conference on Management of Data. (1981).
10. Phillips, C.L., Nagle. H.T.: Digital Control System Analysis And Design. 3rd Edition, Prentice Hall (1995).
11. Heiss, H. U.: Overload Effects and Their Prevention. Performance Evaluation, (1991).
12. Moenkeberg, Weikum, G.: Conflict-Driven Load Control for the Avoidance of Data-Contention Thashing. ICDE (1991).
13. Son, S. H.: Supporting the Requirements for Multilevel Secure and Real-time Databases in Distributed Environments. Annual IFIP WG 11.3 Conference of Database Security, Lake Tahoe, CA (1997) 57-71.
14. Son, S. H., Mukkamala, R., David, R.: Integrating Security and Real-Time Requirements using Covert Channel Capacity. IEEE Transactions on Knowledge and Data Engineering (2000) 12(6).
15. Jajodia, S., Mancini, L. Setia. S.: A fair locking protocol for multilevel secure databases. 11th IEEE Computer Security Foundations Workshop(1998) 68 -178.
16. Shannon, C. E.: A Mathematical Theory of Communications", Bell System Technical Journal(1948), Vol. 27.
17. Carey M., Livny. : Conflict Detection Tradeoffs for Replicated Data ACM Transactions on Database Systems (1991) vol 16/4.

# Optimistic Anonymous Participation in Inter-organizational Workflow Instances

Joachim Biskup and Joerg Parthe

University of Dortmund, Computer Science Department, 44221 Dortmund, Germany
{biskup,parthe}@ls6.cs.uni-dortmund.de

**Abstract.** Electronic business applications are often structured by work-flow declarations that span potentially numerous generic activities in different organizations. Such declarations are used to assign activities to specific entities, and to dynamically grant and revoke access to the resources according to the execution state of the workflow instance. If competing organizations cooperate in common workflow instances for achieving a joint purpose, they might want to let entities participate anonymously. Anonymous participation demands a restricted flow of identifying information, whereas state dependent access control requires the flow of specific control information. In this paper we introduce the 'Anonymous SDSD' approach (State-Dependent Security Decisions) balancing the conflicting requirements by combining techniques like onion routing, logging, bulletin boards, pseudonyms and proxies.

## 1 Introduction

Electronic business applications are often structured by workflow declarations that span potentially numerous generic activities in different organizations. While a workflow instance is executed, generic activities are bound to specific entities that belong to the organizations involved. Although the respective organizations have agreed to cooperate in common workflow instances for achieving a joint purpose (e.g. as a virtual organization [18]), the organizations as a whole as well as individual entities might be interested in concealing those details of their contribution that are not necessary for the agreed purpose. In particular, there might be an interest to let entities participate anonymously in workflow instances – say by employing user pseudonyms – as far as possible under functional requirements and compatible with other security interests.

With regard to functional requirements, we need a mechanism of binding entities to generic activities. Regardless of whether the mechanism is centralistic or – for the sake of anonymity – somehow distributed, it has to respect certain qualifications. Accordingly, the mechanism must ensure that the properties needed to perform an activity, as specified in the workflow declaration, are actually held by the assigned entity. Thus, in this context a candidate entity for a binding should provide evidence of its properties, even if the entity is acting under some user pseudonym. More technically, each user pseudonym should inherit a subset of the properties held by the represented entity. In general, however,

A. Bagchi and V. Atluri (Eds.): ICISS 2006, LNCS 4332, pp. 86–100, 2006.

given an open workflow declaration, some a priori knowledge about properties of entities, and a suitable observation of a pseudonymized activity within a workflow instance, this functional requirement might enable inferences about the relationships of entities and the pseudonym under consideration. Speaking in general terms, such inferences are possible whenever under the sketched conditions the cardinality of the anonymity set of the potential entities is too small. Thus, any attempt to provide for anonymous participation in workflow instances is limited by the need of respecting qualifications, and accordingly requires an appropriate setting to make the discussed anonymity sets sufficiently large.

With regard to other security interests, we need a control mechanism that permits a specific activity to be performed by a specific entity only according to a declared security policy. Preferably, following the principle of least privileges, permissions should be dynamically granted and revoked according to the progress in executing a workflow instance. More technically, decisions on permissions or prohibitions should be based on an appropriate notion of a state (of a workflow instance execution). As an example, the security policy might demand that the activity 'read data of customer $x$' is only permitted if the activity 'order good' has been previously executed by the customer $x$.

In this work, more extensively reported in [5], we analyze the problem of anonymous participation in inter-organizational workflow instances in depth. As far as needed for a concise presentation, the analysis is based on our specific proposal for State-Dependent Security Decisions (SDSD) [2,3,4]. Moreover, we outline a solution to the problem by extending our proposal accordingly. The primary novel contributions are the following.

– Our solution aims at hiding not only the relationship between entities and pseudonyms, but additionally the binding between pseudonyms and activities. Consequently, we get a second chance to enlarge the anonymity set of potential entities which might be involved in an activity.
– Due to the lack of trust between the involved organizations, we neither use a central control (CC) nor shift critical functionality to a trusted third party. Instead, we maintain only the relevant parts of the assignment of activities to pseudonyms by the locally involved entities. Additionally, if the security policy prescribes that two or more specified activities are called or executed by the same entity, the relevant information is transferred into the context of the second activity after the necessity is proven.

The outlined solution is optimistic in the following sense. Whenever all participating entities behave honestly, anonymity is provided, only subject to the limitation mentioned above. However, for the case that some entity is complaining about a suspected violation of the security policy, a trusted third party is needed for the inspection of the logs. All participants have to agree in advance that this third party will be able to identify entities during its investigation, possibly even if the affected entities have been honest. To simplify the description we assume that all communication channels are reliable, all sites are online and operating. These conditions have to be guaranteed by additional mechanisms.

## 2    Considered Problem

In our introduction, we already sketched a small scenario in which entities participate in activities while satisfying qualification requirements. Before we introduce our solution, we first describe the considered problem within a simple model.

### 2.1    SDSD Model

The *entities* form a set $EN$ (ENtity). Each $en \in EN$ *holds* a subset of certain *properties* taken from the set $PR$ (PRoperty) expressed by the function *hold* : $EN \longrightarrow \mathcal{P}(PR)$ (hold). Generic activities are described using *formal participants* $P$ (Participant), which are essentially variables for entities. The function *req* : $P \longrightarrow \mathcal{P}(PR)$ (require) describes the *qualification requirements* an entity has to meet for acting as a certain formal participant.

A generic activity is called *step* and is composed of two formal participants of set $P$ and a *formal action* of set $AC$ (ACtion). A generic activity sequence is then a family $SS = (s_k)_{k=1,...,n}$ (Step Sequence) with $s_k \in P \times P \times AC$. Sometimes we refer to the first formal participant $p_1$ of a step $p_1 p_2 ac$ as the *activator* and to the second formal participant $p_2$ as the *executor* of the pertinent action $ac$.

A *protocol* specifies a set of allowed generic activity sequences. The core of a protocol is a regular expression on steps. Thus, we restrict to sets that can be recognized by finite automatons. Such an automaton is used to keep track of the relevant part of the execution history: a state represents the already executed part of the activity sequence and each outgoing transition a possible next activity.

**Fig. 1.** In state $z_2$ the execution of step $s_4$ or step $s_5$ is permitted

For example, as shown in Figure 1, state $z_2$ represents the completed execution of activity sequence ($s_1 = p_{1,1} p_{1,2} ac_1$, $s_2 = p_{2,1} p_{2,2} ac_2$) or of sequence ($s_3 = p_{3,1} p_{3,2} ac_3$). In $z_2$ the execution of $s_4$ or $s_5$ is permitted, but – following the principle of least privilege – the execution of $s_1, s_2$ or $s_3$ is prohibited.

A concrete activity sequence is allowed, if it results from applying the present binding and an action mapping (which maps formal actions to concrete method calls) on an allowed generic activity sequence. Roughly speaking, a *binding* assigns formal participants to entities in a consistent manner, which respects qualification requirements. The formal definition follows in Section 2.2.

The details of the distributed approach of SDSD, which dynamically grants and revokes permissions to enforce such security policies, as well as the theoretical foundations are described in [2,3,4]. This approach captures basic features of workflow management systems, except for handling parallel executions.

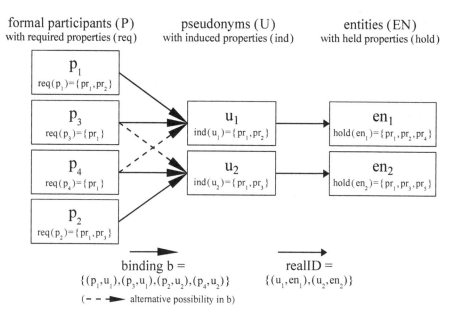

**Fig. 2.** Example setting

## 2.2   Privacy Problem

Suppose a pseudonymizer provides pseudonyms $U$ and keeps track of the association between entities and pseudonyms, $realID : U \longrightarrow EN$ (real identity).

We then argue that a central control (CC) (e.g. wf-engine) would endanger the privacy of entities, even if pseudonyms are used. First, we observe that the CC needs at least some information about the properties held by the associated entities to respect qualifications. Thus the CC must have access to a function $ind : U \longrightarrow \mathcal{P}(PR)$ (induce) with $ind(u) \subseteq hold(realID(u))$. Then a binding is a function $b : P \longrightarrow U$ with $req(p) \subseteq ind(b(p))$ (bind). Second, let us further assume that the CC has partial knowledge of $EN$ and $hold$. This is a realistic assumption in the sense that business partners often know parts of each other's staff. Furthermore properties such as diplomas, social functions, professional qualifications and so on are often publicly known. The setting depicted in Figure 2 exemplifies the dangers.

*Example 1.* Entity $en_1$ holds properties $pr_1$, $pr_2$ and $pr_4$. Entity $en_2$ holds properties $pr_1$, $pr_3$ and $pr_5$ (e.g. imagine a public authority: $pr_1$ stands for 'is staff member', $pr_2$ for 'is construction engineer', $pr_3$ for 'is lawyer', $pr_4$ and $pr_5$ for something else). The CC knows $EN = \{en_1, en_2\}$, $\{pr_1, pr_2\} \subseteq hold(en_1)$ and $\{pr_1, pr_3\} \subseteq hold(en_2)$ (not shown in the figure). The pseudonymizer provides the pseudonyms $U = \{u_1, u_2\}$ and the function $ind$, both also known by the CC. This means, in this case $u_1$ and $u_2$ are poor pseudonyms, since the CC knows $ind$ and parts of $hold$, and thus for the CC $RealID$ is fully revealed.

*Example 2.* Now suppose previous participation at certain activities demanded the pseudonyms $u_1$ and $u_2$, e.g., $en_1$ previously acted as $p_1$ (e.g. involved in an activity 'granting a building licence') and $en_2$ as $p_2$ (e.g. involved in an activity 'furnishing a legal opinion'). Thus $p_1$ was bound to $u_1$ and $p_2$ to $u_2$. Since the CC is responsible for binding participants and therefore knows the binding $b$, the CC has full knowledge of the connection between entities and formal participants. This means, in this simple centralized approach the anonymity of entities w.r.t. to the activities is not supported.

The example setting exhibits an artificial worst case scenario. But anonymity is a relative term which is closely related to the *size* of the anonymity set and also to the *probability distribution* concerning the connections between items of interest (pseudonyms, formal participants or activities) and entities. Often even partial knowledge endangers the ideal of a large anonymity set and an equal probability distribution. Consequently, in general it is worthwhile not only to hide information about the pseudonyms but also to hide information concerning the binding.

## 3   Anonymous SDSD

### 3.1   Requirements

Often, information such as the current execution state of an activity sequence has to be made publicly available. Thus a facility for *'information publishing'* is needed. Sometimes, knowing the reader and/or the creator of a message threatens the anonymity of an entity. In these situations *'reader hiding'* and/or *'creator hiding'* are needed. In the distributed message based SDSD approach entities rely on and refer to received messages. Thus *'accountability'*, *'authenticity'* and *'integrity'* of messages are required. *'Confidentiality'* is also needed, because sometimes the content of a message reveals parts of the binding. Thus only the intended receiver should be able to read the message. Even though the creator of a message might be hidden, often entities have to send an answer to a messsage via a *'back channel'*.

Our approach uses well-known techniques like 'pseudonyms', 'onion routing', 'logging', 'bulletin boards' and 'proxies' to address these requirements at different levels. We mark these places with the previously introduced headwords.

### 3.2   Architecture

An *entity* actually consists of two parts: a *functional object* (FO, or application object) and a *security object* (SO). The FO is the object which has to be monitored by the system. The SO is a part of our distributed access control monitor. It encapsulates the FO in the sense, that every call to the FO is intercepted, inspected and – if necessary – blocked by the SO. The security objects synchronize each other and share necessary information like system states and binding information by especially typed messages. Entities normally act on behalf of their own purpose (more precisely, for the application). Sometimes the entities act as

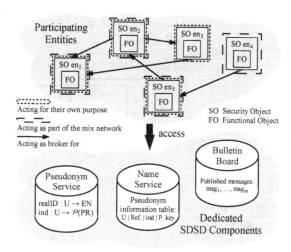

**Fig. 3.** Architecture example with five entities $en_1, \ldots, en_5$

a part of the SDSD mechanisms, e.g. as a node in a *mix network* (described in Section 3.3) or as *broker* (proxy) for another entity (described in Section 3.5). Figure 3 shows an architecture example with five entities $en_1, \ldots, en_5$.

A *pseudonym service* manages the pseudonyms, i.e., it maintains $U$ and $realID$. On behalf of each entity $en$ the pseudonym service verifies selected properties of $en$ and assigns them to the appropriate pseudonym, i.e., for $en = realID(u)$ the service defines $ind(u)$ as a subset of $hold(en)$. The function $ind$ is digitally signed by the pseudonym service ('authenticity'). This signature can be verified by everyone. The pseudonym service has to be a trusted third party in the sense, that one can trust the correctness of its assignments and that it reveals the relevant parts of $realID$ only in case of proven cheating ('accountability'). The pseudonyms provide 'creator hiding' for anybody except the pseudonym service. The already mentioned brokers address this remaining problem.

A publicly accessible *bulletin board* (bb) is used to publish information (e.g. the execution state of an activity sequence) system-wide or even beyond ('information publishing'). This could be realized, e.g., as a broadcast message ('reader hiding'). As a guideline the information published on the bb must not violate the privacy requirements of the entities.

A publicly accessible *name service* (e.g. realized as a part of the bb) provides a pseudonym information table, which is digitally signed by the pseudonym service ('authenticity'). The table assigns to each pseudonym $u$ a reference to the entity $en$ with $realID(u) = en$, the $ind(u)$ value and a public key $pk_u$. The secret key $sk_u$ for $pk_u$ is held by $en$ (asymmetric encryption and signature scheme for 'accountability', 'authenticity' and 'integrity'; in an actual implementation different key pairs for encryption and signature have to be used). The reference does not point directly to $en$, but it is covered by the onion routing technique.

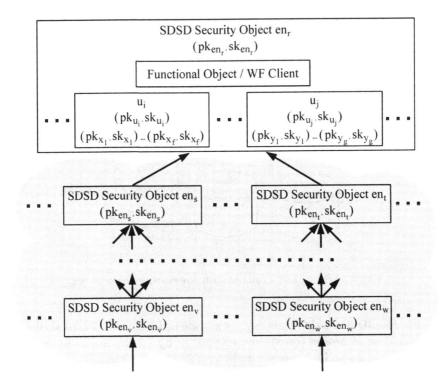

**Fig. 4.** Example mix network

### 3.3   References and Routing

A reference comprises the *IOR of the next mix node*, the encrypted *information for the next mix node*, and a *public message modification key that has to be used to modify the message for the next sub route*. For example, suppose the entities form the mix network sketched in Figure 4. Then the reference *ref* to $en_r$ acting as $u_i$ could be:

$$\Big( IOR_{en_v}, enc \Big( \dots$$
$$\Big( IOR_{en_s}, enc \big( (IOR_{en_r}, enc(u_i, pk_{en_r}), pk_{x_f}), pk_{en_s} \big), pk_{x_{f-1}} \Big) \dots, pk_{en_v} \Big), pk_{x_1} \Big)$$

$IOR_{en_v}$ is the communication reference to $en_v$. Since SDSD uses the middleware CORBA, this is a CORBA interoperable object reference. The encryption function *enc* expects the content to be the first and the encryption key to be the second argument. The message modification keys are used to modify the message appearence on each subroute. These modifications can only be removed by the final receiver. Thus, if at least one mix node is trustworthy, then the sent messages cannot be linked. Note that each entity *en* knows its secret key $sk_{en}$, the secret keys $sk_{u_i}, sk_{u_j}, \dots$ of all pseudonyms used by *en* and all secret keys for the public message modification keys of references to its pseudonyms.

A message $msg_{k_0}$ that should be sent to $u_i$ is first sent as message $msg_{k_1} = enc(enc(enc(msg_{k_0}, pk_{u_i}), pk_{x_1}), pk_{en_v})$ to the first planned mix node $en_v$, which is able to decrypt the 'outer onion skin' of $ref$ and $msg_{k_1}$. Then $en_v$ finds the next subroute and sends the updated message as $msg_{k_2} = enc(enc(enc(enc(msg_{k_0}, pk_{u_i}), pk_{x_1}), pk_{x_2}), pk_{en_{nextMixNode}}$ with an updated reference accordingly. After some time, $en_s$ receives message $msg_{k_0}$ encrypted as $msg_{k_{f-1}} = enc(enc(\dots(enc(enc(enc(msg_{k_0}, pk_{u_i}), pk_{x_1}), pk_{x_2}), \dots), pk_{x_{f-1}}), pk_{en_s})$ and the remaining part of $ref$ (i.e. $enc((IOR_{en_r}, enc(u_i, pk_{en_r}), pk_{x_f}), pk_{en_s}))$. With $sk_{en_s}$ entity $en_s$ removes the 'outer encryption' of $msg_{k_{f-1}}$ and of the part of $ref$. In the remaining part $en_s$ finds the $IOR$ of the next mix node and $pk_{x_f}$. Thus, $en_s$ sends $msg_{k_l} = enc(enc(\dots(enc(enc(enc(msg_{k_0}, pk_{u_i}), pk_{x_1}), pk_{x_2}), \dots), pk_{x_{f-1}}), pk_{x_f})$ and $enc(u_i, pk_{en_r})$ to $en_r$. Eventually $en_r$ receives the message and after decrypting the reference with $sk_{en_r}$ entity $en_r$ notices that no further message sending is necessary, because the only remaining reference $u_i$ belongs to itself. Now it is able to recover the actual message $msg_{k_0}$ with $sk_{u_i}$ and $sk_{x_1}, \dots, sk_{x_f}$.

Apart from the known attacks on mix networks, no one but $en_r$ should be able to identify the final destination of the sent message ('reader hiding'), because $en_r$ is the only entity which knows that no further message sending is necessary. Furthermore if two or more pseudonyms are associated with the same entity, a different route can be declared for each pseudonym to avoid linking of pseudonyms. To prevent attacks which exploit the length information of the reference, the reference can be padded up to a fixed length.

## 3.4 Messages

We adapt the basic SDSD approach, which grants and – after usage – immediately revokes permissions to execute activities. An entity gets such a *dynamic* permission in form of a conceptual security token. To exploit the permission, the entity has to pass the token and therefore loses the permission.

First, the token is offered to the activators of all possible next steps by sending offer messages (offer msgs for short). An activator which wants to execute its step answers with a get msg. Then, one of these answering activators gets the token in form of a put msg. Finally, this activator calls the step action on the executor by handing over the token to the executor by means of an invoke msg. Subsequently, the next offer msgs are sent and so on. The Anonymous SDSD approach uses these and some additional message types:

1. offer(automat_id, sender, receiver, step_id, step_counter):
   to offer the execution permission to an activator of a possible next step
2. get(automat_id, sender, receiver, step_id, step_counter):
   to express the wish to get the execution permission for a step (answer to an offer)
3. put(automat_id, sender, receiver, step_id, step_counter, signature_of_invoke_msg):
   to give the execution permission for a step to its activator (answer to a get)

4. invoke(automat_id, sender, receiver, step_id, step_counter, signature_of_put_msg):
   to give the execution permission for a step to its executor (reaction to a put)
5. who(automat_id, sender, receiver, formal_participant_of_interest):
   to ask for uncovering the binding of a formal participant
6. inform(automat_id, sender, receiver, formal_participant_of_interest, bound_to):
   to uncover the binding of a formal participant (answer to a who)
7. publish(automat_id, sender, receiver, content):
   to publish the content
8. revoke(automat_id, sender, receiver, content):
   to revoke a content, this means to mark it outdated
9. deliver(automat_id, sender, receiver, msg_to_deliver, msg_to_deliver_receiver):
   to deliver a message via a broker to its intended receiver
10. bound(automat_id, sender, receiver, formal_participant_of_interest):
    to inform that a formal participant is bound, but without revealing to whom

To accumulate evidence, any sent message is logged both by its sender and by its receiver. Furthermore, before sending a message the sender digitally signs the message ('authenticity', 'integrity'). Sometimes, a message is embedded in another message, then the embedded message is often deliberately not signed. In all cases, before sending a message the 'outer' message is encrypted with the key of the intended receiver ('confidentiality'). When an entity receives a message, the entity decrypts the message, verifies the signature, checks that it is not a replayed message, and finally checks that the step_counter value – if contained – is not less than the step_counter values of all previously received messages.

### 3.5   Usage of Messages

In a technical report [5] we describe what messages are sent in which order to enable the SOs to locally take their access decisions. In this paper, we exemplify a part of these protocols by means of the steps and messages shown in Figure 5.

#### 3.5.1   Initialize a Protocol Instance

Some entity which acts as an *initializer* instantiates a protocol. As a result the initializer gets an unbound automaton with $b = \emptyset$. The formal participants will be bound on demand in the local contexts. The initializer signs the automaton and finally publishes it on the bb (so far, not shown in Figure 5). Then some entity which acts as a *starter* starts this automaton by offering the permission to execute one of the steps which lead off the start state.

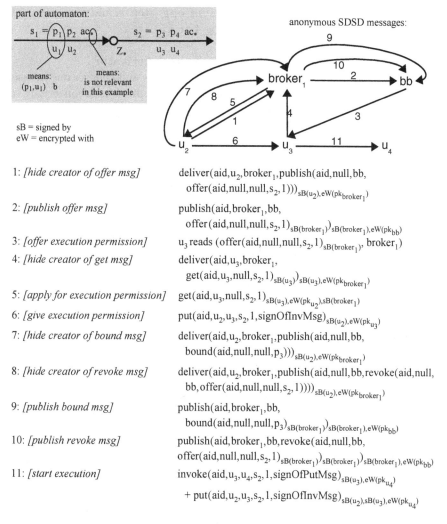

part of automaton:

$s_1 = \boxed{p_1 \; p_2 \; ac_*}$     $s_2 = p_3 \; p_4 \; ac_*$

$u_1 \; u_2$     $z_*$     $u_3 \; u_4$

means: $(p_1,u_1)$ b

means: is not relevant in this example

sB = signed by
eW = encrypted with

anonymous SDSD messages:

1: *[hide creator of offer msg]*     deliver(aid,$u_2$,broker$_1$,publish(aid,null,bb,
  offer(aid,null,null,$s_2$,1)))$_{sB(u_2),eW(pk_{broker_1})}$

2: *[publish offer msg]*     publish(aid,broker$_1$,bb,
  offer(aid,null,null,$s_2$,1)$_{sB(broker_1)})_{sB(broker_1),eW(pk_{bb})}$

3: *[offer execution permission]*     $u_3$ reads (offer(aid,null,null,$s_2$,1)$_{sB(broker_1)}$, broker$_1$)

4: *[hide creator of get msg]*     deliver(aid,$u_3$,broker$_1$,
  get(aid,$u_3$,null,$s_2$,1)$_{sB(u_3)})_{sB(u_3),eW(pk_{broker_1})}$

5: *[apply for execution permission]*     get(aid,$u_3$,null,$s_2$,1)$_{sB(u_3),eW(pk_{u_2}),sB(broker_1)}$

6: *[give execution permission]*     put(aid,$u_2$,$u_3$,$s_2$,1,signOfInvMsg)$_{sB(u_2),eW(pk_{u_3})}$

7: *[hide creator of bound msg]*     deliver(aid,$u_2$,broker$_1$,publish(aid,null,bb,
  bound(aid,null,null,$p_3$)))$_{sB(u_2),eW(pk_{broker_1})}$

8: *[hide creator of revoke msg]*     deliver(aid,$u_2$,broker$_1$,publish(aid,null,bb,revoke(aid,null,
  bb,offer(aid,null,null,$s_2$,1))))$_{sB(u_2),eW(pk_{broker_1})}$

9: *[publish bound msg]*     publish(aid,broker$_1$,bb,
  bound(aid,null,null,$p_3$)$_{sB(broker_1)})_{sB(broker_1),eW(pk_{bb})}$

10: *[publish revoke msg]*     publish(aid,broker$_1$,bb,revoke(aid,null,bb,
  offer(aid,null,null,$s_2$,1)$_{sB(broker_1)})_{sB(broker_1)})_{sB(broker_1),eW(pk_{bb})}$

11: *[start execution]*     invoke(aid,$u_3$,$u_4$,$s_2$,1,signOfPutMsg)$_{sB(u_3),eW(pk_{u_4})}$
  + put(aid,$u_2$,$u_3$,$s_2$,1,signOfInvMsg)$_{sB(u_2),sB(u_3),eW(pk_{u_4})}$

**Fig. 5.** Example of the usage of messages: $u_2$ acts as the last executor; $s_2$ is the next executed step; $u_3$ acts as the next activator; $u_4$ acts as the next executor

### 3.5.2   Offering the Execution Right

The starter, and later on the pertinent *last executor*, respectively, creates an offer msg and prepares to publish it on the bb. In order to hide himself as creator, the offer msg is embedded into a deliver msg (step 1) and sent via a so-called *broker*, using a further embedding into a publish msg (step 1). The broker unpacks the deliver msg, and forwards the publish msg to the bb, which actually publishes the offer (step 2).

When an entity reads an offer msg (step 3) and wants to act as the activator of the respective step, it answers with a new signed get msg. Again, this get msg is embedded in a new signed deliver msg (step 4) and returned to the last executor via the involved broker (steps 4 and 5).

### 3.5.3  Giving the Execution Right to a Step Activator

The last executor collects all get msgs which it receives and chooses one message for a positive put msg answer. Before, it does a plausibility check concerning the correctness of the get msg w.r.t. the underlying SDSD protocol. If the formal participant is still unbound, then the last executor verifies that the qualification requirements are complied, creates a new put msg, signs it and sends it directly to the creator of the get msg (step 6). The put msg permits its receiver to activate the next step. Consequently the previously published offer msgs have to be marked outdated on the bb. Furthermore a bound msg has to be published on the bb to reveal which formal participant is bound but not to whom. Similar as before, the publications are mediated by a broker (steps 7 to 10).

If the activator of the next step – more precisely the designated formal participant – is already bound to a pseudonym, then the last executor has to verify that the sender of the get msg is equal to this pseudonym (this case is not shown in Figure 5). If the binding is unknown, the last executor analyses the bound msgs on the bb. The bound msg that refers to the pertinent formal participant reveals the broker that was involved in the relevant local context, because the broker is publicly associated with this message on the bb. Then the last executor obtains the necessary binding information by asking this broker with a who msg. To prove the necessity of the request the get msg is forwarded, too.

### 3.5.4  Giving the Execution Right to a Step Executor

The received put msg permits its receiver to act as the activator of the step. After checking the plausibility of the put msg w.r.t. the underlying SDSD protocol, the activator has to invoke the executor of this step. If this executor is already bound – more precisely the designated formal participant – then the activator has to ask for the relevant binding similarly to the above described procedure with one difference.

If the activator knows the executor's pseudonym, it creates a signed invoke msg and sends it to the executor, together with a put msg to improve the plausibility (step 11). Then the executor executes the action of the step. If the executor is not yet bound, the activator chooses one of the candidates (according to the *ind* function) listed at the name service. Then, as described before, the step is executed with the help of an invoke msg. Because a formal participant has just been bound, the executor has to publish this information on the bb.

## 4   Security Properties

We only state basic security claims, whose justifications are omitted for space restrictions but documented in a technical report [5]. Furthermore, Table 1 summarizes how the requirements, as presented in Section 3.1, are met by the employed mechanisms, as surveyed in Sections 3.2 and 3.3. The claims and justifications

Table 1. Survey on justifications of security properties

| requirement / mechanism | information publishing | reader hiding | creator hiding | accountability | providing back channel | confidentiality | authenticity |
|---|---|---|---|---|---|---|---|
| **bulletin board / name service (broad-casting)** | publicly providing: • execution state of activity sequence • info which formal participants are bound • communication references, induced properties and public keys *broadcasting provides public access* | hiding need of information, because this fact (+ public automaton description + public execution state) can reveal bindings *broadcasting hides need of information* | | reader of a published information is relying on and refering to this information *msg deliverer is associated (verifiable by signature)* | providing back channel for reactions (get, who) *provided by associated deliverer* | | |
| **broker (proxy)** | | | hiding msg creator, because this information (+ public automaton description + public execution state) can reveal bindings *entities which trust a broker form a anonymity set* | receiver of a delivered msg is relying on and refering to this msg *msg signature reveals broker as deliverer broker has a signed order to deliver* | providing back channel for reactions (get, who) *broker knows creator of msg to which the reaction refer* | | |
| **pseudonym service** | | | hiding msg creator, because this information (+ public automaton description + public execution state) can reveal bindings *pseudonyms cover the real identity but only against parties which don't know realID (i.e. not against the pseudonym service)* | *signature of msg reveals pseudonym and pseudonym service knows entity hidden by pseudonym* | | | qualification requirements have to be respected communication reference and public key have to refer to correct entity *some properties of entity are induced to its pseudonym pseudonym service verifies and signs property induction, communication reference and public key* |
| **mix network** | | hiding need of information and the intended receiver, because these facts (+ public automaton description + public execution state) can reveal bindings *mix network hides intended receiver* | hiding msg creator, because this information (+ public automaton description + public execution state) can reveal bindings *mix network hides creator* | | | | |
| **asymmetric encryption and signature schemes** | | | | | | hiding content of msgs which contain binding information *msg isn't readable without private decryption key pseudonym service + name service provide PKI* | reader of a msg is relying on and refering to authentic and unchanged msgs *msg signature indicates authenticity of the creator + unchanged msg* |

assume that all communication channels are reliable, all sites are online and operating. These conditions have to be guaranteed by additional mechanisms.

*Claim.* If security is violated, then a referee (i.e. a trusted third party) is able to name the pseudonym under which the last fraudulent behaviour occurred that took place before executing a forbidden activity.

*Claim.* No central component obtains binding information, except the binding information which the component can infer before any binding has taken place.

*Claim.* Information concerning the bindings in a local execution context is only transferred to entities (and their involved brokers) which (a) participate in this context or (b) answer binding questions of entities participating in this context. Furthermore, (c) the binder that answers a binding question of an entity from this context reveals to the questioner (and its involved broker) under which formal participant the binder has made the binding.

*Claim.* In the worst case a *local execution context* consists of four formal participants and therefore of at most four entities.

## 5   Related Work

Hansen/Pfitzmann [10] provide an extensive terminology proposal regarding anonymity, pseudonymity and related terms. Their definitions mostly correspond to our view. Steinbrecher/Koepsell [17] suggest an entropy based measure for the degree of anonymity, which we can transfer to our setting. Further proposals for anonymity measures can be found e.g. in Diaz et al [9] or Serjantov/Danezis [16].

WIDE [7] uses workflow authorization constraints for a flexible assignment of tasks to roles and agents. The workflow security model W-RBAC [20] is a RBAC-based permission service and a workflow component, using a logic based language and providing a mechanism for controlled overriding of constraints. Tucupi [21] is a prototype, which makes use of the W-RBAC model. The administrative activity of overriding constraints is treated in the same way as a normal activity. This idea of a self administrative mechanism is viable in the SDSD proposal as well [4]. Moreover, there are several publications dealing with security for workflows, e.g. by Huang/Atluri (SecureFlow) [11], Oh/Park (T-RBAC) [14], Knorr [13], Sun/Pan [19] and Bertino et al. [1]. All these approaches are centralistic, thus suffering from the problems described in Section 2.

METEOR [22] is a web-based wfms which has a distributed enactment service, but without addressing anonymity issues. SALSA [12] is a distributed wfms for inter-organizational workflows, addressing the specific security problems for such workflows. To support state dependent access control, SALSA uses so-called monitor servers which log the execution history. These servers can be queried by the enforcement mechanism and prevent anonymous participation. By some suitable restrictions, it may be possible to support anonymous participation.

Schulz/Orlowska [15] treat privacy requirements of cross-organizational wfs, distinguishing between private wfs, wf views and coalition wfs. The proposed architecture has the potential to effectively meet certain privacy requirements. Since the monitors are controlled by their owning organizations the pretence of false wf execution states can neither be prevented nor detected.

The increasing need of quick response to market opportunities led to the idea of virtual organizations (e.g. Strader et al. [18], [6]), where different companies temporarily collaborate in a loosely-coupled way. Our Anonymous SDSD approach addresses some requirements of virtual organizations: participation in workflow instances across company boundaries, hiding the organizational details which are not necessary for the cooperation, a decentralized access control enforcement system which works under limited trust between the companies.

The development of state dependent access control for web services seems to be in an early phase. Coetzee/Eloff [8] demand access control decisions based on results of previous actions without offering a solution. Yang et al. [23] suggest a trust-based security model and an enforcement mechanism which uses event trigger rules that enable certain dynamic constraints. But – unlike our approach – restrictions like, e.g., 'an entity has access to a web service $x$, if and only if this entity has previously accessed another web service $y$', cannot be enforced.

# 6    Conclusion

The cooperation across different security domains raises various challenges regarding the confinement of information flows. As an important example, we identified and analysed the problem of anonymous participation in inter-organizational workflow instances. We presented and justified a general concept for a solution: Replacing a traditional central control by an innovative distributed combination of known techniques like onion routing, logging, bulletin boards, pseudonyms and proxies, we achieved the hiding not only of the identities but also of the pseudonyms of the actual participants, as far as possible in a specific situation.

# References

1. Elisa Bertino, Elena Ferrari, and Vijay Atluri. The specification and enforcement of authorization constraints in workflow management systems. *ACM Trans. Inf. Syst. Secur.*, 2(1):65–104, 1999.
2. Joachim Biskup and Christian Eckert. About the enforcement of state dependent security specifications. In T.F. Keefe and C.E. Landwehr, editors, *Database Security VII*, pages 3–17, Boston, etc., 1994. Kluwer.
3. Joachim Biskup and Thomas Leineweber. State-dependent security decisions for distributed object-systems. In Martin S. Olivier and David L. Spooner, editors, *Database and Application Security XV*, pages 105–118. Kluwer, 2002.
4. Joachim Biskup, Thomas Leineweber, and Jörg Parthe. Administration rights in the sdsd-system. In Sabrina De Capitani di Vimercati, Indrakshi Ray, and Indrajit Ray, editors, *Data and Applications Security XVII: Status and Prospects*, pages 149–162. Kluwer, 2004.
5. Joachim Biskup and Jörg Parthe. Optimistic anonymous participation in inter-organizational workflow instances. http://ls6-www.cs.uni-dortmund.de/issi/publications/2006.html.de, 2006.

6. L. M. Camarinha-Matos and H. Afsarmanesh, editors. *Processes and Foundations for Virtual Organizations*, volume 134 of *IFIP International Federation for Information Processing*. Springer, Berlin, 2003.

7. Fabio Casati, Silvana Castano, and Maria Grazia Fugini. Managing workflow authorization constraints through active database technology. *Information Systems Frontiers*, 3(3):319–338, 2001.

8. M. Coetzee and J.H.P. Eloff. Towards web service access control. *Computers & Security*, 23(7):559–570, 2004.

9. Claudia Diaz, Stefaan Seys, Joris Claessens, and Bart Preneel. Towards measuring anonymity. In Roger Dingledine and Paul Syverson, editors, *Privacy Enhancing Technologies 2002*, LNCS, pages 54–68, Berlin Heidelberg, 2003. Springer.

10. Marit Hansen and Andreas Pfitzmann. Anonymity, unlinkability, unobservability, pseudonymity, and identity management   a consolidated proposal for terminology. version v0.23. `http://dud.inf.tu-dresden.de/Literatur_V1.shtml`, 2005.

11. Wei-Kuang Huang and Vijayalakshmi Atluri. Secureflow: a secure web-enabled workflow management system. In *Proceedings of the Fourth ACM Workshop on Role-based Access Control*, pages 83–94. ACM Press, 1999.

12. Myong H. Kang, Joon S. Park, and Judith N. Froscher. Access control mechanisms for inter-organizational workflow. In *Proceedings of the Sixth ACM Symposium on Access Control Models and Technologies*, pages 66–74. ACM Press, 2001.

13. Konstantin Knorr. Dynamic access control through petri net workflows. In *Proceedings of the 16th Annual Computer Security Applications Conference*, pages 159–167. IEEE Computer Society, 2000.

14. Sejong Oh and Seog Park. Task-role-based access control model. *Information Systems*, 28(6):533–562, September 2003.

15. Karsten A. Schulz and Maria E. Orlowska. Facilitating cross-organisational workflows with a workflow view approach. *Data & Knowledge Engineering*, 51(1):109–147, 2004.

16. Andrei Serjantov and George Danezis. Towards an information theoretic metric for anonymity. In Roger Dingledine and Paul Syverson, editors, *Privacy Enhancing Technologies 2002*, LNCS, pages 41–53, Berlin Heidelberg, 2003. Springer.

17. Sandra Steinbrecher and Stefan Köpsell. Modelling Unlinkability. `http://www.inf.tu-dresden.de/~ss64/Papers/PET-Unlinkability.pdf`, 2003.

18. Troy J. Strader, Fu-Ren Lin, and Michael J. Shaw. Information infrastructure for electronic virtual organization management. *Decision Support Systems*, 23:75–94, 1998.

19. Yuqing Sun and Peng Pan. Pres: a practical flexible rbac workflow system. In *ICEC '05: Proceedings of the 7th International Conference on Electronic Commerce*, pages 653–658, New York, NY, USA, 2005. ACM Press.

20. Jacques Wainer, Paulo Barthelmess, and Akhil Kumar. W-rbac – a workflow security model incorporating controlled overriding of constraints. *International Journal of Cooperative Information Systems*, 12(4):455–485, 2003.

21. Jacques Wainer, Fabio Bezerra, and Paulo Barthelmess. Tucupi: a flexible workflow system based on overridable constraints. In *Proceedings of the 2004 ACM Symposium on Applied Computing*, pages 498–502, 2004.

22. Shengli Wu, Amit Sheth, John Miller, and Zongwei Luo. Authorization and access control of application data in workflow systems. *J. Intell. Inf. Syst.*, 18(1):71–94, 2002.

23. S. Yang, H. Lam, and S. Y. W. Su. Trust-based security model and enforcement mechanism for web service technology. In *Technologies for E-Services. Third International Workshop, TES 2002.*, pages 151–160. Springer, 2002.

# O2O: Virtual Private Organizations to Manage Security Policy Interoperability

Frédéric Cuppens, Nora Cuppens-Boulahia, and Céline Coma

GET/ENST Bretagne, 2 rue de la chataîgneraie,
35576 Cesson-Sévigné Cedex, France
{frederic.cuppens,nora.cuppens,celine.coma}@enst-bretagne.fr

**Abstract.** Nowadays, the interaction between systems is absolutely essential to achieve business continuity. There is a need to exchange and share services and resources. Unfortunately, this does not come without security problems. The organizations (companies, enterprizes, etc.) have to manage accesses to their services and resources by external opponents. O2O is a formal approach we suggest in this paper to deal with access control in an interoperability context. It is based on two main concepts: *Virtual Private Organization* (VPO) and Role Single-Sign On (RSSO). A VPO enables any organization undertaking an inter-operation with other organizations to keep control over the ressources accessed during the interoperability phases. The RSSO principle allows a given subject to keep the same role when accessing to another organization but with privileges defined in the VPO. Thus, using O2O, each organization can define and enforce its own secure interoperability policy. O2O is integrated in the OrBAC model (Organization based access control).

**Keywords:** Virtual Organization (VO), Virtual Private Organization (VPO), Role Single Sign On (RSSO), OrBAC, Access Control, Authority spheres, Interoperability.

## 1 Introduction

Current information systems are more and more distributed and require more interactions with external components or services. Classical client/server architecture is no longer adapted to manage these systems when several organizations have to exchange information or provide service interoperability. For this purpose, the concept of *Virtual Organization* (VO) has been suggested [13,18]. A VO is created by several organizations and is formed with some users, services or resources from the different organizations.

To interact securely in a VO, each organization has to define its security policy and every interaction must be compliant with the policies of organizations involved in the interaction. Classical security models such as the RBAC model [19] are not suited to model these requirements. They only apply to centralized management of security in which some servers implement their security policy to control the access of some clients. However, in a VO, each principal wants to have some guarantee that information provided to other principals are processed securely. Thus, every principal implements

A. Bagchi and V. Atluri (Eds.): ICISS 2006, LNCS 4332, pp. 101–115, 2006.
© Springer-Verlag Berlin Heidelberg 2006

its own policy and the interaction will only take place if it does not violate their policy. Access control models have to be adapted to manage such symmetric behavior.

In this paper, we suggest a new approach called O2O (for *Organization to Organization*) to manage interoperability between components having their own policies defined by different organizations. To explain the basic principals of O2O, let us consider that a given organization Alice.org wants to interoperate with another organization Bob.org. In this case, each organization has to define a *Virtual Private organization* (VPO) respectively called Alice2Bob (A2B for short) and Bob2Alice (B2A for short). The VPO A2B is associated with a security policy that manages how subjects from organization Alice.org may have an access to organization Bob.org. We say that the VPO A2B manages the *interoperability* security policy from Alice.org to Bob.org. The VPO B2A is similarly defined to control accesses of subjects from Bob.org to Alice.org. Hence, a VPO is a dynamic organization created to achieve a given purpose of interoperability and disappears once this purpose in no more needed. VPO is the basic concept used to enforce our O2O approach.

O2O is formally defined as an extension of the OrBAC model [1,8]. The concept of organization is central in this model. In OrBAC, each organization can define its own security policy which does not directly apply to concrete subjects, actions and objects. Instead, the policy is defined using the organizational concepts of role, activity and view which are respectively abstractions of subject, action and object (this is further detailed in section 3 below). The concrete policy that applies to subjects, actions and objects is then derived from the organizational policy specification.

We suggest extending the OrBAC model so that an organization can also define interoperability security policies with other organizations using O2O. One advantage of the approach is that a given subject who is assigned to a given role in an organization A can keep his or her role when accessing to another organization B but possibly with different privileges as defined in the interoperability policy of A2B. By analogy with Single-Sign On used for identity management, we call this principle RSSO for Role Single-Sign On. For instance, let us assume that a given subject is assigned to role physician in a given hospital A. Then, when this subject attempts to have an access to another hospital B, this subject is assigned to role physician, not in hospital B, but in the VPO A2B. By doing so, this subject can keep his or her role but possibly with different privileges than other subjects that are directly assigned to role physician in B. Notice that privileges of role physician in the virtual private organization A2B are also generally different from those of role physician in organization A.

The remainder of this paper is organized as follows. Section 2 further motivates our approach and compares it with other proposals. Section 3 gives an overview of the OrBAC model. Section 4 defines the confinement principle. We argue that this principle must be enforced so that secure interactions between organizations may take place. Section 5 presents our O2O approach and shows how it is used to manage security in a virtual organization. We formally define inter-organization compatibility in section 6 which makes it easy interactions between organizations that need to interoperate. Section 7 shows how our O2O model applies to manage security of a Virtual Organization. Finally, section 8 concludes the paper.

## 2   Motivation

Federation of identity currently facilitates the subject's authentication through the Internet. For example, using Liberty Alliance [4], some subject has not to repeatedly identify himself or herself with a new password each time he or she wants to have an access to a service managed by a different organization. Hence, this subject only manages a single password (single-sign on [15]) and then, through certificate exchanges, he or she can access to other organizations that belong to the Alliance without the halting delays of redundant entry.

However, at first glance, except the real advantage that the authentication is done once for all, this process is not fully satisfactory as it is based on a high level consideration of Alliance membership. Hence, if A and B are two members of the alliance then (1) all authenticated subjects of B will have the same set of rights when accessing to A and (2) the access control is not fine grained as it is based on some characteristics shared by all B's subjects vis-à-vis of A. For instance, let us consider a subject John who is assigned to role customer into a first organization A and that another organization B gives a special discount to the customers of organization A. Once John is logged in organization A, if both A and B are members of Liberty Alliance, then B will trust in the certificate delivered by the Alliance that says that John comes from organization A. However, this certificate does not guarantee that John is assigned to role customer in organization A.

This need for finer grained dynamic access control has been identified by Liberty Alliance and is included in the SAML 2.0 specification. The solution is based on exchange of *credentials* [12]. A credential contains attribute information used to establish trust between two parties A and B. Traditionally, the credential is sent as a whole. In this way, though not necessary, all information contained in the credential is disclosed. To avoid this disclosure, the other drastic measure is to reveal nothing about the information contained in the credential. In these traditional approaches, interaction between some parties A and B belonging to some Alliance can fail though for both A and B the amount of information that has to be disclosed is acceptable.

Some works have been done to manage a more subtle access control policy to the information contained in the credentials and to define classes of negotiation strategies to control disclosure of credentials during the interaction. TrustBuilder [10,22] provides a set of language-independent protocols that ensures the interoperability of the negotiation strategies. During a negotiation, a local security agent uses a negotiation strategy to determine which local resources to disclose next and to accept new disclosure from other participants. Trust-X [3] also supports different strategies for trust negotiations to determine the order in which credentials should be disclosed.

Besides the definition of negotiation strategies, we also need high level languages to enable parties who intend to inter-operate to specify authorization requirements that must be met to access to all or part of the information contained in the credential. An example of such a language is presented in the work by J. Li, N. Li and W. Winsborough [11]. Though this language that defines security policies based on credential are inspired by the well known access control model RBAC, it is not free of ambiguity. There is no clear separation between the security policy specification and credential that are used to implement this policy. A similar comment applies to other approaches such as the Dynamic Coalition-Based Access Control (DCBAC) model [21].

Moreover, as we said in the introduction, the use of RBAC as access control model is not judicious. As a matter of fact, the role approach leads to a more fine grained access control to attribute information transmitted in the credential than the Liberty Alliance or Micro Passport [14] access control do. But the interoperability enabled by such a role approach is static; all the roles needed for this interaction must be anticipated and have to be defined in advance.

We actually need approaches that allow organizations to specify more dynamic access control policies. This is typically the case when several organizations interoperate through a Virtual Organization. Grid computing is especially concerned with the sharing and coordinated use of resources in such distributed VOs [9]. In a VO, one must guarantee interoperability of diverse local mechanisms, support dynamic creation of services and enable dynamic creation of trust domains. For instance, the CAS server [16] allows VOs to express policies and communicates these policies to various local organizations involved in the VO. Thus, CAS implicitly assumes a centralized administration of the VO security policy and does not answer the following questions [17]: (1) Who is in charge of defining the security policy associated with the VO, (2) Who is responsible for administrating this security policy?

Since there are several organizations involved in the VO having possibly conflicting interests, it is not easy to answer these two questions if we assume a centralized administration of the VO security policy. This is why we argue for a decentralized administration of the VO and we suggest our O2O approach whose objectives are the following:

- In O2O, each organization involved in a VO is responsible for controlling interoperability with other organizations through the definition and administration of a Virtual Private Organization (VPO). VPO provides a fully decentralized administration of a VO.
- In a VPO, it is not necessary to define new roles. When accessing to another organization, a given subject can keep the same role as in its own organization, but the VPO will define the security policy associated with this role in this other organization. Thus, in some sense, VPO generalizes the concept of single sign on already defined for subject identity to *role* identity. This is why we call this principle RSSO (Role Single-Sign On).
- In a VPO, it is possible to specify dynamic and fine grained access control. In particular, the *organization* concept as it is defined in the OrBAC model brings the *dynamical* dimension through our O2O approach.
- Our O2O model clearly separates the security policy specification from its implementation. In this paper, we only present the policy specification part of our model. We do not address its implementation through trust negotiation by exchange of credentials.

## 3   Outline of the OrBAC Model

Since O2O is actually defined as an extension of the OrBAC model, we first briefly present the basic principles of OrBAC.

The concept of *organization* is central in OrBAC. Intuitively, an organization is any entity that is responsible for managing a security policy. Each organization can use Or-BAC to specify its own security policy at the *organizational* level, that is abstractly from the implementation of this policy. Thus, instead of modelling the policy by using the concrete and implementation-related concepts of subject, action and object, the OrBAC model suggests reasoning with the roles that subjects, actions or objects are assigned in the organization. The role of a subject is simply called a *role* as in the RBAC model. On the other hand, the role of an action is called an *activity* whereas the role of an object is called a *view*.

Each organization can then define security rules which specify that some roles are permitted or prohibited to carry out some activities on some views. These security rules do not apply statically but their activation may depend on contextual conditions. For this purpose, the concept of *context* is explicitly introduced in OrBAC. Thus, using a formalism based on first order logic, security rules are modelled using a 6-places predicate:

- security_rule(type, org, role, activity, view, context) where type belongs to {permission, prohibition}.

For instance, the following security rule:

- security_rule(permission, a_hosp, nurse, consult, medical_record, urgency) means that, in organization a_hosp, a nurse is permitted to consult a medical record in the context of urgency.

The organizational policy is then used to automatically derive concrete configurations of PEP's (Policy Enforcement Point, see the AAA architecture). For this purpose, we need to assign to subjects, actions and objects, the roles they are assigned in the organization. In the OrBAC model, this is modelled using the following 3-places predicates:

- empower(org, subject, role): means that in organization org, subject is empowered in role.
- consider(org, action, activity): means that in organization org, action is considered an implementation of activity.
- use(org, object, view): means that in organization org, object is used in view.

For instance, the fact empower(a_hosp,john,physician) means that organization a_hosp empowers john in role physician.

Notice that, instead of enumerating facts corresponding to instances of predicate empower, it is also possible to specify *role definitions* which correspond to logical conditions that, when satisfied, are used to derive that some subjects are automatically empowered in the role associated with the role definition. Role definition may be viewed as an extension of the Attribute-Based User-Role assignment suggested in [2]. For instance, a bookshop bs may consider that a subject is empowered in role gold_customer if this subject is empowered in role customer and if he or she has been a customer for more than ten years. This is modelled by the following role definition:

- empower(bs, X, gold_customer) :-
  empower(bs, X, customer), membership(bs,X,Y), Y >= 10.

Activity and view definitions are similarly used to automatically manage assignment of action to activity and object to view. Role definition (resp. activity and view definition) are used in our O2O approach for managing federations of roles (resp. activity and view) as specified in interoperability security policy (see section 5).

Regarding context, we have also to define logical conditions to characterize when contexts are active. In the OrBAC model, this is represented by logical rules that derive the following predicate:

- hold(org, subject, action, object, context): means that in organization org, subject performs action on object in context context.

Using the model, one can then derive concrete privileges that apply to subject, action and object from organizational security rules. This corresponds to the following general principle of derivation:

- concrete_privilege(Type,S,Act,Obj) :-
  security_rule(Org,Type,R,A,V,Cxt),
  empower(Org,S,R) use(Org,Obj,V), consider(Org,Act,A),
  hold(Org,S,Act,Obj,Cxt).

that is a subject S has a concrete privilege of type Type to perform an action Act on object O if (1) organization Org assigns to role R a security rule of type Type to perform activity A on view V in context Cxt and (2) if Org empowers subject S in role R and (3) Org uses object O in view V and (4) Org considers that action Act implements the activity A and (5) in Org, the context Cxt is active when subject S is performing action Act on object Obj.

This general principle of derivation of concrete privileges from organizational authorizations is used to automatically generate concrete configurations (see [5] for further details in the case of network security policies). We actually restrict our model to be compatible with a stratified Datalog program [20], so that derivation in our model is computable in polynomial time.

## 4   Confinement Principle

Since OrBAC can explicitly manage several security policies related to different organizations, it provides an adequate framework to define security policies for organizations that have to interoperate. For instance, let us consider two hospitals a_hosp and b_hosp. We assume that each hospital manages its own medical records into a view medical_record and that there is no medical record shared by the two hospitals. We also assume that each organization manages a role physician and that a physician is permitted to consult medical records handled by his or her hospital in every situation (corresponding to a context called nominal). In OrBAC, this is modelled by the following security rule:

- security_rule(permission, a_hosp, physician, consult, medical_record, nominal). and similarly for b_hosp.

Up to now, notice that a physician from a given hospital cannot have an access to medical records managed by the other hospital. More precisely, OrBAC actually implements a *confinement* principal so that the scope of every security rule is restricted to the organization in which the rule applies. Thus the rule above specifies that a physician is permitted to consult medical records of a_hosp but prevents him to have an access to medical records of b_hosp (except if some medical records are physically shared by both a_hosp and b_hosp but this is not our assumption here).

Confinement is a good security principle. When dealing with interoperability requirements, we have to be compatible with this principle. For instance, let us assume that, in a context of urgency, a_hosp wants to grant to physician from b_hosp the permission to consult its medical records. A first possibility, which preserves the confinement principle, would be that a_hosp creates a new role b_physician and specifies the following security rule:

- security_rule(permission, a_hosp, b_physician, consult, medical_record, urgency).

and the following role definition:

- empower(a_hosp, X, b_physician) :- empower(b_hosp, X, physician).

This role definition rule says that a subject X is empowered in role b_physician in organization a_hosp if this subject is empowered in role physician in organization b_hosp.

So let us consider a subject Alice who is empowered in role physician in organization b_hosp and that context urgency is active in organization a_hosp. If Alice asks for an access to an a_hosp's medical record, then she will have to give her credential that proves that she is empowered in role physician in organization b_hosp. By doing so, she will automatically be empowered in role b_physician in organization a_hosp and thus will be permitted to have an access to a_hosp's medical records since we assumed that the context urgency is active.

However, this first solution to manage interoperability is not satisfactory for at least three reasons:

1. From the security administration point of view, it will create many "artificial" roles related to interoperability, such as the b_physician role. At the end, this may significantly complicate administration of the security policy.
2. From the usability point of view, physicians from organization b_hosp will have to manage several different roles: role physician in organization b_hosp, role b_physician in organization a_hosp, etc. This is not satisfactory.
3. From the interoperability point of view, physicians from organization b_hosp may be *temporarily* permitted to have an access to a_hosp (for instance they are asked to intervene after some catastrophic event). When the need for interoperability ends, it is necessary to revoke physicians from their role b_physician. This is not convenient and a more dynamic approach is necessary.

Thus, one of the objectives of our O2O approach is to provide a more adequate management of role (and also of activity and view).

## 5   O2O and Virtual Private Organization

In some sense, our O2O model is similar to management of identity provided by federations of identity such as Liberty Alliance. When a given organization A wants to interoperate with another organization B, it has first to create a Virtual Private Organization (VPO) B2A and associate B2A with a security policy to control interoperability from B to A (see figure 1 for an application of the O2O approach with three organizations). Similarly organization B will create another VPO A2B to control interoperability from A to B.

Thus, each VPO is associated with two attributes: o-grantor and o-grantee. The o-grantor attribute represents the organization which has created the VPO in order to grant some accesses to subjects coming from another organization represented by the o-grantee attribute.

As shown in figure 1, a VPO is within the *sphere of authority* [7] of the o-grantor attribute. A sphere of authority defines an oriented relation between organizations whose meaning is the following: An organization A is in the sphere of authority of another organization B if the security policy that applies to A is defined and administrated by B. This administration is done thanks to the AdOrBAC model principles (see [6] for more details).

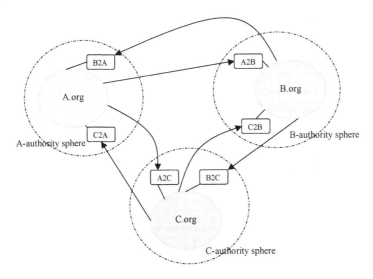

**Fig. 1.** Security policy interoperability between three organizations

Thus, in a VPO, the o-grantor organization can define roles, activities and views and associate these roles, activities and views with contextual security rules as in a classical organization of the OrBAC model. When assigning subjects, actions and objects to the respective roles, activities and views defined in the VPO, the following restrictions apply:

– If a given role is assigned to a given subject in a VPO, then this subject must come from the o-grantee organization of this VPO. This is because a VPO is designed to control how subjects from the o-grantee organization may have an access to the o-grantor organization.

- If a given object is used in a given view in a VPO, then this object must be used in some view in the o-grantor organization. This is because, in a VPO, the o-grantor organization can only grant access to its "own" objects.
- If a given action is considered an implementation of an activity, then this action must be controlled by the o-grantor organization. This will be the case when this action is directly implemented by the o-grantor organization (for instance, a web service provided by the o-grantor). When this action actually comes from the o-grantee organization (for instance a mobile code such as an applet), the situation is more complex. In this case, the o-grantor organization will choose either to (1) not trust this code and to reject it or (2) execute it in a confined space or (3) ask some guarantee to the o-grantee organization. In this latter case, we consider that this must be part of the negotiation protocol.

In the above example, since a_hosp wants to interoperate with b_hosp, a VPO b_hosp2a_hosp is created (bh2ah for short in the following). To grant to physicians from b_hosp the permission to consult medical records in organization a_hosp in the context urgency, we have to add to the VPO bh2ah security policy the following security rule:

- security_rule(permission, bh2ah, physician, consult, medical_record, urgency).

and the following role definition:

- empower(bh2ah, X, physician) :- empower(b_hosp, X, physician).

In particular, notice that physicians from b_hosp will keep their role when accessing to a_hosp (RSSO principle). Notice also that the O2O approach clearly separates the physician's permissions in the VPO bh2ah from their permissions in both a_hosp and b_hosp.

This is a simple example. We can imagine more complex examples. For instance, in September, a bookshop bs may grant special discount on scientific books to students of university u who have a credit card and are more than 18 years old. This is modelled as follows:

- security_rule(permission,    u2bs,    student,    special_discount,    scientific_book, september).
- empower(u2bs, X, student) :-
    empower(u, X, student), age(X,Y), Y >= 18, credit_card_holder(X).

Of course, implementation of the O2O is based on credential exchange. For instance, in the above example, a student will have to exchange her credential to prove she is actually a student from university u, is more than 18 years old and is a credit card holder. However, compared with previous approaches such as [11,21], one advantage of O2O is that it clearly separates the specification of the interoperability security policy from its implementation with credentials.

# 6   Security Policies Compatibility

One of the advantages of the OrBAC model is that the security policy specification of an organization is structured using the concepts of role, activity, view and context. To ease the definition of interoperability security policies, it is possible that some organizations will agree that some correspondances exist between their respective roles, activities, views and contexts.

Let us first present the concept of role compatibility. If a given organization B agrees that a given role role_A of another organization A is compatible with one of its role role_B, then every subject empowered in role role_A in organization A will automatically be granted the privileges of role_B when accessing to organization B.

To model role compatibility, we introduce the following predicate:

– compatible_role(A2B,role_A,role_B): in the virtual organization A2B, organization B agrees with organization A that role_A defined in organization A is compatible with role_B defined in organization B.

Using this predicate, we can automatically derive some part of the interoperability policy by considering the following rule:

R1: security_rule(Type,A2B,Role_A,Activity,View,Context) :-
       o-grantee(A2B,A), o-grantor(A2B,B),
       security_rule(Type,B,Role_B,Activity,View,Context),
       role_compatible(A2B,Role_A,Role_B).

This rule says that if organizations A and B agree that Role_A is compatible with Role_B, then every security rule assigned to Role_B in the organization B are also assigned to Role_A in the VPO A2B.

The approach based on view, activity and context compatibility is different. Thus, let us assume that a given organization B agrees to consider that a given view view_A (resp. activity activity_A) (resp. context context_A) of organization A is compatible with one of its view view_B (resp. activity activity_B) (resp. context context_B). Now, if a given role role_A of organization A is permitted to perform activity_A on view_A in context context_A, then this role role_A will be automatically permitted to perform activity activity_B on view view_B in context context_B in organization B.

This is modelled by using three other predicates compatible_view, compatible_activity, and compatible_context whose meaning is similar to predicate compatible_role. We then consider the following rule which is used to automatically derive some part of the interoperability policy:

R2: security_rule(Type,A2B,Role,Activity_B,View_B,Context_B) :-
       o-grantee(A2B,A), o-grantor(A2B,B),
       security_rule(Type,A,Role,Activity_A,View_A,Context_A),
       activity_compatible(A2B,Activity_A,Activity_B),
       view_compatible(A2B,View_A,View_B),
       context_compatible(A2B,Context_A,Context_B).

This rule says that if organizations A and B agree that Activity_A, View_A and Context_A are respectively compatible with Activity_B, View_B and Context_B, then security rules that apply in the organization A also applies in the VPO A2B after replacing Activity_A in Activity_B, View_A in View_B and Context_A in Context_B.

To illustrate rules R1 and R2, let us consider two organizations french and nato that respectively correspond to French and Nato Defense Organizations. The policy of the nato organization includes the following security rules:

S1: security_rule(permission,nato,nato_confidential,read,nato_confid_doc,need_to_know).
S2: security_rule(permission,nato, nato_secret, read, nato_secret_doc, need_to_know).

Rule S1 says that in organization nato, subjects empowered in role nato_confidential (correspond to subjects cleared at level nato_confidential) are permitted to read documents in view nato_confid_doc (correspond to documents classified at level nato_confidential) in context need_to_know. Rule S2 is similar to rule S1 but applies to subjects cleared at level nato_secret that are permitted to read documents classified at level nato_secret.

Let us now assume that organizations french and nato create two VPOs fr2nato and nato2fr to manage their interoperability and that they agree about the following compatibilities:

F1: role_compatible(fr2nato, confidentiel_defense, nato_confidential).
F2: activity_compatible(nato2fr, read, lire).
F3: view_compatible(nato2fr, nato_confidential_doc, doc_cd).
F4: view_compatible(nato2fr, nato_secret_doc, doc_cd_special_fr).
F5: context_compatible(nato2fr, need_to_know, besoin_de_connaitre).

Then from R1, S1 and F1, we can derive the following security rule:

security_rule(permission,fr2nato,confidentiel_defense,read,nato_confid_doc,need_to_know).

Actually, from F1, we can derive that, when accessing to organization nato, subjects empowered in role confidentiel_defense in organization fr will get the same permissions as subjects empowered in role nato_confidential in organization nato.

From R2, S1, F2, F3 and F5, we can derive:

security_rule(permission,nato2fr, nato_confidential, lire, doc_cd, besoin_de_connaitre).

And from R2, S2, F2, F4 and F5, we can derive:

security_rule(permission,nato2fr,nato_secret,lire, doc_cd_special_fr,besoin_de_connaitre).

# 7 Application to VO Policy Administration

In a Virtual Organization (VO), several organizations share some of their subjects, actions and objects to achieve a common purpose. Usually, an initiator organization, which wants to create a VO, will have to issue a query to other organizations it wants to interoperate with. The VO will be created if all the organizations that receive this query agree to be a member of this VO. Each of these organizations will require that the access to its resources must be compliant with some security policy. We claim that these interoperability security policies defined by the different organizations actually correspond to VPOs.

Thus, in our O2O approach, the security policy of the VO is the union of all these VPOs. The problem is then to define how to manage the security policy of the VO. There are three main approaches:

- Decentralized VPO management: This closely corresponds to the approach sketches in figure 1. After defining its VPOs to control interoperability with other organizations in the VO, each organization will manage these VPOs that are inside its sphere of authority. Thus, when a subject of a given organization A wants to have an access to another organization B, this subject will issue a query. Organization B will apply the VPO A2B to check whether this query is authorized. This will generally require exchanging credentials between A and B for negotiating the access. If this negotiation phase succeeds, then the access will be granted.

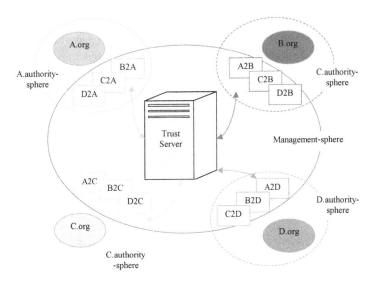

**Fig. 2.** Centralized VPO Management

- Centralized VPO management: In this case, a VPO is both in the authority sphere of a given organization which is in charge of defining its interoperability policies and in the *management sphere* of a server (see figure 2) which is in charge of managing all the interoperability policies of those organizations that trust this server. So, managing the VPOs is delegated to a unique trust server, which may be viewed as an extension of a CAS server (Globus toolkit) [16] or an advanced PEP, say PMP for Policy Management Point. Once a VO is created, each organization involved in this VO will have to send its VPOs to this server. When a subject s_A from a given organization A wants to have an access to another organization B, this subject must send its query to the server. The server will first authenticate this subject to get the proof that this subject is member of one of those organizations involved in the VO. Then the server will apply the VPO A2B and negotiate the access on behalf of organization B. If this negotiation succeeds, the server will sign the query so that the subject can then present this query to organization B for evaluation.

– Hybrid VPO management: The sensitivity of interoperation may vary. In the case of organizations (governmental or military for instance) that deal with high sensitive information, assigning the task of managing the interoperability policies to a server may not meet the high confidentiality requirements of such organizations. When some Virtual Organization is created, these organizations may not entrust the server used in the Centralized VPO Management approach and/or may not accept to send its interoperability policy to this server because this may disclose some sensitive information and/or may not agree to interoperate with some organizations involved in this VO. In both case, Hybrid VPO management may be used (see figure 3). In this figure, three organizations A.org, B.org and C.org agree to interoperate through Centralized VPO management, whereas the fourth organization D.org only accepts to interoperate with organization A.org using Decentralized VPO management.

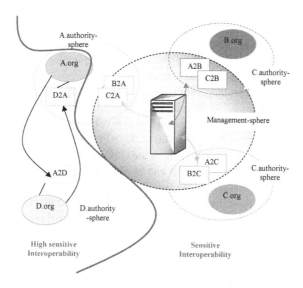

**Fig. 3.** Hybrid VPO Management

In every approach, the interoperability policies are specified using the OrBAC model. The authority or the management sphere checks for each query(s,a,o) if a concrete permission for subject s to do action a on the object o can be derived from the specified VPO policies (see [8] for further details on the concrete permission derivation process).

The main advantage of the centralized management approach over the decentralized one is that, since the trust server has a global view of all the VPOs, it can manage possible conflicts between these VPOs. For instance, let us come back to the example of section 5 and consider that a bookshop a grants a special discount on scientific books to students of university b who have a credit card and are more than 18 years old. If the policy of the university b denies the access to the fact that a student is more than 18 years old, then the negotiation between the bookshop a and the university b will always fail. By analyzing the interoperability policies a2b and b2a, the trust server can detect these conflicts and warn the organizations about the impossibility to interoperate in this case.

# 8    Conclusion

Several works investigate interoperability between entities that have not a priori compatible access control policies. The delicate problem that faces both industrialists and researchers is to identify and enforce minimal requirements so that these interactions continue to be compliant with each security policy of those entities involved in this interoperation. In this paper, we claim that most of these works do not establish a clear separation between (1) the definition of the security policy to be applied in this context of interoperation, (2) how to express it, (3) how to administer it and (4) how to manage it. Our O2O approach gives a response to each of these interrogations. We introduce the concept of VPO to designate the sub-organization in charge of the interoperability access control. This interoperability access control policy is constrained by the access control policy of the parent organization of this VPO but perceptibly differs from it. In the O2O approach, VPO policies are expressed using the OrBAC model. Its built-in confinement principle ensure a secure interoperation and its structure around organizations, roles, activities, views and contexts entities makes it easier to specify dynamic fine grained access control. Moreover, the RSSO principle allows a subject to keep his or her role when accessing to another organization.

In the O2O approach, interoperability policies are always defined and administered by the VPO parent organization. In this way, the VPO controls all the external accesses to the resources of the parent organization that is involved in an interoperation. The VO policy can be actually viewed as the union of the VPO policies.

The management of the VPO policies in the O2O approach can be done by the VPO itself (decentralized management) or it can be delegated to a trust server (centralized management) or a combination of the two (hybrid management). In the case of an interoperation involving more than two organizations, the centralized approach is clearly advised as it is able to efficiently manage conflicts and control negotiations. However, the hybrid approach is sometimes necessary when some organizations do not entrust the server used in the centralized approach.

Due to space limitation, we have not tackle, in this paper, the problem of negotiation and the exchange of credentials. Of course, the negotiation protocols like those used by TrustBuilder or Trust-X have to be adapted to handle OrBAC policy expressions.

The collaboration of several organizations in a VO may lead to creation of new objects. Clearly, these new objects do not belong to any members of the VO. Managing accesses to new resources created in a VO represents further work to be done.

**Acknowledgements.** This work was supported by funding from the French RNRT project Politess and by a grant from the GET (Groupe des Ecoles des Télécommunications).

# References

1. A. Abou El Kalam, R. E. Baida, P. Balbiani, S. Benferhat, F. Cuppens, Y. Deswarte, A. Miège, C. Saurel, and G. Trouessin. Organization Based Access Control. In *Policy'03*, Como, Italie, June 2003.
2. M. A. Al-Kahtani and R. Sandhu. A Model for Attribute-Based User-Role Assignment. In *18th Annual Computer Security Applications Conference (ACSAC '02)*, Las Vegas, Nevada, December 2002.

3. E. Bertino, E. Ferrari, and A. Squicciarini. X-TNL: An XML Based Language for Trust Negotiations. In *4th IEEE International Workshop on Policies for Distributed Systems and Networks*, pages 81–84, 2003.

4. S. Cantor, J. Hodges, J. Kemp, and P. Thompson. *Liberty ID-FF Architecture Overview*. Thomas Wason ed., https://www.projectliberty.org/resources/specifications.php#box1, 2005. Version 1.2.

5. F. Cuppens, N. Cuppens-Boulahia, T. Sans, and A. Miège. A formal approach to specify and deploy a network security policy. In *Second Workshop FAST*, Toulouse, France, 26-27 August, 2004.

6. F. Cuppens and A. Miège. Administration Model for Or-BAC. *Computer Systems Science and Engineering (CSSE'04)*, 19(3), May, 2004.

7. T. Davies. Spheres of Control. *IBM Systems Journal*, 17:179–198, 1978.

8. O. et al. *The OrBAC Model Web Site*. http://www.orbac.org, 2006.

9. I. Foster, C. Kesselman, G. Tsudik, and S. Tuecke. A Security Architecture for Computational Grids. In *5th Conference on Computer and Communications Security*, pages 83–91, San Francisco, CA, 1998.

10. A. Hersberg, Y. Mihaeli, D. Naor, and Y. Ravid. Access Control System Meets Public Infrastructure, Or: Assigning Roles to Strangers. In *IEEE Symposium on Security and Privacy*, Oakland, CA, May 2000.

11. J. Li, N. Li, and W. H. Winsborough. Automated Trust Negotiation Using Cryptographic Credentials. In *12th ACM Conference on Computer and Communications Security (CCS'05)*, November 7-11 2005.

12. M. C. Mont, R. Thyne, K. Chan, and P. Bramhall. Extending HP Identity Management Solutions to Enforce Privacy Policies and Obligations for Regulatory Compliance by Enterprises. In *12th HP OpenView University Association Workshop*, July 10-13 2005.

13. A. Mowshowitz. Virtual organization. *Communications of the ACM*, 40(9):30–37, 1977.

14. R. Oppliger. Microsoft .net passport: A security analysis. *Computer*, 36(7):29–35, 2003.

15. A. Pashalidis and C. J. Mitchell. A Taxonomy of Single Sign-On Systems. In *Lecture Notes in Computer Science*, volume 2727, pages 249 – 264, Junary 2003.

16. L. Pearlman, C. Kesselman, V. Weich, I. Foster, and S. Tuecke. The Community Authorization Service: Status and Future. In *CHEP03*, La Jolia, CA, March 2003.

17. C. Philips, T. C. Ting, and S. Demurjian. Information Sharing and Security in Dynamic Coalitions. In *SACMAT*, Monterey, CA, June 2002.

18. M. Rittenbruch, H. Kahler, and A. Cremers. Supporting Cooperation in a Virtual Organization. In *ICIS*, 1998.

19. R. S. Sandhu, E. J. Coyne, H. L. Feinstein, and C. E. Youman. Role-Based Access Control Models. *Computer*, 29(2):38–47, 1996.

20. J. D. Ullman. *Principles of Database and Knowledge-Base Systems, Volume II*. Computer Science Press, 1989.

21. J. Warner, V. Atluri, and R. Mukkamala. A Credential-Based Approach for Facilitating Automatic Resource Sharing among Ah-Hoc Dynamic Coalitions. In *19th Annual IFIP WG 11.3 Working Conference on Data and Applications Security*, Storrs, CT, August 2005.

22. T. Yu, M. Winslett, and K. Seamons. Supporting Structured Credentials and Sensitive Policies through Interoperable Strategies for Automated Trust Negociations. *ACM Transactions and Information System Security*, 6(1), February 2003.

# Privacy Preserving Web-Based Email

Kevin Butler, William Enck, Jennifer Plasterr,
Patrick Traynor, and Patrick McDaniel

Systems and Internet Infrastructure Security Laboratory
The Pennsylvania State University
University Park, PA 16802 USA
{butler,enck,plasterr,traynor,mcdaniel}@cse.psu.edu

**Abstract.** Recent web-based applications offer users free service in exchange for access to personal communication, such as on-line email services and instant messaging. The inspection and retention of user communication is generally intended to enable targeted marketing. However, unless specifically stated otherwise by the collecting service's privacy policy, such records have an indefinite lifetime and may be later used or sold without restriction. In this paper, we show that it is possible to protect a user's privacy from these risks by exploiting mutually oblivious, competing communication channels. We create virtual channels over online services (e.g., Google's Gmail, Microsoft's Hotmail) through which messages and cryptographic keys are delivered. The message recipient uses a shared secret to identify the shares and ultimately recover the original plaintext. In so doing, we create a wired "spread-spectrum" mechanism for protecting the privacy of web-based communication. We discuss the design and implementation of our open-source Java applet, Aquinas, and consider ways that the myriad of communication channels present on the Internet can be exploited to preserve privacy.

## 1 Introduction

Internet users hemorrhage personal information. Almost every interaction on the web is scanned (directly or indirectly) by some party other than those directly involved in the transaction. Tracking cookies, web bugs, and other tools are used by advertisers to follow users as they move from site to site across the Internet [21]. Less scrupulous groups rely upon spyware to surreptitiously acquire personal information. Such information can be warehoused, collated with other sources, and stored indefinitely.

Recently, however, a more active means of collecting personal information has become common: users expose their personal communications to service providers in exchange for free online applications such as email and instant messaging. As promoted, access to this information allows online providers to personalize the user experience by offering targeted advertisements [16]. The revenue generated by connecting users and vendors has historically fueled much of the growth of the Internet, and is the major source of revenue for many websites. Hence, user profiling is an often positive and possibly necessary element of online life.

A. Bagchi and V. Atluri (Eds.): ICISS 2006, LNCS 4332, pp. 116–131, 2006.
© Springer-Verlag Berlin Heidelberg 2006

However, the communications provided by users of these new services such as free email can be used to develop profiles that extend far beyond simply online habits. By allowing these services to scan the contents of every message that passes through their system, they provide commercial interests with insight into their daily and sometimes highly personal lives. The contents of such communications are further susceptible to interception and examination by repressive regimes [1,19]. Such practices are becoming the norm in web-based applications. Unfortunately, the legal devices for protecting user privacy against abuse or sale of this information are few, and those that do exist are often ineffective [7].

We assert that users need not sacrifice their right to privacy in exchange for any service. Just as customers of the postal service have come to expect that their messages will only be read by the intended recipient, so too should users of web-based services be guaranteed privacy in their communications. We demonstrate that strong confidentiality is attainable for all Internet users, regardless of the privacy policy of these online services.

In this paper, we introduce *Aquinas*, an open source tool designed to provide email privacy while maintaining plausible deniability against the existence of the unobservable (covert) communication. The Aquinas client provides privacy using a hybrid scheme; we employ cryptography to secure communication, steganography to hide the existence and substance of ciphertext, and multipath delivery to ensure compromised accounts or intercepted messages provide little information to an adversary. All email messages are initially encrypted and protected with a *message authentication code* (MAC) to ensure confidentiality and integrity. The key and ciphertext are then carefully divided into *shares*. The shares are embedded in emails using steganographic tools and sent to the recipient via multiple email accounts established at competing services such as Yahoo! Mail, Gmail, and Hotmail. When the recipient receives the ciphertext and key shares, Aquinas reconstructs the key and ciphertext. The ciphertext is decrypted and the contents validated to obtain the plaintext message.

Aquinas is an open-source Java applet. While the mechanisms and distributed nature of content delivery make the current iteration of Aquinas highly robust against multi-party collusion and third-party scanning, it is our intention to allow anyone to contribute additional algorithms and functionality to the codebase. This diversity of operation means that ultimately, the ability of any entity to detect or prevent private communications through web-based email services will be severely curtailed.

Through its use of multiple channels for message delivery, Aquinas's design mimics wireless "spread-spectrum" protocols, which use a pseudo-random pattern of radio channels in order to prevent eavesdropping and jamming. Even with the observation of some subset of channels, an adversary gains no usable information about the true nature of a message's contents. In Aquinas, an adversary needs to intercept email on all used mail accounts to gain *any* information about the user communication. Because no web-service can feasibly intercept all communication, user profiling is not possible.

Aquinas differs significantly from existing email privacy tools such as PGP [28]. Existing tools seek to secure the missives between known users typically using highly secure keys, i.e., public keys. Conversely, Aquinas seeks to enable mobile and lightweight communication; users need not have any physical data beyond a single password in their head. Moreover, Aquinas seeks to secure communication in environments where integration with existing tools is not available, e.g., free email accounts. That is not to say that Aquinas provides a superset of features of these tools. Specifically, Aquinas does not provide all the guarantees that other systems may, e.g., non-repudiation. Moreover, Aquinas is robust to compromise due to the generation of new keys for each message. We believe that this forward-security in combination with portability make this mechanism a highly attractive means of addressing the privacy.

The remainder of this paper is organized as follows: Section 2 gives an overview of our approach to solving these issues; Section 4 discusses additional issues facing the use of privacy preserving software; Section 3 examines the specifics of the our implementation; Section 5 examines the related work in this field; Section 6 offers concluding thoughts and future directions for this work.

## 2   Design

We first define the goals of Aquinas and consider the threats and adversaries we seek to protect against. The latter parts of this section describe the protections in Aquinas and the mechanisms for their implementation.

### 2.1   Goals

The high-level design goals of Aquinas include:

**Confidentiality:** No adversary should be able to obtain information about the existence or content of email communication.

**Integrity:** The integrity of all communication must also be preserved, i.e., any modification of the message should be detectable by the recipient.

**Ease of use:** Aquinas should not require that the user understand or directly use any sophisticated concepts such as cryptography or steganography. Additionally, the tool should provide a user experience consistent with traditional email applications.

The systemic requirements of Aquinas are somewhat more mundane. We do not want to place a requirement on the user for having to install software beyond a simple web browser, or to provide complex data, e.g., maintain keyrings. The implications of this are that all security-relevant data needed to receive email from a single user should be derivable from a password. The second implication is that the tool should be able to execute on arbitrary platforms.

In addition, we want to maximize the flexibility of the services that can be used; to that end, we wish to be able to easily integrate Aquinas with any communication service available on the Internet. Finally, we require the tool to be extensible in order to accommodate future functionality.

## 2.2   Threat Analysis

Users of web-based email services are subject to a variety of threats against their privacy and security. Below, we consider possible adversaries and the motivation and attacks they may employ.

Threats may arise from corporate adversaries. For the application providers that run web-based email services, there is a strong interest in profiling their users for revenue generation. Information about users can be sold to marketing agencies or directly to other companies interested in advertising products to their target demographics. The information gleaned about a user through profiling email can be arbitrarily detailed; through sufficiently optimized data-mining techniques, even users reticent to reveal personal information may unwittingly divulge many more personal details than they realize. If information is sent without any form of obfuscation, it is trivial for the adversary to intercept communications; any party between the user and the application provider will also have unfettered access to this information.

There are environments where protections such as message confidentiality may not be allowed: the email provider may disallow encrypted or unrecognizable content, or the network used for information transmission may have similar restrictions. Even when hidden channels are used, vulnerabilities may still be manifested. As information flows to and from an email account, the account will be subject to *channel decay* over time: an adversary collecting copies of the transferred information will be able to use the amassed data to more easily mount an attack against the channel. In addition, the probability of an adversary learning of a channel's existence will increase with time.

An additional adversary with a similar reward model to the application provider can be the webmail user's ISP. Defending against these attacks presents a tangential set of challenges. We consider adversarial ISPs in greater detail in section 2.5.

While the goals of adversarial companies are largely financially-based, political adversaries may represent a greater threat to some users. Repressive political states have shown little compunction about using Internet activity logs to target and persecute dissidents [1,19]. These adversaries can be significantly more determined to discover information about their target than businesses, and have full access to all records and logs of activity. We can consider the political adversary to have all of the same tools at their disposal as the corporate adversary, plus the ability to compel multiple application providers to turn over all information they possess, or force those companies into collusion. This could create very serious consequences for a dissident attempting to keep their communications hidden from a regime.

## 2.3   Email Protection

Figure 1 provides an overview of how email messages are protected by Aquinas. After a message is composed, the email is encrypted and steganographic techniques are applied to conceal the nature of the information being sent. We use *symmetric cryptography* as the encryption mechanism, in contrast to alternative

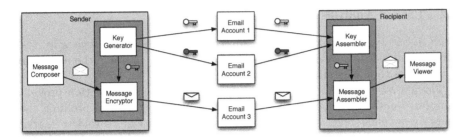

**Fig. 1.** A sample message and key delivery flow. The sender encrypts the plaintext and then embeds it into carefully select covertext using steganography. The message containing the hidden content is then sent as shares to one or more accounts owned by the recipient. Each of the key shares used to create the encryption key are then sent to different destination email accounts. The recipient's client checks all of the accounts, reassembles the key and ciphertext from the shares, and recovers the plaintext. The separate emails from different SMTP servers to prevent reassembly by adversaries.

email schemes, which use public-key cryptography. Because public-key systems require the use of a trusted third party for endorsing user identities, selecting parameters for key encryption, and proving credentials—a non-trivial problem that has not been entirely solved in a satisfactory manner [8]—as well as a full associated infrastructure, we found that this architecture would not fit within the goals of our system. While use of symmetric cryptography necessitates initial establishment of a shared secret (typically in an out-of-band fashion), we felt this was an adequate tradeoff.

Symmetric cryptography requires both the sender and recipient to agree on a key. Obviously, we do not want to send the key in the same email as the ciphertext. A simple solution is to send the key and ciphertext is separate emails, but if both are sent through the same mail service, the adversary still has access to both. The solution is to split both the key and ciphertext into multiple shares and send each part through multiple mail services.

The encryption process is straightforward. The sender begins by creating some number of keys. These keys are combined via XOR (herein noted as $\oplus$) to create the encryption key[1]. Using some symmetric cryptographic algorithm, e.g. AES, the message ciphertext is created. However, encryption alone is not sufficient protection for the email, as a service provider could easily detect that an encrypted message was sent. A sender may wish to plausibly deny that sensitive information has been transmitted, and the presence of ciphertext in a message alludes to the transmission of unknown information. To make the emails appear innocuous, the message and key shares are passed through a steganographic filter (e.g., SNOW [26]), obscuring the email with *covertext* that provides no insight as to the real message contents.

Once the message has been encrypted and protected with a MAC, it is steganographically obscured with covertext. The resulting message is sent in an email to

---

[1] The encryption key cannot be determined unless *all* of the key shares are known.

one of the recipient's accounts. The key shares are also hidden through steganographic techniques, and these messages are sent to different accounts. At this point, the message and key shares are distributed among multiple, independently administered email servers, and the message contents, mass collusion notwithstanding, are secured from unauthorized observers.

The recipient begins the decryption process by downloading both the message and key shares. From the recipient's point of view, the key to decrypt the message is the recipient email accounts. Once downloaded, the recipient applies the steganographic filter to eliminate the covertext and retrieve the ciphertext and key shares. The key shares are combined with $\oplus$ to create the decryption key, and the ciphertext is decrypted.

## 2.4   Design Detail

Our key distribution approach is an example of *multipath delivery*. This method leverages the distributed nature of Internet services to create and multiplex orthogonal channels in the form of multiple email accounts. An analogous means of communications, known as *spread spectrum*, has been used for more than fifty years. Given some range of radio spectrum with $x$ discernible frequencies, messages are transmitted using some pseudorandom sequence of frequencies known only to sender and receiver. An adversary attempting to eavesdrop on communications has a probability $(1/x)^p$ of overhearing the entire message over $p$ time periods. As $x$ and $p$ increase, the ability of an attacker to successfully intercept communications quickly approaches zero. The application of such a technique to the Web makes interception by an adversary an even more daunting task. While the radio spectrum arguably has a limited number of frequencies, the number of channels in which data can be injected into and across the Internet are arguably infinite. We demonstrate the use of Aquinas with key shares carried across multiple email addresses; however, with little additional extension, we can store key shares and messages in web log comments, chat rooms, newsgroups, and a variety of other locations. If we consider each of these particular channels equivalent to a different frequency in the spread-spectrum analogy, then we see the vast number of virtual frequencies afforded to us.

Each of these email accounts used to send the shares should be located at domains operated by different providers. This method of key delivery is robust to collusion for a number of reasons. Competition will deter collusion: any information about a user that a provider is able to garner or derive that is not known to the provider's competitors generates a competitive advantage. Because providers are competing for revenue from advertisers, having unique insights into customer profiles will be rewarded by allowing more targeted marketing to those users, making advertising more lucrative and profitable. Hence, providers desire to keep this information as private as possible, and colluding with other providers would necessitate providing information on the user. This creates a *competitive disincentive* for the provider to engage in collusion. Additionally, even if an adversary is to discover that a message is hidden within an email, they must still recover all $n$ key shares along with the message in order to decrypt it, making this system robust to the compromise of up to $n - 1$ key shares.

The recipient, using the Aquinas client, checks her disparate *message* and *key* email accounts for shares. Aquinas downloads all of the messages and then searches through the headers for a flag identifying the keys for a specific message. Demultiplexing via the $\oplus$ operation is performed on all $n$ key shares, providing the recipient with key $K$. The actual data contained within the email is then uncovered and decrypted using $K$. The real message from the sender is then displayed for the recipient.

The communication process is no more difficult from a user's standpoint than using a traditional mail program. Specifically, a user must enter the multiple outgoing (SMTP) and incoming (POP3) email servers that are to be used to deliver messages. With the *address book* feature in Aquinas, allowing storage of multiple users per email address, this information only needs to be entered once.

## 2.5  Adversarial ISPs

Many users rely on a single service provider to transit their information to the greater Internet. The consequence, however, is that this ISP has access to all of the information sent through its network. By implication, this means that all of the messages sent by the Aquinas user will pass through their home provider who can collect data, even though the destinations of these messages may be disparate email services providers.

Key management does not help in this case because all $n$ channels are implicitly revealed. However, the user has recourse through use of the SSL protocol. SSL provides end-to-end data protection between the user and the email provider, making information unreadable to an ISP attempting to passively eavesdrop on messages. Aquinas supports the use of SSL in order to thwart the ISP threat. With SSL, however, there is some information leakage; the adversary can learn the destination of the packets (but not the destination of the email) by examining the IP header. Thus, while the content of the messages will be unknowable, the fact that information is being transferred to an email provider will be leaked. By observing this information, the ISP could learn all of the providers used and instantiate collusion with them. To hide evidence of the destination, the user could make use of proxies, such as anonymous remailers and other anonymous routing services [27,9]. Additionally, to lower the probability of an adversary detecting the existence of a channel formed by the email account, the user can periodically abandon their accounts and set up new ones for communication.

An alternative solution to the ISP threat exists that does not require the use of SSL between a user and their email provider. Security can be implemented through *chaffing and winnowing* [20] with email accounts. By including email accounts not used during the email communication, the adversarial ISP will have to choose the correct subset of accounts that correspond to a message. A brute-force approach based on combinatorics rapidly becomes infeasible for the adversary. For example, if the user transmits a message with 40 shares, but only

20 of those are used to construct the message, the adversary will be required to search through the $\binom{40}{20}$, or nearly 138 billion, combinations.

## 2.6   Key Negotiation and Management

Bootstrapping communication between users requires a mechanism outside of Aquinas to be used. Out-of-band key communication through methods such as speaking over the phone or meeting in person is possible; alternately, a mechanism such as PGP could be used for the initial setup. While the user would have to be on a trusted machine that has PGP installed to perform this transaction, once the initial key setup was complete, the user can then communicate using any terminal with the recipient.

We propose that a directory of users be stored in a publicly accessible repository. Each set of email addresses associated with a user can be stored within this space. The addresses can be public because it is their particular combination used for an email transmission that is the secret. Part of the initial communication between two users can include transmission of a shared secret between the two parties. This can be very simple, such as the word "dog". A permutation sequence can then be calculated by using this secret as a key. For example, AES-128 has a keyspace of $2^{128}$ entries. Encoding the secret as a value (e.g., converting "dog" in its decimal representation) allows us to use it as a key. If there are 40 email addresses associated with a user, the keyspace can be binned into 40 intervals, and the generated number will fall into one of these bins, generating one of the email addresses that will comprise the key share. The resulting value is then encrypted with the key and another interval is selected based on the new output. This process is repeated until there are 20 unique addresses selected. By negotiating a new secret (for example, through email communication), a new combination of addresses used as key shares can be selected. The following matrix illustrates the series of transformations that generates the values to be binned:

$$\begin{bmatrix} k_0 = h(\text{``}dog\text{''}) \\ k_1 = E(k_0, k_0) \\ k_2 = E(k_1, k_1) \\ \vdots \\ k_{20} = E(k_{19}, k_{18}) \end{bmatrix}$$

Note that email is not the only method by which key and ciphertext can be delivered. The open functionality inherent to the Internet allows any means of sending data to become a covert channel for communication. A combination of keys placed in weblog referrer logs, instant messages, BitTorrent [2] and other P2P file sharing systems, streaming audio and video, newsgroup postings, and any number of disposable or community email accounts can be used to keep the contents of any message secret. This method of key and content distribution creates a wired "spread-spectrum" effect, effectively using servers across the Internet like unique "frequencies". This technique thereby obfuscates the

**Fig. 2.** A screenshot of the content of an email sent from Aquinas to a Gmail account

ability to determine that communication has occurred at all. Because of the sheer vastness of the web, the ability to prohibit privacy on this medium is *virtually impossible.*

## 3   Implementation

Aquinas is principally designed to support a simple and user-friendly interface. In order to retain the convenience of web-based email, Aquinas is required to be accessible via the Internet. Ideally, this portability should be machine independent to allow use by the widest possible community. For these reasons, we developed Aquinas using Java. Our goals, however, were not merely to allow use on their primary home or work machines (although this use is encouraged); rather, we wanted to ensure that users could protect their communications no matter where they were or what machine they were using, such as a terminal at an Internet cafe[2]. Accordingly, we have designed Aquinas to run as an applet. The Aquinas Java applet and source-code are freely available from:

<code>http://siis.cse.psu.edu/aquinas.html</code>

For reasons of space, the complete details of the implementation have been made available in the technical report [3], which is also available at the above address.

Figure 2 shows a screenshot of what the Gmail scanner sees as the content of an email sent using Aquinas. The plaintext of the message, however, is displayed in Figure 3. We performed extensive tests with emails protected by different steganographic covertexts, to determine how they would be handled by Gmail and other providers. While Gmail sometimes showed advertisements pertaining

---

[2] Note that users must still be cognizant of their surroundings and the machines they use if Aquinas is used in an untrusted location such as a remote kiosk. We cannot and do not protect against physical attacks such as keystroke loggers on remote terminals.

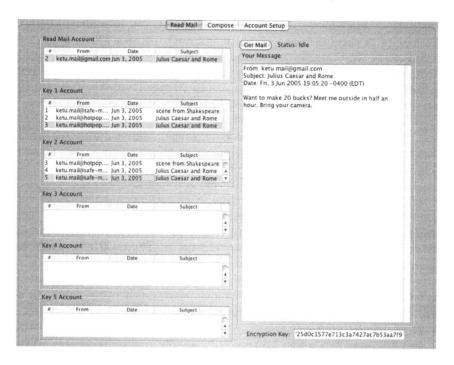

**Fig. 3.** A screenshot of the recovered plaintext of the email displayed in Figure 2

to the content of the covertext, none of these advertisements reflected the keywords or terms found in the plaintext message. This indicates to us that the real message transmitted stayed private and was protected from profiling.

## 4 Discussion

Aquinas extends the confidential nature of email by allowing message contents to remain secret until being read by the intended recipients thereby redefining the endpoint of web-based email as the user. Its portability, imperceptibility and forward-security through unique session keys make the use of Aquinas more attractive than many more traditional schemes. We therefore consider several issues of the secure use and implementation of Aquinas in the following subsections.

### 4.1 Preserving Privacy

Although the mechanisms discussed in this paper can provide security against profile generation and data mining, users of these solutions must still be cognizant of other privacy issues. Specifically, in spite of the use of encryption and steganography, it is still possible for information leakage to occur. The selection of cover text, for example, provides data that can be scanned and associated with a user. If a user were to select text from a website with radical political statements or adult material, that information may still be affiliated with the user in spite of there being no actual relationship between the two parties in the real world. To mitigate this threat, we suggest using neutral text, such as the "Terms of Service" or "Frequently Asked Questions" pages available at the websites hosting the email. By doing this, a user exposes only the fact that they use a service (which is already known to the service provider).

The sender should also be aware of the paths that key shares take. For example, if all data were to cross a particular domain either during the sending or receiving process, all of the data necessary to create the keys for decryption would be readily available. It is therefore critical that users take advantage of as many unique channels as possible to provide maximum security.

Users should take additional precautions when deciding upon names for email accounts. While identically named accounts at a number of major free email providers would be easy for people to remember, they also increase the ease with which collusion between providers can occur. The tradeoff between ease and security must be carefully considered by each user. Much of this tradeoff can be mitigated by using the address book feature provided in Aquinas. As a standard security practice, the use of unique passwords across accounts in also highly recommended. In addition to providing robustness to a single compromise, the use of unique passwords also prevents one service provider from logging in to a user's account at another provider (i.e., unapproved collusion [11]). Simple methods to increase the security of password re-use include browser extensions such as those presented by Ross et al. [22].

The number of accounts used to achieve privacy can be set by the user and should be based upon their perceived threats. For example, someone simply wanting to avoid being profiled by free web-based email providers and advertisers may decide to rely upon two accounts. Because it is extremely unlikely that competing forces including Hotmail and Gmail will willingly share trade secrets (for economic and potentially anti-trust reasons), the effort required to protect the average account using Aquinas is minimal. If the consequence of content compromise is more dangerous, the number of accounts used should be increased. While the Chinese government was able to put pressure on Yahoo! Mail to turn over information on suspected members of the political opposition, the ability of a government to achieve the same if Aquinas is used is minimized. Because it is unlikely that every provider will be compliant with foreign governments, communications can be protected from this sort of interception. One way to realistically implement a significant increase in the number of accounts would be for users to aggregate and share accounts within larger communities. In a design similar to the Crowds [18], users could receive and forward mail on behalf of other users within their community while maintaining plausible deniability of the communication details.

Techniques leveraging the temporal spacing of messages can also help to protect against traffic analysis attacks. As mentioned in Section 2.5, a user can include chaffing and winnowing techniques to increase their security. For example, slowly sending shares over the course of an hour forces an adversary to consider all egress traffic during that period. A small alteration to the current version of Aquinas would allow it to continuously emit low volumes of traffic to randomly chosen websites and accounts. Shares included within this stream would be significantly more difficult to detect.

Due to the nearly infinite number of ways in which data can be injected into the Internet, the probability of an adversary selecting all of the correct repositories is incalculably small. Even in the unlikely event of an adversary having perfect knowledge of the accounts used for communication, a user can still be protected. Assuming that 40 messages are again used, but that the number of keys used is decided out of band (perhaps as part of account selection as in Section 2.6), an adversary is would be required to try up to $2^n - 1$, or nearly 1.1 trillion, combinations of messages. The action of selecting accounts therefore becomes equivalent to encryption by an additional, unrelated key. If the accounts are unknown, the size of this key is arguably infinite. In the worst case, the key size of the secondary in this example is 40-bits. Users uncomfortable with such a key length can increase robustness by changing the algorithm used to generate the encryption key from the key shares. If the $\bigoplus$ operation is replaced by an order-dependent technique (such as alternating multiplication and division of key shares according to the account selection scheme in Section 2.6), the adversary will instead have to try $\sum_{k=1}^{n} {}_nP_k$ permutations, as between 1 and $n$ shares in the correct order could be required to reassemble the key. This operation has time complexity $O(n!)$. With 40 messages, more than $1.6 * 10^{48}$ permutations would be required to uncover the key. As this is much larger than the number of brute-force attempts to recover a 128-bit key, a user is sufficiently protected against even the strongest adversaries.

## 4.2   Resiliency

While offering robustness to the collusion of multiple service providers, the multi-path key and message delivery mechanism described in this paper is not without its own limitations. For example, if an email service provider were to determine that a message contained a key, simply deleting the message would prevent the intended recipient from decrypting and reading their mail. A message mistakenly classified as spam would have similarly deleterious effects, as the user would have difficulty differentiating real messages amongst the torrent of spam messages most email users receive.

Shamir's *threshold secret sharing* [25] could be used to make Aquinas robust against share-loss. This technique works by creating the key $K$ from the combination of $n$ key shares. $K$ can be reconstructed as long as $k$ key shares (where $n = 2k - 1$) are in the possession of the recipient. The advantage to this scheme is that it allows for $k-1$ key shares to be lost (or delivered late) without affecting the ability of the recipient to decrypt and read their email. If spam filtering were to become an issue, this scheme would be more robust, as it would allow the intended recipient to still read their encrypted messages without all $n$ keys. While this approach is secure to the compromise of up to $k - 1$ key shares, if $k < n$, messages can be decrypted with fewer keys than in the currently implemented scheme.

Robustness based upon the perceived threat of an adversary could also be incorporated as a keying mechanism. For example, a user may decide that the overhead of increasing the number of email accounts is greater than the protection offered from a keying scheme based on threshold secret sharing. One simple extension to the multipath mechanism is to increase the number of accounts to which copies of key shares are sent. A user could opt to send the same key share to multiple accounts. In so doing, fewer cooperating adversaries would be necessary to reconstruct keys. A more elegant solution would be to use a mechanism based on *error correcting codes* (ECC). By attaching tags containing a few extra bytes to the end of each key, it becomes possible to reconstruct $K$ with only a subset of all $n$ key shares. The size of this subset (and the attached ECC) needed to recreate $K$ can be adjusted to suit the specific expected adversary. The threshold secret sharing, multi-share delivery and error correcting code alternatives are all under consideration for future versions of this software.

## 5   Related Work

Privacy on the Internet is not guaranteed for users in general, and can be ambiguously defined even where it exists [15]. Often, users believe that they have online privacy but really have no guarantees to that effect [14]. To mitigate these shortcomings, many privacy-preserving tools have been created and deployed, protecting numerous aspects of a user's online activities.

Methods of securing non-web-based email have been extensively studied. Solutions such as Privacy Enhanced Mail (PEM) [12] and its successor, Secure MIME (S/MIME) [17], provide confidentiality, integrity, and non-repudiation for email messages. With PEM, this is accomplished through the construction of a full certificate hierarchy within a public key infrastructure (PKI); this has proven to be unwieldy in practice. For S/MIME, cryptographically transformed messages are sent as attachments within email, with key validation performed through a PKI. Pretty Good Privacy (PGP) [28] is another system for providing confidentiality and integrity of email that does not rely on the use of a PKI. A user forms a *web of trust* by trusting certain entities she communicates with, which in turn has other trusted relationships. The transitive certification paths of trust among these relationships are used to authenticate the source of email. Confidentiality can be provided by the mailer itself, with tools such as *ssmail*, a patch for the *sendmail* [5] mail transfer agent.

The *Off-the-record Email* (OTR) system [10] works at the user level, with dynamic key management performed between the two parties using it. Additionally, OTR provides non-recoverability of email messages once they have been deleted, even if the private keys used to generate the cryptographic operations have been revealed. However, while forward secrecy is assured, plausible deniability is not: an agent monitoring traffic will observe that encrypted information is being transmitted to the recipient.

While privacy within web-based email services has been largely absent, one solution is offered by SAFe-mail.net [23]. This system supplies confidentiality and integrity through the use of a PKI that is run by SAFe-mail themselves. Because the service handles both certificates and user email, however, it has access to all of a user's information, allowing them to arbitrarily link and use this data.

Secure publication of data is another area where privacy can be crucial, in order to protect the authors of controversial documents from reprisal. The ability to publish without the fear of retribution has been tremendously important to citizens throughout history. The Federalist papers in the United States brought forth the ideals that ultimately became enshrined in the Constitution, but many of the authors published anonymously to avoid reprisal. More recently, the former Soviet-bloc countries witnessed the rise of *samizdat*, the process of anonymously publishing and distributing information banned by the government [24]. Publius [13] is a tool that facilitates secure publishing on the Internet, using threshold keying (discussed further in Section 4) to preserve anonymity. Other systems, including Free Haven [6], provide anonymous storage and retrieval. Similarly, Freenet [4], a distributed system for storage, provides anonymous content storage and dynamic growth of the network through the addition of new nodes.

Many of these tools have been useful in keeping communications private and secure; in particular, PGP has been extensively used by human rights organizations around the world. However, in virtually all cases, the fact that communication has taken place can be divined through the presence of encrypted data, or information has been transferred through private services. To this point, there have not been any solutions that allow for encrypted and steganographically concealed communications that transmit information solely through public channels and publicly available services.

## 6   Conclusion

This work has introduced Aquinas, an open source tool for preserving the privacy of user communication carried by web-email services. Each message is initially encrypted with a random symmetric key. The resulting ciphertext and key are both divided into shares. Each share is hidden in randomly chosen cover-text using steganography and sent through an independent web email account. Clients reconstitute the ciphertext and keys from shares received via the appropriate accounts. The result is decrypted to obtain the original message. We use email accounts in an analogous manner to the multiple channels employed in spread-spectrum communications. More generally, we show that the retention of one's privacy is possible regardless of the policies imposed by the providers of these web-based services.

Future extensions to this work will incorporate a variety of new image and linguistic steganography techniques, allowing users to more fully obfuscate their communications. Additionally, we will implement features that support the distribution of ciphertext shares across multiple accounts, and will continue to improve the usability of our interface as directed by user input. Such an approach also begs extension to the panoply of channels available throughout the Internet.

Our future work will not only explore these diverse channels, but also develop a formal framework for reasoning about the security provided by them.

# References

1. BBC News. Chinese man 'jailed due to Yahoo'. http://news.bbc.co.uk/2/hi/asia-pacific/4695718.stm, February 2006.
2. BitTorrent. http://www.bittorrent.com.
3. K. Butler, W. Enck, J. Plasterr, P. Traynor, and P. McDaniel. Privacy Preserving Web-based Email. Technical report, Technical Report NAS-TR-0009-2005, Network and Security Research Center, Department of Computer Science and Engineering, Pennsylvania State University, University Park, PA, June 2005.
4. I. Clarke, O. Sandberg, B. Wiley, and T. W. Hong. Freenet: a distributed anonymous information storage and retrieval system. In *International workshop on Designing privacy enhancing technologies*, pages 46–66, New York, NY, USA, 2001. Springer-Verlag New York, Inc.
5. B. Costales and E. Allman. *Sendmail(2nd ed.)*. O'Reilly & Associates, Inc., Sebastopol, CA, USA, 1997.
6. R. Dingledine, M. J. Freedman, and D. Molnar. The Free Haven Project: Distributed Anonymous Storage Service. In *International workshop on Designing privacy enhancing technologies*, pages 67–95, New York, NY, USA, 2001. Springer-Verlag New York, Inc.
7. Electronic Frontier Foundation. http://www.eff.org.
8. C. M. Ellison and B. Schneier. Ten Risks of PKI: What You're Not Being Told About Public-Key Infrastructure. *Computer Security Journal*, 16(1):1–7, 1999.
9. D. Goldschlag, M. Reed, and P. Syverson. Onion routing for anonymous and private Internet connections. *Commun. ACM*, 42(2):39–41, 1999.
10. P. Henry and H. Luo. Off-the-record email system. In *Proceedings of IEEE INFO-COM 2001*, pages 869–877, Anchorage, AK, USA, Apr. 2001.
11. E. Jordan and A. Becker. Princeton officials broke into Yale online admissions decisions. http://www.yaledailynews.com/article.asp?AID=19454, July 25, 2002.
12. S. T. Kent. Internet privacy enhanced mail. *Commun. ACM*, 36(8):48–60, 1993.
13. A. D. R. Marc Waldman and L. F. Cranor. Publius: A robust, tamper-evident, censorship-resistant, web publishing system. *Proc. 9th USENIX Security Symposium*, pages 59–72, August 2000.
14. R. L. Mcarthur. Reasonable expectations of privacy. *Ethics and Inf. Tech.*, 3(2):123–128, 2001.
15. L. Palen and P. Dourish. Unpacking "privacy" for a networked world. In *CHI '03: Proceedings of the SIGCHI conference on Human factors in computing systems*, pages 129–136, New York, NY, USA, 2003. ACM Press.
16. D. Peppers and M. Rogers. *The One to One Future: Building Relationships One Customer at a Time*. Doubleday, 1993.
17. B. Ramsdell. S/MIME version 3 message specification. RFC 2633, IETF, June 1999.
18. M. K. Reiter and A. D. Rubin. Crowds: anonymity for Web transactions. *ACM Transactions on Information and System Security*, 1(1):66–92, 1998.
19. Reporters Without Borders. Information supplied by Yahoo! helped journalist Shi Tao get 10 years in prison. http://www.rsf.org/article.php3?id_article=14884, September 2005.

20. R. L. Rivest. Chaffing and Winnowing: Confidentiality without Encryption. *RSA CryptoBytes*, 4(1), Summer 1998.
21. W. Roger. Surfer beware: Advertiser's on your trail, DoubleClick tracks online movements. *USA Today*, page 01.B, 26 Jan. 2000.
22. B. Ross, C. Jackson, N. Miyake, D. Boneh, and J. Mitchell. Stronger Password Authentication Using Browser Extensions. In *Proceedings of the 14th USENIX Security Symposium*, 2005.
23. SAFe-mail.net. SAFe-Mail features. http://www.safe-mail.net/help/SAFeMail-http://www.safe-mail.net/help/SAFeMailFeatures.html Features.html, May 2005.
24. G. Saunders. *Samizdat: Voices of the Soviet Opposition*. Pathfinder Press, Atlanta, GA, USA, 1974.
25. A. Shamir. How to share a secret. *Commun. ACM*, Vol 22:612–613, 1979.
26. SNOW. The SNOW Home Page. http://www.darkside.com.au/snow/.
27. The Anonymizer. http://www.anonymizer.com.
28. P. R. Zimmermann. *The official PGP user's guide*. MIT Press, Cambridge, MA, USA, 1995.

# Context-Aware Provisional Access Control

Amir Reza Masoumzadeh, Morteza Amini, and Rasool Jalili

Computer Engineering Department
Sharif University of Technology
Tehran, Iran
{masoumzadeh@ce.,m_amini@ce.,jalili@}sharif.edu

**Abstract.** High heterogeneity and dynamicity of pervasive computing environments introduces requirement of more flexible and functional access control policies. The notion of provisional actions has been defined previously to overcome the insufficient grant/denial response to an access request and has been incorporated in the provision-based access control model (PBAC). Based on PBAC, we propose a context-aware provision-based access control model, capable of dynamic adaptation of access control policy according to the changing context. In particular, the model facilitates the definition of context-aware policies and enriches the access control by enforcing provisional actions in addition to common permissions.

## 1 Introduction

Pervasive computing sketches a pleasant vision for the future computing environments, as the computing power is provided anywhere, anytime, and using any device. Mobile and stationary devices spread in the environment trying to assist humans in their tasks unnoticeably. The main enabling technology of this vision is context-awareness, i.e. extract, interpret, and use context information and adapt functionality of the system to the current context of use [1]. Due to high heterogeneity and dynamicity in such environments, some requirements are introduced in expressiveness and flexibility of security policies. Therefore, a new trend of research in computer security formed towards designing context-aware security infrastructures and access control models.

It is necessary to define what can be considered as context accurately. Context as defined expressively by Dey [2] is: *"any information that can be used to characterize the situation of an entity."* An entity is a person, place, or object that is considered relevant to the interaction between a user and an application, including the user and applications themselves. There are many ways to leverage contextual information in an access control system [3]; two of which are of our interest in this paper. Contextual information can be used by an access control policy to utilize environmental factors specifying how and when the policy is enforced [4]. In addition, the system can express its policy flexibly based on the context of subjects and objects, moving from identity-based towards attribute-based and context-based authorization. Existence of various entities and high dynamicity of future environments urges such flexibility.

A. Bagchi and V. Atluri (Eds.): ICISS 2006, LNCS 4332, pp. 132–146, 2006.
© Springer-Verlag Berlin Heidelberg 2006

On the other hand, ordinary access control models assume a binary decision upon an access request, either grant or deny, which seems to be non-satisfactory in new environments. The idea of provisional authorization states that the user requests will be authorized provided he (and/or the system) takes certain actions prior to authorization of his request [5]. In this manner, a decision upon an access request consists of two components; a permission denoting grant or denial, and a set of provisional actions to be performed before the access decision. Provisional actions, also called provisions, empower policy rules to enforce required actions such as logging and encryption prior to access.

We argue that incorporating the above concepts, namely provisional actions and context-awareness, into a well-structured access control model would be a good candidate to control access in new distributed environments. In this paper, we propose the CA-PBAC as a context-aware provision-based access control model. Access decision in this model is aware of the context, and provisions enable enforcing more powerful and efficient security policies.

The rest of this paper is organized as follows. In section 2, some access control models are surveyed which consider either provisions or context-awareness. Section 3 gives an informal description of CA-PBAC. An access control framework is extended in section 4 to meet our model requirements. In section 5, we present a formal definition of the CA-PBAC model. The formal description prevents any ambiguity in the model and makes implementation and application of the model straightforward. Finally, Section 6 provides a simple system based on CA-PBAC model and explain its function in an access scenario, followed by our conclusion and future works.

## 2   Related Work

Kudo proposed provision-based access control model (PBAC) to include provisional actions in addition to the common grant or denial decision [6]. He provided a foundation model that addresses fundamental principles of access control, e.g. multiple hierarchies and typical policies for property propagation through hierarchies. The model contains a foundation data set including multiple hierarchical and non-hierarchical sets, and also a relation among these sets that corresponds to access control policy rules. The foundation model decides some properties in response to a property query based on its data set. On the basis of the foundation model, a conventional authorization model and a provisional authorization model were presented to determine binary authorization decision and a set of provisional actions, respectively. PBAC uses a combination of these two authorization models to determine the access decision containing a permission and some provisional actions. Bettini et al. introduced the notion of obligation in addition to provisions [7]. Obligations are those conditions or actions that must be fulfilled by either the users or the system after the access decision is rendered. They proposed a rule-based framework to select the appropriate set of provisions and obligations based on numerical weights assigned to provisions and obligations as well as on semantic relationships among them. Park et al. introduced a family of $UCON_{ABC}$ models for usage control which integrate authorizations, obligations, and conditions [8]. Usage control covers continuity of access control. Similar to provisions, obligations are functional predicates that verify mandatory requirements a subject has to perform before or during a usage exercise. The model is abstract in that expresses only its semantics and does not define the authorization procedure.

Han et al. proposed a basic definition of context-sensitive access control [9], which consists of extendible context model, authorization policy model, request model, and the relevant algorithms. Some ordinary contexts like time and location were formally defined. The model is very basic and lacks fundamental features of an access control model such as groups, hierarchies, and conflict resolution. Kouadri et al. introduced contextual graphs as a new modeling approach for specifying context-based policies [10]. It is a variation of decision tree that allows branching based on contextual information, instead of making a decision. The branched paths are recombined after specifying some security actions or more branching. Although it is an expressive way to define context-based policies, management of such policies seems to be complicated.

Many researches are targeted to applying context-awareness to the RBAC model. Al-Kahtani et al. proposed the RB-RBAC model, performing role assignment dynamically based on users' attributes or other constraints on roles [11]. GRBAC [12] incorporates three type of roles; subject roles corresponds to traditional RBAC roles, object roles which are used to categorize objects, and environment roles to capture environmental or contextual information. Zhang et al. proposed DRBAC, a dynamic context-aware access control for pervasive applications [13]. In DRBAC, there is a role state machine for each user and a permission state machine for each role. Changes in context trigger transitions in the state machines. Therefore, user's role and role's permissions are determined according to the context.

# 3 Narrative Description of CA-PBAC

In order to provide context-awareness, we incorporated a formal specification of contextual information into CA-PBAC. It follows the general form of (<entity>, <context type>, <relator>, <value>) as context predicates. A context predicate describes a *context type* about an *entity* by associating a *value* through a *relator*. For example, (John, location, entering, ConferenceRoom) states that John is entering the conference room, or (Bob, position, is, secretary) expresses Bob's position. The basic idea of such context predicates has been adopted from Gaia project which provides the infrastructure for constructing smart spaces [14]. Therefore, contextual information are expressed by a set of context predicates in the model. The special characteristic of this specification is decomposability, i.e. a predicate can be decomposed into an entity and its context (including a context type, a relator, and a value). Inversely, an entity and a context can be composed to make a contextual information entry.

Hierarchies have been widely employed in access control models. They simplify authorization management by organizing entities and propagating properties through the links among them. The ability to define different propagation strategies [6] or derivations [15] makes hierarchies more efficient. Although CA-PBAC does not provide the generality of the foundation model in [6], it is capable of defining multiple subject group hierarchies and object group hierarchies. There exists a context-assignment function for each hierarchy which assigns a contextual condition including some contexts to each group. A subject requesting an access on an object is mapped to some subject groups according to its context. It is mapped to a subject group, if it's context matches all the contexts in the group contextual condition. Similar context-aware mapping is done for the object.

In practice, it is more likely to construct each hierarchy based on a particular set of context types. The semantics on which hierarchies are defined may vary. This leads to the requirement of different propagation strategies. Selection of an appropriate propagation strategy for each hierarchy, avoids any concern in the model about what actually the mentioned semantics are. In addition to propagation strategies defined in [6], i.e. *"most specific"* and *"path traversing"*, we also consider the *"most general"* strategy. The "most specific" strategy is appropriate to specify exceptions against more general policies. The "path traversing" strategy states that the policies of each ancestor is applicable. We argue that there are some cases in which the "most specific" strategy is not desirable [16], neither is the "path traversing". Actually, the "most general" strategy is useful when there is a need to override more specific policies. As an example, consider specifying a temporary policy to grant authorization to every user in a general group, overriding previously specified denials for more specific groups.

In addition to propagation, hierarchies simplifies conflict resolution based on contextual information. Consider an authorization decision about an access requested by a secretary. Let the first rule state that access is denied if he or she is an employee and the second one state that access is granted if he or she is is a secretary. Clearly, the two rules are in conflict, i.e. a secretary is also an employee. It is common to resolve such conflict by selecting the alternative that states more specific condition, i.e. the second rule. Association of the first rule and the second rule conditions to a parent and a child node in a hierarchy respectively, defining the rules on corresponding nodes, and using "most specific" as propagation strategy avoids such conflicts.

The CA-PBAC model is rule-based. So, the access control policy consists of multiple access control policy rules. Each rule is composed of a group in each subject/object group hierarchy, the requested action on the object, a contextual constraint to limit the context in which the rule is applicable, the permission specified for such action, and the provisions to be executed. Specifying the permission as *"NIL"* enables the rule to apply some provisions to an access request without defining a permission for such access. That is appropriate to execute common provisions such as logging for accesses regardless of permission result.

Receiving a request from a subject to access an object, a decision including a permission and some provisions is made. Firstly, the subject and the object are mapped to corresponding groups according to their context. Then, according to the policy rules and propagation policies on each hierarchy applicable rules are selected and their permissions are retrieved. The final permission is determined by resolving possible conflict among the retrieved permissions.

In order to determine provisions, a similar procedure is used. However, we consider a difference between propagation of permissions and provisions. Since provisions are obligatory actions, it seems that propagation strategies such as "most specific" are not suitable. For example, "most specific" strategy prevents enforcement of provisions in more general rules even they have no conflicts with the provisions in a selected rule. Actually, we consider full propagation for provisions but restricted to those specified in rules whose permission have no conflict with the decided permission. However, there may be some conflicts among provisions retrieved which are resolved by a domain specific conflict resolution function.

## 4    Context-Aware Provision-Based Access Control Framework

Illustrated in Figure 1, we suggest a framework to address both data elements and sequences of operations required to provide context-aware provision-based access control. It is based on the PBAC architecture, which itself is a modified version of "Access Control Framework", an international standard [17]. We attempted to use the standard notations according to [17] but adapt their interpretations to meet our model requirements. Extending the standard framework, we introduce two new components. The Contextual Information (CI), which represents all contextual information available to the system. It is assumed that a context infrastructure or simply a context engine provides such information. It includes information that have been stored, sensed from environment, or interpreted from other information. The Access Control Meta Policies (ACMP), which are high-level policies that often used to mediate other policies and are changed less frequently than conventional policies. Conflict resolution and default policies are examples of ACMP.

In this framework, the basic entities and functions involved in an access control scenario are the initiator, the Access Control Enforcement function (AEF), the Access Control Decision Function (ADF), and the target. Initiator, also referred to as *subject* in the access control literature, submits an access request to the system. An access request specifies an operation to be performed on a target, which is referred to as *object* in the access control literature. AEF submits the access request to ADF. ADF decides about the access request using Access Control Decision Information (ADI), Access Control Policy Rules (ACPR), Contextual Information (CI), and Access Control Meta Policies (ACMP). ADI consists of information which is local to access control system, such as group hierarchies. ACPR consists of rules specifying the system current policy. CI is used to interpret both ADI and ACPR. ACMP is used to mediate ACPR and resolve conflicts, in case there is. Based on such inputs, ADF makes the decision

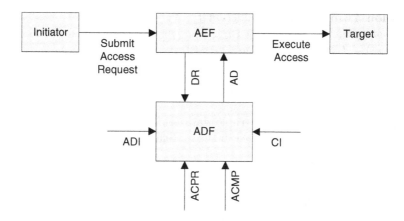

**Fig. 1.** Context-Aware Provision-Based Access Control Framework

consisting of a usual binary decision as well as a set of provisions. Finally AEF enforces the access decision on the target.

# 5   Context-Aware Provision-Based Access Control (CA-PBAC) Model

In order to have a formal definition of CA-PBAC, we define some basic concepts and then the CA-PBAC data set and access decision function are formally defined. Considering these definitions and also the context-aware provision-based access control framework, a formal definition of our model is presented.

## 5.1   Basic Definitions

**Definition 1 (hierarchy).** *Let $H$ be a set forming a partial order, i.e. $\langle H, \leq \rangle$. Formally, $H$ is a hierarchy if and only if $\forall a \in H[\forall x \in H, x \leq a, \forall y \in H, y \leq a[x \leq y \vee y \leq x]]$. Hierarchy $H$ is denoted by $\langle H, \leq^{Tr} \rangle$.*

**Definition 2 (Maximal function).** *Let $H$ be a hierarchy, i.e. $\langle H, \leq^{Tr} \rangle$ and $A$ be a set such that $A \subseteq H$. The function $Maximal(H, A)$ returns the maximal elements of the hierarchy $H$ restricted to the elements in the set $A$. Formally, $Maximal(H, A) = \{x \mid x \in A \wedge (\nexists y \in A[y \neq x \wedge x \leq^{Tr} y])\}$.*

**Definition 3 (Minimal function).** *Let $H$ be a hierarchy, i.e. $\langle H, \leq^{Tr} \rangle$ and $A$ be a set such that $A \subseteq H$. The function $Minimal(H, A)$ returns the minimal elements of the hierarchy $H$ restricted to the elements in the set $A$. Formally, $Minimal(H, A) = \{x \mid x \in A \wedge (\nexists y \in A[y \neq x \wedge y \leq^{Tr} x])\}$.*

**Notation 1 (tuple element).** *Let $T$ be a tuple $(t_1, t_2, \ldots, t_k)$. The notation $T.t_i, 1 \leq i \leq k$ corresponds to the element $t_i$ of $T$.*

**Definition 4 (mapping).** *A function* $f : X_1 \times \ldots \times X_m \to Y_1 \times \ldots \times Y_n$ *is called a mapping if it satisfies:* $\forall (x_1, \ldots, x_m) \in X_1 \times \ldots \times X_m [\exists (y_1, \ldots, y_n) \in Y_1 \times \ldots \times Y_m, f(x_1, \ldots, x_m) = (y_1, \ldots, y_n)]$.

## 5.2   CA-PBAC Data Set: CAPDS

The CA-PBAC model uses a 4-tuple data set $(DS, CI, ACMP, ACPR)$ that formalizes any data structure used in the system.

1. $DS = BDS \cup CDS \cup HDS$; defines required data sets including basic access control data sets, context-related data sets, and hierarchy-related data sets. We introduce each group sets in the following paragraphs.
   - $BDS$ (Basic Data Sets) corresponds to the sets that define the basic components of a provision-based access control model and propagation strategies. It includes
     - $ActSet$ is a set of available actions that can be performed on objects in $ObjSet$.
     - $PvnSet$ is a set of provisions defined according to the application domain.
     - $PrmSet = \{+, -, NIL\}$; is the set of permission results. They correspond to grant, denial, and unspecified permissions, respectively.
     - $PrpStgSet = \{most\_specific, most\_general, path\_traversing\}$; is the set of alternative authorization propagation strategies on a hierarchy. According to a given member $h$ of a hierarchy, "$most\_specific$" means only authorization specified for the most specific member is applicable, "$most\_general$" means only authorization specified for the most general member is applicable, and "$path\_traversing$" means that every authorization specified for members from the root "$any$" to $h$ are applicable.
   - $CDS$ (Context-related Data Sets) formalize the contextual information used in the system. It includes
     - $EntSet$ is a set of entities that information about their situation can be considered as context in the system. According to Dey's definition of context [2], subjects and objects of the access control system are also considerable as entities that have context. Therefore, $SbjSet$ is a subset of entities ($SbjSet \subseteq EntSet$) that can act actively in the system. Similarly, $ObjSet$ is a subset of entities ($ObjSet \subseteq EntSet$) that can act passively in the system.
     - $CtxTypeSet$ is a set of possible context types, e.g. location, time.
     - $CtxValueSet$ is a set of possible values, e.g. room1, 8pm.
     - $CtxRelatorSet$ is a set of possible relators which relate context types to values, e.g. entering, $\geq$.
     - $CtxSet = CtxTypeSet \times CtxRelatorSet \times CtxValueSet$; forms all possible contexts without binding to a specific entity, e.g. (location, entering, room1).

- $EntCtxSet=EntSet \times CtxTypeSet \times CtxRelatorSet \times CtxValueSet$; forms all possible contextual information about entities in the system, e.g. (Bob, location, entering, room1) considering Bob in $EntSet$.

 - $HDS = \{SH_1, \ldots, SH_n, OH_1, \ldots, OH_m, SC_1, \ldots, SC_n, OC_1, \ldots, OC_m\}$; (Hierarchy-related Data Sets) composed of subject and object group hierarchies and their corresponding context-assignments.

   - $\forall i, 1 \leq i \leq n, SH_i$ is a set of subject groups forming a hierarchy, i.e. $\langle SH_i, \leq^{Tr} \rangle$. There is a special subject group "$any$" $\in SH_i$ which is the root of the hierarchy.
   - $\forall j, 1 \leq j \leq m, OH_j$ is a set of object groups forming a hierarchy, i.e. $\langle OH_j, \leq^{Tr} \rangle$. There is a special object group "$any$" $\in OH_j$ which is the root of the hierarchy.
   - $\forall i, 1 \leq i \leq n, SC_i : SH_i \rightarrow \mathcal{P}(CtxSet)$; is a mapping which assigns some contexts to each subject group. Note that $SC_i(any)$ is fixed and equals to $\emptyset$. The function result is used to map subjects in $SbjSet$ to subject groups in $SH_i$.
   - $\forall j, 1 \leq j \leq m, OC_j : OH_j \rightarrow \mathcal{P}(CtxSet)$; is a mapping which assigns some contexts to each object group. Note that $OC_j(any)$ is fixed and equals to $\emptyset$. The function result is used to map objects in $ObjSet$ to object groups in $OH_j$.

2. $CI \in \mathcal{P}(EntCtxSet)$; corresponds to the set of all contextual information in the current state of the system.

3. $ACMP = (P_{SH_1}, \ldots, P_{SH_n}, P_{OH_1}, \ldots, P_{OH_m}, HsPr, PrmConfRes, DefPrm, PvnConfRes)$; is a tuple corresponding to access control meta-policy. Its elements are defined as:

   - $\forall i, 1 \leq i \leq n, P_{SH_i} \in PrpStgSet$; specifies authorization propagation strategy for the $i$th subject hierarchy.
   - $\forall j, 1 \leq j \leq m, P_{OH_j} \in PrpStgSet$; specifies authorization propagation strategy for the $j$th object hierarchy.
   - $HsPr : \{1, \ldots, n+m\} \rightarrow \{SH_1, \ldots, SH_n, OH_1, \ldots, OH_m\}$; is a bijective (one-to-one and onto) function that associates a distinguished subject or object hierarchy to an input rank, establishing a total order among hierarchies. This order affects the selection of applicable policy rules due to different propagation strategies on hierarchies.
   - $PrmConfRes \in \{denials\_take\_precednece, grants\_take\_precedence\}$; specifies which permission overrides when a conflict occurs. "$denials\_take\_precednece$" means that "$-$" permission takes precedence over "$+$" permission, and "$grants\_take\_precedence$" means that "$+$" permission takes precedence over "$-$" permission.
   - $DefPrm \in PrmSet - \{NIL\}$; specifies default permission for an access when no authorization is specified. "$+$" indicates an open system and "$-$" corresponds to a close one.
   - $PvnConfRes : \mathcal{P}(PvnSet) \rightarrow \mathcal{P}(PvnSet)$; is a domain specific conflict resolution function for provisions.

4. $ACPR \in \mathcal{P}(SH_1 \times \ldots \times SH_n \times OH_1 \times \ldots \times OH_m \times ActSet \times \mathcal{P}(EntCtxSet) \times PrmSet \times \mathcal{P}(PvnSet))$; corresponds to the set of access control policy rules.

Each policy rule $r \in ACPR$, structured as $(g_{SH_1}, \ldots, g_{SH_n}, g_{OH_1}, \ldots, g_{OH_m},$ $act, c, prm, pvns)$, is composed of a member of each subject and object hierarchy, an action, a constraint defined by some contextual information entries, a permission specified for such request, and some provisions.

Note that when "$NIL$" used as the permission in a rule it indicates that no permission is specified by the rule and only provisions are considered.

### 5.3 Access Control Framework Components

Components of the access control framework defined in section 4 are formally defined by the set $\{DR, AD, ADI, CI, ACPR, ACMP\}$ as follows.

- $DR = (sbj, obj, act) \in SbjSet \times ObjSet \times ActSet$; Decision request consists of a subject $sbj$, an object $obj$, and an action $act$ requested by the subject to be performed on the object.
- $AD = (prm, pvns) \in (PrmSet - \{NIL\}) \times \mathcal{P}(PvnSet)$; Access decision consists of a permission $prm$ and a set of provisions $pvns$ to be enforced.
- $ADI = (SC_1, \ldots, SC_n, OC_1, \ldots, OC_m)$; Access decision information consists of subject and object context-assignments.
- $CI$, $ACPR$, and $ACMP$ are exactly as defined in $CAPDS$.

### 5.4 Access Decision Function

The access decision function is the mapping $ADF : CAPDS \times DR \to PrmSet \times \mathcal{P}(PvnSet)$. It consists of the following steps:

1. *Context-Aware Mapping Step:*
   In this step, groups of subjects and objects to which $DR.sbj$ and $DR.obj$ can be mapped respectively are selected. To achieve this, each subject group $g$ in the hierarchy $SH_i$ is considered. The subject $DR.sbj$ is mapped to $g$ if it satisfies the contexts defined by the hierarchy context-assignment function $SC_i$, i.e. $\{(DR.sbj, t, r, v) | (t, r, v) \in SC_i(g)\} \subseteq CI$. Since it is possible to have more than one group from each hierarchy selected for a subject, the set of such subject groups in the hierarchy $SH_i$ are collected in $SG_i$. Formally, $\forall i, 1 \leq i \leq n, SG_i = \{g \in SH_i \mid \forall(t, r, v) \in SC_i(g)[(DR.sbj, t, r, v) \in CI]\}$. Note that according to the definition of $SC_i$ function, group "$any$" $\in SH_i$ will be selected by default for any subject; i.e. $\{(DR.sbj, t, r, v) | (t, r, v) \in SC_i(any)\} = \emptyset \subseteq CI$.
   Analogously, $OG_j$ is formed for each object hierarchy $OH_j$. Formally, $\forall j, 1 \leq j \leq m, OG_j = \{g \in OH_j \mid \forall(t, r, v) \in OC_j(g)[(DR.obj, t, r, v) \in CI]\}$. Similarly, group "$any$" $\in OH_j$ will be selected by default for any object.

2. *Hierarchy Pruning Step:*
   In this step, each hierarchy $SH_i$ is pruned to form a sub-hierarchy $Q_{SH_i}$ limited to the elements in $SG_i$. Formally, $\forall i, 1 \leq i \leq n, Q_{SH_i} = \{s \mid s \in SH_i \wedge \exists g \in SG_i[s \leq^{Tr} g]\}$. Analogously, a sub-hierarchy $Q_{OH_j}$ is formed for each hierarchy $OH_j$. Formally, $\forall j, 1 \leq j \leq m, Q_{OH_j} = \{o \mid o \in OH_j \wedge \exists g \in OG_j[o \leq^{Tr} g]\}$.

3. *Context-Aware Permission Retrieval Step:*
   Firstly, acceptable rules are gathered in a temporary set $R_1$. A rule is acceptable if its subject/object groups are in the pruned hierarchies resultant from the previous step, its action is equal to the requested action, its permission is definite, and finally its condition is satisfied. Recalling the definition of a single rule $r \in ACPR$, constraint $r.c$ consists of some contextual propositions. Constraint $r.c$ is satisfied if current contextual information include contents of the constraint, i.e. $r.c \subseteq CI$. Next, according to the order defined by $ACMP.HsPr$, the set $R_1$ is refined considering the propagation strategy of each hierarchy. The resulting set $R_{PRM}$ expresses the applicable rules according to the propagation strategies. Finally, the permission result set $PRM$ is retrieved from the refined rule set. The following algorithm describes this step formally:

   (a) $R_1 = \{r \in ACPR \mid \forall i, 1 \leq i \leq n[r.g_{SH_i} \in Q_{SH_i}] \wedge \forall j, 1 \leq j \leq m[r.g_{OH_j} \in Q_{OH_j}] \wedge r.act = DR.act \wedge r.prm \neq \text{"NIL"} \wedge r.c \subseteq CI\}$
   (b) $\forall k, 1 \leq k \leq n + m$
      i. $H = HsPr(k)$
      ii. $A = \{r.g_H \mid r \in R_1\}$
      iii. $B = \begin{cases} Maximal(Q_H, A) & \text{if } ACMP.P_H = \text{"most\_specific"} \\ Minimal(Q_H, A) & \text{if } ACMP.P_H = \text{"most\_general"} \\ A & \text{if } ACMP.P_H = \text{"path\_traversing"} \end{cases}$
      iv. $R_1 = \{r \in R_1 \mid r.g_H \in B\}$
   (c) $R_{PRM} = R_1$
   (d) $PRM = \{r.prm \mid r \in R_{PRM}\}$

   Note that $Maximal$ and $Minimal$ functions are defined in section 5.1.

4. *Permission Conflict Resolution Step:*
   If no permission could be retrieved, the meta-policy $ACMP.DefPrm$ becomes the permission decision. It is also possible that conflict occurs in the retrieved permission set $PRM$, i.e. both "+" and "−" permissions are retrieved. In this case, conflict is resolved according to the meta-policy $ACMP.PrmConfRes$. Formally, the access permission is decided as

   $$AD.prm = \begin{cases} ACMP.DefPrm & \text{if } |PRM| = 0 \\ p \in PRM & \text{if } |PRM| = 1 \\ \text{"+"} & \text{if } |PRM| = 2 \wedge \\ & ACMP.PrmConfRes = \\ & \text{"grants\_take\_precedence"} \\ \text{"−"} & \text{if } |PRM| = 2 \wedge \\ & ACMP.PrmConfRes = \\ & \text{"denials\_take\_precedence"} \end{cases}$$

5. *Context-Aware Provision Retrieval Step:*
   The set of applicable rules for retrieving provisions are formally stated by $R_{PVN} = \{r \in ACPR \mid \forall i, 1 \leq i \leq n, r.g_{SH_i} \in Q_{SH_i} \wedge \forall j, 1 \leq j \leq m, r.g_{OH_j} \in Q_{OH_j} \wedge r.act = DR.act \wedge (r.prm = AD.prm \vee r.prm = \text{"NIL"}) \wedge r.c \subseteq CI\}$. Note that $AD.prm$ was a result of previous step. Therefore the set of provision result is computed as $PVN = \{p \in r.pvns \mid r \in R_{PVN}\}$.

6. *Provision Conflict Resolution Step:*
The calculated set in the previous step, $PVN$, may have some conflicting provisions. Such conflicts are domain specific and relevant to semantics of defined provisions. Therefore the domain specific function $ACMP.PvnConfRes$ : $\mathcal{P}(PvnSet) \to \mathcal{P}(PvnSet)$ resolves these conflicts. Finally, $AD.pvns$ is computed by $ACMP.PvnConfRes(PVN)$.

## 5.5 CA-PBAC Access Control Model

The CA-PBAC model uses an authorization model formally defined by a 4-tuple $(CAPDS, ADF, DR, AD)$. Based on the framework explained in section 4, CA-PBAC controls accesses by sending an access request as $DR$ into $ADF$, which itself makes the access decision $AD$ based on the model data set $CAPDS$, and finally enforcing $AD$. Enforcing $AD$ includes fulfilment of some provisions prior to statement of permission decision.

# 6    Application Example

In order to illustrate applicability of CA-PBAC, controlling accesses to the internet applications in a university department is given as an example. The required data sets according to section 5.2 are explained very briefly. Basic data sets in $BDS$ are defined as:

$ActSet = \{use\}$,
$PvnSet = \{Log, LimitBW, SetMaxSecurity, NotifyTeacher, NotifyManager\}$

Context-related data sets in $CDS$ are defined as:

$$EntSct = \{Alice, Bob, MsnMessenger, InternetExplorer, Emule,$$
$$RealPlayer, env, network\}$$
$$SbjSet = \{Alice, Bob\}$$
$$ObjSet = \{MsnMessenger, InternetExplorer, Emule, RealPlayer\}$$
$$CtxTypeSet = \{occupation, position, resources, type, traffic, time\}$$
$$CtxValueSet = \{student, employee, professor, staff, class, laboratory, internet,$$
$$P2P, messenger, multimedia, browser, low, launch\_time\}$$
$$CtxRelatorSet = \{is, in, not\_in\}$$

Figure 2 illustrates subject and object hierarchies in the system, namely $SH_1$, $SH_2$, and $OH_1$. For instance according to Figure 2.a, we have $EMP \leq^{Tr} PROF$ in $SH_1$. The formal definition of each hierarchy and its context-assignment function follows:

$$SH_1 = \{any, STU, EMP, PROF, STAF \mid any \leq^{Tr} STU \wedge any \leq^{Tr} EMP \wedge$$
$$EMP \leq^{Tr} PROF \wedge EMP \leq^{Tr} STAF \}$$
$$SC_1 = \{(any, \emptyset), (STU, \{(occupation, is, student)\}),$$
$$(EMP, \{(occupation, is, employee)\}), (PROF, \{(position, is, professor)\}),$$

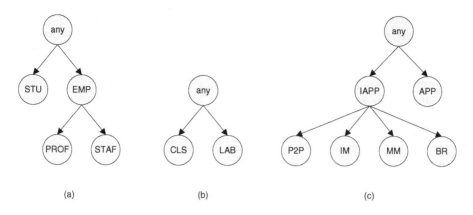

**Fig. 2.** Example hierarchies in a university department: a)$SH_1$ b)$SH_2$ c)$OH_1$

$(STAF, \{(position, is, staff)\})$ }

$SH_2=\{any, CLS, LAB \mid \ldots\}$

$SC_2=\{(any, \emptyset),(CLS, \{(location, in, class)\}),(LAB, \{(location, in, laboratory)\})\}$

$OH_1=\{any, IAPP, APP, P2P, IM, MM, BR \mid \ldots\}$

$OC_1=\{(any, \emptyset),$

$(IAPP, \{(resources, include, internet)\}),$

$(APP, \{(resources, not\_include, internet)\})$

$(P2P, \{(resources, include, internet), (type, is, P2P)\}),$

$(IM, \{(resources, include, internet), (type, is, messenger)\}),$

$(MM, \{(resources, include, internet), (type, is, multimedia)\}),$

$(BR, \{(resources, include, internet), (type, is, browser)\})\}$

The $CI$ component should be considered when an access request is made. Elements of the $ACMP$ tuple containing meta-policies is defined as:

$P_{SH_1} = $ "$most\_specific$", $P_{SH_2} = $ "$most\_specific$", $P_{OH_1} = $ "$path\_traversing$",
$HsPr = \{(1, SH_1), (2, SH_1), (3, OH_1)\}$, $PrmConfRes = $ "$denials\_take\_precedence$",
$DefPrm = $ "$+$", $PvnConfRes = \{(pvns, pvns) \mid pvns \in \mathcal{P}(PvnSet)\}$

Finally, the system has following policy rules defined in $ACPR$:

$ACPR = \{r_1, r_2, r_3, r_4, r_5, r_6\}$

$r_1 = (STU, any, MM, use, \{(network, traffic, is, low)\}, +, \{LimitBW(128kbps)\}),$

$r_2 = (STU, CLS, IAPP, use, \{\}, -, \{NotifyTeacher\}),$

$r_3 = (STU, CLS, any, use, \{\}, +, \{log\}),$

$r_4 = (EMP, any, IM, use, \{\}, NIL, \{log\}),$

$r_5 = (EMP, any, IAPP, use, \{\}, +, \{SetMaxSecurity\}),$

$r_6 = (STAF, any, IM, use, \{(env, time, not\_in, launch\_time)\}, -, \{NotifyManager\}).$

$r_1$ states that if the network traffic is low students are allowed to use multimedia applications, provided that their bandwidth is limited to 128kbps. $r_2$ states that students in class are not allowed to use internet applications, but their teacher is notified of their request. $r_3$ states that students can use anything (here any applications), but prior to use it is logged. $r_4$ states that employees' request of using instant messaging applications will be logged. $r_5$ states that employees are allowed to use internet applications, provided that the security level of their application is set to maximum. $r_6$ states that staff are not allowed to use instant messaging applications out of launch time, however their manager is notified of such request.

Now consider the following scenario. Alice, who is a student, wants to use Real Player application to watch news online in class. The decision request $DR = (Alice, RealPlayer, use)$ is submitted to the $ADF$ function. The contextual information $CI$ at the time of the request consists of

$$CI = \{(Alice, occupation, is, student),\ (Alice, location, in, class),$$

$$(RealPlayer, resources, include, internet),\ (RealPlayer, type, is, multimedia),$$

$$(network, traffic, is, low),\ \ldots\}$$

The following steps are taken in the $ADF$:

1. The result of mappings becomes $SG_1 = \{any, STU\}$, $SG_2 = \{any, CLS\}$, and $OG_1 = \{any, IAPP, IM\}$
2. Pruning each hierarchy according to the above sets results to $Q_{SH_1} = \{any, STU \mid any \leq^{Tr} STU\}$, $Q_{SH_2} = \{any, CLS \mid any \leq^{Tr} CLS\}$, and $Q_{OH_1} = \{any, IAPP, IM \mid any \leq^{Tr} IAPP \wedge IAPP \leq^{Tr} IM\}$
3. Policy rule $r_1$ is acceptable because $STU \in Q_{SH_1} \wedge any \in Q_{SH_2} \wedge MM \in Q_{OH_1} \wedge DR.act = "use" \wedge "+" \neq "NIL" \wedge \{(network, traffic, is, low)\} \subseteq CI$. Similarly, $r_2$ and $r_3$ are selected. Therefore, in step (a) of the algorithm $R_1 = \{r_1, r_2, r_3\}$. The following table shows the execution of loop at step (b):

| $k$ | $R_1$ | $H$ | $A$ | $ACMP.P_H$ | $B$ |
|---|---|---|---|---|---|
| 1 | $\{r_1, r_2, r_3\}$ | $SH_1$ | $\{STU\}$ | $most\_specific$ | $\{STU\}$ |
| 2 | $\{r_1, r_2, r_3\}$ | $SH_2$ | $\{any, CLS\}$ | $most\_specific$ | $\{CLS\}$ |
| 3 | $\{r_2, r_3\}$ | $OH_1$ | $\{any, IAPP, MM\}$ | $path\_traversing$ | $\{any, IAPP, MM\}$ |
| 4 | $\{r_2, r_3\}$ | - | - | - | - |

The applicable rules $R_{PRM}$ becomes $\{r_2, r_3\}$ and the retrieved permission set $PRM$ becomes $\{-, +\}$.

4. Since there is a permission conflict and $ACMP.PrmConfRes$ equals to "denials_take_precedence", $AD.prm$ becomes "$-$".
5. The set of applicable rules to retrieve provisions $R_{PVN}$ becomes $\{r_2\}$. So the set of provisions becomes $PVN = \{NotifyTeacher\}$.
6. Since $ACMP.PvnConfRes$ is defined as a reflexive function, the final provisions becomes:
$AD.pvns = ACMP.PvnConfRes(\{NotifyTeacher\}) = \{NotifyTeacher\}$.

Eventually, the access decision is composed from results of steps 4 and 6, i.e. $AD = (" - ", NotifyTeacher)$. Alice is denied to use Real Player application and also her teacher is notified of her request.

Consider another scenario; A staff named Bob requests to use MSN messenger application in launch time. $CI$ at the time of the request consists of

$$CI = \{(Bob, occupation, is, employee), (Bob, position, is, staff),$$
$$(MsnMessenger, resources, include, internet), (MsnMessenger, type, is, messenger),$$
$$(env, time, in, launch\_time), ...\}$$

Following the steps in $ADF$, it is decided that Bob is allowed to use MSN messenger application provided its security level is set to maximum and the access is logged.

## 7   Conclusion

In this paper, we extended a standard access control framework to include contextual information, access control meta policies, and provisions. Based on the framework, we proposed and formally specified our CA-PBAC model which enables definition of context-aware policy and enriches the access control by enforcing provisions in addition to common permissions. Context is incorporated into group hierarchies using contextual condition assignment to each group. Actually, hierarchies are formed over contextual groups to which subjects and objects are mapped. Constructing multiple hierarchies, each probably based on a particular set of context types, allows high flexibility in defining subjects and objects based on their context. In addition, different propagation strategies enable different hierarchical definition semantics. Moreover, specification of contextual constraints in policy rules controls the applicability of rules according to the context, i.e. the overall policy is dynamically adapted to the current context.

Enhancements to the model can be considered as future works. These include 1) separation of the access control model from the context model, 2) contextual provisions which are determined according to the context, and 3) conflict resolution based on the context of rules.

## References

1. Korkea-aho, M.: Context-aware applications survey. Technical report, Helsinki University of Technology (2000)
2. Dey, A.K.: Understanding and using context. Personal and Ubiquitous Computing 5(1) (2001) 4–7
3. Thomas, R.K., Sandhu, R.S.: Models, protocols, and architectures for secure pervasive computing: Challenges and research directions. In: 2nd IEEE Conference on Pervasive Computing and Communications Workshops (PerCom 2004 Workshops), Orlando, FL, USA (2004) 164–170
4. McDaniel, P.D.: On context in authorization policy. In: 8th ACM Symposium on Access Control Models and Technologies (SACMAT 2003), Villa Gallia, Como, Italy, ACM (2003)

5. Jajodia, S., Kudo, M., Subrahmanian, V.S.: Provisional authorizations. In: 1st Workshop on Security and Privacy in E-Commerce, Athens, Greece (2000)
6. Kudo, M.: Pbac: Provision-based access control model. International Journal of Information Security **1**(2) (2002) 116–130
7. Bettini, C., Jajodia, S., Sean Wang, X., Wijesekera, D.: Provisions and obligations in policy management and security applications. In: 28th International Conference on Very Large Data Bases (VLDB 2002), Hong Kong, China, Morgan Kaufmann (2002) 502–513
8. Park, J., Sandhu, R.S.: The ucon$_{abc}$ usage control model. ACM Transactions on Information and System Security **7**(1) (2004) 128–174
9. Han, W., Zhang, J., Yao, X.: Context-sensitive access control model and implementation. In: Fifth International Conference on Computer and Information Technology (CIT 2005), Shanghai, China, IEEE Computer Society (2005) 757–763
10. Kouadri Mostéfaoui, G., Brézillon, P.: Modeling context-based security policies with contextual graphs. In: 2nd IEEE Conference on Pervasive Computing and Communications Workshops (PerCom 2004 Workshops), Orlando, FL, USA, IEEE Computer Society (2004) 28–32
11. Al-Kahtani, M.A., Sandhu, R.S.: A model for attribute-based user-role assignment. In: 18th Annual Computer Security Applications Conference (ACSAC 2002), Las Vegas, NV, USA, IEEE Computer Society (2002) 353–364
12. Moyer, M.J., Ahamad, M.: Generalized role-based access control. In: 21st International Conference on Distributed Computing Systems. (2001) 391–398
13. Zhang, G., Parashar, M.: Context-aware dynamic access control for pervasive applications. In: Communication Networks and Distributed Systems Modeling and Simulation Conference, San Diego, USA (2004)
14. Roman, M., Hess, C., Cerqueira, R., Ranganathan, A., Campbell, R.H., Nahrstedt, K.: A middleware infrastructure for active spaces. IEEE Pervasive Computing **1**(4) (2002) 74–83
15. Jajodia, S., Samarati, P., Subrahmanian, V.S.: A logical language for expressing authorizations. In: IEEE Symposium on Security and Privacy, Oakland, CA, USA, IEEE Computer Society (1997) 31–42
16. Dunlop, N., Indulska, J., Raymond, K.: Methods for conflict resolution in policy-based management systems. In: 7th IEEE International Enterprise Distributed Object Computing Conference, Brisbane, Australia, IEEE Computer Society (2003) 98–109
17. ITU-T: Security Frameworks for Open Systems: Access Control Framework. ITU-T Recommendation X.812. (1995)

# LRBAC: A Location-Aware Role-Based Access Control Model*

Indrakshi Ray, Mahendra Kumar, and Lijun Yu

Department of Computer Science
Colorado State University
Fort Collins, CO 80523-1873
{iray,kumar,lijun}@cs.colostate.edu

**Abstract.** With the growing use of wireless networks and mobile devices, we are moving towards an era where location information will be necessary for access control. The use of location information can be used for enhancing the security of an application, and it can also be exploited to launch attacks. For critical applications, a formal model for location-based access control is needed that increases the security of the application and ensures that the location information cannot be exploited to cause harm. In this paper, we show how the Role-Based Access Control (RBAC) model can be extended to incorporate the notion of location. We show how the different components in the RBAC model are related with location and how this location information can be used to determine whether a subject has access to a given object. This model is suitable for applications consisting of static and dynamic objects, where location of the subject and object must be considered before granting access.

## 1  Introduction

With the increase in the growth of wireless networks and sensor and mobile devices, we are moving towards an age of ubiquitous computing where location information will be an important component of access control. For instance, when a user moves away from his computer in a smart room, the access should be automatically denied. When a computer containing top secret information is placed in a public place, the computer should automatically become inaccessible. The traditional access control models, such as Discretionary Access Control (DAC) or Role-Based Access Control (RBAC), cannot provide such location-based access control. These traditional models need to be augmented so that they can provide location-based access.

Denning and MacDoran [4] and other researchers have advocated that location information can be used to provide additional security. For instance, a user should be able to control or fire a missile from specific high security locations only. Moreover, the missile can be fired only when it is in a certain location. For such critical applications, we can include additional checks, such as verification of the location of the user and the location of the missile, that must be satisfied before the user is granted access. With the reduction in cost of Geo-Positional Systems (GPS) and infra-red sensors, this indeed is a viable option.

* This material is based upon work funded by AFOSR under Award No. FA9550-04-1-0102.

A. Bagchi and V. Atluri (Eds.): ICISS 2006, LNCS 4332, pp. 147–161, 2006.

Using location information for providing security has its own drawbacks as well. For example, information about the location of a user can compromise his privacy. Alternately, malicious users can observe the presence of a person in a certain location and infer the activities being performed by the person. The use of location information must be carefully controlled to prevent malicious users from launching attacks. Such attacks may have disastrous consequences for critical applications such as the military. In short, a formal model is needed for performing location-based access control.

In this paper we propose one such formal model that is suitable for commercial applications. Our model is based on RBAC. We show how RBAC can be extended to incorporate the concept of location. We illustrate how the different components in RBAC are related with location and how location impacts these different components. Finally, we show how this location information can be used to determine whether a user has access to a given object. The correct behavior of the model is formulated in terms of constraints that must be satisfied by any application using this model.

The remainder of the paper is organized as follows. Section 2 illustrates how we represent location in our model, and how to protect location information. Section 3 shows how the different components of RBAC are related with location and the constraints that location-based access control imposes on these components. Section 5 mentions some work related to this area. Section 6 concludes the paper with pointers to future directions.

## 2   Our Approach to Location Formalization

In order to perform location-based access control, we need to perform operations on location information and protect the location information. We begin by formalizing the concept of location. Locations can be specified at different levels of granularity. The smallest granularity of location is a point. A location is formally defined as follows.

**Definition 1 [Location].** *A location $Loc_i$ is a non-empty set of points $\{p_i, p_j, \ldots, p_n\}$ where a point $p_k$ is represented by three co-ordinates.*

We define three kinds of relations that may exist between a pair of locations. The first one is the *contained in* relation, the second one is the *overlapping* relation, and the third one is the *equality* relation. . The contained in relation formalizes the idea whether one location is enclosed by another. The overlapping relation formalizes the idea whether two locations have one or more points in common. The equality relation determines whether a given pair of locations are the same. These are formally defined below.

**Definition 2 [Contained in Relation].** *Location $Loc_j$ is said to be contained in $Loc_k$, denoted as, $Loc_j \subset Loc_k$, if the following condition holds: $\forall p_i \in Loc_j, p_i \in Loc_k$. The location $Loc_j$ is called the contained location and $Loc_k$ is referred to as the containing or the enclosing location.*

**Definition 3 [Overlapping Relation].** *Location $Loc_j$ is said to overlap $Loc_k$, denoted as, $Loc_j \bowtie Loc_k$, if the following condition holds: $\exists p_i \in Loc_j$ such that $p_i \in Loc_k$.*

**Definition 4 [Equality Relation].** *Two locations $Loc_i$ and $Loc_j$ are equal, denoted as $Loc_i = Loc_j$ if $Loc_i \subset Loc_j$ and $Loc_j \subset Loc_i$.*

The contained in relation is reflexive, transitive, and anti-symmetric. The overlapping relation is reflexive, symmetric, and non-transitive. The equality relation is reflexive, symmetric, and transitive. Note that, for any two locations $Loc_i$ and $Loc_j$, the following holds true: (i) $Loc_i = Loc_j \Rightarrow Loc_i \bowtie Loc_j$ and (ii) $Loc_i \subset Loc_j \Rightarrow Loc_i \bowtie Loc_j$.

We denote the set of all locations as **Loc**. The locations form a partial order where the ordering is described by the contained in relation $\subset$. Since the set of locations **Loc** form a partial order, they can be arranged in the form of a hierarchy. If $Loc_i \subset Loc_j$ and $Loc_i \neq Loc_j$, then $Loc_j$ is higher up in the hierarchy than $Loc_i$ and $Loc_j$ is said to be an ancestor of $Loc_i$. If $Loc_i \subset Loc_j$ and there is no $Loc_k$ such that $Loc_i \subset Loc_k \subset Loc_j$, then $Loc_j$ is said to be the parent of $Loc_i$. The root of this hierarchy is occupied by a special location termed "*universe*" that contains every other location.

# 3   Extending RBAC to Incorporate Location-Based Access Control

Core RBAC embodies the essential aspects of RBAC. The constraints specified by Core RBAC are present in any RBAC application. The model requires that users (human) be assigned to roles (job function), roles be associated with permissions (approval to perform an operation on an object), and users acquire permissions by being members of roles. The model does not place any constraint on the cardinalities of the user-role assignment relation or the permission-role association. Core RBAC also includes the notion of user sessions. A user establishes a session during which he activates a subset of the roles assigned to him. Each user can activate multiple sessions; however, each session is associated with only one user. The operations that a user can perform in a session depend on the roles activated in that session and the permissions associated with those roles.

In this section we show how RBAC can be extended to incorporate location-based access control. The different components of RBAC are *Users*, *Roles*, *Sessions*, *Permissions*, *Objects* and *Operations*. We discuss how each of these components are associated with location. Figure 1 illustrates how these components are related with *Location*. The multiplicity of these relationships are indicated by presence or absence of an arrowhead. The absence of an arrowhead indicates a multiplicity of "one" and the presence of arrowhead indicates a multiplicity of "many". Later in Section 4 we formalize these relationships and list the constraints imposed by our model. The operations in Core RBAC that need modification to provide location-aware access are also described in details Section 4.

**Users**

We assume that each valid user carries a locating device which is able to track the location of a user. The association between user and location is indicated by the edge labeled *UserLocation* in Figure 1. Each user is associated with one location at any given instant of time. However, a single location may be associated with multiple users. Our formalization of this relationship includes defining a function in Section 4 called *UserLocation* that gives the location associated with a valid user. That is, $UserLocation(u)$ returns the location of user $u$ where $u$ is a valid user.

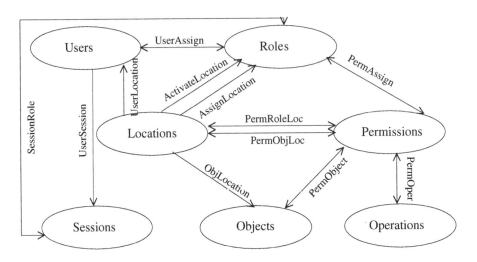

**Fig. 1.** Relationship of RBAC entities with Location

### Roles

In our model, roles are associated with locations. In fact, there are two kinds of associations roles can have with locations. These associations are indicated by the labeled edge *AssignLocation* and *ActivateLocation* in Figure 1. In the following we explain these associations.

Often times, the assignment of user to roles is location dependent. For instance, a person can be assigned the role of U.S. citizen only in certain designated locations. To get the role of conference attendee, a person must register at the conference location. Thus, for a user to be assigned a role, he must be in certain designated locations. In our model, each valid role is associated with a set of locations where the role can be assigned. We define a function *AssignLocation* that takes as input a role and returns the set of locations in which that role can be assigned. In other words, *AssignLocation*($r$) returns the set of locations where a user can be assigned the role $r$. The assignment of some role $s$ may not be location dependent. In such cases, *AssignLocation*($s$) = *universe*, which implies that the location of the user can be anywhere for it to be assigned the role $s$. The location of a user $u$ must be contained within *AssignLocation*($r$) for $u$ to be assigned the role $r$. Since users can be assigned to roles only if they have satisfied the location constraint, the function *AssignUser* in the core RBAC must be changed to include the extra precondition that verifies this.

Some roles can be activated only if the user is in some specific locations. For instance, the role of audience of a theater can be activated only if the user is in the theater. The role of conference attendee can be activated only if the user is in the conference site. Each role is associated with a set of locations from where this role can be activated. The function *ActivateLocation* takes as input a role $r$ and returns the set of locations where the role $r$ can be activated. For a role $s$ whose activation is not location dependent, *ActivateLocation*($s$) equals universe. Before a user $u$ can activate a role $r$, we must check whether the location of $u$ is contained in *ActivateLocation*($r$). This requires an additional precondition check in the operation *ActivateRole* in the Core RBAC.

**Sessions**

A user initiates a session. To create a session, a user submits a set of roles that must be activated in that session. If the location of the user satisfies the location constraints for all the roles he is trying to activate, then the session will be created. Otherwise he is notified and the session will not be created. The location associated with the session is the location associated with the user when he created that session. The function *CreateSession* in the Core RBAC needs to be changed because the session creation depends on successful role activation, which, in turn, depends on the location of the user.

**Objects**

Objects can be physical or logical. Example of physical object is a computer. Files are examples of logical objects. Physical objects have devices that transmit their location information. Logical objects are stored in physical objects. The location of a logical object is the location of the physical object containing the logical object. For the sake of simplicity, we assume that each object is associated with one location only. Each location can be associated with many objects. This is shown by the association *ObjLocation* in Figure 1. The function *ObjLocation* takes as input an object and returns the location associated with the object. Formally, *ObjLocation*($o$) returns the location of object $o$.

**Permissions**

Location-based access control models provide more security than their traditional counterparts. This happens because the location of a user and that of an object are taken into account before making the access decisions. Location-based access control also allows us to model real-world requirements where access is contingent upon the location of the user and object. For example, a vendor may provide some free services only to the local customers. Our model should be capable of expressing such requirements.

In the Core RBAC model, permissions are associated with roles, objects and operations. These associations are labeled as *PermAssign*, *PermObject* and *PermOper* respectively in Figure 1. *PermAssign* is a function that takes as input a permission and returns the set of roles assigned to that permission. *PermOper* is a function that takes as input a permission and returns the set of operations associated with this permission. *PermObj* is a function that takes as input a permission and returns the set of objects associated with the permission. A role can perform an operation on an object, if there is a permission that authorizes the role to perform the operation on the object. To incorporate location-aware access, we associate a permission with two locations: allowable role location and allowable object location. These associations are indicated by the edges labeled *PermRoleLoc* and *PermObjLoc* in Figure 1. The function *PermRoleLoc* takes as input a permission $p$ and returns the set of allowable locations for the role associated with this permission. The function *PermObjLoc* takes as input a permission $p$ and returns the set of allowable locations for the object.

In location based access control, a user $u$ is allowed to perform an operation $op$ on an object $o$ in a session $s$, if there is a permission $p$ such that *PermAssign*($p$) includes an activated role $r$, *PermOper*($p$) includes $op$, *PermObject*($p$) includes $o$, the *UserLocation*($u$) is contained in *PermRoleLoc*($p$) and the *ObjLocation*($o$) is contained in *PermObjLoc*($p$). This requires changing the operation *CheckAccess* in Core RBAC.

**Table 1.** Relevant Z Notation

| | |
|---|---|
| $\mathbb{N}$ | Set of Natural Numbers |
| $\mathbb{P}A$ | Powerset of Set $A$ |
| $\backslash$ | Set Difference (Also schema 'hiding') |
| $x \mapsto y$ | Ordered Pair $(x, y)$ |
| $A \nrightarrow B$ | Partial Function from $A$ to $B$ |
| $B \lhd A$ | Relation $A$ with Set $B$ Removed from Domain |
| $A \rhd B$ | Relation $A$ with Range Restricted to Set $B$ |
| $\text{dom}\,A$ | Domain of Relation $A$ |
| $\text{ran}\,A$ | Range of Relation $A$ |
| $A \oplus B$ | Function $A$ Overridden with Function $B$ |
| $x?$ | Variable $x?$ is an Input |
| $x!$ | Variable $x!$ is an Output |
| $x$ | State Variable $x$ before an Operation |
| $x'$ | State Variable $x'$ after an Operation |
| $\Delta A$ | Before and After State of Schema A |
| $\Xi A$ | $\Delta A$ with No Change to State |

$[USER, ROLE, SESSION, LOCATION, OBJECT, OPERATION, PERMISSION]$
$BOOLEAN ::= True \mid False$

# 4   A Formal Model

In this section, we propose a formal model that extends the core RBAC with location constraints. We use the Z specification language [7] for presenting our formal model. Z is based on set theory, first order predicate logic, and a schema calculus to organize large specifications. Table 1 briefly explains the Z notations used in our examples. Other specification and analysis conventions peculiar to Z are explained as the need arises.

The specification assumes the given types *USER, ROLE, SESSION, PERMISSION, LOCATION, OBJECT, OPERATION*, which enumerate all possible users, roles, sessions, permissions, locations, objects and operations respectively. In addition, we have the enumerated type BOOLEAN that can take on any two values *True* or *False*.

In Z, states, as well as operations, are described with a two-dimensional notation called a *schema*. The declarations for the various objects appear in the top part and the constraints on these objects appear at the bottom part. The objects in the location-aware RBAC are listed in the schema *LRBAC*, which defines the state of the access control system. The objects *Users, Roles, Sessions, Permissions, Objects, Operations* and *Locations* store the set of users, roles, sessions, permissions, objects, operations, and locations, respectively, of the system. The object *UserLocation* and *ObjLocation* are functions that record the location of the user and the location of the object respectively. The function *AssignLocation* maps a role to a set of locations – these are the locations in which the role can be assigned to some user. *ActivateLocation* is a function mapping a role to the set of locations from where the role can be activated. *UserSession* is a function that returns the set of sessions associated with any user. The function

*UserAssign* maps a user to the set of roles assigned to the user. *SessionRole* maps a session to the set of roles that are activated in a session. The function *SessionUser* maps a session to the user associated with that session. The functions *PermObject*, *PermOper*, and *PermAssign* give the set of objects, operations, and roles, respectively, associated with a given permission. The functions *PermRoleLoc* and *PermObjLoc* give the set of allowable locations for the role and object respectively associated with a given permission.

---

_____LRBAC_____

$Users : \mathbb{P}(USER)$; $Roles : \mathbb{P}(ROLE)$; $Sessions : \mathbb{P}(SESSION)$; $Objects : \mathbb{P}(OBJECT)$
$Permissions : \mathbb{P}(PERMISSION)$
$Operations : \mathbb{P}(OPERATION)$; $Locations : \mathbb{P}(LOCATION)$
$UserLocation : USER \nrightarrow LOCATION$; $ObjLocation : OBJECT \nrightarrow LOCATION$
$AssignLocation : ROLE \nrightarrow \mathbb{P}(LOCATION)$; $ActivateLocation : ROLE \nrightarrow \mathbb{P}(LOCATION)$
$UserSession : USER \nrightarrow \mathbb{P}(SESSION)$; $UserAssign : USER \nrightarrow \mathbb{P}(ROLE)$
$SessionRole : SESSION \nrightarrow \mathbb{P}(ROLE)$; $SessionUser : SESSION \nrightarrow USER$
$PermObject : PERMISSION \nrightarrow \mathbb{P}(OBJECT)$; $PermOper : PERMISSION \nrightarrow \mathbb{P}(OPERATION)$
$PermAssign : PERMISSION \nrightarrow \mathbb{P}(ROLE)$; $PermRoleLoc : PERMISSION \nrightarrow \mathbb{P}(LOCATION)$
$PermObjLoc : PERMISSION \nrightarrow \mathbb{P}(LOCATION)$

---

$\mathrm{dom}\, UserLocation = Users$; $\mathrm{dom}\, ObjLocation = Objects$; $\mathrm{ran}\, ObjLocation \subseteq Locations$
$\mathrm{dom}\, AssignLocation = Roles$; $\forall l : \mathrm{ran}\, AssignLocation \bullet l \subseteq Locations$
$\mathrm{dom}\, ActivateLocation = Roles$; $\forall l : \mathrm{ran}\, ActivateLocation \bullet l \subseteq Locations$
$\mathrm{dom}\, UserSession \subseteq Users$; $\forall l : \mathrm{ran}\, UserSession \bullet l \subseteq Sessions$
$\mathrm{dom}\, UserAssign \subseteq Users$; $\forall r : \mathrm{ran}\, UserAssign \bullet r \subseteq Roles$
$\mathrm{dom}\, SessionRole = Sessions$; $\forall r : \mathrm{ran}\, SessionRoles \bullet r \subseteq Roles$
$\forall s : Sessions \bullet (SessionRole(s) \subseteq UserAssign(SessionUser(s)))$
$\mathrm{dom}\, SessionUser = Sessions$; $\mathrm{ran}\, SessionUser \subseteq Users$; $\mathrm{dom}\, UserSession = \mathrm{ran}\, SessionUser$
$\mathrm{dom}\, PermObject = Permissions$; $\forall r : \mathrm{ran}\, PermObject \bullet r \subseteq Objects$
$\mathrm{dom}\, PermOper = Permissions$; $\forall r : \mathrm{ran}\, PermOper \bullet r \subseteq Operations$
$\mathrm{dom}\, PermAssign = Permissions$; $\forall r : \mathrm{ran}\, PermAssign \bullet r \subseteq Roles$
$\mathrm{dom}\, PermRoleLoc = Permissions$; $\forall r : \mathrm{ran}\, PermRoleLoc \bullet r \subseteq Locations$
$\mathrm{dom}\, PermObjLoc = Permissions$; $\forall r : \mathrm{ran}\, PermObjLoc \bullet r \subseteq Locations$

---

The bottom of the schema *LRBAC* gives the constraints that are imposed on the objects. The first one states that the domain of *UserLocation* equals the set of users in the system. In other words, all users are associated with a location. The next one states that the domain of *ObjLocation* equals the set of objects in the system – this is because all objects are associated with locations. Each location associated with an object must be in an allowable location. This is imposed by requiring that the set of locations in the range of function *ObjLocation* is a subset of *Locations*. The next one states that the domain of *AssignLocation* equals the set of *Roles*. This implies that each role in *Roles* is associated with a set of locations where the role can be assigned. Each set in the range of *AssignLocation* must be a subset of locations of interest in the system.

Similar constraints are imposed for the function *ActivateLocation*. Since all users in the set *Users* may not have an active session, the domain of *UserSession* is a subset of the set *Users*. Each set in the range of *UserSession* denotes the sessions associated with a particular user. Each such set must be a subset of *Sessions*. The function *UserAssign* maps a user to the set of roles assigned to him. Not all users in *Users* may have roles assigned to them, hence the domain of *UserAssign* is a subset of *Users*. Each set in the range *UserAssign* corresponds to roles associated with a user – each such set is a subset of *Roles*. The function *SessionRole* maps a session to a set of roles associated with the session. Each session must be associated with some roles; the domain of *SessionRole* therefore equals *Sessions*. Moreover, each set in the range of *SessionRole* is a subset of *Roles*. The domain of *SessionUser* must equal *Sessions* because every session in *Sessions* must be associated with a user. The range of *SessionUser* is a subset of *Users* because not all users in the system may have an active session. Also, the domain of *UserSession* must equal the range of *SessionUser*. For all sessions, the roles associated with the session must be a subset of the roles assigned to the user associated with that session. Each permission must be associated with a set of objects; thus the domain of *PermObject* equals *Permissions*, and each set in the range of *PermObject* is a subset of *Objects*. Similar constraints are placed for *PermOper*, *PermAssign*, *PermRoleLoc*, and *PermObjLocation*.

---

**_AddRoleAssignLocation_**
$\Delta LRBAC$; $r?$ : $ROLE$; $l?$ : $\mathbb{P}\,LOCATION$

---

$r? \in Roles$; $l? \subseteq Locations$; $Operations' = Operations$; $Permissions' = Permissions$
$Roles' = Roles$; $Users' = Users$; $ActivateLocation' = ActivateLocation$
$AssignLocation' = AssignLocation \oplus \{r \mapsto AssignLocation(r?) \cup l?\}$
$Locations' = Locations$; $UserLocation' = UserLocation$; $UserSession' = UserSession$
$PermAssign' = PermAssign$; $SessionRole' = SessionRole$; $SessionUser' = SessionUser$
$PermObject' = PermObject$; $PermOper' = PermOper$; $PermRoleLoc' = PermRoleLoc$
$ObjLocation' = ObjLocation$; $PermObjLoc' = PermObjLoc$
$UserAssign' = UserAssign$; $Sessions' = Sessions$; $Objects' = Objects$

---

We next describe the operations for performing the administration commands for the Location Aware RBAC. For lack of space, we do not specify all the operations. We show only those operations that are significantly different from the Core RBAC and those that are not present in the Core RBAC. The operations *AddUser*, *DeleteUser*, *AddRole*, *DeleteRole* are similar to that specified in CoreRBAC. Since roles are associated with an assignment location and an activation location, we must have operations that add and delete these associations. The operation *AddRoleAssignLocation* associates a new set of locations with a role. The operation takes as input a role $r?$ and a set of locations $l?$. It has two preconditions. The first verifies whether $r?$ is a valid role by checking whether $r?$ is in the set *Roles*. The second checks whether $l?$ is a subset of *Locations*. The post condition changes the object *AssignLocation*. The role $r?$ is now mapped to the set of original locations union $l?$. All the other objects remain unchanged.

The operation *DeleteRoleAssignLocation* also takes as input a role $r$? and a set of locations $l$?. This has two preconditions. The first one verifies role $r$? is a valid role by checking whether $r$? is in the set *Roles*. The second one checks whether $l$? is a subset of the locations that are associated with the assignment of role $r$?. The postcondition removes $l$? from the set of roles associated with $r$?. No other objects are changed. The operations *AddRoleActivateLoc* and *DeleteRoleActivateLoc* are specified in a similar fashion.

---
___DeleteRoleAssignLocation_____

$\Delta LRBAC$; $r$? : $ROLE$; $l$? : $\mathbb{P}\,LOCATION$

---
$r$? $\in$ *Roles*; $l$? $\subseteq$ *AssignLocation*($r$?); *Users'* = *Users*; *Roles'* = *Roles*
*AssignLocation'* = *AssignLocation* $\oplus$ $\{r \mapsto AssignLocation(r?) \setminus l?\}$
*Permissions'* = *Permissions*; *Sessions'* = *Sessions*; *Objects'* = *Objects*
*Operations'* = *Operations*; *Locations'* = *Locations*; *UserLocation'* = *UserLocation*
*UserSession'* = *UserSession*; *SessionRole'* = *SessionRole*; *PermAssign'* = *PermAssign*
*ActivateLocation'* = *ActivateLocation*; *SessionUser'* = *SessionUser*; *PermOper'* = *PermOper*
*PermObject'* = *PermObject*; *PermRoleLoc'* = *PermRoleLoc*; *ObjLocation'* = *ObjLocation*
*PermObjLoc'* = *PermObjLoc*; *UserAssign'* = *UserAssign*

---
___AddRoleActivateLoc_____

$\Delta LRBAC$; $r$? : $ROLE$; $l$? : $\mathbb{P}\,LOCATION$

---
$r$? $\in$ *Roles*; $l$? $\subseteq$ *Locations*; *PermObjLoc'* = *PermObjLoc*; *Users'* = *Users*
*ActivateLocation'* = *ActivateLocation* $\oplus$ $\{r \mapsto ActivateLocation(r?) \cup l?\}$; *Objects'* = *Objects*
*Operations'* = *Operations*; *Locations'* = *Locations*; *UserLocation'* = *UserLocation*
*UserSession'* = *UserSession*; *PermAssign'* = *PermAssign*; *Sessions'* = *Sessions*
*Roles'* = *Roles*; *AssignLocation'* = *AssignLocation*; *ObjLocation'* = *ObjLocation*
*Permissions'* = *Permissions*; *SessionRole'* = *SessionRole*; *SessionUser'* = *SessionUser*
*PermObject'* = *PermObject*; *PermOper'* = *PermOper*; *PermRoleLoc'* = *PermRoleLoc*

---
___DeleteRoleActivateLoc_____

$\Delta LRBAC$; $r$? : $ROLE$; $l$? : $\mathbb{P}\,LOCATION$

---
$r$? $\in$ *Roles*; $l$? $\subseteq$ *AssignLocation*($r$?); *Users'* = *Users*; *Operations'* = *Operations*
*AssignLocation'* = *AssignLocation* $\oplus$ $\{r \mapsto AssignLocation(r?) \setminus l?\}$
*Objects'* = *Objects*; *Locations'* = *Locations*; *UserLocation'* = *UserLocation*
*Sessions'* = *Sessions*; *UserSession'* = *UserSession*; *PermAssign'* = *PermAssign*
*ActivateLocation'* = *ActivateLocation*; *ObjLocation'* = *ObjLocation*; *PermOper'* = *PermOper*
*SessionRole'* = *SessionRole*; *SessionUser'* = *SessionUser*; *PermObject'* = *PermObject*
*PermRoleLoc'* = *PermRoleLoc*; *Roles'* = *Roles*; *PermObjLoc'* = *PermObjLoc*

---

___AddPermission_____

$\Delta LRBAC$; $p?$ : $PERMISSION$; $obj?$ : $\mathbb{P}\,OBJECT$
$r?$ : $\mathbb{P}\,ROLE$; $op?$ : $\mathbb{P}\,OPERATION$; $rl?, ol?$ : $\mathbb{P}\,LOCATION$

---

$p? \notin Permissions$; $obj? \subseteq Objects$; $op? \subseteq Operations$; $rl? \subseteq Locations$
$AssignLocation' = AssignLocation$; $ol? \subseteq Locations$; $ActivateLocation' = ActivateLocation$
$Users' = Users$; $Permissions' = Permissions \cup \{p?\}$; $Sessions' = Sessions$
$PermAssign' = PermAssign \cup \{p? \mapsto r?\}$; $PermObject' = PermAssign \cup \{p? \mapsto obj?\}$
$PermOper' = PermAssign \cup \{p? \mapsto op?\}$; $PermRoleLoc' = PermRoleLoc \cup \{p? \mapsto rl?\}$
$PermObjLoc' = PermObjLoc \cup \{p? \mapsto ol?\}$; $Objects' = Objects$; $Roles' = Roles$
$ObjLocation' = ObjLocation$; $Operations' = Operations$
$Locations' = Locations$; $UserLocation' = UserLocation$; $UserSession' = UserSession$
$UserAssign' = UserAssign$; $SessionRole' = SessionRole$; $SessionUser' = SessionUser$

---

___DeletePermission_____

$\Delta LRBAC$; $p?$ : $PERMISSION$

---

$p? \in Permissions$; $Users' = Users$; $Roles' = Roles$; $Sessions' = Sessions$
$Permissions' = Permissions - \{p?\}$; $PermAssign' = \{p?\} \lhd PermAssign$
$PermObject' = \{p?\} \lhd PermObject$; $PermOper' = \{p?\} \lhd PermOper$
$PermRoleLoc' = \{p?\} \lhd PermRoleLoc$; $PermObjLoc' = \{p?\} \lhd PermObjLoc$
$Operations' = Operations$; $UserLocation' = UserLocation$; $UserAssign' = UserAssign$
$Locations' = Locations$; $Objects' = Objects$; $AssignLocation' = AssignLocation$
$ActivateLocation' = ActivateLocation$; $UserSession' = UserSession$
$ObjLocation' = ObjLocation$; $SessionRole' = SessionRole$; $SessionUser' = SessionUser$

---

The operation *AddPermission* adds a new permission to the set *Permissions*. It takes as input the new permission $p?$, the set of roles $r?$ which must be assigned this permission, the set of objects $obj?$ and the set of operations $op?$ associated with this permission, the set of role locations $rl?$ and the set of object locations $ol?$ associated with this permission. There are five preconditions associated with this operation. The first one checks that $p?$ is not an existing permission, the second and third check whether $obj?$ and $op?$ are valid sets of objects and operations respectively, and the fourth and fifth check whether $rl?$ and $ol?$ are valid sets of locations. The postconditions change the set *Permissions* to include $p?$, change the function *PermAssign* to include the new mapping $p? \mapsto r?$. The function *PermObject*, *PermOper*, *PermRoleLoc*, and *PermObjLoc* are updated to include the mappings of permission $p?$ to object $obj?$, operation $op?$, role location $rl?$, and object location $ol?$ respectively. The other objects remain unchanged.

The operation *DeletePermission* removes a permission $p?$ from the set *Permissions*. It takes in one input: the permission $p?$ to be removed. The precondition checks whether $p?$ is an existing permission by checking if it is in the set *Permissions*. The postcondition removes $p?$ from *Permissions*. It also changes the objects *PermAssign*, *PermObject*, *PermOper*, *PermRoleLoc*, *PermObjLoc* by removing the entries associated with $p?$ in each of these objects.

The operation *AssignUser* must also be changed. It takes in two inputs: the user $u$? to whom the role $r$? must be assigned. This operation has four preconditions. The first two check whether $u$? and $r$? are valid user and role respectively. The third one ensures that $r$? is not in the set of roles assigned to $u$?. Since $r$? can be assigned only in certain locations, the last precondition checks whether the location of the user is contained in the locations where $r$? can be assigned. The postcondition is that the function *UserAssign* is changed so that $u$? maps to the set consisting of the roles previously assigned to $u$? and $r$?. The other objects remain unchanged.

---
**AssignUser**

$\Delta LRBAC$; $u$? : $USER$; $r$? : $ROLE$

---

$u? \in Users$; $r? \in Roles$; $r? \notin UserAssign(u?)$; $UserLocation(u?) \in AssignLocation(r?)$
$PermObjLoc' = PermObjLoc$; $Roles' = Roles$; $Objects' = Objects$; $Operations' = Operations$
$UserAssign = UserAssign \oplus \{u? \mapsto UserAssign(u?) \cup \{r?\}\}$; $PermRoleLoc' = PermRoleLoc$
$Locations' = Locations$; $Permissions' = Permissions$; $UserLocation' = UserLocation$
$UserSession' = UserSession$; $PermAssign' = PermAssign$; $ObjLocation' = ObjLocation$
$ActivateLocation' = ActivateLocation$; $SessionRole' = SessionRole$; $SessionUser' = SessionUser$
$PermObject' = PermObject$; $PermOper' = PermOper$; $Users' = Users$; $Sessions' = Sessions$

---
**AddLocation**

$\Delta LRBAC$; $l$? : $LOCATION$

---

$l? \notin Locations$; $Users' = Users$; $Roles' = Roles$; $Locations' = Locations \cup \{l?\}$
$Objects' = Objects$; $Operations' = Operations$; $UserLocation' = UserLocation$
$UserSession' = UserSession$; $PermAssign' = PermAssign$; $ActivateLocation' = ActivateLocation$
$Sessions' = Sessions$; $SessionRole' = SessionRole$; $SessionUser' = SessionUser$
$PermObject' = PermObject$; $PermOper' = PermOper$; $PermRoleLoc' = PermRoleLoc$
$ObjLocation' = ObjLocation$; $PermObjLoc' = PermObjLoc$; $Permissions' = Permissions$

---
**DeleteLocation**

$\Delta LRBAC$; $l$? : $LOCATION$

---

$l? \in Locations$; $l? \notin \mathrm{ran}\, ObjLocation$; $l? \notin \mathrm{ran}\, PermRoleLoc l? \notin \mathrm{ran}\, PermObjLoc$
$l? \notin \mathrm{ran}\, AssignLocation$; $l? \notin \mathrm{ran}\, ActivateLocation$; $Locations' = Locations \setminus \{l?\}$
$Operations' = Operations$; $UserLocation' = UserLocation$; $UserSession' = UserSession$
$PermAssign' = PermAssign$; $ActivateLocation' = ActivateLocation$; $ObjLocation' = ObjLocation$
$SessionRole' = SessionRole$; $SessionUser' = SessionUser$; $PermObject' = PermObject$
$PermOper' = PermOper$; $Permissions' = Permissions$; $Roles' = Roles$; $PermRoleLoc' = PermRoleLoc$
$Users' = Users$; $PermObjLoc' = PermObjLoc$; $Sessions' = Sessions$; $Objects' = Objects$

---

Two operations, not present in the Core RBAC, are added to this model. The first is *AddLocation* which adds a new location to the set *Locations*. The precondition is that the input $l$? is not among the existing set *Locations*. The postcondition is that the set *Locations* is changed to include $l$?. The rest of the objects remain unchanged. The second operation is *DeleteLocation*. It removes a location $l$? from the set *Locations*. The first precondition is that $l$? must be an existing location. The second one checks that $l$? must not be the location of any object. The next four preconditions check that $l$? must not be a location which is associated with some permission, role assignment or role activation. The postcondition removes $l$? from the set *Locations*. Other objects remain unchanged.

```
__CreateSession_____
ΔLRBAC; u? : USER; s? : SESSION; rset? : P(ROLE)
_____
u? ∈ Users; rset? ⊆ Roles; s? ∉ Sessions; rset? ∈ UserAssign(u?)
∀r ∈ rset? • (UserLocation(u) ∈ ActivateLocation(r)); Sessions' = Sessions ∪ {s?}
Users' = Users; UserSession' = UserSession ⊕ {u? ↦ UserSession(u?) ∪ {s?}}
SessionRole' = SessionRole ∪ {s? ↦ rset?}; SessionUser' = SessionUser ∪ {s? ↦ u?}
AssignLocation' = AssignLocation; Objects' = Objects; Operations' = Operations
Permissions' = Permissions; PermAssign' = PermAssign; ActivateLocation' = ActivateLocation
Roles' = Roles; PermObject' = PermObject; UserLocation' = UserLocation
PermOper' = PermOper; UserAssign' = UserAssign; PermRoleLoc' = PermRoleLoc
PermObjLoc' = PermObjLoc; Sessions' = Sessions; ObjLocation' = ObjLocation
```

```
__ActivateRole_____
ΔLRBAC; u? : USER; r? : ROLE; s? : SESSION
_____
u? ∈ Users; r? ∈ Roles; s? ∈ Sessions; r? ∈ UserAssign(u?); s? ∈ UserSession(u?)
UserLocation(u?) ∈ ActivateLocation(r?); Users' = Users; Objects' = Objects
Sessions' = Sessions; SessionRole' = SessionRole ⊕ {s? ↦ SessionRole(s?) ∪ {r?}}
Operations' = Operations; UserLocation' = UserLocation; UserSession' = UserSession
Roles' = Roles; PermAssign' = PermAssign; ActivateLocation' = ActivateLocation
SessionRole' = SessionRole; SessionUser' = SessionUser; PermObject' = PermObject
PermOper' = PermOper; UserAssign' = UserAssign; PermRoleLoc' = PermRoleLoc
PermObjLoc' = PermObjLoc; ObjLocation' = ObjLocation; Permissions' = Permissions
```

```
__CheckAccess_____
ΞLRBAC; s? : SESSION; op? : OPERATION; o? : OBJECT; res! : BOOLEAN
_____
s? ∈ Sessions; o? ∈ Objects; op? ∈ Operations
∃r : ROLE • (r ∈ SessionRole(s?) ∧ (∃p : PERMISSION • (r ∈ PermAssign(p) ∧ op? ∈ PermOper(p)
    ∧ o? ∈ PermObject(p) ∧ ObjLocation(o?) ∈ PermObjLoc(p)
    ∧ UserLocation(SessionUser(s?)) ∈ PermRoleLoc(p)) ⇒ res! = TRUE
∄r : ROLE • (r ∈ SessionRole(s?) ∧ (∃p : PERMISSION • (r ∈ PermAssign(p) ∧ op? ∈ PermOper(p)
    ∧ o? ∈ PermObject(p) ∧ ObjLocation(o?) ∈ PermObjLoc(p)
    ∧ UserLocation(SessionUser(s?)) ∈ PermRoleLoc(p))) ⇒ res! = FALSE
```

Next, we specify the operations for system functions for the Location Aware RBAC. Here again, we specify only those operations that differ from the Core RBAC. The first one is the *CreateSession* operation. This operation takes as input a user $u$? whose session is being created, the session $s$? that must be created, and a set of roles $rset$? that must be activated. This operation has three preconditions. The first ensures that

$u$? is a valid user, that is, it must belong to the set *Users*. The second checks whether *rset*? is a subset of *Roles*. The third ensures that $s$? is not an existing session. The fourth precondition checks that *rset*? is a subset of the roles assigned to the user. The fifth checks that for each role $r$ in the set *rset*?, the location of user $u$? is contained in the activation location of $r$. The post condition changes *Sessions* by including $s$?. The function *UserSession* is changed – user $u$? is now associated with the set of pre-existing sessions of $u$? together with the session $s$?. The function *SessionRole* is also changed; a new mapping $s$? $\mapsto$ *rset*? is added to *SessionRole*. Similarly *SessionUser* is changed to include the mapping $s$? $\mapsto$ $u$?. All other objects remain unchanged.

The other operation that is significantly different is *ActivateRole*. The input to this operation are the user $u$?, the role $r$?, and the session $s$? in which the role must be activated. The first three preconditions check whether $u$?, $r$?, and $s$? are existing user, role and session respectively. The fourth and fifth preconditions check whether $r$? is a role assigned to the user $u$?, and $s$? is a session initiated by user $u$?. The last precondition checks that the location of $u$? is within the activation location of $r$?. The postcondition is that the function *SessionRole* is updated; $s$? is now associated with $r$? and also the roles that were previously activated. The other operations remain unchanged.

The next operation is the *CheckAccess* operation. This function takes in three inputs: the session $s$?, the operation *op*? and the object $o$?. The operation has three preconditions that check whether $s$?, *op*? and $o$? are valid session, operation, and object, respectively. The postcondition does not change any object. This operation produces an output *res*! which is BOOLEAN. If there is a role $r$ that is activated in the session $s$?, and there is a permission $p$ such $r$, *op*? and $o$? are associated with permission $p$, and the location of the user and the object are contained in *PermRoleLoc*($p$) and *PermObjLoc*($p$), respectively, then *res*! returns true. Otherwise *res*! returns false.

## 5   Related Work

Denning and MacDoran [4] propose many motivating examples as to why location-based security is important for applications. Their argument is that use of location information can enhance the security of applications. The authors discuss how location-based authentication can be achieved using GPS and a tool called Cyberlocator.

Hengartner and Steenkiste [5] design an access control mechanism for a people location system. The authors say that an individual is associated with two kinds of location policies. The first are the location policies that are specified by individuals. The second are the policies that are specified by institutions. For instance, if a person is at the mall, his individual location policies are in effect. When he is at work, the institutional policies of the organization are in effect. The access control policy is enforced using digital certificates.

Leonhardt and Magee [6] discuss how location-based access can be provided over existing matrix-based access control models and mandatory access control models. The proposed approach consists of three parts: controlling access, controlling visibility and controlling anonymity. The visibility policy specifies what location information gets returned to the user who is querying about the location of an entity. The anonymity policy specifies what information gets returned to the user querying about some other user. The access policy specifies how location information can be used to control access. Although this paper has presented some nice ideas, it lacks details and formalisms. For instance, the authors do not discuss how the different components of an access control model are impacted by location and what constraints are necessary on the location-based model. In our work we try to address these issues and complement the above mentioned work.

Sampemane et al. [9] present a new access control model for active spaces. Active space denotes the computing environment integrating physical spaces and embedded computing software and hardware entities. The active space allows interactive exchange of information between the user and the space. Environmental aspects are adopted into the access control model for active spaces, and the space roles are introduced into the implementation of the access control model based on RBAC. The model supports specification of RBAC policies in which system administrator maintains the access matrix and DAC policies in which users create and update security policies for their devices.

Covington et al. [3] introduce environment roles in a generalized RBAC model (GR-BAC) to help control access control to private information and resources in ubiquitous computing applications. The environments roles differ from the subject roles in RBAC but do have similar properties including role activation, role hierarchy and separation of duty. In the access control framework enabled by environment roles, each element of permission assignment is associated with a set of environment roles, and environment roles are activated according to the changing conditions specified in environmental conditions, thus environmental properties like time and location are introduced to the access control framework. In a subsequent work [2], Covington et al. describes the Context-Aware Security Architecture (CASA) which is an implementation of the GR-BAC model. The access control is provided by the security services in the architecture. In CASA, polices are expressed as roles and managed by the security management service, authentication and authorization services are used to verify user credentials and determine access to the system resources. The environmental role activation services manage environmental role activation and deactivation according to the environment variables collected by the context management services.

Ray et al.[8] briefly describe the impact that location has on the various components of RBAC. However, the paper does not provide any formal treatment of the topic. Bertino et al.[1] describe the GEO-RBAC model which extends RBAC to incorporate spatial and location information. Each role is associated with an extent which defines the boundary at which the role is effective. Our model not only associates locations with role activations, but also associates locations with role assignments and permissions.

## 6   Conclusion

In this paper, we have proposed a location-based access control model that is based on RBAC. This model will be useful for pervasive computing applications in which the role of the user as well as his location will be used to determine if the user has access to some resource. We have shown how the different components of the core RBAC model are related with location, what new operations are needed and how existing operations must be changed to perform location-based access. We have formalized our model using the Z specification language. In future, we would like to extend this model by taking into account the effects of the constraints imposed by role hierarchy, static separation of duty, and dynamic separation of duty. We also plan to propose mechanisms by which such a model can be implemented. Typically location of a user or an object changes with time. Our future plans include proposing a model that takes into account these kinds of temporal constraints.

# References

1. Elisa Bertino, Barbara Catania, Maria Luisa Damiani, and Paolo Perlasca. GEO-RBAC: A Spatially Aware RBAC. In *Proceedings of the ACM Symposium on Access Control Models and Technologies*, Stockholm, Sweden, June 2005.
2. Michael J. Covington, Prahlad Fogla, Zhiyuan Zhan, and Mustaque Ahamad. A Context-Aware Security Architecture for Emerging Applications. In *Proceedings of the Annual Computer Security Applications Conference* , pages 249–260, Las Vegas, NV, USA, December 2002.
3. Michael J. Covington, Wende Long, Srividhya Srinivasan, Anind Dey, Mustaque Ahamad, and Gregory Abowd. Securing Context-Aware Applications Using Environment Roles. In *Proceedings of the 6th ACM Symposium on Access Control Models and Technologies*, pages 10–20, Chantilly, VA, USA, May 2001.
4. Dorothy E. Denning and Peter F. MacDoran. Location-Based Authentication:Grounding Cyberspace for Better Security. In *Computer Fraud and Security,Elsevier Science Ltd*, February 1996.
5. Urs Hengartner and Peter Steenkiste. Implementing Access Control to People Location Information. In *Proceeding of the SACMAT'04 Yorktown Heights,California,USA*, June 2004.
6. Ulf Leonhardt and Jeff Magee. Security Consideration for a Distributed Location Service. *Imperial College of Science, Technology and Medicine, London, UK*, 1997.
7. B. Potter, J. Sinclair, and D. Till. *An Introduction to Formal Specification and Z*. Prentice-Hall, New York, NY, 1991.
8. Indrakshi Ray and Lijun Yu. Short Paper: Towards a Location-Aware Role-Based Access Control Model. In *Proceedings of the IEEE Conference on Security and Privacy for Emerging Areas in Communications Network*, Athens, Greece, September 2005.
9. Geetanjali Sampemane, Prasad Naldurg, and Roy H. Campbell. Access Control for Active Spaces. In *Proceedings of the Annual Computer Security Applications Conference* , pages 343–352, Las Vegas, NV, USA, December 2002.

# Extending Context Descriptions in Semantics-Aware Access Control

E. Damiani, S. De Capitani di Vimercati, C. Fugazza, and P. Samarati

Dipartimento di Tecnologie dell'Informazione
Università degli Studi di Milano
v. Bramante 65, 26013 Crema, Italy
{damiani,decapita,fugazza,samarati}@dti.unimi.it

**Abstract.** Security is a crucial concern for commercial and mission critical applications in Web-based environments. In our model, context information associated with *Access Control* management policies is defined according to basic operators that can be represented using the *Web Ontology Language*. Standard inference procedures of *Description Logics* are being used to check the consistency of context information referred to by policy conditions and, more interestingly, to pre-process context information for grounding policy propagation and enabling conflict resolution. In this paper, we extend the model to encompass part-of relations between entities in context descriptions and, consequently, revise the policy propagation criteria being applied to the model to take into account the newly introduced relations. Finally, we exemplify modality conflicts arising from part-of relations, a category of *extensional* conflicts (i.e., inconsistencies related to individuals) that cannot be foreseen by looking at the terminology underlying context information.

## 1 Introduction

Security is a crucial concern for commercial and mission critical applications in Web-based environments. Recently, a number of advanced models and languages have been proposed for protecting Web resources and services, specifying and enforcing policies and *Access Control* (AC) constraints based on Semantic Web-style context descriptions [12] aimed at supporting widespread distribution of resources and cooperation of autonomous agents on the Web in a secure way. Ontologies, rule languages and Semantic Web reasoning are important ingredients of this infrastructure to enable distributed peers to negotiate access to distributed resources and services.

In our previous work [18], context information associated with AC management policies (e.g., subjects, actions, target objects) is defined according to basic operators (namely, subsumption, union, intersection, and complement) that can be represented using the *Web Ontology Language* (OWL) [8]. The same primitives are used, in the specification of authorizations, to compose *domain scope expressions* i.e., constructs combining entities defined by context descriptions. By doing this, authorizations can be directly mapped with branches of the hierarchical representation of context information and, under the assumption of

A. Bagchi and V. Atluri (Eds.): ICISS 2006, LNCS 4332, pp. 162–176, 2006.

a closed-world reasoning (i.e., complete knowledge), it is possible to regulate access to resources with only positive authorizations. Standard inference procedures of *Description Logics* (DL) [13] have been used to check the consistency of context information referred to by policy conditions and, more interestingly, to pre-process context information for grounding policy propagation and enabling conflict resolution. Specifically, authorizations are propagated along partially ordered structures obtained by classifying context descriptions.

In this paper, we first extend our basic model [18] to encompass part-of relations between context entities. With respect to authorization objects, partonomy can express logical or physical containment between resources (consider, respectively, images included in a XHTML page and time-delimited fragments of a movie clip) and also more fine-grained assertions related to the informative content itself, such as "Text of Note123 contains the data associated with AccountXYZ". On the other hand, authorization subjects can model more complex social structures, such as the Workgroup concept considered in Sec. 4. In this paper, we extend the policy propagation criteria being applied to our model to take into account part-of relations. Moreover, in [18] we primarily investigated modality conflicts arising from the classification taxonomy, which we indicate by *terminological* conflicts; instead, the examples in this paper belong to the category of *extensional* conflicts, i.e. inconsistencies related to individuals that cannot be foreseen by looking at the terminology underlying context information.

The paper is structured as follows. Sec. 2 introduces the context of our work and provides the rationale for re-using high-level modeling techniques, such as UML, for deriving the structure of domain information. In Sec. 3 we give a primer on mereology, the theory of part-of relations, and pinpoint the characteristics interesting in our context that can be expressed with OWL. In Sec. 4 we extend the expressiveness achievable with our model to represent this category of relations. Sec. 5 recalls the authorization model that will be used throughout the paper and explains the criteria adopted for policy propagation and conflict resolution w.r.t. the extension to the model. Sec. 6 draws the conclusions and introduces future work.

## 2   Motivation and Background

In [18] we introduced an ontology-based model for context description to investigate modality conflicts in semantics-aware AC architectures. We also drew a comparison with traditional models, such as RBAC [28], to pinpoint the similarities and distinguishing features, particularly with respect to the distinct semantics that can be considered when interpreting a *knowledge base* (KB). Specifically, we combine the traditional negation-as-failure interpretation of closed-world systems (e.g., relational databases) with the open-world semantics of the DLs underlying OWL Lite and OWL DL. This approach widens the scope of our model, making it suitable for environments like inter-organizational systems or the open net, where information is under the control of different owners and no assumptions can be made on the time of its release. With regards to the integration of existing paradigms with our model, in this paper we will consider the UML modeling language [5] as a possible source for re-usable context descriptions. Indeed, a major motivation for adopting a semantics-aware representation is that a) administrative and business processes within an organization are often modeled by means of expressive, high-level abstractions such as UML diagrams and b) the translation to Semantic Web formats is technically achievable through the XML Metadata Interchange (XMI) format and any XML conversion technique e.g., the eXtensible Stylesheet Language Transformations (XSLT). In order to express with UML class diagrams more fine-grained properties, such as disjointeness between class extensions, we consider the *inter-relationship constraints* [19] that can be used in conjunction with generalization and association structures. More complex constraints achievable with the *Object Constraint Language* (OCL) [16] are not considered by our model.

A straightforward way of structuring context information is using a subsumption hierarchy combining different kinds of entities. Firstly, concept descriptions categorize the entities known to the system that will be referenced by authorizations. In our working example, we consider subjects and objects of access requests, but the model can be immediately extended to encompass further components of AC authorizations (e.g., the different actions that a subject can execute on an object). Secondly, domain scope expressions introduced by authorization subjects and objects are integrated with the former in order to identify the concepts being addressed by authorizations. This structure can be used to detect and resolve terminological conflicts i.e., those conflicts due to inheritance of colliding authorizations from super-concepts. They are resolved, wherever possible, by applying either the *specificity principle* [25] or *semantic similarity measures* [27,17]. We also need to reconcile extensional conflicts that cannot be spotted simply by inspecting the subsumption hierarchy because they are due to multiple type relationships of individuals. In this case, the *most specific concept* (*msc*) [13] related to an individual is computed and inserted into the hierarchy to reconduce the conflict to the former typology. In this work, we extend the previously defined model by adding meronymic inclusion (i.e., part-of relations) for expressing heterogeneous aggregate entities. In the example presented in Sec. 4, the Workgroup concept is introduced as a nestable structure grouping employees in a company workforce. Similarly, different kinds of containment relations between resources are investigated. Authorizations are propagated according to the newly introduced relations and the modality conflicts arising from them are discussed.

## 2.1   Defining Ontologies with UML

The OMG Ontology Definition Metamodel (ODM) [4] provides UML-compliant modeling tools for representing the "specifications of conceptualizations" named *ontologies*. The ODM aims at bridging heterogeneous formats (e.g., OWL, RDF(S), Topic Maps, and Common Logic [8,7,11,1]) that may also feature different underlying semantics. We are primarily interested in the compatibility between UML and OWL with respect to the generalization structures introduced in [18] and the

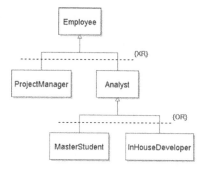

**Fig. 1.** A simple UML diagram describing a company structure

composition/aggregation structures investigated in this work. More exhaustive translation criteria can be found in [4,15,20]. Albeit more general, the notion of UML *class* comprises the OWL notion of class as a set of *instances*. Some properties can be immediately translated, such as multiple inheritance and subclasses covering the superclass. Binary UML associations can be translated into Object-Property and DatatypeProperty constructs from the OWL palette, according to the entities on both sides of the association. Instead, modeling n-ary associations and multiplicities requires, respectively, the insertion of a new class representing the association and the creation of an inverse property to model the multiplicities on both sides of the association. The owl:oneOf construct corresponds, in UML, to the explicit enumeration of a class as a set of individuals. Finally, OWL constructs such as symmetric and transitive properties cannot be directly translated into UML and require the adjoint OCL for specification. Other than relying on OCL for constraint specification, UML generalization hierarchies may also take advantage of a set of inter-relationship constraints to specify properties on subconcepts [19]. These constraints can be assimilated to well known operators in *Propositional Logic* (PL) and have been effectively modeled with OWL [22].

### 2.2 Modeling Constraints in Logics

Let us briefly examine how logic modeling of constraints is performed. The {OR} constraint, requiring a superclass instance to be an instance of at least one subclass, can be expressed with the owl:unionOf construct and has exactly the same semantics of the OR operator in PL. The {XR} constraint, requiring a superclass instance to be an instance of at most one subclass, can be expressed as the union of mutually disjoint subclasses. The similarity with the XOR (exclusive-or) operator of PL ends if we consider three or more subclasses: as an example, $a \, XOR \, b \, XOR \, c$ is true even when all three variables are true, while the {XR} constraint requires that a superclass individual belongs to exactly one subconcept. Fig. 1 shows a small section of company organization structuring concepts according to a generalization hierarchy. Inter-relationship constraints have been added to express that:

– Analysts are either MasterStudents or InHouseDevelopers. An Analyst can be both of them.
– Employees are made up by ProjectManagers and Analysts. ProjectManagers cannot be Analysts and vice-versa.

The structure depicted in Fig. 1 can be translated into the following set of DL axioms, substituting more verbose OWL constructs:

$$Analyst \doteq MasterStudent \sqcup InHouseDeveloper$$

$$Employee \doteq ProjectManager \sqcup Analyst$$

$$ProjectManager \sqsubseteq \neg Analyst$$

Other inter-relationship constraints are less interesting w.r.t. our specific task. Firstly, the {ND} constraint requires an instance to be member of at most $n-1$ of the $n$ subclasses of a concept. When considering only two subclasses, it is equivalent to the NAND operator of PL and can be expressed by disjointness. The {EQ} constraint is based on the logical equivalence operator and can be applied to concepts, properties, and instances by means of the OWL owl:equivalentClass, owl:equivalentProperty, and owl:sameAs constructs, respectively. Finally, the {IP} constraint models the implication operator by requiring an instance of the subclass indicated by the constraint to be also an instance of the previous $n - 1$ subclasses. Unfortunately, this constraint cannot be modeled properly with OWL concept definitions.

## 3    An Introduction to Mereology

Mereology, the theory of part-of relations, has an enormous background in early, medieval, and modern philosophy. There are also different meanings for "a portion of a given entity", according to a wide range of properties (whether the "part" can be detached from the "whole", whether the former is arbitrarily demarcated, etc.). Also the characterization of the partially ordered structures stemming from part-of relations (i.e., being a reflexive, antisymmetric, and transitive relation) has been debated. As an example, transitivity might be argued upon when considering the functional aspects of parthood (e.g., wheels can be considered functional parts of a vehicle but are clearly not functional parts of the car park hosting the vehicle). With respect to the specific scope of our research, we are primarily interested in a general notion of *cognitively salient* [3] components of an object i.e., those parts that can be distinguished as individual units, regardless of their interaction with the "whole". The functional aspects of meronymic inclusion can be separated from more generic membership properties as in [29], distinguishing between a) *component-object*, b) *feature-event*, and c) *member-collection* part-of relations. Typologies a) and b) can respectively be exemplified by images included in XHTML [9] pages and time-delimited fragments of movie clips. In our scenario, they can be merged for the purpose of structuring composite objects because we are essentially interested in whether an element can be part of more than one composite element or, referring to UML, whether the structure should be modeled as aggregation or composition. In Sec. 4 we will address this distinction when evaluating the enforcement options for authorizations. Finally, member-collection relations can be expressed with aggregation, are exemplified by the traditional notion of work group, and specifies no restriction on multiple relations of the same kind.

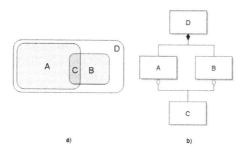

**Fig. 2.** a) Overlapping of parts; b) one possible representation in UML

In this work, we limit our scope to *proper parthood* (i.e., when it holds that $X$ being part of $Y$ automatically implies that $Y$ is not part of $X$) and *proper overlapping* (i.e., when $X$ overlapping $Y$ also implies that neither $X$ or $Y$ is a proper part of the other). In our model, proper overlapping is modeled by nesting proper parts: in the example of Fig. 2, $A$, $B$, and $C$ are parts of $D$, and $C$ is part of both $A$ and $B$. The inclusion properties relating $A$ and $B$ with $D$ can be exclusive (i.e., they can be modeled with composition); on the contrary, both $A$ and $B$ aggregate $C$ and none of these properties can be exclusive. The work presented in [14] proposes a model of part-of relations to be specifically used in Access Control infrastructures: it distinguishes between functional and non-functional part-of relations (named *shared* and *exclusive* aggregation), but also takes into account whether individual parts are bound to the life-cycle of the composite object. The *independent* aggregation of images included in a XHTML page, surviving the removal of the latter, can then be distinguished from the *dependent* aggregation of (logical) fragments of a movie clip that would cease to exist once the movie clip is removed. This is particularly important when implementing, other than a tout-court grant or denial of a resource, the sanitization of this (e.g., the removal of images in XHTML pages). We model this kind of dependence by introducing a new concept in the context ontology for typing atomic individuals that cannot be physically divided into components by the system.

### 3.1   Composition and Aggregation in OWL

Semantic Web languages primarily rely on generalization to build up data structures. Datatype and object properties, in conjunction with their possible characterizations (e.g., functionality, cardinality restrictions, etc.) provide the general-purpose means for modeling associations between individuals. Both composition and aggregation (respectively, functional and non-functional part-of relations) have no reserved construct in OWL. Although it is possible to define a class as the enumeration of its members, the notion of aggregation and composition that *enumerated classes* convey is limited. Firstly, we are interested in representing individuals (e.g., the work group ProjectABC in Fig. 3) that constitute composite structures grouping individuals (e.g., MaryJones and JohnSmith) and not in defining new concepts on the basis of individuals, because the terminology should not change as a consequence of the creation of new entities in the system's context representation. Moreover, nesting this category of structures amounts to considering classes as instances, resulting in OWL Full ontologies that cannot be considered for actual deployment of Semantic Web applications because they lack terminating decision procedures.

Representing composite entities as enumerated classes corresponds to the *set of sets* solution (SOS) presented in [30], that also presents another straightforward representation, the *union of sets* solution (UOS), in which also components are represented by class definitions. Since all these definitions are concept-level, it is awkward to apply the same technique to our use case because the entities in the context description are prone to change dynamically and this would imply radical changes in the terminology. Moreover, none of these representations takes into account the distinct notions of part-of relations our model aims to portray, presented in the beginning of this section. The work [30] also proposes an *instance solution* (IS) by adding a parallel class hierarchy to model the different relations. Object properties memberOf and its inverse hasMember are also added to relate composite entities, modeled as individuals, to the composing individuals. A more general approach for translating UML diagrams into OWL ontologies [20] also rules out the possibility of representing part-of relations with OWL built-in constructors and, similarly to the IS approach, relies on object properties and also distinguishes between functional and non-functional relations by considering both composition and aggregation. Number restrictions on properties can then represent cardinality constraints, as for more general associations. Integrating both the approaches, we will express composition and aggregation with object properties, and take advantage of a role hierarchy to consider composition and aggregation as one property for the purpose of policy propagation.

## 4   Extending Modelling Primitives

Using existing ontology-based representations to ground AC management policies over traditional AC structures, like RBAC *domains*, fosters reuse of expensive metadata [18]. Also, when using OWL sub-languages such as OWL Lite and OWL DL, well-known results of *Description Logics* [21] can be applied to check the consistency of policies and derive implicit information. In our model, context information is stored as a OWL ontology, whose root concept DomainConcept is sub-classed by:

- SubjectConcepts representing the categorization of subjects that will issue access requests to the system.

- ObjectConcepts modeling the actual resources referenced by authorizations as target objects.

Of course, the ontology can be extended with more DomainConcept subclasses to represent essentially any property that programming logics can bind to the model. As an example, in this paper we will add the CompositeEntity and CoherentEntity concepts for expressing, respectively, individuals aggregating individuals and, among them, those that cannot be separated from their parts. SubjectConcepts and ObjectConcepts are processed separatedly to carry out policy propagation and then compared for the purpose of conflict detection. Context descriptions are created by sub-classing existing concepts in a top-down approach or else by using union (⊔), intersection (⊓), and complement (¬) operators of DL. The same expressiveness can be used for defining domain scope expressions in authorizations. In this paper, we enrich context description with object properties representing composition and aggregation. Fig. 3 portrays the extended context information considered by our example w.r.t. subject entities: the categorization of employees introduced in Sec. 2.1 is extended with concept Workgroup, modeling groups of Employees within the organization. ProjectABC and BetaTestersABC are nested instances of Workgroup modeling, respectively, the employees participating in a software project and, among them, the employees participating in the testing of the application. These Workgroup instances aggregate individuals MaryJones and JohnSmith which are, respectively, instances of ProjectManager and MasterStudent. On the other hand, Fig. 4 portrays the context information associated with object entities: mutually disjoint concepts ClassifiedData and SecretData are the clearance levels that can characterize SensitiveData. Document and Footage represent typologies of resources stored by the system while Chart123 (a

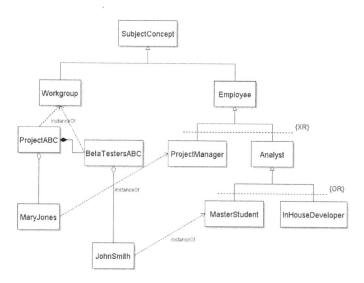

**Fig. 3.** UML diagram displaying context information associated with authorization subjects

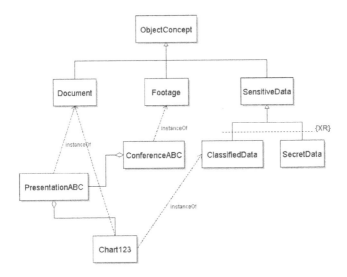

**Fig. 4.** UML diagram displaying context information associated with target objects

typical raster image), PresentationABC (which we assume to be in the XHTML file format[1]), and ConferenceABC (a recorded video) are individuals instantiated from these concepts. Aggregation links indicate that Chart123 has been embedded in PresenationABC and the presentation has been recorded in the ConferenceABC video footage.

### 4.1   Expressing Part-of Relations

The composition link in Fig. 3 corresponds, in the context ontology, to the pair of object properties componentOf and hasComponent, that are one the inverse of the other. We model the semantics of composition by requiring componentOf to be a functional property (i.e., an individual can be component of at most one individual). Should another Workgroup instance (say, DummyInstance) contain BetaTestersABC, the reasoner will assert that:

$$\text{ProjectABC } \textsf{owl:sameAs } \text{ DummyInstance}$$

This happens because of the functional (resp., inverse functional) restriction on property componentOf (resp., hasComponent). Should Workgroup instances be declared as distinct entities in the KB (with the owl:allDifferent construct), the reasoner will report the inconsistency of the terminology (TBox) w.r.t. the assertions in its extension (ABox). Object properties memberOf and hasMember (again, one the inverse of the other) model the aggregation links in Fig. 3 and 4, with no restriction on the number of distinct individuals an individual can be member of.

---

[1] We specify a XML file format to exemplify the sanitization of composite resources.

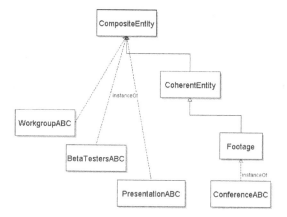

**Fig. 5.** The categorization of subjects and objects grounding policy propagation in part-of structures

In order to generalize inclusion relations for AC policy propagation, we group pairwise the object properties modeling composition and aggregation: property partOf (resp., hasPart) is introduced as a super-property of componentOf and memberOf (resp., hasComponent and hasMember). Moreover, authorizations are propagated across heterogeneous part-of relations by making partOf, and consequently hasPart, transitive properties. Finally, in order to model composite object that can only be released as a whole, we introduce the cross-cutting categorization of SubjectConcepts and ObjectConcepts shown in Fig. 5. Specifically, the CompositeEntity concept is defined as:

$$\mathsf{CompositeEntity} \doteq \exists\ \mathsf{hasPart.DomainConcept}$$

By doing this, it is not necessary to declaratively assert individuals as members of class CompositeEntity; instead, it will be the DL reasoner to derive this information. This concept is further sub-classed by CoherentEntity to represent composite entities that cannot be separated from their parts (in the example, instances of the Footage resource type). Unfortunately, it is up to the system administrator to determine which concepts or individuals should be considered entities of this kind, as for the Footage definition in Fig. 5.

## 5   Policy Propagation and Modality Conflict Detection

We are now ready to summarize the simple authorization model we use to exemplify modality conflict detection[2]. In order to represent authorization policies we need to identify the subject/object pair the authorization is applying to and the authorization mode (+ or −). Fig. 6 displays the authorizations considered by the example of conflict detection presented in this paper. Authorization A1 ap-

---

[2] Note that, as explained in [18], it is straightforward to extend the authorization model to encompass obligations.

```
Auth.  | Mode | Subject      | Object
============================================
   A1  |  +   | ProjectABC   | ObjectConcept
   A2  |  -   | Employee     | SensitiveData
```

**Fig. 6.** The authorizations considered by the example

plies, with positive mode, to the specific subject instance ProjectABC and to the most generic target object ObjectConcept. Authorization A2 applies, with negative mode, to the Employee concept as the subject and to the SensitiveData object concept. As in our previous work [18], authorizations are propagated to subsumed concepts in the domain representation model and to the corresponding individuals. Therefore, authorization A1 will apply to any ObjectConcept class and individual in the domain representation; particularly, Chart123. In a similar way, authorization A2 will apply to all Employee individuals in Fig. 3 and to individuals being categorized as either ClassifiedData or SecretData, comprising Chart123. In order to ground policy propagation, both the context ontology and domain scope expressions introduced by authorizations are classified with the Pellet DL reasoner [6]. Authorizations themselves are also featured in the ontology, in order to be related with subject and object expressions, but their definition do not represent the focus for explaining policy propagation criteria and is therefore not further described.

As a next step, traditional forward- and backward-chaining production rules, implemented in the Jena framework [2], carry out propagation of authorizations according to the classification structure processed by the DL reasoner. The results described in this article stem from the addition to these criteria of production rules propagating authorizations across part-of relations between concept instances. As an example, authorization A1 is directly propagated to subject MaryJones because she is member of ProjectABC. By virtue of the role hierarchy described in Sec. 4, the authorization will also propagate to BetaTestersABC along the composition link and then propagate to its member JohnSmith. Considering now the objects being addressed by authorizations, see Fig. 4, Chart123 is the only individual subjected to the negative authorization A2. However, production rules take care of back-propagating the authorization to individuals featuring Chart123 as a direct or indirect component. It is important to remark that, whereas the chain linking individuals in Fig. 4 is made of homogeneous relation types (both are aggregations), the enforcement of policy rules will behave differently according to the different notion of aggregation being considered. Specifically, the XPath [10] expression marking the position of Chart123 within PresentationABC allows to sanitize the latter resource before releasing it, thus avoiding authorization A2 to prevent access to the composite resource. Also, the part-of relation between Chart123 and PresentationABC i.e., the following assertion:

Chart123  memberOf  PresentationABC

may also be the product of an automated process parsing PresentationABC to determine its composing parts. On the contrary, the movie clip ConferenceABC is supposed to be accessible only as a whole and that a specific segment cannot be removed without human intervention[3]. Note that, individual ConferenceABC is inferred as member of class CoherentEntity by the DL reasoner because Footage has been defined as a subclass of the latter.

## 5.1   Detecting Modality Conflicts

After carrying out policy propagation, it is sufficient to query the KB for subjects being granted authorizations of opposite sign on the same object to obtain a listing of possible modality conflicts. As shown in [12], conflicts applying to whole concepts may sometimes be pruned from the list because they are implied by other conflicts. With regard to propagation due to the part-of relations introduced by our sample context, the different enforcement behaviors that the specific nature of resources allow for is reflected in the list of collisions shown in Fig. 7. The tuples are listing, respectively, the colliding policies (necessarily, the only pair we defined), the subject concepts, and the target objects addressed by the conflict. Note that PresenationABC is not flagged as a possible source of conflict because of the sanitization process the resource can be subjected to. Applying the specificity principle to target objects in Fig. 6, authorization A2

```
(+,-)   | Subject        | Object
=========================================
(A1,A2) | JohnSmith      | Chart123
(A1,A2) | JohnSmith      | ConferenceABC
(A1,A2) | MaryJones      | Chart123
(A1,A2) | MaryJones      | ConferenceABC
```

**Fig. 7.** The conflicts generated by the authorizations in Fig. 6

should generally override A1 because ObjectConcept is the root (i.e., least specific) concept modeling resources. On the contrary, authorization subjects ProjectABC and Employee cannot be easily compared: *domain nesting precedence* [25] or semantic similarity measures based on *path distance* [23,31] and *information content* [26,24] cannot be straightforwardly applied to resolve conflicts involving non-taxonomic relations, such as our extended context description model. Consequently, we compute the most specific concept ($msc$) [13] associated with individuals referenced by authorizations and conflicts, and integrate these concepts with the context hierarchy. Note that, in our model, the $msc$ can be finitely computed because we do not allow for cyclic concept definitions. Specifically, to resolve the first conflict in Fig. 7, we need to compute $msc$(ProjectABC) (referred to by authorization A1) and $msc$(JohnSmith). It is now possible to apply more general semantic similarity measures $s(.,.)$ [17] and compare authorization subjects with the entity addressed by the conflict:

---

[3] Of course, it is possible to achieve this automatically (knowing the time delimiters of the sensitive fragment) by embedding the movie in a SMIL presentation.

$$s(msc(\mathsf{ProjectABC}), msc(\mathsf{JohnSmith}))$$

$$s(\mathsf{Employee}, msc(\mathsf{JohnSmith}))$$

Should $msc(\mathsf{ProjectABC})$ prove to be more specific than Employee with respect to $msc(\mathsf{JohnSmith})$, the conflict would involve authorizations whose subjects and objects are, respectively, more and less specific than each other. In this case, the conflict cannot be resolved on the basis of the specificity principle and then different techniques or default behaviors (e.g., deny-takes-precedence) should be applied. We are currently evaluating, among the possible semantic similarity measures, the ones best fitting the specific requirements of modality conflicts resolution.

# 6    Conclusions and Outlook

A huge effort is being made to establish fully declarative, standard descriptions of contexts, environments and systems by means of semantic-Web style, logic-based formalisms like OWL. This process is now only beginning to show its impact on access control models and languages; but it is gaining importance, as it is widely acknowledged that organizations will not be able nor willing to maintain multiple, incompatible representations of their internal structure and resources for related purposes like access control and business process engineering. Still, evaluating access control policies based on Semantic Web metadata is not straightforward; rather, it poses a number of problems due to the high expressive power of DL-based languages. Evaluating the semantic status of a resource, e.g. along a path in the part-of relation graph, is a basic step toward taking an access description consistent with available knowledge about the resource itself. In this paper, we stated and addressed some crucial (though preliminary) problems posed by policy statement and evaluation in a Semantic Web scenario. However, much work remain to be done toward being able to perform this kind of computation efficiently, identifying and preventing conflicts on arbitrary ontologies. Our current research is aimed at providing a complete framework for Semantic Web-style access control.

# Acknowledgments

This work was supported in part by the European Union within the PRIME Project in the FP6/IST Programme under contract IST-2002-507591.

# References

1. The Common Logic Standard (CL). http://cl.tamu.edu/.
2. Jena, A Semantic Web Framework for Java. http://jena.sourceforge.net/.
3. Mereology, Stanford Encyclopedia of Philosophy. http://plato.stanford.edu/archives/spr2004/entries/mereology/.

4. OMG Ontology Definition Metamodel (ODM). http://www.omg.org/docs/ad/03-08-01.pdf.
5. OMG Unified Modeling Language (UML), version 2.0. http://www.omg.org/technology/ documents/formal/uml.htm.
6. Pellet OWL reasoner. http://www.mindswap.org/2003/pellet.
7. W3C Resource Description Framework (RDF). W3C Specifications - http://www.w3.org/RDF.
8. W3C Web Ontology Language (OWL). W3C Specifications - http://www.w3.org/2004/OWL.
9. XHTML 1.0 The Extensible Hypertext Markup Language. http://www.w3.org/TR/xhtml1/.
10. XML Path Language (XPath) 1.0. http://www.w3.org/TR/xpath.
11. XML Topic Maps (XTM). http://www.topicmaps.org/xtm/.
12. C. A. Ardagna, E. Damiani, S. De Capitani di Vimercati, C. Fugazza, and P. Samarati. Offline Expansion of XACML Policies Based on P3P Metadata. In *Fifth International Conference on Web Engineering (ICWE'05), July 25 - 29, 2005, Sydney, AU*, pages 363–374, 2005.
13. F. Baader, D. Calvanese, D. L. McGuinness, D. Nardi, and P. F. Patel-Schneider, editors. *The Description Logic Handbook: Theory, Implementation, and Applications*. Cambridge University Press, 2003.
14. E. Bertino, S. Jajodia, and P. Samarati. Access control in object-oriented database systems - some approaches and issues. In *Advanced Database Systems*, pages 17–44, London, UK, 1993. Springer-Verlag.
15. S. Brockmans, R. Volz, A. Eberhart, and P. Löffler. Visual Modeling of OWL DL Ontologies Using UML. In *International Semantic Web Conference (ISWC 2004), November 7-11, Hiroshima, JA*, pages 198–213, 2004.
16. S. Cook, A. Kleppe, R. Mitchell, B. Rumpe, J. Warmer, and A. Wills. The amsterdam manifesto on OCL. In *Object Modeling with the OCL*, pages 115–149, 2002.
17. C. d'Amato, N. Fanizzi, and F. Esposito. A semantic similarity measure for expressive Description Logics. In A. Pettorossi, editor, *Proceedings of Convegno Italiano di Logica Computazionale (CILC05), June 21-22 2005, Rome, IT*, 2005.
18. E. Damiani, S. De Capitani di Vimercati, C. Fugazza, and P. Samarati. Modality Conflicts in Semantics-Aware Access Control. In *Sixth International Conference on Web Engineering (ICWE'06), July 11-14, 2006, Palo Alto, CA, USA*. ACM, July 2006.
19. J. P. Davis and R. D. Bonnell. A Taxonomy of Propositional Logic Constraint Patterns for the Unified Modeling Language. http://www.cse.sc.edu/jimdavis/Research/Papers-PDF/TKDE-paper-040113.pdf.
20. K. Falkovych, M. Sabou, and H. Stuckenschmidt. UML for the Semantic Web: Transformation-Based Approaches. In *B. Omelayenko and M. Klein, editors, Knowledge Transformation for the Semantic Web*, pages 92–106. IOS Press, 2003.
21. I. Horrocks and P. Patel-Schneider. Reducing OWL entailment to description logic satisfiability. *Journal of Web Semantics*, 1(4):345–357, 2004.
22. C. R. Kothari and D. J. Russomanno. Modeling Logic-Based Constraints in OWL. In *IASTED International Conference on Databases and Applications, part of the 22nd Multi-Conference on Applied Informatics, Innsbruck, Austria, February 17-19, 2004*, 2004. http://engronline.ee.memphis.edu/objectoriented/411-160.pdf.
23. C. Leacock and M. Chodorow. Combining local context and WordNet similarity for word sense identification. In C. Fellbaum, editor, *WordNet, An Electronic Lexical Database*, pages 265–283. MIT Press, 1998.

24. D. Lin. An information-theoretic definition of similarity. In *Proc. 15th International Conf. on Machine Learning, July 24-27, 1998, Madison, WI, USA*, pages 296–304. Morgan Kaufmann, 1998.

25. E. C. Lupu and M. S. Sloman. Conflict Analysis for Management Policies. In *Proceedings of the 5th IFIP/IEEE International Symposium on Integrated Network management IM'97, San Diego, CA, USA*, 1997.

26. P. Resnik. Using Information Content to Evaluate Semantic Similarity in a Taxonomy. In *International Joint Conference on Artificial Intelligence (IJCAI), August 20-25 Montréal, Québec, CA*, pages 448–453, 1995.

27. P. Resnik. Semantic Similarity in a Taxonomy: An Information-Based Measure and its Application to Problems of Ambiguity in Natural Language. *Journal of Artificial Intelligence Research*, 11:95–130, 1999.

28. R. Sandhu. Rationale for the RBAC96 family of access control models. In *RBAC '95: Proceedings of the first ACM Workshop on Role-based access control*, pages 9–17, New York, NY, USA, 1996. ACM Press.

29. V. C. Storey. Understanding semantic relationships. *The VLDB Journal*, 2(4):455–488, October 1993.

30. C. Veres. Aggregation in Ontologies: Practical Implementations in OWL. In *Fifth International Conference on Web Engineering (ICWE'05), July 25-29, 2005, Sydney, AU*, pages 285–295, 2005.

31. Z. Wu and M. Palmer. Verb semantics and lexical selection. In *32nd. Annual Meeting of the Association for Computational Linguistics, New Mexico State University, Las Cruces, New Mexico*, pages 133–138, 1994.

# Specification and Realization of Access Control in SPKI/SDSI

N.V. Narendra Kumar[1] and R.K. Shyamasundar[1,2]

[1] School of Technology and Computer Science
Tata Institute of Fundamental Research
Mumbai, India 400005
{naren,shyam}@tcs.tifr.res.in
[2] IBM - India Research Lab
New Delhi, India 110016

**Abstract.** SACL is an access control language based on SPKI/SDSI PKI that has features like group certificates, delegation, threshold certificates etc. In this paper, we show how SACL can be effectively realized in a Security Automata framework. We establish the equivalence of the transformation with the SPKI/SDSI semantics as well as the set-theoretic semantics. The transformation gives an efficient way to enforce the policy being defined and allows inference of authorizations obtained from multiple certificates. Further, we describe algorithms for efficiently solving certificate-analysis problems, resource authentication problems etc. The transformation allows us to capture the authorization of tags while being delegated in an unambiguous way and, define the set of tags permissible under threshold certification. The framework succinctly captures the expressive power of SACL and enables heterogenous integration of SACL with state-based security mechanisms that are widely used for protection/security of classical OS, Databases etc. One of the distinct advantages of the framework is the amenability of using finite state model-checking algorithms for verifying access control. We shall show how very useful properties can be verified using our transformation.

## 1   Introduction

When resources are shared, we need access control mechanisms for protection and security. Sharing resources are needed in centralized systems (file management in an operating system), in distributed systems (sharing resources on internet), in collaborative efforts. Access control in centralized systems is relatively simpler as protection is the main issue and identity is kept outside the access control mechanisms. However, in distributed systems identity management need to be handled in the access control itself as remote access is the normal order. Thus, trust management systems play a vital role. In the technology of trust management systems, public key infrastructure (PKIs) plays a vital role. One of the nicely articulated PKIs is the SPKI/SDSI system proposed in [4] that supports delegation, threshold features etc. SPKI/SDSI is one of the prominently studied

A. Bagchi and V. Atluri (Eds.): ICISS 2006, LNCS 4332, pp. 177–193, 2006.

technologies for trust management systems. Our present work is motivated by issues considered in [3,7,6].

In SPKI/SDSI, name certificates define the names available in an issuers local name space; authorization certificates grant authorizations, or delegate the ability to grant authorizations. SPKI/SDSI Access Control specification (SACL) is a set of name and authorization certificates specified in terms of rewrite systems. In [3], Clarke et al considered the problem of discovering a certificate chain for an authorization with respect to a set of SPKI/SDSI certificates; a certificate chain provides a proof that a client's public key is one of the keys that has been authorized to access a given resource either directly or transitively, via one or more name-definition or authorization-delegation steps.

Schneider [8] has proposed security automata model for arriving at computational characteristics of security policies. One such class is the category of security policies enforceable with mechanisms that work just by monitoring system execution.

In this paper, we shall show how an SACL can be realized via security automata [8] - one of the well established models of realizing ACL. The crux of such a realization is based on first transforming SACL to a finite state transition system. We establish the equivalence of the transformation with the SPKI/SDSI semantics as well as set-theoretic semantics and describe algorithms for efficiently solving certificate-analysis, resource authentication problems. An additional advantage of such a transformation is that it is possible to capture the authorization of tags while being delegated in an unambiguous way and further, makes it possible to define the set of tags (and also possible implications of combinations whenever defined) permissible under threshold certification. The underlying finite state transformation permits the use of efficient model checking algorithms for verifying properties of SACL. We shall illustrate the uses of approach for resource authentication etc, and provide a comparison with other models such as Li et.al [7], Jha et.al el [6].

Rest of the paper is organized as follows: In section 2 we define SACL. In section 3 we show how SACL can be transformed into a finite state transition system which allows us to realize the control through the security automata framework. We end with a discussion, in section 4, on how our approach can lead to efficient enforcement of possible extensions to SACL and other access control policies.

## 2    SACL

In this section we define SACL, an access control language based on SPKI/SDSI PKI. We start by giving a brief overview of SPKI/SDSI in section 2.1.

### 2.1    SPKI/SDSI

In this section we provide the basic definitions of SPKI/SDSI as in [3,6].

**Names.** In SPKI/SDSI, all principals are represented by their public keys. A *principal* is an individual, process or any other active entity. $\mathcal{K}$ denotes the set of all public keys. An *identifier* is a word over some alphabet $\Sigma$. The set of all identifiers is denoted by $\mathcal{A}$.

A *term* is a key followed by 0 or more identifiers. $\mathcal{T}$ denotes the set of all possible terms. A *local name* is of the form K A, where $K \in \mathcal{K}$ and $A \in \mathcal{A}$.

**Certificates.** SPKI/SDSI has two types of certificates, or certs. The first type of certificate called a *name cert*, provides definitions of local names. Authorizations are specified using *authorization certs* (or *auth certs*, for short).

**Name Certificates.** A name cert provides a definition of a local name in the issuer's local name space. A name cert $C$ is a signed four-tuple(K,A,S,V):

- The issuer K is a public key and the certificate is signed by K.
- A is an identifier.
- The subject S is a term in $\mathcal{T}$. Intuitively, S gives additional meaning for the local name K A.
- The *validity specification* V provides information regarding the validity of the certificate. Usually, the validity specification V takes the form of an interval $[t_1, t_2]$, i.e., the cert is valid from time $t_1$ to $t_2$ inclusive. A validity specification can also take the form of an on-line check to be performed.

A name cert $(K, A, S, V)$ can also be denoted by the rewrite rule $K A \mapsto S$. The purpose of name certs is to associate principals with local names, thereby also associating principals with terms. Given a name $K A_1 A_2 ... A_n$, we can use the name cert $(K, A_1, K', V)$ to reduce it to $K' A_2 ... A_n$. By repeatedly applying this reduction we get the set of principals associated with the name $K A_1 A_2 ... A_n$, called the valuation of the name. Two name certs $C_1 = (K, A, K_1 A_1 A_2 ... A_n, V)$ and $C_2 = (K_1, A_1, K_2 B_1 ... B_m, V')$ can be combined to yield a name cert $C_3 = C_1 C_2 = (K, A, K_2 B_1 ... B_m A_2 ... A_n, VI(V, V'))$. $VI$ is defined as validity intersection, succeeds if intersection is well defined.

**Authorization Certificates.** An Auth cert grants or delegates a specific authorization from an issuer to a subject. Specifically, an auth cert $C$ is a five-tuple (K,S,D,T,V):

- The issuer K is a public key, which signs the cert. The issuer is the one granting a specific authorization.
- The subject S is a term. All the public keys that are in the valuation of S are granted authorization.
- If the *delegation bit* D is turned on, then the key receiving this authorization can delegate this authorization to other keys.
- The *authorization specification* or *authorization tag* T specifies the specific permission or permissions being granted.
- The *validity specification* V, for an auth cert is the same as that for a name cert.

The auth certs $(K, S, 1, T, V)$, $(K, S, 0, T, V)$ can be denoted by the rewrite rules $K \square_T \mapsto S \square_T$ and $K \square_T \mapsto S \blacksquare_T$ respectively. The meaning of an authorization cert $(K, S, D, T, V)$ is that all the principals associated with the name $S$ are authorized by the principal $K$ to access the resource $T$. In addition if $D = 1$, these principals may further delegate this authority. Given an auth cert $C_1 = (K, K_1 A_1 A_2 ... A_n, D, T_1, V_1)$ and a name cert $C_2 = (K_1, A_1, K_2 B_1 ... B_m, V_2)$, they can be combined to yield an auth cert $C_3 = C_1 C_2 = (K, K_2 B_1 ... B_m A_2 ... A_n, D, T_1, VI(V_1, V_2))$ provided $VI$ succeeds.

Given two auth certs $C_1 = (K_1, K_2, 1, T_1, V_1)$ and $C_2 = (K_2, S_2, D, T_2, V_2)$, they can be combined to yield an auth cert $C_3 = C_1 C_2 = (K_1, S_2, D, TI(T_1, T_2), VI(V_1, V_2))$ provided $TI$ and $VI$ succeed. In our presentation we assume that the authorization tags are sets of strings that represent permissions over a resource. So, $TI$ succeeds only if $T_1$ and $T_2$ represent permissions over the same resource, and their intersection is well defined. $VI$ is defined as validity intersection, succeeds if intersection is well defined.

We assume that each resource $T$ has a unique owner denoted $K_{owner[T]}$. A principal $K$ will be granted permission to access resource $T$, if the cert $(K_{owner[T]}, K, D, T, V)$ can be derived from the given set of certs using the reduction rules. It is the responsibility of the principal $K$ requesting access, to find the Graph of certs that will be used in the derivation, and to submit it along with request.

## 2.2  SACL

SACL is the language in which we give access control specifications. An access control specification in SACL consists of a set of name certs and auth certs. Access control specifications in SACL have features like group certificates, authorization delegation, threshold certificates etc. Authorization certificates in SACL include threshold certificates like $(K, \theta_m(S_1, S_2, ..., S_n), D, T', V)$. This certificate means that a request to access permissions in $T'$ will be granted only if the set of keys signing the request are in the valuations of at least m out of the n names.

**SACL example.** The set of certificates given in Figure 1, is an example of how an access control specification will be given in SACL. Suppose that $K_3$ wants to *read, write* and *execute* a file $F$. Given the following SACL $\mathcal{E}$, $K_3$ has to prove that he is authorized to do so.

$C_1 = (K_{owner[F]}, A, K_1, \cdot)$, $C_2 = (K_{owner[F]}, B, K_1 C, \cdot)$, $C_3 = (K_1, C, K_3, \cdot)$
$C_4 = (K_1, C, K_4, \cdot)$, $C_5 = (K_2, A, K_{owner[F]} AC, \cdot)$, $C_6 = (K_3, E, K_2, \cdot)$
$C_7 = (K_{owner[F]}, K_1 C, 0, \{read\}, \cdot)$, $C_8 = (K_{owner[F]}, K_1, 1, \{read, write\}, \cdot)$
$C_9 = (K_{owner[F]}, K_2, 1, \{exec\}, \cdot)$, $C_{10} = (K_1, K_3, 1, \{read, write\}, \cdot)$
$C_{11} = (K_4, K_3, 0, \{read\}, \cdot)$, $C_{12} = (K_3, K_2, 1, \{write\}, \cdot)$
$C_{13} = (K_2, K_3, 0, \{write, exec\}, \cdot)$

**Fig. 1.** Set $\mathcal{E}$ of certs

# 3  Transforming SACL into Security Automata Framework

In this section we show that a given SACL can be modeled as a **Finite State Transition System**(referred to as *FSTS* henceforth). We also show how this model can be used to answer various certificate-analysis problems.

*Notation*

- $Id = \{N_1, N_2, ..., N_l\}$ denotes the set of name certs
- $Au = \{D_1, D_2, ..., D_m\}$ denotes the set of auth certs
- $\mathcal{C} = Id \cup Au$ denotes the set of certificates that specifies an SACL
- $\mathcal{K}_\mathcal{C}$ denotes the set of public keys appearing in $\mathcal{C}$
- $\mathcal{A}_\mathcal{C}$ denotes the set of identifiers appearing in $\mathcal{C}$
- $T_\mathcal{C}$ denotes the set of authorization tags appearing in $\mathcal{C}$.

## 3.1  Finite State Transition System Equivalent of SACL

Let $\mathcal{C}$ be the SACL. For simplicity, let us assume that all invalid certs are removed.
We construct a *FSTS* $\mathcal{M}_\mathcal{C} \triangleq (Q, \Sigma, \delta)$ where

- $Q = \mathcal{K}_\mathcal{C}$ public keys act as states
- $\Sigma = \mathcal{A}_\mathcal{C} \cup (T_\mathcal{C} \times \{0,1\})$

We systematically construct the transition function (initially empty) $\delta : Q \times \Sigma \to 2^Q$. Let $\hat{\delta} : Q \times \Sigma^* \to 2^Q$, be the extended transition function corresponding to $\delta$, defined in the standard way.

### Algorithm for constructing the model

1. For each name cert of the form $(K, A, K_1, V)$ do
   $\delta(K, A) := \delta(K, A) \cup \{K_1\}$
2. For each name cert of the form $(K, A, K_1 A_1...A_n, V)$, n $\geqslant$ 1, do
   $\delta(K, A) := \delta(K, A) \cup \hat{\delta}(K_1, A_1...A_n)$
3. Repeat Step 2 until no further changes
4. For each auth cert of the form $(K, K_1, D, T, V)$ do
   $\delta(K, (T, D)) := \delta(K, (T, D)) \cup \{K_1\}$
5. For each auth cert of the form $(K, K_1 A_1...A_n, D, T, V)$, n $\geqslant$ 1, do
   $\delta(K, (T, D)) := \delta(K, (T, D)) \cup \hat{\delta}(K_1, A_1...A_n)$

The above algorithm can be easily seen to be terminating, since a certificate in step2 can add at most $|\mathcal{K}|$ edges and at least one edge gets added in each iteration of step2. FSTS obtained for the SACL described in Figure 1 is shown in Figure 2. For simplicity we denote $K_{owner[F]}$ as $K_F$.

The intended meaning in our model is that $\delta(K, A)$ captures the set of principals associated with the local name $KA$. Now, we proceed to prove that, $\delta$ as

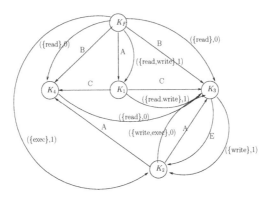

**Fig. 2.** FSTS for the example in Figure 1

we have defined in our model correctly captures the set-theoretic semantics of name certs formalized by Li and Mitchell [7].

Given any function $f : \mathcal{K} \times \mathcal{A} \to 2^{\mathcal{K}}$ mapping local names to sets of principals, $f$ can be extended to a valuation $\mathcal{V}_f : \mathcal{K} \times \mathcal{A}^* \to 2^{\mathcal{K}}$ on all name strings as follows:

$$\mathcal{V}_f(K) = \{K\}$$
$$\mathcal{V}_f(KA) = f(KA)$$
$$\mathcal{V}_f(K_1 A_1 ... A_l) = \bigcup_{K_2 \in f(K_1 A_1)} \mathcal{V}_f(K_2 A_2 ... A_l) \text{ where } l > 1.$$

The semantics $\mathcal{M}[\mathcal{C}] : \mathcal{K} \times \mathcal{A} \to 2^{\mathcal{K}}$ of a set $\mathcal{C}$ of name certs is the least function $f : \mathcal{K} \times \mathcal{A} \to 2^{\mathcal{K}}$ that satisfies the system of set containments

$$S_{\mathcal{C}} = \{f(KA) \supseteq \mathcal{V}_f(S) | KA \mapsto S \in \mathcal{C}\}$$

**Proposition 1.** *Given a set $\mathcal{C}$ of name certs, a local name $KA$, and a principal $K'$, $\delta(K, A) \ni K'$ iff $\mathcal{M}[\mathcal{C}](K, A) \ni K'$. As an immediate consequence we have, for any term $K_1 A_1 ... A_n$, and a principal $K'$, $\hat{\delta}(K_1, A_1, ..., A_n) \ni K'$ iff $\mathcal{V}_{\mathcal{M}[\mathcal{C}]}(K_1, A_1, ..., A_n) \ni K'$.*

In our model, we intend that $\delta(K, (T, 0))$ captures the set of principals authorized by $K$ to access resource $T$, also that $\delta(K, (T, 1))$ captures the set of principals authorized by $K$ to access resource $T$ and further delegate this authority. Now we prove that $\delta$ as defined in our model correctly captures the meaning of certs, by proving it equivalent to the name reduction closure algorithm by Clarke et.al [3].

A cert $C = L \mapsto R$ is said to be reducing if $|L| > |R|$, where $|X|$ denotes the length of the sequence $X$. If $\mathcal{C}$ is a set of certs, then the name-reduction closure $\mathcal{C}^{\sharp}$ of $\mathcal{C}$ is defined to be the smallest set of certs containing $\mathcal{C}$ and closed under *name-reduction*(composing with reducing certificates).

**Proposition 2.** *Let $\mathcal{C}$ be a set of certs. Let $\mathcal{C}^{\sharp}$ be the name reduction closure of $\mathcal{C}$.*

1. *A cert $KA \mapsto K' \in \mathcal{C}^{\sharp}$ iff $\delta(K, A) \ni K'$.*
2. *A cert $K\square \mapsto K'\square \in \mathcal{C}^{\sharp}$ iff $\delta(K, (T, 1)) \ni K'$.*
3. *A cert $K\square \mapsto K'\blacksquare \in \mathcal{C}^{\sharp}$ iff $\delta(K, (T, 0)) \ni K'$.*

## 3.2   Verifying Authorizations in SACL Using FSTS

In this section, we show how the FSTS model can be used to verify the authorization requests in the given SACL. The authorization problem can be described as follows:

Given an SACL, in order that the request $(K', T')$ be honored, principal $K'$ needs to provide a proof (which is in the form of a Graph of certificates) to the principal $K_{owner[T']}$ that $K'$ is authorized to access $T'$.

Li et.al [7] has argued that the semantics of authorization as defined in [3,6] are incomplete, compared to the logical characterization they presented. The example given was that consider the two 5-tuples $(K, K_1, 0, (* \ set \ read \ write), V)$ and $(K, K_1, 0, (* \ set \ delete), V)$, then the query $(K, K_1, 0, (* \ set \ read \ delete), V)$ should be true. However, there is no rule that lets us combine authorizations received from multiple 5-tuples.

To be able to handle the above case, we introduce a new rule that lets us combine authorizations received from multiple auth certs. Given two auth certs $C_1 = (K_1, K, D_1, T_1, V_1)$ and $C_2 = (K_1, K, D_2, T_2, V_2)$, they can be combined to yield an auth cert $C_3 = C_1 + C_2 = (K_1, K, min(D_1, D_2), TU(T_1, T_2), VI(V_1, V_2))$, provided $TU$ and $VI$ succeed. $TU$ is defined as tag union, succeeds only if $T_1$ and $T_2$ represent permissions over the same resource. $VI$ is defined as validity intersection, succeeds if intersection is well defined.

Now we give an algorithm for the authorization problem in which we also make use of the rule for combining authorizations obtained from multiple certificates described above.

### Algorithm for Authorization problem

#### Remove useless edges from the model:

1. From $\mathcal{M}_C$ remove those edges which correspond only to name certs, to get $\mathcal{M}'_C$
2. Remove those edges from $\mathcal{M}'_C$ such that $\delta(K, (T, D)) \ni K_1$ where $T \cap T' = \emptyset$, to get $\mathcal{M}''_C$
3. Remove those edges from $\mathcal{M}''_C$ such that $\delta(K, (T, 0)) \ni K_1$ where $K_1 \neq K'$, to get $\mathcal{M}'''_C$
4. Let $\mathcal{M}_0 = \mathcal{M}'''_C \cap T'$ ie, let $\mathcal{M}_0$ be the graph obtained from $\mathcal{M}'''_C$ after intersecting the tag in the label on each edge with $T'$

#### Label the nodes with auth tags they are allowed to access:

5. Set the label of $K_{owner[T']}$ to $T'$, and that of every other node(principal) in $\mathcal{M}_0$ other than $K'$ to $\emptyset$ and mark all the edges *red*. $K'$ will have two labels associated with it, label1 corresponds to auth tags it can delegate and label2 corresponds to auth tags it can not delegate, both initially $\emptyset$. Whenever we talk about the label of $K'$ we are referring to label1. We also associate rank with the edges of $\mathcal{M}_0$. Let $i = 1$.
6. If a node $K$ is labeled $T$ currently, and there is a *red* edge from $K$ to $K_1$ labeled $(T_1, 1)$ or $K$ to $K'$ labeled $(T_1, 0)$, such that $T_1 \subseteq T$, then mark the edge *green* and set the rank of the edge to $i$.

7. If there is a green edge of rank $i$ with label $(T, 1)$ into node $K$, then set $label(K) = label(K) \cup T$. If there is a green edge of rank $i$ with label $(T, 0)$ into node $K'$, then set $label2(K') = label2(K') \cup T$.
8. $i = i + 1$
9. Repeat steps 6,7 and 8 until convergence
10. If now the $label1(K') \cup label2(K') = T'$, then we conclude that principal $K'$ has authorization to $T'$, else terminate with FAIL. To actually find the Graph that serves as a proof of authorization do the following

**Find the graph that serves as a proof of the required authorization:**

11. Remove all the *red* edges from the final graph and initialize a queue $Q'$ to contain $(K', T', \infty)$ as its only element, and define $\infty$ to be greater than the rank of any edge
12. Let the entry at the front of the $Q'$ be $(K, T, r)$, if $K = K_{owner[T']}$, remove it from the $Q'$, move on to next element in the $Q'$, else, set $current = T$ and do the following
13. Let $K_1$ be a predecessor of $K$ in the graph and let $(T_1, D)$ be the label on an edge of rank $r'$ between them, if $r > r'$, mark that edge *blue*, set $current = current - T_1$ and insert $(K_1, T_1, r')$ into the $Q'$
14. Repeat step13 until $current$ becomes $\emptyset$
15. Remove $(K, T, r)$ from $Q'$, go to step12 if $Q'$ is nonempty
16. The *blue* subgraph of the final graph obtained gives us the required proof, from this we can compute the set of certificates and indicate which rule was applied to which certificates, see the section 3.5 below

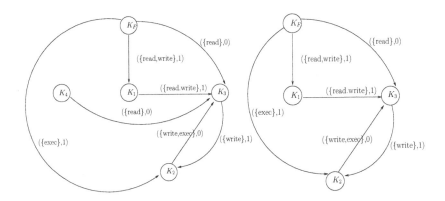

**Fig. 3.** Intermediate graphs during model checking

Iterations of steps 6,7 and 8 of the algorithm will terminate, because in each iteration of step6 at least one red edge will be marked green and there are only finitely many red edges. Also, because of this rank of any edge will be a finite number. An entry $(K, T, r)$ in $Q'$ causes only finitely many entries to be made into $Q'$, and if $(K, T, r)$ causes an entry $(K_1, T_1, r_1)$ then $r_1 < r$ is guaranteed.

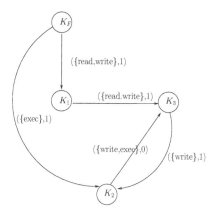

**Fig. 4.** Final graph obtained after model checking

Because of this and the fact that rank is bounded from below by 0, we can argue that iterations of steps 12,13 and 14 will terminate. Thus it can be seen that our algorithm for authorization problem terminates.

The following theorem establishes the correctness of the algorithm by establishing the equivalence with the certificate chain discovery algorithm of [3].

**Theorem 1.** *Given a set $\mathcal{C}$ of certs, a principal $K'$ is granted authorization to access resource $T'$ by our model checking procedure if $K'$ is granted authorization to access resource $T'$ by Clarke et.al's [3] Certificate-chain discovery algorithm.*

*Proof.* Proposition 2, together with the fact that their certificate chain discovery algorithm is a special case of the model checking algorithm described above, prove the claim.

In fact, our system achieves a stronger inference as it can use the semantic information associated with authorization tags. Thus, we will be able to conclude that principal $K$ is authorized to perform an operation $T$ on a resource, if we can derive that $K$ is authorized to perform the set of operations $T'$ on the same resource and if $T$ is implied by $T'$. We shall not go into further details for lack of space.

### 3.3   Implementing SACL Using Security Automata

Schneider [8] has proposed a class of automata referred to as Security Automata and has characterized various families based upon properties of the underlying security policies. In this section, we shall provide a basic definition as given in [8] and show that an SACL can be efficiently implemented as a security automata.

A *security automata* is a Buchi automata defined by:

- a countable set $Q$ of *automaton states*
- a countable set $Q_0 \subseteq Q$ of *initial automaton states*

- a countable set $I$ of *input symbols*
- a transition function, $\delta : Q \times I \to 2^Q$

Set $I$ of input symbols is dictated by the security policy being enforced and the manner in which target executions are being represented. To process a sequence $s_1, s_2, \ldots$ of input symbols, the *current state* $Q'$ of the security automaton starts equal to $Q_0$ and the sequence is read one input symbol at a time. As each input symbol $s_i$ is read, the security automaton changes $Q'$ to $\bigcup_{q \in Q'} \delta(q, s_i)$. If $Q'$ is ever the empty set, then the input is rejected; otherwise the input is accepted.

We now show how an SACL specification can be realized in a security automata. Let *construct_FSTS* be transition system equivalent generated for the given SACL, after removing the invalid certs. Let *label* be a procedure that labels the nodes of an FSTS with two labels *label1* and *label2*. *label1(k)* denotes the set of auth tags that $k$ has access to and can further delegate, and *label2(k)* denotes the set of auth tags that $k$ has access to but can not further delegate.

Since the state space is huge and the transition relation $\delta$ is complex, we use an alternate representation for the security automata. We encode the current state information of the security automata using **state variables**, and use **guarded commands** to describe the transitions of the automata. Transitions in the security automaton are specified using predicates defined on the input symbols that correspond to a next step of the targets execution. The following predicates will be useful:

$req(K, T)$ : principal $K$ invoked an operation requiring authorization to $T$
$add\_Id(K, A, S, V)$ : principal $K$ invoked an operation to define local name $KA$
$rm\_Id(K, A, S, V)$ : principal $K$ invoked an operation to remove the association of the local name $KA$ to the name $S$
$add\_Au(K, S, D, T, V)$ : principal $K$ invoked an operation to delegate authorization for tag $T$ to the term $S$
$rm\_Id(K, S, D, T, V)$ : principal $K$ invoked an operation to delegate authorization for tag $T$ to the term $S$

Let **Date** be the date domain.

### Security Automata definition

### State Variables

$\mathcal{K}$ : set of **keys** initially $\mathcal{K}^*$
$\mathcal{A}$ : set of **idents** initially $\emptyset$
$T_*$ : set of auth **tags** initially $\emptyset$
$Id$ : set of name certs, initially $\emptyset$,
   ⟨K:**keys**,A:**idents**,S:**keys** ×**idents**\*,V:**Date**×**Date**⟩
$Au$ : set of auth certs, initially $\emptyset$
   ⟨K:**keys**,S:**keys**×**idents**\*, D:{0,1},T:**tags**,V:**Date**×**Date**⟩
$M = (Q, \Sigma, \delta)$, where $Q = \mathcal{K}$, $\Sigma = \mathcal{A} \cup (T_* \times \{0,1\})$ and $\delta \subseteq Q \times \Sigma \times Q$, initially $(\mathcal{K}^*, \emptyset, \emptyset)$
$label1 : \mathcal{K} \to 2^{T_*}$ initially $\emptyset$
$label2 : \mathcal{K} \to 2^{T_*}$ initially $\emptyset$

**Transitions:**

1. $req(K,T) \wedge (T \subseteq TU(T',T''))$ for some $T' \in label1(K) \wedge T'' \in label2(K)) \rightarrow$
   $skip$
2. $add\_Id(K,A,K_1A_1...A_n,V) \rightarrow Id := Id \cup \{(K,A,K_1A_1...A_n,V)\}, \mathcal{K} := \mathcal{K} \cup$
   $\{K,K_1\}, \mathcal{A} := \mathcal{A} \cup \{A,A_1,...,A_n\}, M = construct\_FSTS(Id,Au), label(M)$
3. $rm\_Id(K,A,K_1A_1...A_n,V) \rightarrow Id := Id - \{(K,A,K_1A_1...A_n,V)\},$
   $M = construct\_FSTS(Id,Au), label(M)$
4. $add\_Au(K,K_1A_1...A_n,D,T,V) \rightarrow Au := Au \cup \{(K,K_1A_1...A_n,D,T,V)\},$
   $\mathcal{K} := \mathcal{K} \cup \{K,K_1\}, \mathcal{A} := \mathcal{A} \cup \{A_1,...,A_n\}, \mathcal{T}_* := \mathcal{T}_* \cup \{T\},$
   $M = (Q,\Sigma,\delta')$ where $\delta' = \delta \cup \{\langle K,(T,D),K'\rangle | K' \in \hat{\delta}(K_1,A_1...A_n)\}, label(M)$
5. $rm\_Au(K,K_1A_1...A_n,D,T,V) \rightarrow Au := Au - \{(K,K_1A_1...A_n,D,T,V)\},$
   $M = construct\_FSTS(Id,Au), label(M).$

## 3.4    Complexity of the Algorithm

Let $n_{\mathcal{K}}$ be the number of public keys that appear in the set $\mathcal{C}$ of certs. Let $n_{\mathcal{L}}, n_{\mathcal{A}}$ be the number of name certs and auth certs in $\mathcal{C}$ respectively. Let $m_1, m_2$ be the sum of the lengths of the righthand sides of the name certs, auth certs in $\mathcal{C}$ respectively.

First, let us analyze the time taken to construct the model $\mathcal{M_C}$. Iterations of Step 2 will clearly be the bottleneck. To compute $\hat{\delta}(K_1, A_1...A_l)$ will take time $O(n_{\mathcal{K}}l)$. So, each iteration of Step 2 will take time $O(n_{\mathcal{K}}m_1)$. Also, each local name ie, $\delta(K,A)$ can have utmost $n_{\mathcal{K}}$ keys associated to it. So the overall running time for steps 1,2 and 3 will be $O(n_{\mathcal{K}}^2 m_1)$. Time taken for steps 4 and 5 is clearly $O(n_{\mathcal{K}}m_2)$. So, the overall running time to construct the model $\mathcal{M_C}$ will be $O(n_{\mathcal{K}}^2 m_1 + n_{\mathcal{K}}m_2)$.

The time complexity of the model checking algorithm described in section 3.2 is obtained as follows: The number of keys that can be associated to a local name by a defining name cert can utmost be $n_{\mathcal{K}}$. So, there can be at most $O(n_{\mathcal{K}}n_{\mathcal{L}})$ of edges labeled with identifiers in $\mathcal{M_C}$. So, step 1 of the algorithm can be carried out in time $O(n_{\mathcal{K}}n_{\mathcal{L}})$. Steps 2,3,4 and 5 can be done in $O(n_{\mathcal{K}}n_{\mathcal{A}})$ time. In each execution of step 6 at least one edge is marked *green*. So, iterations of steps 6,7 and 8 can also be executed in $O(n_{\mathcal{K}}n_{\mathcal{A}})$ time. Step 11 can be executed in time $O(n_{\mathcal{K}}n_{\mathcal{A}})$. Steps 12,13,14 and 15 can be performed in time $O(n_{\mathcal{K}}|T'|)$. Step 16 can be executed in time $O(n_{\mathcal{K}}n_{\mathcal{A}})$. So the overall time taken to model check $\mathcal{M_C}$ would be $O(n_{\mathcal{K}}n_{\mathcal{L}} + n_{\mathcal{K}}n_{\mathcal{A}})$.

So, the basic authorization question: should an authorization request be honored can be answered in time $O(n_{\mathcal{K}}^2 m_1 + n_{\mathcal{K}}m_2)$.

## 3.5    Certificate-Graph Reconstruction

As discussed in section 2.1, a principal $K$ will be granted permission to access resource $T$, if the cert $(K_{owner[T]}, K, D, T, V)$ can be derived from the given set of certs. It is the responsibility of the principal $K$ requesting access, to find the set of certs that will be used in the derivation, and to submit it along with request in the order in which they are combined.

Now, we augment the model $\mathcal{M_C}$ with auxiliary information to find the certificate-Graph which gives us the proof of authorization. First, let us label the certificates in $\mathcal{C}$ as $C_1, C_2, ... C_m$. Let us also assume that the transitions in the model are labeled $t_1, t_2, ... t_l$. We associate a structure consisting of a certificate and a sequence of transitions with every transition in $\mathcal{M_C}$.

1. If $(K, A, K')$ was added during step 1 of the construction of $\mathcal{M_C}$, then there must be a cert
   $C_i = (K, A, K', V)$ in $\mathcal{C}$. Associate $(K, A, K')$ with $< C_i, null >$
2. If $(K, A, K')$ was added during an iteration of step 2 of the construction of $\mathcal{M_C}$, then there must be a cert $C_i = (K, A, K_1 A_1 ... A_n, V)$ in $\mathcal{C}$, and there must be $K_2, ... K_n$, such that $K_2 \in \delta(K_1, A_1)$, ..., $K_n \in \delta(K_{n-1}, A_{n-1})$ and $K' \in \delta(K_n, A_n)$, let these transitions be labeled $t_{i_1}, t_{i_2}, ..., t_{i_n}$ respectively. Then associate $(K, A, K')$ with the following structure $< C_i, t_{i_1}, t_{i_2}, ..., t_{i_n} >$.
3. If $(K, (T, D), K')$ was added during Step 4 of the construction of $\mathcal{M_C}$, then there must be a cert
   $C_i = (K, K', D, T, V)$. Associate $(K, (T, D), K')$ with $< C_i, null >$.
4. If $(K, (T, D), K')$ was added during Step 5 of the construction of $\mathcal{M_C}$, then there must be a cert $C_i = (K, K_1 A_1 ... A_n, D, T, V)$. Let $t_{i_1}, t_{i_2}, ..., t_{i_n}$ be as defined in step 2 above. Associate $(K, (T, D), K')$ with the structure $< C_i, t_{i_1}, t_{i_2}, ..., t_{i_n} >$.

To compute the certificate-Graph that proves the authorization of principal $K$ for $T$, we associate an expression with the pair $(K, T)$. During step 13 of the model-checking algorithm given in section 3.2 let the entry $(K, T)$ cause the following entries to be inserted into the queue $(K_1, T_1)$, $(K_2, T_2)$, ..., $(K_n, T_n)$, also let $t^1, t^2, ..., t^n$ be the corresponding transitions that are marked *blue*, then set $expr(K, T) = expr(K_1, T_1)t^1 + expr(K_2, T_2)t^2 + ... + expr(K_n, T_n)t^n$. The expression associated with $(K_{owner[T]}, -)$ would be $null$, and the result of $(null)t$ would be $t$.

Now we explain how the structure associated with the transitions and the expressions associated with pairs $(K, T)$ help us prove that the principal $K'$ is authorized to $T'$.

We define $expand(t)$ for a transition $t$ as follows:

- if the structure associated with $t$ is $< C, null >$ then $expand(t) = C$
- if the structure associated with $t$ is $< C, t^1 ... t^n >$ then $expand(t) = C \; ||$
  $expand(t^1) || ... || expand(t^n)$, where $||$ denotes string concatenation

$expand(t)$ for a transition $t$ gives us the certificate chain. To obtain the certificate-Graph that proves that the principal $K'$ is authorized to $T'$, compute $expr(K', T')$ and replace each occurrence of a transition $t$ in it by $expand(t)$.

For the example given in Figure 1, we show how the certificate graph can be constructed. The following table gives the structure associated with each of the transitions of Figure 2.

**Table 1.** The structure associated with each transition in Figure 2

| Transition Label | Transition | Structure associated |
|---|---|---|
| $t_1$ | $(K_F, A, K_1)$ | $< C_1, null >$ |
| $t_2$ | $(K_1, C, K_3)$ | $< C_3, null >$ |
| $t_3$ | $(K_1, C, K_4)$ | $< C_4, null >$ |
| $t_4$ | $(K_F, B, K_3)$ | $< C_2, t_2 >$ |
| $t_5$ | $(K_F, B, K_4)$ | $< C_2, t_3 >$ |
| $t_6$ | $(K_2, A, K_3)$ | $< C_5, t_1 t_2 >$ |
| $t_7$ | $(K_2, A, K_4)$ | $< C_5, t_1 t_3 >$ |
| $t_8$ | $(K_3, E, K_2)$ | $< C_6, null >$ |
| $t_9$ | $(K_F, < \{read\}, 0 >, K_3)$ | $< C_7, t_2 >$ |
| $t_{10}$ | $(K_F, < \{read\}, 0 >, K_4)$ | $< C_7, t_3 >$ |
| $t_{11}$ | $(K_F, < \{read, write\}, 1 >, K_1)$ | $< C_8, null >$ |
| $t_{12}$ | $(K_F, < \{exec\}, 1 >, K_2)$ | $< C_9, null >$ |
| $t_{13}$ | $(K_1, < \{read, write\}, 1 >, K_3)$ | $< C_{10}, null >$ |
| $t_{14}$ | $(K_4, < \{read\}, 0 >, K_3)$ | $< C_{11}, null >$ |
| $t_{15}$ | $(K_3, < \{write\}, 1 >, K_2)$ | $< C_{12}, null >$ |
| $t_{16}$ | $(K_2, < \{write, exec\}, 0 >, K_3)$ | $< C_{13}, null >$ |

The certificate sequence associated with transition $t_6$ would be $expand(t_6) = C_5 || expand(t_1) || expand(t_2) = C_5 C_1 C_3$. For the example shown in Figure 1 $expr(K_3, \{read, write, execute\})$ would be $t_{11} t_{13} + (t_{11} t_{13} t_{15} + t_{12}) t_{16}$. From this we get the certificate graph $C_8 C_{10} + (C_8 C_{10} C_{12} + C_9) C_{13}$.

## 3.6   Handling Multiple Requests

Given a set $\mathcal{C}$ of SPKI/SDSI certs, we want to answer a set of questions of the form 'Is $K_i$ authorized to access $T_i$?' for $i = 1, ..., m$. We now describe how our framework can be extended to handle multiple requests. Assume that we are given $m$ requests, $r_i = (K_i, T_i)$ for $1 \leqslant i \leqslant m$.

1. Construct the model $\mathcal{M}_\mathcal{C}$ as described in section 3.1
2. From $\mathcal{M}_\mathcal{C}$ remove those edges which correspond only to name certs, to get $\mathcal{M}'_\mathcal{C}$
3. Remove those edges from $\mathcal{M}'_\mathcal{C}$ such that $\delta(K, (T, D)) \ni K'$ where $T \cap T_i = \emptyset$ for all $i$, $1 \leqslant i \leqslant m$, to get $\mathcal{M}''_\mathcal{C}$
4. Remove those edges from $\mathcal{M}''_\mathcal{C}$ such that $\delta(K, (T, 0)) \ni K'$ where $K' \neq K_i$ and $T \cap T_i \neq \emptyset$ , to get $\mathcal{M}'''_\mathcal{C}$
5. In $\mathcal{M}'''_\mathcal{C}$ apply steps 5 to 9 of our model checking algorithm described in 3.2. If $K_i$ is labeled $T_i$ then $req(r_i)$ would be granted, else not granted.

Let $n_\mathcal{K}$ be the number of public keys that appear in the set $\mathcal{C}$ of certs. Let $m_1, m_2$ be the sum of the lengths of the righthand sides of the name certs, auth certs in $\mathcal{C}$ respectively. Then the time taken by the procedure described above would be $O(n_\mathcal{K}^2 m_1 + n_\mathcal{K} m_2)$.

### 3.7    Threshold Subjects

Threshold subjects can be used to specify a requirement that 'm out of n' keys must sign a request in order for it to be honored. More precisely, the public keys signing the request must belong to m out of n groups; there may be fewer than m keys signing the request if some keys belong to more than one of n groups. A set of principals attempt to determine if they are authorized if they collectively sign an access request, based on a set of certificates that may contain auth certs with *threshold subjects*.

A *threshold subject* is an expression of the form $\theta_m(S_1, S_2, ..., S_n)$, where $1 \leqslant m \leqslant n$ and each $S_i$ is a term or another threshold subject.

A threshold subject can appear only as a subject in an auth cert; it can not appear in a name cert. Now we define the notion of a set of keys *satisfying* a threshold subject. A set of keys $\mathcal{K}_*$ satisfy a term $S$ if $\mathcal{K}_* \cap \hat{\delta}(S) \neq \emptyset$. A set of keys $\mathcal{K}_*$ satisfy a threshold subject $\theta_m(S_1, S_2, ..., S_n)$ if it satisfies at least m out of the n subjects $S_1, S_2, ..., S_n$.

Now we are ready to describe how to handle the following authorization question: will a given set $\mathcal{K}_*$ of principals be authorized to access $T'$ if they collectively sign an access request, based on a given set $\mathcal{C}$ of certs?

1. Remove from $\mathcal{C}$ all the invalid certs, and those auth certs which are of the form $(K, S, D, T, V)$ where $T \cap T' = \emptyset$
2. Temporarily set aside those auth certs which have a threshold subject
3. Construct $\mathcal{M}_\mathcal{C}$, let $\mathcal{K}^* = \mathcal{K}_*$
4. For each auth cert $C = (K, \theta_m(S_1, S_2, ..., S_n), D, T', V)$ set aside in step 2 above, do the following, if $\mathcal{K}_*$ satisfies $\theta_m(S_1, S_2, ..., S_n)$, then $\mathcal{K}^* = \mathcal{K}^* \cup \{K\}$
5. From $\mathcal{M}_\mathcal{C}$ remove those edges which correspond only to name certs, to get $\mathcal{M}'_\mathcal{C}$
6. Remove those edges from $\mathcal{M}'_\mathcal{C}$ such that $\delta(K, (T, 0)) \ni K_1$ where $K_1 \notin \mathcal{K}_*$, to get $\mathcal{M}''_\mathcal{C}$
7. Run steps 4 to 9 of our model checking algorithm (section 3.2) on $\mathcal{M}''_\mathcal{C}$ and collect all the nodes labeled $T'$, call that set $\mathcal{K}_{T'}$
8. If $\mathcal{K}^* \cap \mathcal{K}_{T'} \neq \emptyset$ then honor the request else not.

### 3.8    Certificate-Set Analysis Problems

Now we discuss how our model checking algorithm described in section 3.2 can be applied to the certificate-set analysis problems described in [6]. For a resource $T'$, let $\mathcal{K}_{T'}$ be the set of principals who are authorized to access resource $T'$. Note that we can construct this set efficiently by a small modification to our model checking algorithm described in section 3.2. In analysis problems involving multiple resources we use the encoding given in section 3.6.

**Authorized access1:** Given a resource $T$ and a principal $K$, is $K$ authorized to access $T$?

$$K \in \mathcal{K}_T$$

**Authorized access2:** Given a resource $T$ and a term $S$, is $S$ authorized to access $T$?

$$\hat{\delta}(S) \subseteq \mathcal{K}_T$$

**Authorized access3:** Given resource $T$, what names are authorized to access $T$?

1. Construct $\mathcal{M}_\mathcal{C}$
2. Construct $\mathcal{K}_T$
3. Construct a finite automata $M = (Q, \Sigma, f, Q, Q)$ where $Q = \mathcal{K}_T$, $\Sigma = \mathcal{A}_\mathcal{C}$, $f : Q \times \Sigma \to 2^Q$, and $f(K, A) \ni K'$ iff $\delta(K, A) \ni K'$
4. The set of names authorized to access $T$ is
   $\{KA_1...A_n | \hat{f}(KA_1...A_n) \neq \emptyset\}$

**Shared access1:** For two given resources $T_1$ and $T_2$, what principals can access both $T_1$ and $T_2$?

$$\mathcal{K}_{T_1} \cap \mathcal{K}_{T_2}$$

**Shared access2:** Given two principals $K_1$ and $K_2$, and a resource $T$, can both $K_1$ and $K_2$ access $T$?

$$K_1 \in \mathcal{K}_T \text{ and } K_2 \in \mathcal{K}_T$$

**Shared access3:** For two given principals $K_1$ and $K_2$, and a finite set of resources $T_* = \{T_1, T_2, ..., T_n\}$, which resources can be accessed by both $K_1$ and $K_2$?

$$\{T_i \in T_* \mid K_1 \in \mathcal{K}_{T_i} \text{ and } K_2 \in \mathcal{K}_{T_i}\}$$

**Compromisation assessment1:** What resources from a finite set $T_* = \{T_1, T_2, ..., T_n\}$, could principal $K$ have gained access to(solely) due to the presence of maliciously or accidentally issued certificate set $\mathcal{C}' \subseteq \mathcal{C}$?

To explicitly note the dependence of the set $\mathcal{K}_{T_i}$ on the set $\mathcal{C}$ of certificates we represent it by $\mathcal{K}_{T_i}^{\mathcal{C}}$

$$\{T_i \in T_* | K \in (\mathcal{K}_{T_i}^{\mathcal{C}} - \mathcal{K}_{T_i}^{\mathcal{C}-\mathcal{C}'})\}$$

**Compromisation assessment2:** What principals could have gained access to resource $T$(solely) due to the presence of maliciously or accidentally issued certificate set $\mathcal{C}' \subseteq \mathcal{C}$?

$$\mathcal{K}_{T_i}^{\mathcal{C}} - \mathcal{K}_{T_i}^{\mathcal{C}-\mathcal{C}'}$$

**Expiration vulnerability1:** What resources from a finite set $T_*=\{T_1, T_2, ..., T_n\}$ will principal $K$ be prevented from accessing if certificate set $\mathcal{C}' \subseteq \mathcal{C}$ expires?

Same as Compromisation assessment1.

**Expiration vulnerability2:** What principals will be excluded from accessing resource $T$ if certificate set $\mathcal{C}' \subseteq \mathcal{C}$ expires?

Same as Compromisation assessment2.

### 3.9  Comparison with Other Approaches

The first formalization of SPKI/SDSI was [4] was achieved through rewrite rules. There have been several works formalizing the formulations using variants of FOL. Li et.al [7] established a formal relationship with the first-order semantics and pointed out some of the incompleteness issues.

First formalizations and solutions for the authorization problems for SPKI/SDSI specifications was reported in [3]. Since then there have been several improvements. Jha et.al [6] provided the first model checking approach for checking of resource authentication problems for SPKI/SDSI specifications by using pushdown systems (PDSs) on the specifications and deriving languages from the PDS to check for the required properties; the latter uses a theorem of Buchi that relates regular sets of pushdown configurations and reachability.

In the present paper, we have shown how an SACL can be modeled as a FSTS that effectively captures the set-theoretic semantics defined by Li et.al [7]. This allows us to use simple graph based model checking algorithms to efficiently(in polynomial time) answer a number of certificate-analysis questions. We have also illustrated that the certificate-analysis problems considered by Jha et.al [6] could be answered using our approach. In addition the automata representation for a set of certs is efficient.

Although the asymptotic complexity of our algorithm is the same compared to the other approaches [3,6], in practice we expect our algorithm to show better performance for the following reason: name reduction closure (steps 1 to 3 of our algorithm in section 3.1) can be performed once and the result can be reused as long as the set of name certs remains the same, this for example is not true in Jha et.al's [6] approach. Also note that we do not construct the whole name reduction closure. For the purposes of answering the authorization queries all we need is to be able to evaluate the set of keys corresponding to a given term, so, we are only interested in certs of the form $(K, A, K', \cdot)$. Thus, with respect to space efficiency, our algorithm does better than other approaches.

## 4  Discussion

In this paper, we have shown how an SACL can be effectively transformed into a finite state model and realized via security automata. We have also shown that the transformation preserves the envisaged semantics of [4] as well as the set-theoretic semantics of [7]. The transformation gives us an efficient way to enforce the policy being defined. Such a transformation permits unambiguous variants of capturing the authorization of tags while being delegated and also clearly makes it possible to define the set of tags permissible under threshold certificates. We described algorithms for certificate-chaining and resource discovery requirements. In fact, our approach allows the reuse of closure computation in the context of multiple requests unlike other approaches where the closure needs to be computed fresh every time. Further, such a transformation shows clearly the power of SACL and enables integration of SACL with state-based security mechanisms that are widely used for protection/security of classical

Operating systems, Databases etc. Such an integration would allow issuance of a priori limited uses PKI tokens in a distributed framework. The possibility of heterogeneous integration would provide the much needed flexibility for PKIs which is one of the main factors for the limited adoption of PKIs much below the expected growth.

We are working towards transformation of various security models such as Chinese wall security policy [2], BELL-LaPADULA [1], Role Based Access Control [5] etc. models in the above framework that would allow a nice heterogenous integration of security specifications.

# References

1. D. E. Bell and L. J. LaPadula. Secure computer system: Unified exposition and multics interpretation. *ESD-TR-75-306, rev. 1, Electronic Systems Division, Air Force Systems Command, Hanscom Field, Bedford, MA 01731.*

2. D. F. C. Brewer and M. J. Nash. The chinese wall security policy. In *IEEE Symposium on Security and Privacy*, pages 206–214, 1989.

3. D. E. Clarke, J.-E. Elien, C. M. Ellison, M. Fredette, A. Morcos, and R. L. Rivest. Certificate chain discovery in SPKI/SDSI. *Journal of Computer Security*, 9(4):285–322, 2001.

4. C. Ellison, B. Frantz, B. Lampson, R. Rivest, B. Thomas, and T. Ylonen. RFC 2693: SPKI certificate theory. IETF RFC Publication, September 1999.

5. D. Ferraiolo and R. Kuhn. Role-based access controls. In *15th NIST-NCSC National Computer Security Conference*, pages 554–563, 1992.

6. S. Jha and T. Reps. Model checking SPKI/SDSI. *Journal of Computer Security*, 12:317–353, 2004.

7. N. Li and J. C. Mitchell. Understanding SPKI/SDSI using first-order logic. In *CSFW*, pages 89–103, 2003.

8. F. B. Schneider. Enforceable security policies. *Information and System Security*, 3(1):30–50, 2000.

# Design of Key Establishment Protocol Using One-Way Functions to Avert *insider-replay* Attack

Mounita Saha and Dipanwita RoyChowdhury

Department of Computer Science and Engineering,
Indian institute of Technology, Kharagpur, India

**Abstract.** In this work, we have identified a class of weakness named as *insider-replay* attack in a number of existing protocols and propose a common design principle to avoid the weakness. Also, based on the design principles, we propose three key establishment schemes under two different scenarios. The proposed schemes are efficient in terms of number of nonce used and are based on one-way functions.

## 1 Introduction

In recent times, security is a major concern while designing the communication protocols. Key establishment protocols are the initial step to set up a secure communication. Hence, the design of key establishment protocols has received considerable amount of attention due to their importance in communication protocols. However design of flawless and efficient key establishment protocols is a challenging task. A large number of security protocols have been proposed in the literature. Many of them have subsequently been shown to have different weaknesses.

Key establishment is a process or protocol whereby a shared secret becomes available to two or more parties, for subsequent cryptographic use [2]. A key transport protocol is a key establishment technique where the secret value is created by only one party and transferred to the other(s). If the number of parties involved in a key establishment protocol is two, it is a two party protocol, otherwise with multiple users the protocol becomes a multiparty protocol. The majority of key establishment protocols use either symmetric key cryptosystems or public key cryptosystems. However, one-way functions are also used to design key establishment protocols, without requiring these cryptosystems. We have examined a number of two party server based protocols using both encryption-decryption and one way functions and detected a class of weakness in some of them, including improved Yahalom's protocol [8] and Boyd's protocol [9]. Similar weakness is also noted in the Gong's hybrid protocol [6] using one way functions [1]. The first part of our work is concerned with detecting this class of weakness and providing a common principle to avert it while designing such a protocol.

Gong introduced the idea of using one way functions in designing key establishment protocols in [1]. Later, similar ideas were discussed in [3],[7]. In [3] several existing one-way function based key exchange protocols are analyzed.

A. Bagchi and V. Atluri (Eds.): ICISS 2006, LNCS 4332, pp. 194–204, 2006.

The KryptoKnight authentication and key distribution system has proposed the use of one-way functions in the design for restricted computing environment in [7].

In the second part of our work we have proposed two new protocols using one-way functions, which obey the proposed design principle. The advantage of using one-way functions is that unlike the encryption functions, the one way functions do not need to be reversible. Therefore they are simpler as well as secure from the design and implementation point of view. The proposed protocols are shown to avert the weakness found in Yahalom's, Boyd's and Gong's protocols. At the same time, the proposed protocols satisfy the fundamental goals of a key establishment protocol. They are also shown to be resistant to conventional type of attacks and efficient in terms of number of random values used.

The rest of the paper is organized as follows. Section 2 describes the preliminaries and also describes a weakness called "insider replay" in a number of protocols. In section 3 we propose a design principle to avoid the weakness and also provide the description of the proposed protocols. Finally we conclude with the future plans of the work in section 4.

## 2    Preliminaries

The key issues and goals of a protocol design problem are discussed in detail in [6]. While designing an authentication and key establishment protocols the goals to be met should be specified clearly and the protocol should be able to meet all the specified goals only. The design goals are of two types. These are user oriented goals and key oriented goals. The user oriented goals requires the far end to be operative and the knowledge of peer among the communicating parties. Conforming to the user oriented goals ensures entity authentication. The major key oriented goals are key freshness and key authentication. Key freshness is ensured by the use of three alternative techniques which are nonce value, timestamp or sequence numbers. The key authentication requires the assurance that the key is only known to the communicating users and mutually trusted parties. The other issues of protocol design include key confirmation, key control, reducing number of messages/rounds etc. In subsequent discussions we shall show how these different goals are met by the proposed protocol.

In server based two party symmetric key establishment protocols, the key control can be with any combination of users and server. The server can control the key alone or with one or both of the users. Also, one of the users alone can have the control of the key or all of the users can decide the key together. Thus, along with the other goals of the design, the designer of a protocol has to explicitly mention the key control requirement. However, we have observed certain protocols where the claimed key control goal is not met. The examples of such protocols are given below.

The communication architecture that we consider in rest of the paper consists of a set of users. Only two of the users may wish to communicate at a time to establish a secret key shared between them. We also consider the existence of a server, which engages in the protocol as a trusted third party. Thus our protocol involves three principals consisting of two users and a trusted server. Both the users share a long term secret key with the server. We assume the security model where the adversary is capable of observing all messages sent, alter messages, insert or delete messages and delay messages.

We shall use the following notations for the protocol description.

$A, B$ : The two users who wish to share a new secret key

$S$ : The trusted server

$K_{as}$ : The shared secret between S and A

$K_{bs}$ : The shared secret between S and B

$K_{ab}$ : The secret key established between A and B

$\{M\}_K$ : Encryption of message M with key K

$N_a, N_b$ : Nonce values generated by users A and B respectively

We have addressed one particular scenario where the server sends a message containing the secret key, to one user through the other user. In some cases, the intermediate user has the scope to replay an old key in place of the intended key sent by the server. We name this weakness as *insider-replay*. We have identified this type of weakness in improved Yahalom's and Boyd's protocols.

Improved Yahalom's Protocol

1.    $A \rightarrow B : A, N_a$
2.    $B \rightarrow S : A, \{B, N_a, N_b\}_{K_{bs}}$
3.    $S \rightarrow A : \{B, K_{ab}, N_a, N_b\}_{K_{as}}, \{K_{ab}, A\}_{K_{bs}}$
4.    $A \rightarrow B : \{K_{ab}, A\}_{K_{bs}}, \{N_b\}_{K_{ab}}$

Boyd's protocol

1.    $.A \rightarrow S : A, B, N_a$
2.    $S \rightarrow B : \{A, B, K_s\}_{K_{as}}, \{A, B, K_s\}_{K_{bs}}, N_a$
3.    $B \rightarrow A : \{A, B, K_s\}_{K_{as}}, \{N_a\}_{k_{ab}}], N_b$
4.    $A \rightarrow B : \{N_b\}_{K_{ab}}$

○ The weakness of Yahalom's two party protocol is identified in message 4.
Message 4: $A \rightarrow B$: $\{K'_{ab}, A\}_{K_{bs}}, \{N_b\}_{K'_{ab}}$

In this protocol, the server decides the key and transmits it to both the parties. The server $S$ sends the secret key for B ($\{K_{ab}, A\}_{K_{bs}}$) in the second part the message 3 to A. Finally A sends that value to B. Here A has the scope to replay an old key value in place of the one originally sent by the server.

The weakness here is that the user $B$ has no way to verify that the key was chosen by $A$ not $S$. Here the key control goal of the protocol has been violated and the control has gone to $A$ instead of $S$. Moreover, in absence of key confirmation an adversary is also able to mount an attack by replaying old value of $\{K'_{ab}, A\}_{K_{bs}}$ to $B$.

○ In Boyd's protocol also, $B$ can modify the third message to be sent to $A$ by replacing the value of $K_s$ by an old value $K'_s$.
*Message 3:$B \to A$*: $[A, B, K'_s]_{K_{as}}, [Na]_{k'_{ab}}, N_b$
Moreover this protocol is also vulnerable to replay attack. Any adversary is able to replace the first two parts of message 2 by old values from previous run.

○ Similar weakness of the Gongs hybrid protocol using one way functions is observed in [6].

The Gongs Protocol

1.    $A \to B : A, B, N_a$
2.    $B \to S : A, B, N_a, N_b$
3.    $S \to B : N_s, f(N_s, K_{bs}, N_b, A) \oplus (K_{ab}, H_a, H_b), g(K_{ab}, H_a, H_b, K_{bs})$
4.    $B \to A : N_s, H_b$
5.    $A \to B : H_a$

The detail of the protocol is given in [1]. Here, although an adversary is not able to mount an attack, an insider $B$ is still able to replay an old key value. $B$ is unable to detect that the key is not the one transmitted by server $S$ and is chosen by $A$ instead.

The weakness is as follows.

$3'$: $S \to A(B) : N_s, f(N_s, K_{bs}, N_b, A) \oplus (K_{ab}, H_a, H_b), g(K_{ab}, H_a, H_b, K_{bs})$
$\quad\ A(S) \to B : N_s, f(N_s, K_{bs}, N_b, A) \oplus (K'_{ab}, H'_a, H'_b), g(K'_{ab}, H'_a, H'_b, K_{bs})$
$4'$: $B \to A$: $N_s, H'_b$
$5'$: $A \to B$: $H'_a$

Hence, from the above discussions it is evident that this weakness called *insider-replay* arises is a common scenario where the server sends some message to one user through the other user. A good example of such an attack environment is a public-key scenario where different key sizes or signature schemes might have different legal validity. There, being sure that the key has been chosen by the server itself and not maliciously replaced by an insider is a significant threat. In the next section we provide a principle to prevent this common class of weakness and thereafter construct two efficient protocols based on that.

# 3    Proposed Work

In this section we first describe the common class of weakness called *insider-replay* stated in previous section and propose a design principle to avoid it. We then propose two new schemes of key establishment which obey the principle and are based on one-way functions.

## 3.1    Principle to Avoid the Weakness

In the previous section we have seen that the Yahalom's, Boyd's and Gong's protocols use a common scenario where the server sends the secret key to one user through the other user. This kind of scenario is very common in protocol literature. However, this situation has a prospective vulnerability that, if proper measure is not taken, the intermediate user may be able to alter the message for the intended user. This vulnerability is present in the case of the example protocols described in previous section. Hence, this can be taken as a common class of weakness as described here.

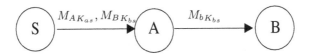

**Fig. 1.** S forwards message for B through A

Suppose server $S$ has constructed messages $M_A$ and $M_B$ for users A and B, containing the session key of $A$ and $B$. It encrypts/creates one-way function using the shared keys $K_{as}$ and $K_{bs}$ and sends $\{M_A\}_{K_{as}} + \{M_B\}_{K_{bs}}$ to user $A$. $A$ forwards $\{M_B\}_{K_{bs}}$ to user $B$ as shown in figure 1.

Here, $B$ must be assured that the received key is freshly generated by the server $S$ and the intermediate user $A$ or some adversary has not changed the value as might happen like the example protocols described earlier. Figure 2(a) and 2(b)describe this weakness.

**Fig. 2.** (a) A is inseider attacker (b) C is an adversary

In case of Yahalom's and Boyd's protocols insider $A$ is able to replay the old value and in absence of key confirmation, replay attack is also possible by an adversary. Gong's protocol is susceptible to replay by the insider $A$.

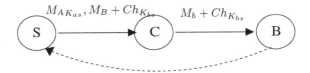

**Fig. 3.** Challenge-response between server and indirectly connecter user

The proposed solution to the problem is that the server has to obtain one challenge previously created by $B$ within the session. $S$ can collect the challenge either directly or indirectly through the other user $A$. Now, in its response to $B$, the server $S$ should include that challenge. The situation is depicted in figure 3. Here $S$ forms the response to $B$ as $M_B + Ch$ in response to the challenge $Ch$. As the challenge is supposed to be fresh, $B$ can immediately check that the response obtained from $S$ is a fresh one and not some replay of an old message.

## 3.2    The Proposed Schemes

In this section, we propose two key establishment protocols preventing the *insider-replay* attack with two different scenarios. Our work is promarily based on Gong's hybrid protocol. Similar to the protocol, we have used one way functions in place of encryption. However, instead of hybrid key control, here in the first scenario the key control lies with the server only. The second scenario deals with key transport protocol where one user decides the key and sends it to the other user through the server. In both of the cases, the protocols resist the *insider-replay* attack on the key control property while preserving the fundamental properties of key establishment. They are efficient in terms of number of nonce used and resistant to conventional attacks.

In the protocol description, we use the notations described earlier. Additionally, $H_a$ and $H_b$ are handshake numbers similar to Gongs protocol [1]. $f()$ and $g()$ are similar one-way functions.

**Schemes under scenario-I**
We propose two schemes under the first scenario as described below. In both the cases, the values of $K_{ab}$, $H_a$, $H_b$ are selected by the server and transmitted to $A$ and $B$.

**Scenario (I) Scheme (A):** *Server controlled key*

Message 1: $A \rightarrow B$: $A, B, N_a$
Message 2: $B \rightarrow S$: $A, B, N_a, N_b$
Message 3: $S \rightarrow B$: $N_s, f2 \oplus K, g2, f1 \oplus K, g1$
$//f2 = f(K_{bs}, N_s, N_b, A); K = (K_{ab}, H_a, H_b)$
$//g2 = g(K_{ab}, H_a, H_b, K_{bs}, N_b)$
Message 4: $B \rightarrow A$: $N_s, H_b, f1 \oplus K, g1$
$//f1 = f(K_{as}, N_s, N_a, B);$
$//g1 = g(K_{ab}, H_a, H_b, K_{as}, N_a);$
Message 5: $A \rightarrow B$: $H_a$

The protocol works in the following way.

○ *Message 1*: Initially at the start of the transaction,$A$ generates a nonce value $N_a$. A nonce is a number that has not been used before i.e. generated only once. $A$ transmits its nonce value and the user identity to $B$.
$A \rightarrow B : A, B, N_a$

○ *Message 2*: B adds its own nonce value and transmits the message to the server.

$B \rightarrow S : A, B, N_a, N_b$

○ *Message 3*: When the server receives the message, it generates its own nonce value $N_s$ and decides the values of $K_{ab}, H_a, H_b$ Then, $S$ computes two one way functions $f()$ and $g()$ for each of the users i.e. $f1, f2$ and $g1, g2$ and sends message 3.

$S \rightarrow B : N_s, f2 \oplus K, g2, f1 \oplus K, g1$

○ *Message 4*: On receipt of message 3, $B$ itself computes $f2 = f(K_{bs}, N_a, N_b, A)$ and extracts the key value by XORing it with the first part of message 3. B then computes $g2 = g(K_{ab}, H_a, H_b, K_{bs}, N_b)$ and compares it with the value of second part of message 3 to check the that key value has not been tampered with. After $B$ is satisfied with the authenticity of the key, it sends the third and fourth part of the message to $A$ along with the handshake number $H_b$ and the servers nonce value $N_s$.

$B \rightarrow A : N_s, H_b, f1 \oplus K, g1$

○ *Message 5*: A forms $f1 = f(K_{as}, N_s, N_a, B)$, finds the key and finally computes $g1 = g(K_{ab}, H_a, H_b, K_{bs}, N_a)$ to check the integrity of the received key. It also checks $H_b$ and finally sends its own handshaking number $H_a$ to B to complete key confirmation.

$A \rightarrow B : H_a$

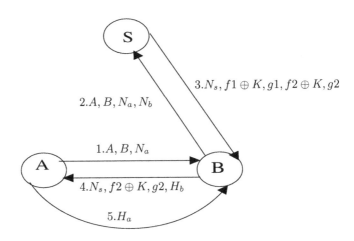

**Fig. 4.** Key establishment scheme I

In the first scheme, $N_s$ is generated by the server as a nonce value. It can be noted that $N_s$ is neither produced as a challenge in any message nor any response using that $N_s$ value reaches the server. Thus, we construct a similar scheme without using $N_s$ as shown in figure 2. The advantage of the scheme is that it involves one less nonce value compared to the other. The requirement of the server to generate a nonce value has been removed here.

**Scenario (I) Scheme (B):** *Server controlled key-without server nonce* (fig. 3)

Message 1: $A \rightarrow B$: $A, B, N_a$
Message 2: $B \rightarrow S$: $A, B, N_a, N_b$
Message 3: $S \rightarrow B$: $f2 \oplus K, g2, f1 \oplus K, g1$
$$// \ f2 = f(K_{bs}, N_b, N_a, A); K = (K_{ab}, H_a, H_b)$$
$$//g2 = g(K_{ab}, H_a, H_b, K_{bs}, N_b)$$
Message 4: $B \rightarrow A$: $N_b, H_b, f1 \oplus K, g1$
$$// \ f1 = f(K_{as}, N_a, N_b, B);$$
$$//g1 = g(K_{ab}, H_a, H_b, K_{as}, N_a);$$
Message 5: $A \rightarrow B : H_a$

The working of the protocol is explained as follows.

○ *Message 1:* Similar to the scheme (A), initially at the start of the transaction, $A$ generates a nonce value $N_a$ and transmits it and the user identities to $B$.
  $A \rightarrow B: A, B, N_a$
○ *Message 2:* B adds its own nonce value and transmits the message to the server.
  $B \rightarrow S: A, B, N_a, N_b$
○ *Message 3:* When the server receives the message, it decides the values of $K_{ab}, H_a, H_b$ and computes $f1$, $f2$, $g1$ and $g2$. However, it does not generate and transmit any nonce value as before.
  $S \rightarrow B: f2 \oplus K, g2, f1 \oplus K, g1$
○ *Message 4:* On receipt of message 3, $B$ extracts and verifies the key value similar to scheme(A). It then sends the $f1 \oplus K, g1$ part to $A$ along with the handshake number $H_b$ and its nonce value $N_b$.
  $B \rightarrow A: N_b, H_b, f1 \oplus K, g1$
○ *Message 5:* Similarly, $A$ finds and verifies the key and also checks $H_b$. Finally $A$ sends its own handshaking number $H_a$ to $B$ to complete key confirmation.

Figure 4 and figure 5 describe the proposed schemes. Both of the protocols use five messages and five rounds. It can be noted from [5] that the minimum number of messages required for a nonce based server controlled authentication and key generation scheme is also five. Hence the proposed schemes meet the lower bound on the number of messages. As an alternative, the server can itself send the values to A and B in parallel. The number of rounds then come down to four, however number of messages becomes six.

**Scheme under scenario-II**
The proposed key transport protocol using one-way function is as follows.

**Scenario (II) Scheme (A):** *Key transport by one of the user*

Message 1: $B \rightarrow A$: $A, B, N_b$
Message 2: $A \rightarrow S$: $A, B, N_a, N_b, f1 \oplus K_{ab}, g1$
$$//f1 = f(K_{as}, N_a, N_b, B);$$
$$//g1 = g(K_{ab}, K_{as}, N_a);$$

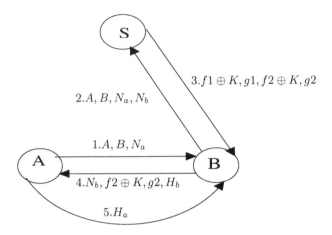

**Fig. 5.** Key establishment scheme II

Message 3: $S \rightarrow B$: $N_a, f2 \oplus K_{ab}, g2$

$$// \ f2 = f(K_{bs}, N_b, N_a, A);$$
$$// \ g2 = g(K_{ab}, K_{bs}, N_b)$$

Message 4: $B \rightarrow A$: $f(K_{ab}, N_a)$

Here $A$ decides the key $K_{ab}$ and transports that value to $B$ through the server $S$. On, initial request from $B$, $A$ generates key $K_{ab}$ and computes $f1$, $g1$. On receipt of message 2, $S$ finds out $f1$ and finds $K_{ab}$. It also verifies the value with $g1$. Then $S$ computes $f2$ and $g2$ and sends message 3 to $B$. $B$ can compute $f2$ and hence find out the key $K_{ab}$. It verifies the key by computing $g2$. $B$'s knowledge of correct key is demonstrated to $A$ by message 4. Figure 6 describes the key transport scheme. The advantage of the scheme is that four messages are required to complete the protocol transactions.

**Analysis against protocol goals**
The basic goals of key establishment protocols are satisfied in proposed protocols in the following way.

- Knowledge of peer: The knowledge of peer is ensured in the initial messages of the protocol where the identities of the communicating parties are included in the messages communicated. Far end operative: The freshly generated nonce values are exchanged between the users. It satisfies the far end operative property.
- Entity authentication: As the protocols satisfy the knowledge of peer and far end operative properties, entity authentication is ensured. Both the users have assurance that the other end is the intended user.
- Freshness: Freshness of key is achieved through nonce values. The nonce values $N_a$ and $N_b$ are used in the computation of the functions $f()$ and $g()$. Hence old values of the functions cannot be replayed.

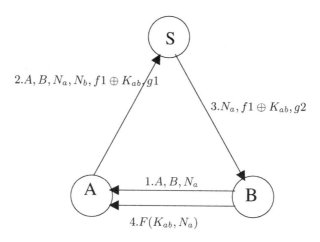

**Fig. 6.** Key establishment with single user control

○ Key authentication: As the key values are communicated by associating them the shared secret $K_{as}$ and $K_{bs}$, it is ensured that the key is known only to the trusted server and users. Hence Key authentication is ensured. Moreover, verification of the receipt of correct key value is achieved by the function values $g1$ and $g2$.

○ Key confirmation: It is achieved by the use of the handshake numbers $H_a$ and $H_b$ in all the schemes.

**Security analysis against conventional attacks**
In this section, we examine the security of the proposed protocols against the *insider-replay* attack as well as the other conventional attacks which are relevant in the proposed framework.

**A.** *Insider-replay attack*
All of the protocols mentioned above avoid the proposed *insider-replay* attack in the following way. Suppose in scenario(I)-schemeB, user $A$ can intercept the message 3, compute $f1$ to obtain the key $K$. Hence it is able to find $f2$ by xor-ing $K$ with $f2 \oplus K$. It can now substitute $K$ by $K'$ and find out $f2 \oplus K'$. Neither $A$ is not able to compute $g2$, as it requires knowledge of the shared secret $K_{bs}$ between $B$ and $S$ nor it can substitute $g2$ by appropriate old value $g2$. as $g2$ involves the fresh nonce $N_b$.
Message 3: $S \rightarrow B$: $f2 \oplus K, g2, f1 \oplus K, g1$
$$//f2 = f(K_{bs}, N_b, N_a, A); K = (K_{ab}, H_a, H_b)$$
$$//g2 = g(K_{ab}, H_a, H_b, K_{bs}, N_b)$$
**B.** *Modification*
In the proposed protocols, modification to the key content is avoided by using the integrity check function $g()$.
**C.** *Replay-attack*
The security of the proposed schemes against the replay attacks is ensured by

the inclusion of nonces $N_a$ and $N_b$. All the $f()$ and $g()$ function values computed involves atleast one nonce, hence old values cannot be replayed.

**D**. *Man-in-the-middle attack*

Next, we examine the possibilities of man-in-the-middle attacks against the proposed protocols.

○ If an adversary impersonates $A$, it cannot find the key without the knowledge of the long term key $K_{as}$ and also cannot participate in key confirmation handshake.

○ Similarly, an adversary also can't impersonate $B$ to fool $A$. The computation of $f1$ and $g1$ values for $A$ requires the knowledge of the long term key $K_{as}$, which is not available to $B$.

○ If an adversary impersonates as $B$ to $S$, it won't be able to calculate the values of key $K_{ab}$ and $H_a$, $H_b$ .

○ Nobody can impersonate server, as only server knows $K_{as}$ and $K_{bs}$ and therefore is able to calculate all the values of $f1$, $f2$ and $g1$, $g2$ correctly.

# 4  Conclusion

In this paper we have observed a class of weakness called *insider-replay* in a number of protocols. We have also proposed a design principle to avert the weakness. We have also proposed three authentication and key establishment protocols using one-way functions which are secure against a number of conventional attack.

# References

1. Gong, L.: Using One-way Functions for Authentication. (1989) 8–11
2. Menezes, Alfred J., Oorschot, Paul C. van., Vanstone, Scott. A.: Handbook of Applied Cryptography. available at http://www.cacr.math.uwaterloo.ca/hac/index.html
3. Boyd, C., Mathuria, A.: Systematic Design of key establishment protocols based on one-way functions. IEE proceedingings on computer and digital technology, **144** No 2, March (1997),
4. Mathuria, A., Jain, V.: On Efficient Key Agreement Protocols, (2005)
5. Gong, L.: Lower bounds on Messages and Rounds for Network Authentication Protocols. (1993)
6. Boyd, C., Mathuria, A.: Protocols for authentication and key establishment, Springer publication, (2003)
7. Bird , R., Gopal, I., Herzberg, A., Janson, P., Kutten, S., Molva, R.: The CryptoKnight Family of light-weight protocols for authentication and key distribution. IEEE/ACM Transaction on networking, **3** (1995), 31–41
8. Paulson, L. C.: Relation between secrets: Two formal analyses of the Yahalom's protocol, Journal of computer security. **9**, (2001) 197–216.
9. Boyd, C.: A class of flexible and efficient key management protocols. In 9th IEEE Computer Security Foundations Workshop, IEEE Press (1996), 2–8

# An Efficient Key Assignment Scheme for Access Control in a Hierarchy

Praveen Kumar Vadnala* and Anish Mathuria

Dhirubhai Ambani Institute of Information and Communication Technology
Gandhinagar, Gujarat, India
{anish_mathuria,praveen_vadnala}@daiict.ac.in

**Abstract.** This paper examines a hash based hierarchical access control scheme proposed by Yang and Li. It is shown that the scheme suffers from the ex-member access problem. A new hash based scheme that avoids the ex-member problem is proposed. Our scheme has the following advantages: (i) it uses less private storage per node; (ii) addition or deletion of nodes and users does not require rekeying of all nodes; and (iii) the static version of the scheme carries a proof of security. A hash based scheme recently proposed by Atallah, Frikken and Blanton also has these properties. Compared to their scheme, our scheme requires less public storage space for tree hierarchies.

## 1 Introduction

In an enterprise, the users are often organized into a hierarchy of security classes, where some security classes have greater access privileges than others. A hierarchical access control scheme ensures that if a class $S_i$ is superior to a class $S_j$, then $S_i$ has access to $S_j$, whereas the opposite is prevented. A poset hierarchy is defined by a partially ordered set $(S, \leq)$, where $S$ is the set of security classes and $\leq$ is a reflexive, anti-symmetric and transitive binary relation on $S$. If $S_j \leq S_i$, then $S_i$ is said to be at a higher security level than $S_j$. A poset hierarchy can be represented as a directed acyclic graph in which the nodes correspond to the security classes and the edges correspond to the partial order relation. Suppose the nodes $U_i$ and $U_j$ correspond to security classes $S_i$ and $S_j$. If $S_i \leq S_j$, then there will be an edge from $U_j$ to $U_i$. In this case, $U_j$ is called a *predecessor* of $U_i$ and $U_i$ is called a *successor* of $U_j$. If there is no node $U_k$ in the hierarchy such that $S_i \leq S_k \leq S_j$, then $U_j$ is called an *immediate predecessor* of node $U_i$ and $U_i$ is called an *immediate successor* of $U_j$. A node with zero predecessors is called a *root* node. A node with zero successors is called a *leaf* node. An example of a poset hierarchy can be seen in Fig. 1.

The cryptographic solution to the hierarchical access control problem involves assigning keys to the nodes. In the most basic scheme, every node is assigned a key by a trusted Central Authority (CA), and is also given the keys of all its successors. The drawback of this approach is that it requires the higher level

---

* Present address: Mindtree Consulting Pvt. Ltd., Bangalore. Work was carried out at DA-IICT.

A. Bagchi and V. Atluri (Eds.): ICISS 2006, LNCS 4332, pp. 205–219, 2006.

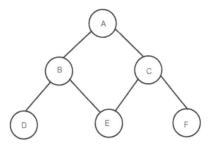

**Fig. 1.** An example of a poset in a User Hierarchy

nodes to store a large number of secret keys. An alternative approach is to give each node only one key and use cryptographic techniques to enable the node to derive the successors' keys with the help of its own key and some public information. The first such scheme was proposed by Akl and Taylor in 1983 [1]. The two main drawbacks of this scheme are that the size of the private information held by the higher level nodes grows when new nodes are added, and it requires a large amount of storage for the public information. Many researchers have proposed alternative schemes to address these problems. Some notable examples are Sandhu's scheme [2] based on one-way functions, the Harn-Lin scheme [3], which uses a bottom-up key derivation method, the Shen-Chen scheme [4] based on the discrete logarithm problem and Newton's polynomial interpolation, the Wu-Wei scheme [5] based on the discrete logarithm problem, and the Yang-Li [6] and Atallah-Frikken-Blanton [7] schemes based on one-way hash functions.

Many schemes proposed in the literature are known to be insecure against a collusion attack, where the nodes at lower levels collude to obtain the key of a higher level node. A recent example is the attack found by Hsu and Wu [8] on the Shen-Chen scheme. The majority of schemes proposed till date do not have security proofs available. Two notable exceptions are the schemes proposed by Wu and Wei [5] and Atallah et al [7].

In this paper we present attacks on the dynamic version of the Yang-Li scheme in the situation where a node or relationship between two nodes is deleted. An alternative hash based scheme that avoids these attacks is proposed. Compared to the hash-based schemes of Yang and Li and Atallah et al, our scheme has the following properties: (i) each node stores only one key, so the total private storage required is $O(n)$ (where $n$ is the number of nodes in the graph), whereas the the private storage required by Yang-Li scheme is $O(n^2)$; (ii) when a user is added/deleted from a class, then that class and all successors of that class are rekeyed; whereas in the Yang-Li scheme, additions/deletion of users require rekeying of all nodes; (iii) the total public storage required by our scheme is $O(n^2)$ for a general non-tree hierarchy, the same as required by the Atallah-Frikken-Blanton scheme. In the case of tree hierarchies, their scheme requires $2n - 1$ public values, whereas our scheme requires $n$ public values of comparable size.

The rest of the paper is organized as follows. Section 2 reviews the Yang-Li scheme. Our attacks on this scheme are described in Section 3. The proposed hash based scheme is described in Section 4. The security proof for the new scheme is given in Section 5. Section 6 concludes the paper by giving a comparison with existing schemes.

## 2   Review of Yang-Li Scheme

We fix $n$ distinct public one-way hash functions $H_1, H_2, \ldots, H_n$, where $n$ is the maximum number of immediate predecessors for any node in the hierarchy. The immediate successors of every node are ordered from left to right.

**Key Generation**

1. The CA assigns an arbitrary key to each root node.
2. For each non-root node $U_j$, the CA performs the following steps:
   (a) If $U_j$ has only one immediate predecessor $U_i$, and $U_j$ is the $k^{\text{th}}$ immediate successor of $U_i$, then the key $K_j$ assigned to $U_j$ is calculated as

   $$K_j = H_k(K_i) \tag{1}$$

   where $K_i$ is the key of $U_i$.
   (b) If $U_j$ has more than one immediate predecessor, say $U_i^1, U_i^2, \ldots, U_i^m$ and $U_j$ is $k^{\text{th}}$ immediate successor of $U_i^1$, $l^{\text{th}}$ immediate successor of $U_i^2$ and so on and $s^{\text{th}}$ immediate successor of $U_i^m$, then the key $K_j$ assigned to $U_j$ is calculated as

   $$K_j = H_k(H_k(K_1)||H_l(K_2)||\ldots||H_s(K_m)) \tag{2}$$

   where $||$ denotes concatenation and $K_1, K_2, \ldots, K_m$ are the keys of $U_i^1, U_i^2, \ldots, U_i^m$, respectively. The CA makes $H_k(K_1)$, $H_l(K_2)$, $\ldots$, $H_s(K_m)$ available to all the immediate predecessors of $U_j$.
3. Repeat step 2 until all nodes are finished.

   In the above scheme if a node has more than one immediate predecessor, then its key is derived jointly from the keys of the predecessors.

*Example*: For the hierarchy given in Fig. 1, the key assignment is shown in Table 1. Since node $E$ has two immediate predecessors, $B$ and $C$, its key is derived jointly from the keys assigned to $B$ and $C$. Note that the values $H_2(K_B)$ and $H_1(K_C)$ must be kept secret to $C$ and $B$, respectively.

**Key Derivation.** Suppose that node $U_i$ wants to derive the key $K_j$ of its immediate successor $U_j$. If $U_i$ is the only immediate predecessor of $U_j$, then $K_j$ is computed using Equation (1), where $k$ is set accordingly. If $U_j$ has more than one immediate predecessor, then $U_i$ calculates its own input to Equation (2) and retrieves the other inputs from the CA. Finally, it computes $K_j$. The keys of other successors of $U_i$ that are at a lower level than $U_j$ can be derived similarly.

**Table 1.** Key assignment in Yang-Li scheme

| Node ID | Key |
|---------|-----|
| A | $K_A$ (chosen by CA) |
| B | $K_B = H_1(K_A)$ |
| C | $K_C = H_2(K_A)$ |
| D | $K_D = H_1(K_B)$ |
| E | $K_E = H_2(H_2(K_B)\|\|H_1(K_C))$ |
| F | $K_F = H_2(K_C)$ |

## 2.1 Dynamic Access Control

In the Yang-Li paper, the algorithms for dynamic access control are loosely specified by means of examples. We will give formal descriptions of these algorithms so that they can be accurately assessed. We model the hierarchy as a directed acyclic graph $G = (V, E)$, where V is the set of vertices (nodes) and E is the set of edges (relationship between the nodes). Recall that an edge $(U_i, U_j) \in$ E represents the relationship $U_j \leq U_i$ between the two nodes. We define the following functions:

- **Immpred**$(U_i)$: Returns all the immediate predecessors of node $U_i$.
- **Immsucc**$(U_i)$: Returns all the immediate successors of node $U_i$.
- **Predecessors**$(U_i)$: Returns all the predecessors of node $U_i$.
- **Successors**$(U_i)$: Returns all the successors of node $U_i$.
- **root**$(U_i)$: Returns 1 if $U_i$ is a root node, and 0 otherwise.
- **ModifiedBFS**$(U_i)$: Returns the set of nodes of the sub-hierarchy of $G$ rooted at $U_i$, by performing Breadth First Search. Note that the BFS used here is different from classical BFS (see Cormen, Rivest, Leiserson and Stein [9]). In classical BFS, the nodes are returned in the order of their first visit. The ModifiedBFS is different in that a node is added to the output only when all its predecessors have been added to the output. This algorithm is described in Appendix A.

**Adding a Relationship.** To add a new relationship between $U_i$ and $U_j$ such that $U_j \leq U_i$, the CA performs Algorithm 1.

---

**Algorithm 1.** Addrelation$(U_i, U_j)$          {comment: $U_j \leq U_i$}

---

1: $E \leftarrow E \cup \{(U_i, U_j)\}$
2: Regenerate the key of $U_j$ from keys of its immediate predecessors.
3: **for all** $U_s \in$ ModifiedBFS$(U_j)$ **do**
4:     Regenerate the key of $U_s$. {regenerate the key of $U_j$'s successors}
5: **end for**

---

*Example*: In Fig. 1 if a new relationship is added between the nodes $C$ and $D$, then the CA regenerates $D$'s key as $H_1(H_1(K_B)\|\|H_3(K_C))$, and secretly transmits $H_1(K_B)$ and $H_3(K_C)$ to $C$ and $B$, respectively.

**Adding a Node.** To add a new node $U_k$ to the hierarchy such that the nodes in the set $V_k$ become immediate predecessors of $U_k$ and the nodes in the set $V_k'$ becomes immediate successors of $U_k$, the CA performs the steps shown in Algorithm 2.

---

**Algorithm 2.** Addnode$(U_k, V_k, V_k')$

---
1: $V \leftarrow V \cup \{U_k\}$
2: **for all** $U_l \in V_k$ **do**
3:    $E \leftarrow E \cup \{(U_l, U_k)\}$
4: **end for**
5: **for all** $U_m \in V_k'$ **do**
6:    $E \leftarrow E \cup \{(U_k, U_m)\}$
7: **end for**
8: **if** root$(U_k)$ **then**
9:    Assign arbitrary key to $U_k$.
10: **else**
11:    Generate key of $U_k$ from the keys of nodes in $V_k$.
12: **end if**
13: **for all** $U_s \in$ ModifiedBFS$(U_k)$ **do**
14:    Regenerate the key of $U_s$.
15: **end for**

---

*Example*: In Fig. 1, if a new root node $G$ is added and $C$ is made an immediate successor of $G$, then $G$'s key is generated by CA and the keys of $C, E, F$ are re-generated. If a node $H$ is added and $H$ is made an immediate successor of $A$ and immediate predecessor of $F$, then $H$'s key is generated from $A$'s key and $F$'s key is re-generated.

When an edge $(U_i, U_j)$ is deleted, the classes that are at the higher level to $U_i$ are given the access to the key of $U_j$. So the algorithm for deleting a relationship adds edges from all the immediate predecessors of $U_i$ to $U_j$. The same operations are performed in the case of deleting a node. When deleting a node $U_k$, edges are added between immediate predecessors of $U_k$ and its immediate successors.

**Deleting a Relationship.** To delete the relationship $U_j \leq U_i$, the CA performs the steps shown in Algorithm 3.

*Example*: In Fig. 1, if the relationship between $A$ and $B$ is deleted, then no keys are regenerated. If the relationship between $C$ and $E$ is deleted, then $A$ is made an immediate predecessor of $A$, and the key of $E$ is re-generated.

**Deleting a Node.** To delete a node $U_k$, the CA performs the steps shown in Algorithm 4.

*Example*: In Fig. 1, if the node $A$ is deleted, then the edges from $A$ to $B$ and $C$ are deleted, but the keys of $B$ and $C$ are not changed. If the node $C$ is deleted, then $E$ and $F$ become immediate successors of $A$, and therefore their keys are re-generated.

---

**Algorithm 3.** Delrelation($U_i, U_j$)    {comment: $U_j \leq U_i$}

---

1: $E \leftarrow E - \{(U_i, U_j)\}$
2: **if** (root($U_i$) = 0 or root($U_i$) = 0) **then**
3:    **for all** $U_r \in$ Immpred($U_i$) **do**
4:       $E \leftarrow E \cup \{(U_r, U_j)\}$
5:    **end for**
6:    **for all** $U_s \in$ ModifiedBFS($U_j$) **do**
7:       Regenerate the key of $U_s$
8:    **end for**
9: **else**
10:   do nothing
11: **end if**

---

**Algorithm 4.** Delnode($U_k$)

---

1: $V' \leftarrow$ Immsucc($U_k$)
2: $V'' \leftarrow$ Immpred($U_k$)
3: **for all** $U_l \in V'$ **do**
4:   $E \leftarrow E - \{(U_k, U_l)\}$
5: **end for**
6: **if** ($V'' \neq \emptyset$) **then**
7:   **for all** $U_l \in V''$ **do**
8:      $E \leftarrow E - \{(U_l, U_k)\}$
9:      **for all** $U_r \in V'$ **do**
10:         $E \leftarrow E \cup \{(U_l, U_r)\}$
11:      **end for**
12:   **end for**
13: **end if**
14: **for all** $U_l \in V'$ **do**
15:   **if** (root($U_l$) = 0) **then**
16:      **for all** $U_m \in$ ModifiedBFS($U_l$) **do**
17:         Re-generate the key of $U_m$
18:      **end for**
19:   **end if**
20: **end for**
21: $V \leftarrow V - \{U_k\}$

---

## 3    Attacks

This section presents our attacks on Yang-Li scheme. We consider four scenarios.

**Attack 1: Deleting a Root Node.** If a root node is deleted and the immediate successors of previous root node become root nodes after the deletion, the keys of the new root nodes and their successors are not changed. The keys of all these nodes are thus accessible to the previous root node which was deleted.

*Example*: In Fig. 1, if we delete the node $A$, then $B$ and $C$ become root nodes and so their keys are not regenerated. The keys of $B$ and $C$ as well as their successors are still accessible to $A$.

**Attack 2: Deleting a Relationship with Root Node.** If the relationship between a root node and its immediate successor is deleted and the successor becomes a root node after the deletion, then no keys are changed. The old root node can still derive the keys of the new root node as well as the keys of the successors of the new root node.

*Example*: In the hierarchy given in Fig. 1, if we delete the relationship between $A$ and $B$, then $A$ will be no longer at the higher level than $B$. However $A$ can still derive the keys of $B$ and all its successors because these keys are not re-generated.

**Attack 3: Deleting a Non-root Node.** If the deleted node is not a root node, then the keys of all its successors are regenerated. However, the old information held by that node may still prove useful in deriving the new keys assigned to its successors.

*Example*: Suppose that we delete node $C$ from the hierarchy given in Figure 1. The key of $E$ before deletion is $H_2(H_2(K_B)||H_1(K_C))$, where $K_B$ and $K_C$ are the keys of $B$ and $C$, respectively. $H_2(K_B)$ is known to $C$ and $H_1(K_C)$ is known to $B$. Now after the deletion the key of $E$ is regenerated, the new key is calculated as $H_2(H_2(K_B)||H_2(K_A))$. Note that $H_2(K_B)$ is known to C and $H_2(K_A)$ is C's key itself. Thus, $C$ can derive the key of $E$.

**Attack 4: Deleting a Relationship Between Non-root Nodes.** This case is similar to the previous one.

## 4   The Proposed Scheme

This section describes the proposed hash based scheme. The scheme has the following properties.

- The private storage is reduced to one key per node. To achieve this we use the fact that *given $x_1 \oplus x_2$ we can not efficiently find either $x_1$ or $x_2$ without the knowledge of one of them*. We assume that $x_1$ and $x_2$ are large integers on which brute force attack is infeasible.
- In the Yang-Li scheme the key of a non-root node is calculated by finding the hash value of its immediate predecessors' keys. In our proposed scheme we concatenate the public identifiers of the node and all its predecessors before the hash operation is performed. This modification not only overcomes the attacks proposed in the previous section, it also decreases the number of hash functions required to one.

**Key Generation.** The CA chooses a public one-way hash function $H$. Every node in the hierarchy is assigned a unique random number. For each node $U_j$ in the hierarchy, the CA assigns the keys as follows:

- If $U_j$ is a root node, then assign an arbitrary key.
- If $U_j$ has only one immediate predecessor $U_i$ with key $K_i$ (so $U_i \leq U_j$), then the key $K_j$ assigned to $U_j$ is calculated as

$$K_j = H(K_i||i||j||R_j) \tag{3}$$

Here $i$ and $j$ are the identifiers of nodes $U_i$ and $U_j$, respectively. $R_j$ is a public random number associated with $U_j$.
- If $U_j$ has more than one immediate predecessors $U_i^1, U_i^2, \ldots, U_i^m$, then its key $K_j$ is calculated as

$$K_j = H(H(K_{i_1}||i_1|| \ldots ||i_m||j)||H(K_{i_2}||i_1|| \ldots ||i_m||j)|| \cdots ||$$
$$H(K_{i_m}||i_1|| \ldots ||i_m||j)||R_j) \tag{4}$$

Here $K_{i_1}, \ldots, K_{i_m}$ are the keys and $i_1, \ldots, i_n$ are the identifiers of nodes $U_i^1, \ldots, U_i^m$, respectively. The CA also computes the following $m - 1$ values and makes them public.

$$H(K_{i_1}||i_1|| \ldots ||i_m||j) \oplus H(K_{i_2}||i_1|| \ldots ||i_m||j),$$
$$H(K_{i_2}||i_1|| \ldots ||i_m||j) \oplus H(K_{i_3}||i_1|| \ldots ||i_m||j),$$
$$\vdots \qquad\qquad \vdots$$
$$H(K_{i_{m-1}}||i_1|| \ldots ||i_m||j) \oplus H(K_{i_m}||i_1|| \ldots ||i_m||j).$$

*Example:* For the hierarchy given in Fig. 1, the keys are assigned as shown in Table 2. The value $(H(K_B||B||C||E) \oplus H(K_C||B||C||E))$ is made public.

**Table 2.** Key assignment in the proposed scheme

| Node ID | Key |
|---------|-----|
| A | $K_A$(chosen by CA) |
| B | $K_B = H(K_A||A||B||R_B)$ |
| C | $K_C = H(K_A||A||C||R_C)$ |
| D | $K_D = H(K_B||B||D||R_D)$ |
| E | $K_E = H(H(K_B||B||C||E)||H(K_C||B||C||E)||R_E)$ |
| F | $K_F = H(K_C||C||F||R_F)$ |

**Key Derivation.** Suppose that node $U_i$ wants to derive the key $K_j$ of its immediate successor $U_j$. Depending on whether $U_i$ is the only immediate predecessor of $U_j$, the key $K_j$ can be computed using the appropriate equation above. When $U_j$ has more than one immediate predecessor, then $U_i$ must calculate the required inputs from the extra public information made available by the CA.

*Example:* Suppose that node $A$ wants to derive $E$'s key. First $A$ computes $B$'s key $K_B$ as $H(K_A||A||B||R_B)$. Further $A$ computes $H(K_B||B||C||E)$ and xors this value with $H(K_B||B||C||E) \oplus H(K_C||B||C||E))$ to get $H(K_C||B||C||E)$. Now $A$ computes $E$'s key $K_E$ by computing the hash of these two values, i.e. $K_E = H(H(K_B||B||C||E)||H(K_C||B||C||E)||R_E)$. Alternatively, $A$ can compute $C$'s key $K_C$ as $H(K_A||A||C)$ and then extract $H(K_B||B||C||E)$.

### 4.1  Dynamic Access Control

Our scheme supports two types of updates to the hierarchy, one at the node level, i.e. addition/deletion of nodes and relationships, and the other at the user level, i.e. addition/deletion of users from a security class.

**Node Level.** The algorithms for addition of nodes and relationships are the same as that in the Yang-Li scheme. In the case where a root node is deleted, if a successor of the root node becomes a root node after the deletion, the Yang-Li algorithm does not do anything. Therefore their scheme suffers from the ex-member problem. We modify the algorithm for deleting a node such that all the successors keys are regenerated when a node is deleted. The same modification applies to the algorithm for deleting a relationship. These modifications prevent Attacks 1 and 2. The algorithm for deleting a a non-root node is not modified. Attacks 3 and 4 are avoided because of the additional information included in the hash input.

*Example:* In Fig. 1, if the node $C$ is deleted then $E$ and $F$ become immediate successors of $A$. The key of $E$ before deletion is

$$H(H(K_B||B||C||E)||H(K_C||B||C||E)||R_E)$$

Note that $H(K_B||B||C||E)$ is known to $C$ and $H(K_C||B||C||E))$ is known to $B$. After the deletion $E$'s key is

$$H(H(K_A||B||A||E)||H(K_B||B||A||E)||R_E) \tag{5}$$

This value can not be obtained from the information held by $C$ in the past. So Attack 3 is prevented. Likewise, if the relationship between $C$ and $E$ is deleted, then the key of $E$ is changed according to Equation (5) and so Attack 4 is also prevented.

**User Level.** When a user is added to a security class or deleted from a security class, the random number associated with that node is changed. This changes the key of the node. And correspondingly, the keys of all the successors are also regenerated. The deleted user cannot obtain the keys of its past successors because it needs to invert the hash function. Likewise, we can also change the key of a node by changing the random number of that node and correspondingly regenerating the keys of the node and all its successors.

*Example:* Suppose we delete a user from class $B$ in Fig. 1. Then the random number corresponding to class $B$ is changed to $B'$. So the keys of $B$, $D$ and $E$ are changed.

## 5    Security Proof

This section presents a proof of security for the proposed scheme using a security model defined by Wu and Wei [5]. We assume a static hierarchy; in other words, we do not consider additions/deletions to the hierarchy. The following definition of Wu and Wei captures the required security property.

> A hierarchical access control scheme for poset hierarchy is secure if for any group of classes in the poset, it is computationally infeasible to derive the key of any class that is not a member of that group, nor a successor of any member of that group.

Assume that $H$ is a strong hash function with the following properties :

1. It is computationally infeasible to differentiate between the output of $H$ and output of a truly random function.
2. It is computationally infeasible to compute the inverse of $H$, i.e. to find $x$ given $H(x)$.
3. It is computationally infeasible to find two values $x_1$ and $x_2$ which hash to the same value, i.e. $H(x_1) = H(x_2)$.

We use the same notations as Wu-Wei. Suppose that $P$ is the set of all nodes in the hierarchy with a cardinality of $n$. We fix an arbitrary node $T$ with key $K_t$. Let $A$ be the set of predecessors of $T$. We will prove that even if all the nodes in $P - A - \{T\}$ collude they cannot compute $K_t$. The set $P - A - \{T\}$ is divided into three parts defined below:

- $D$ is the set of immediate successors of $T$.
- $B$ is the set of nodes in $P - A - \{T\} - D$ which share a common predecessor or a common immediate successor with $T$, plus all their predecessors.

$$B' = \{x \mid x \in P - A - \{T\} - D \text{ and } (x \in \text{Immsucc}(A) \text{ or } x \in \text{Immpred}(D))\}$$
$$B = B' \cup \{x \mid x \in \text{Predecessors}(B') \text{ and } x \notin A \cup \{T\}\}$$

- The remaining set $R = P - A - \{T\} - B - D$.

First we establish four lemmas which prove that even if all users in $B$, $D$, $B \cup D$, $B \cup D \cup R$ collude they can not efficiently compute $K_t$. Then we establish the main theorem which is consequence of these lemmas, thus proving the secrecy of our scheme.

**Lemma 1.** *Even if all users in the set $B$ collude they cannot compute $K_t$ in polynomial time with non-negligible probability.*

*Proof.* There are only two ways by which the nodes in $B$ can compute $K_t$. One is through common immediate predecessors and another through common immediate successors. We shall prove the lemma for the two cases.

**Case 1 Finding $K_t$ through immediate successors:** The information about $K_t$ known to nodes in $B$ is represented as

$$\{H(K_t||T||(B_j)^+||S_j) \mid S_j \in S \text{ and } 1 < j < n\}$$

Here $S$ is set of nodes in $D$ (immediate successors of $T$) which have $T$ and one or more nodes from $B$ as immediate predecessors, and $(B_j)^+$ is concatenation of identifiers of those nodes in $B$ which are immediate predecessors of $S_j$. As all the node ids are public we can specify the information held by nodes in $B$ as

$$\{H(K_t||Pub_j) \mid S_j \in S \text{ and } 1 < j < n\}$$

where $Pub_j$ is concatenation of node ids of $T$ and all its immediate predecessors. Now we prove the lemma by contradiction. Suppose that there exists a probabilistic polynomial time algorithm $Z$ which computes $K_t$ from the above known information with non negligible probability $\rho$.

$$Pr(Z(H(K_t||Pub_j)\forall S_j \in S, \ K_t)) = \rho$$

Then we show that we can invert the hash function. Suppose that $y = H(x)$ and $x$ is represented in binary as $x_0 x_1 .... x_{l-1}$. Then we can give $H(x_0 x_1 \ldots x_{l-1}||x_l)$ as input to $Z$ and find $x_0 x_1 .... x_l$. Now we can find $x$ by checking the value of $y$ with $H(x_0 x_1 .... x_{l-1}||0)$ and $H(x_0 x_1 .... x_{l-1}||1)$. So we end up with a way to find the inverse of $H$, which contradicts the assumption about $H$.

**Case 2 Finding $K_t$ through immediate predecessors:** The key of node $T$ is generated as follows:

$$K_t = H(K'_t)$$

where $K'_t = Concat(H(K_{A_i}||(A_i)^+||T)) \mid A_i \in Immpred(T)$

*Concat*: Returns concatenation of the elements given as input.
$(A_i)^+$: Concatenation all node ids of Immediate predecessors of $T$.

As all node ids are public we write:

$$K'_t = Concat(H(K_{A_i}||Pub_i)) \mid A_i \in Immpred(T)$$

The keys of nodes in $B_i \in B$ which have same immediate predecessor as T are generated as follows:

$$K_{B_i} = H(K'_{B_i})$$

where $K'_{B_i} = Concat(H(K_{A_j}||(A_j)^+||B_i)) \mid A_j \in Immpred(B_i), \ B_i \in B$

We then write:

$$K'_{B_i} = Concat(H(K_{A_j}||Pub'_i)) \mid A_j \in \text{Immpred}(B_i),\ B_i \in B$$

Suppose that there exists a probabilistic polynomial time algorithm which computes $K_t$ from all $K_{B_i}$'s with non-negligible probability $\rho$. As output of $H$ is indistinguishable from the output of a random function the only way to find $K_t$ is to find $K_{A_i}$ for all $A_i \in \text{Immpred}(T)$. Let the algorithm that computes $K_{A_i}$'s from $K_{B_i}$'s be $Z_1$. Then we can use $Z_1$ to invert H. Give $H(H(x_0x_1 \ldots x_{l-1}||x_l)|| H(y_0y_1 \ldots y_{l-1}||y_l))$ as input to $Z_1$ which outputs $(x_0x_1 \ldots x_{l-1})$ and $(y_0y_1 \ldots y_{l-1})$. Now we can try four possibilities, two each for $x_l$, $y_l$ and compute $x$, $y$. That means we are able to compute inverse of $H$, which contradicts the assumption about $H$.

**Lemma 2.** *Even if all users in the set $D$ collude they cannot compute $K_t$ in polynomial time with non-negligible probability.*

*Proof.* The information that the users in $D$ know about $K_t$ can be represented as:

$$\{H(H(K_t||T||(B_i)^+||D_i)||(H(K_{B_i}||T||(B_i)^+)||D_i)^+) \mid D_i \in D\}$$

as all the node ids are stored publicly we can simplify it as:

$$\{H(H(K_t||Pub_i)||(H(K_{B_i}||(Pub_i)'))^+) \mid D_i \in D\}$$

Suppose that there exists an algorithm $Z_2$ which can compute $K_t$ from the above information with non-negligible probability. Then we show that we can find $x$ from $H(x)$. Find $H(y)$ for an arbitrary y and give $H(H(x_0x_1 \ldots x_{l-1}||x_l)||H(y))$ as input to $Z_2$. Then $Z_2$ outputs $x_0x_1 \ldots x_{l-1}$. From this we can find $x$ by trying two possibilities for $x_l$, which yields a contradiction.

**Lemma 3.** *Even if all users in the set $B \cup D$ collude they cannot compute $K_t$ in polynomial time with non negligible probability.*

*Proof.* The users in $B$ can obtain the information known to all the immediate successors of $B$. So to find the information known to the users of $B \cup D$ it is enough to find the information known to the users of $B$ and the information known to the users of $D$ who do not have any immediate predecessors in $B$ (let this set be $S$). This can be represented as:

$$\{H(K_t||T||S_i) \mid S_i \in S\}$$

and

$$\{H(K_t||T||(D_i)^+||(B_i)^+) \mid B_i \in B\}$$

This can be simplified as

$$\{H(K_t||Pub_i) \mid S_i \in S,\ H(K_t||Pub'_j) \mid B_j \in B\}$$

Suppose that there exists an algorithm $Z_3$ which computes $K_t$ from above information in polynomial time with non-negligible probability. As we know $Pub_i$ and $Pub'_j$, we can find $(K_t||Pub_i)$ and $(K_t||Pub'_j)$, which is essentially equivalent to inverting H.

**Lemma 4.** *Even if all users in the set $B \cup D \cup R$ collude they cannot compute $K_t$ in polynomial time with non negligible probability.*

*Proof.* Since the users in $R$ are either successors of $B \cup D$, whatever information about $K_t$ that is known to the users in $R$ is also known to users in $B \cup D$. Therefore if the users in $B \cup D \cup R$ can derive $K_t$, then the users in $B \cup D$ can also derive $K_t$, which contradicts Lemma 3. Thus the users in $B \cup D \cup R$ cannot derive $K_t$ efficiently.

From the above lemmas it follows that the only way for a user to derive the key of other user is that the latter must be successors of the former. Therefore we arrive at the following theorem.

**Theorem 1.** *The proposed scheme is secure for a static hierarchy.*

## 6   Conclusions

We have shown that Yang-Li scheme is insecure in the dynamic case. We proposed a new hash based scheme which avoids the attacks, and also formally proved its security for a static hierarchy.

Table 3 compares our modified scheme against the Yang-Li scheme and the Atallah-Frikken-Blanton scheme; the latter has performance closest to our scheme. For a $n$-node non-tree hierarchy, the number of edges $e$ is $O(n^2)$. If we let $f$ to be the sum of the in-degrees of all the nodes having in-degree of at least 2, then $f \leq e - 1$. The total private storage required by the Yang-Li scheme

**Table 3.** Comparison of schemes

| Property | Yang-Li [6] | Proposed | Atallah et al [7] |
|---|---|---|---|
| Key Derivation operation | Hashing | Hashing | Hashing |
| Private Storage | $O(n^2)$ | $n$ keys | $n$ keys |
| Public Storage | $O(n)$ | $O(n^2)$ | $O(n^2)$ |
| Dynamic access control | Requires rekeying of only successors | Requires rekeying of only successors | Requires rekeying of only successors |
| Security proof | No | Yes | Yes |
| Ex-Member problem | Yes | No | No |
| User level dynamics | Not Supported | Supported | Supported |
| Changing secret key | Requires rekeying of all nodes | Requires rekeying of only successors | Requires rekeying of only successors |

is $O(f)$; that is, $O(n^2)$; whereas the private storage required by the Atallah-Frikken-Blanton is $O(n)$. From the table we can see that our modified scheme is as efficient as the Atallah-Frikken-Blanton scheme. The Yang-Li scheme does not have a proof of security, whereas both our scheme and the scheme of Atallah et al have security proofs. There is a slight advantage that our scheme has over their scheme. If we assume a tree hierarchy, i.e. a hierarchy where every node has at most one immediate predecessor, then our scheme does not require any extra public storage (beyond the random numbers associated with each node), whereas their scheme requires an additional public value for every edge, in addition to the public values associated with each node. Thus for the tree hierarchies our scheme is more efficient in terms of public storage compared to their scheme.

**Acknowledgments.** We are grateful to the anonymous referees for valuable comments and suggestions. One referee pointed out a problem with the proof of Lemma 4, which led us to a new definition of the set $B$, for which the proof works. We are thankful to Ashok Amin for answering our questions about properties of graphs.

# References

1. Akl, S., Taylor, P.: Cryptographic solution to a problem of access control in a hierarchy. J-TOCS **1**(3) (1983) 239–248
2. Sandhu, R.: Cryptographic implementation of a tree hierarchy for access control. Information Processing Letters **27**(2) (1988) 95–98
3. Harn, L., Lin, H.: Cryptographic key generation scheme for multilevel data security. Computers and Security **9**(6) (1990) 539–546
4. Shen, V.R.L., Chen, T.S.: A novel key management scheme based on discrete logarithms and polynomial interpolations. Computers and Security **21**(2) (2002) 164–171
5. Wu, J., Wei, R.: An access control scheme for partial ordered set hierarchy with provable security. Selected Areas in Cryptography 2005, LNCS 3897 (2006) 221–232
6. Yang, C., Li, C.: Access control in a hierarchy using one-way hash functions. Computers and Security **23**(8) (2004) 659–664
7. Atallah, M., Frikken, K., Blanton, M.: Dynamic and efficient key management for access hierarchies. ACM Conference on Computer and Communications Security (CCS'05) (2005) 190–202
8. Hsu, C.L., Wu, T.S.: Cryptanalyses and improvements of two cryptographic key assignment schemes for dynamic access control in a user hierarchy. Computers and Security **22**(5) (2003) 453–456
9. Cormen, T., Leiserson, C., Rivest, R., Stein, C.: Introduction to Algorithms. Second edn. MIT Press (2001)

# A   ModifiedBFS

---

**Algorithm 5.** ModifiedBFS($U_i$)                 { $G_1$ is the graph rooted at $U_i$}

---

1: **for all** $v \in G_1 - \{U_i\}$ **do**
2:     color $[v] \leftarrow 0$          {used for checking the vertex is visited already}
3: **end for**
4: color $[U_i] \leftarrow 1$
5: ENQUEUE($Q, U_i$)      {Insert into queue $Q$}
6: **while** $Q \neq \phi$ **do**
7:     $u \leftarrow$ DEQUEUE($Q$)       {Delete from queue $Q$}
8:     color $[u] \leftarrow 1$
9:     **for all** $v \in$ Immsucc(u) **do**
10:         Let $u'$ be the rightmost predecessor of $v$
11:         **if** color $[u']$=1 **then**
12:             color $[v] \leftarrow 1$
13:             ENQUEUE($Q, v$)
14:         **else**
15:             Do nothing
16:         **end if**
17:     **end for**
18: **end while**

---

# Adaptation of IEEE 802.1X for Secure Session Establishment Between Ethernet Peers

Purificación Sáiz, Jon Matías, Eduardo Jacob, Javier Bustamante,
and Armando Astarloa

Dep. of Electronics and Telecommunications, University of the Basque Country
Faculty of Engineering of Bilbao, Alda. Urquijo s/n, 48013 Bilbao, Spain
{puri.saiz,jon.matias,eduardo.jacob,armando.astarloa}@ehu.es

**Abstract.** Network connectivity has undergone a significant change
since the appearance and increasing deployment of IEEE 802.11 technology. Wireless links are inherently insecure and, in order to secure them,
the IEEE 802.11i amendment has defined the security mechanisms to be
used. The solution described in IEEE 802.11i is applicable, in theory,
to both infrastructure and ad-hoc networks. Nevertheless, the great deployment of wireless access points and the potential economical benefits
derived from it impelled the standardization bodies to provide a security solution for IEEE 802.11 access links. Therefore, IEEE 802.11i has
been designed as an infrastructure-oriented solution, and some of the
design decisions are not the most appropriate for its use in peer-to-peer
communications, showing several limitations to secure ad-hoc networks.
We have found the same drawbacks when trying to adapt the IEEE
802.1X model for providing end-to-end security at the link layer between
Ethernet peers. We have identified the shortcomings of the standardized
solution for its application in securing peer-to-peer communications, and
we propose some modifications to the IEEE 802.1X model that help to
overcome those limitations. These modifications have been implemented
and functionally tested for establishing secure communications between
end stations in Ethernet networks.

## 1 Introduction

According to the original Local Area Network (LAN) philosophy, network access
was allowed to any device that could connect to a network attachment point.
Provided that the switch port was enabled, there was no means of restricting the
connectivity service to authorized users. To address the security concerns raised
by this unauthorized access, the Institute of Electrical and Electronics Engineers
(IEEE) developed the 802.1X standard [1] to enable port-based network access
control. This standard defines how to authenticate and authorize devices connected to a LAN port, preventing the connected device from exchanging traffic
through that port if the result of the authentication and authorization processes
is unsuccessful.

Today, IEEE 802.11 wireless LANs (WLAN) [2] are widely deployed in public
or semi-public sites. In these wireless access networks, the same access control

A. Bagchi and V. Atluri (Eds.): ICISS 2006, LNCS 4332, pp. 220–234, 2006.

issues have to be considered, but particularized to a more vulnerable scenario: the usage of a share media based on radiofrequency makes the information accessible to any device in the surroundings of the transmitting station. Therefore, a successful authentication is a pre-requisite for authorizing a port, as in the wired case, but additionally the exchanged traffic should be cryptographically protected by means of some keying material that should be previously established. The security mechanisms to be applied in these networks are defined in the IEEE 802.11i standard [3]. It specifies how to use IEEE 802.1X in IEEE 802.11 WLANs for authentication, defines a handshake protocol for key management, and establishes the use of TKIP and AES-CCMP for data protection.

The IEEE 802.11i standard describes the operation of the security procedures for IEEE 802.11 networks in infrastructure and ad-hoc modes, defining the functional models and the security association and key management procedures for both cases.

The specified model and procedures are well-suited for the infrastructure case. In fact, the infrastructure case is an evolution of a wired access network, where the access switch is replaced by a wireless access point (AP) and the access link is a radio link. Therefore the access control model defined in IEEE 802.1X is valid, in the basics, for the infrastructure mode: the AP controls the access of the mobile stations (MSs) to the network. This is the reason why IEEE 802.11i reuses the port-based access control scheme defined in IEEE 802.1X. The novelties come due to the usage of a shared media LAN for accessing the network, having to ensure the reliability of the authentication exchange and the confidentiality and integrity of exchanged data.

The ad-hoc case is completely different, however. There is no longer one device wanting to gain access to a service provided by another one, but two devices wanting to communicate with each other. In this case, a security association has to be established between each pair of stations who want to communicate. The adoption of the existing authentication, authorization and key management model, without a review, implies not considering the particularities of this new scenario: the establishment of secure peer-to-peer communications.

We are working on offering end-to-end security at the link layer between stations of an Ethernet network. When we analyzed the requirements for the security association management in this scenario, we found that they were similar, to a large extent, to those of the IEEE 802.11 ad-hoc networks. And we identified the limitations of the model described in IEEE 802.1X and IEEE 802.11i for its application to establish secure connections between pairs of stations.

In this paper, we firstly summarize the basic principles of IEEE 802.1X and IEEE 802.11i, intended to provide security in IEEE 802 LANs. Next, we analyze this model from the perspective of its application for securing peer-to-peer communications at the link layer, identifying some weak points. Afterwards we propose some modifications in order to overcome those limitations and we report our experience in a test bed where the described modifications have been implemented. Finally we summarize the conclusions and outline the future work to be made.

# 2    Background: IEEE 802.1X Basic Concepts

The operation of IEEE 802.1X and IEEE 802.11i is thoroughly described in [1] and [3]. In this section, a summary of the access control operation defined in them is provided in order to ease the understanding of our analysis and proposal to readers not familiarized with these standards.

## 2.1    Motivation of IEEE 802.1X

Many LANs are deployed in environments where attachment points are very easily accessible, so any device or user can attach to the network. This posed an important problem with the original definition of IEEE 802.1, because there wasn't any mechanism to authenticate the devices or users intending to access the network, neither to authorize the access to the network in a specific port according to the identity of the device or user connected to that port.

This problem of controlling network access through public network ports was tackled by the IEEE 802.1X "Port-Based Network Access Control" standard [1]. This standard defines the mechanisms that allow a device to control the authorizing state of a port. The decision of authorizing or not a port is determined by the result, successful or unsuccessful, of a process of authentication of the user or device connected to the port.

However, IEEE 802.1X doesn't define the contents of the exchanged authentication information, neither the type of authentication to be performed. Instead, it makes use of EAP (Extensible Authentication Protocol) [4] to exchange authentication messages. EAP, in turn, doesn't define a specific authentication procedure, but provides a common framework which supports multiple authentication methods; hence the term "extensible" in its name.

## 2.2    IEEE 802.1X Operation

There are two basic concepts in the IEEE 802.1X design. First, it defines a **port-based** access control, assuming that each port provides point-to-point connectivity with only one device. Therefore, once the device connected to that port has successfully authenticated, the port can be authorized and the traffic allowed through that port.

The other important point is the clear separation between **authentication and authorization**. Initially, there is an authentication message exchange. Afterwards, the access switch establishes the state of the port as Authorized or Unauthorized, according to the result of the previous authentication. This function separation enables the use of a back-end authentication server during the authentication phase, in which case the switch transparently forwards the authentication messages between the device connected to the port and the authentication server. This solution is easy to integrate with existing AAA infrastructure, facilitating the deployment of IEEE 802.1X [5].

In short, IEEE 802.1X defines the protocol (EAPOL – EAP over LAN) used to carry authentication information between the two devices connected to the

LAN, and the mechanisms to control the state of both systems' ports depending on the result of the authentication procedure.

Following IEEE 802.1X terminology, the devices connected to a LAN (*systems*) may have one or more points of attachment to the LAN (*ports*). The port of a system can adopt one of two roles:

- **Authenticator:** the port that enforces authentication before allowing access to the services accessible via that port. In an Ethernet switched network, an Authenticator is associated to each physical port of the access switch through which a device can gain access to the network.
- **Supplicant:** the port that wishes to access the services offered by the Authenticator. In an Ethernet switched network, the Supplicant is the LAN port on the network adapter of the device requesting access to the network.

The *Port Access Entity* (PAE) is the logical entity that performs the algorithms and protocols associated to the access control mechanisms for a port. A PAE can support the functionality associated with an Authenticator, a Supplicant, or both.

Additionally, there is a third role, the **Authentication Server**. The Authentication Server performs the authentication functions to verify the credentials of the Supplicant on behalf of the Authenticator, and then indicates to the Authenticator whether or not the Supplicant is authorized to access the Authenticator's services.

The access control defined in IEEE 802.1X has the effect of splitting a port into two access points: an *uncontrolled port*, which allows the uncontrolled exchange of traffic at any time, regardless the authorization state of the port; and a *controlled port*, which allows the exchange of traffic only when the port is in an Authorized state. The Authenticator and Supplicant PAEs exchange authentication protocol messages via the uncontrolled port. The messages of other protocols are exchanged via the controlled port, if it is in the Authorized state.

Figure 1 shows the described operation of IEEE 802.1X. Uncontrolled and controlled ports in both Authenticator and Supplicant systems are depicted: the uncontrolled port for the authentication exchange, the controlled port for the rest of protocols. The authentication messages are exchanged between the uncontrolled ports of the Supplicant and the Authenticator in the access LAN, and between the Authenticator and Authentication Server in the internal network. The result of the authentication procedure conditions the state of the controlled port: Authorized if successful, Unauthorized if unsuccessful. When the controlled port is Authorized, the traffic generated at or destined to the Supplicant that requires the services offered by the Authenticator is allowed via the controlled port.

## 2.3   IEEE 802.1X Operation in IEEE 802.11 Networks

Due to the nature of radio media, wireless networks are insecure and vulnerable. The original IEEE 802.11 standard included a set of security features that soon proved to be quite easily vulnerable [6]. The IEEE 802.11i standard [3] improved

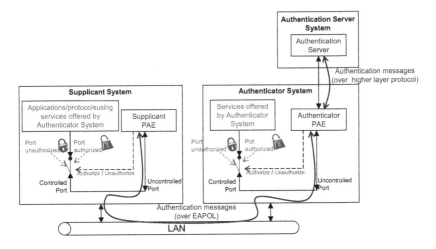

**Fig. 1.** IEEE 802.1X basic operation

WLAN security, addressing all the identified vulnerabilities. Essentially, it separates authentication and message protection (integrity and privacy), linking the two parts, however, in a security context [7].

IEEE 802.11i specifies the use of IEEE 802.1X for authentication and reuses its controlled/uncontrolled port model for controlling the traffic flow. A key generating EAP method should be used with IEEE 802.1X to allow both communicating stations to authenticate and derive a common master key. The master key provides prove of identity and is used to derive session keys that will be used for encryption and data protection as long as the security context is active. IEEE 802.11i defines a key management handshake protocol to derive the session keys from the master key, and two data confidentiality and integrity protocols, TKIP and AES-CCMP.

With regard to the use of IEEE 802.1X in WLAN, an important consideration has to be made. The original scenario for which the IEEE 802.1X standard was designed refers to a switched wired LAN, where the devices attach to the network via a dedicated link to a port of an access switch. The fact that only one device connects to each port of the switch contributes to an easy access control: Once the device has successfully authenticated, its traffic can be allowed authorizing the port, with the certainty that the device sending and receiving frames via that port is the one that has been authenticated and authorized, and that no other device can eavesdrop or modify that traffic.

This key assumption is no longer valid in shared media LANs, such as IEEE 802.11 networks, where one physical port of a system provides connectivity to more than one device. If the port were authorized when a device has successfully authenticated, access would be granted to any device connected through that port. Therefore, in order to use IEEE 802.1X in shared media LAN segments, access control should be based on logical ports, instead of physical ports. From the access control point of view, a physical port can be viewed as a set of independent logical ports, each one controlling the access of a different device.

Nevertheless, this per-device authentication is not enough to authorize the traffic on that port. In a shared media LAN, it is necessary to apply independent encryption in order to protect the traffic exchanged through each authorized logical port, providing at least confidentiality, integrity, and data origin authentication services. In consequence, a successful authentication in a logical port should be followed by a key establishment procedure before the port is authorized. This way, a security context can be established between the two concerned systems, enabling the subsequent secure exchange of traffic between each other.

The explained behavior can be obtained thanks to some features of the IEEE 802.1X standard aimed to support port-based access control in shared media LANs, and some additional features defined in IEEE 802.11i.

First, IEEE 802.1X allows the use of individual MAC addresses as the destination address in frames that carry authentication and key management information (as a complement to the use of a PAE group address in point-to-point LAN access). In the case of IEEE 802.11, a MS must associate to an AP before it can make use of the LAN. This association procedure makes both the MS and AP learn each other's MAC address, and create the logical port that will be used for controlling the access of the system identified by that address. For the port-based access control to work, the destination MAC address of the EAPOL messages exchanged between the two PAEs will have to be the destination system's individual MAC address, instead of the generic PAE group address.

IEEE 802.1X also allows the exchange of cryptographic material between Authenticator and Supplicant after a successful authentication exchange, for its use in scenarios where encryption is available between the Authenticator and Supplicant systems. For that purpose, IEEE 802.1X defines a type of EAPOL message, EAPOL-Key. However, it doesn't define which key values should be transmitted within EAPOL-Key messages or what the Authenticator and Supplicant systems should do with those keys.

It is the IEEE 802.11i standard that defines the content of the EAPOL-Key messages exchanged between an Authenticator and a Supplicant in a wireless LAN, and the functions to be performed with the exchanged information in order to establish a secure channel. IEEE 802.11i defines a 4-way handshake protocol, that is, the exchange of 4 EAPOL-Key messages whose contents allow the Authenticator and Supplicant systems to derive in a secure manner the transient keys that will be used to protect that session's pairwise traffic between both systems. It also defines a group handshake that allows an Authenticator to deliver group keys to a Supplicant, so that the Supplicant system can receive broadcast messages sent by the Authenticator system.

IEEE 802.11i completes the revised access control scheme by defining the key management state machines for the Authenticator and the Supplicant, and redefining the port access control state machines so that a port is not authorized until the keys have been established in that port.

The security model described in IEEE 802.11i perfectly fits the infrastructure mode, where the AP (Authenticator) controls the access of the MNs (Supplicants) to the network, as it can be seen in Fig. 2.

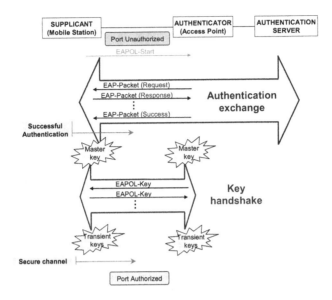

**Fig. 2.** IEEE 802.11i authentication and key establishment in infrastructure network

But IEEE 802.11i gives also indications about how to secure communications in ad-hoc networks, composed of stations within mutual communication range of each other via the wireless medium. In this case, when a station wishes to establish a security association with a peer, each one creates an Authenticator and a Supplicant for that association. Therefore, either a preshared master key is used or two authentication exchanges should take place, each between one station's Authenticator and the peer's Supplicant, in order to satisfy both roles' requirements at each station. In any of both cases, two key management handshake exchanges have to be performed afterwards so that each station provides its peer with its group key. The reason is that different group keys are used to protect the broadcast traffic sent by each station, even if the same pairwise key can be used to protect unicast traffic in both directions. Unfortunately, this results also in two pairwise keys, so one of them is discarded.

It can be seen that, for a secure link to exist between two stations of an IEEE 802.11 ad-hoc network, both authentication procedures and both handshake exchanges have to be completed successfully. In order to achieve this behavior, the Supplicant and Authenticator state machines have to interact so the port is not authorized until both handshakes have finished.

## 3   Target Peer-to-Peer Scenario

eEurope2005 action plan [8] has as a main target "the widespread availability and use of broadband networks throughout the Union by 2005, and the security of networks and information". In line with the established priorities within the

European organizations, the scientific community is working in the bottlenecks that nowadays avoid the provisioning of broadband solutions to the users.

The first conclusions identify "protocol translations" as the source of the complexity and cost in the local loop and the MANs. In order to avoid protocol conversions, the Telecom Network architectural model is moving to networks based on the same link layer end-to-end. Many telecom operators are working on business models based on the provisioning of Ethernet services within Metropolitan environments for the interconnection of business network. Wideband services for end users with a first mile link based on Ethernet are also considered. In this scenario, we will be soon talking of end-to-end Ethernet networks with no protocol translation.

However, in order to provide commercial Ethernet services, it is of vital importance that a security environment is provided. We are working in line with this objective to define a protocol architecture to provide security in end-to-end Ethernet communications regarding data confidentiality and integrity and authentication of data origin. As a required condition for a dynamic link layer end-to-end encryption mechanism to be secure, both communicating ends should have previously established a security association at the Ethernet level.

After an analysis of different possibilities, we reached the evidence that securing Ethernet end-to-end communications presented a similar problem to that of securing communications in an IEEE 802.11 ad-hoc network. Therefore, the security association model to be used could be based on the one defined in IEEE 802.11i. In the following subsections, the similarities and differences between both scenarios are explained

### 3.1   Similarities to IEEE 802.11 Ad-Hoc Networks

In IEEE 802.11i, traffic encryption is performed at link layer, with the keys that have been obtained after authentication and key management exchanges at the same link layer making use of 802.1X. In our target scenario, MAC layer encryption was within the original objectives. In consequence, it makes sense to perform authentication and key management also at link level, with the same basic principles defined in IEEE 802.1X and IEEE 802.11i.

Another important coincidence is that the stations that are part of the secure network have usually only one network interface, and all the traffic exchanged with any other station belonging to the same network have to go through it. Therefore, it is not possible to apply restrictions based on the physical port, because it is shared by all the communications with every station in the network. Instead, the logical port concept could be used: a system should create a different logical port for every station with which it wishes to establish a security association, and keep separately the state information needed for a correct secure operation with every peer.

The two points mentioned above expose similarities between the Ethernet end-to-end scenario and IEEE 802.11 wireless networks in general, not specifically ad-hoc networks. But there is a very important issue where our target scenario is different to the wireless infrastructure case and similar to the ad-hoc one: each station has to maintain separate security associations with each communicating peer, unlike in infrastructure networks where a station has a security association only with the AP.

With these evidences, the previously described access control and key management model seems to be adequate for the scenario we are concerned with. Each station will create a separate logical port for controlling whether secure traffic to/from each other station is authorized, depending on the result of authentication and key establishment exchanges. But, in contrast to the stated in section 2.3, EAPOL frames should carry the individual MAC address of the peer station as the destination address although it is not a shared media LAN, so that each frame is processed by the correct PAE at the right destination system.

## 3.2   Differences with IEEE 802.11 Ad-Hoc Networks

Apart from the obvious physical difference –wired Ethernet media instead of wireless radio links–, there are some others that might have some impact in the adaptation of the authentication and key exchange scheme.

First, two communicating stations within a switched Ethernet network need more than one hop to reach each other, whereas there is only one hop between two stations in an ad-hoc network, as considered in IEEE 802.11i. This could represent a problem, because IEEE 802.1X was designed so that an Authenticator is able to control whether the Supplicants that are at one hop's distance could have access to the services it provides, and this is the reason why:

- IEEE 802.1X selected one of the reserved set of group MAC addresses that are not forwarded by switches for its use as the destination MAC address of EAPOL frames (01-80-C2-00-00-03).
- IEEE 802.1X recommends that switches don't forward EAPOL frames, identified by a special EtherType value (0x888E), for security's sake.

The first item doesn't represent a matter in our case because, as stated at the end of Section 3.1, individual MAC addresses should be used instead of the group address. Regarding the second item, as some switches may not bridge IEEE 802.1X frames, a distinct EtherType could be used to enable such devices to bridge Ethernet end-to-end EAPOL frames.

Another important difference is that, in our case, stations attach to an existing network infrastructure, in contrast to the temporary existence of the wireless ad-hoc networks. This reality may be useful for facilitating the execution of certain tasks, because a specialized server may be introduced in order to ease some functions or to give support at others that are natively solved in a IEEE 802.11 wireless network but not in an Ethernet one.

For example, an IEEE 802.11 station can learn the peer's MAC address and security capabilities during the association procedure. This allows both stations to create the logical port and to select the proper security mechanisms to be used. In Ethernet, on the other hand, there is not a standard way for a station to advertise its presence or security policy. A new announcement message could be defined, or alternatively rely on an external server where every station could register its presence and capabilities, allowing the other stations to learn them.

The same or another server could be responsible, for instance, of creating, managing and distributing the broadcast key. The presence of this server would allow all the stations to share a common key for protecting all the broadcast traffic exchanged in the network, instead of having a separate broadcast key for each station that is used only for the broadcast traffic sent by that particular station, which is the case in IEEE 802.11i ad-hoc networks.

## 4   Issues for the Use of IEEE 802.1X in Peer-to-Peer Scenarios

Although the authentication and key management mechanisms defined in IEEE 802.11i seem a good starting point for creating security associations between Ethernet end stations, a further analysis reveals that there are some issues that could be enhanced, not only for the Ethernet case but also for wireless ad-hoc networks.

First of all, the definition of two roles, Authenticator and Supplicant, is totally meaningful when the purpose is to control network access: there is access controlling equipment, such as an access switch in an Ethernet network or an AP in an IEEE 802.11 infrastructure network, which act as Authenticators; and stations that attempt to access the LAN through them, which act as Supplicants. The Supplicant requesting access has to give prove of its identity to the Authenticator, who controls network access and will grant the Supplicant's access only after successfully authenticating and authorizing it.

On the contrary, if the purpose is to establish a secure communication between peers, this separation is not so clear. The two stations are functionally identical, the only difference being that the process is driven by the station wishing to establish communication with the targeted one. Both stations need to authenticate each other and establish cryptographic keys in order to allow the secure traffic exchange with the peer. Therefore, the Authenticator and Supplicant roles would not be strictly necessary, since both stations could be considered as "Supplicating Authenticators".

The second issue is that the requirement of each station having an Authenticator and a Supplicant talking with the peer station's Supplicant and Authenticator respectively, in order to establish a pairwise association with that peer, represents a waste of resources: processing and storage resources within each station, because each role has its own state machines and a number of structures to control the security context and state related to that port; and communication resources, because each pair of stations have to maintain two coupled dialogs to perform the correspondent authentication and key management exchange in opposite directions. Moreover, mutual authentication may not be achieved simply running a one-way authentication protocol twice, once in each direction. The reason is that messages communicated in one run could be exploited by an attacker to compromise the run in the other direction.

Even if a mutually authenticating EAP method is carried over IEEE 802.1X frames, allowing the Supplicant and Authenticator to mutually authenticate with only one exchange, this would only satisfy the Authenticator role at one station and the Supplicant one at the other station. Then, what reasons may exist to have both roles at each station, forcing two opposite authentication and key management exchanges to have place, one in each direction? Section 6.7 of [1] and section 2.4 of [4] show some cases. Two of them are directly applicable to IEEE 802.11i ad-hoc networks:

- When the devices require the creation of separate key material in each direction but the keying protocol is unidirectional. This is the case of the group handshake in IEEE 802.11 ad-hoc networks. It could be avoided using a bidirectional group key handshake that derives different keys for each direction. Anyway, it does not represent any problem for the Ethernet end-to-end case if the group key is managed and distributed by a third equipment, as suggested at the end of Section 3.2.
- When there is no support for "tie breaking" wherein two hosts initiating authentication with each other will only go forward with a single authentication. This implies that even if IEEE 802.11 were to support a bidirectional group key handshake, two authentications, one in each direction, might still occur. But "tie breaking" could be supported with small modifications to the IEEE 802.1X state machines.

Lastly, IEEE 802.1X state machines associated to an Authenticator or Supplicant never disappear. When the Authenticator or Supplicant is created, its state machines are started. From then on, they keep permanently running and transition between different states depending on the events that occur, even if the peer has died or doesn't answer to the authentication dialog, or if both stations don't support a compatible set of security capabilities or don't have the required credentials for the authentication and key management to be successful. The *Held* state is the most similar to the death of the state machine, let's say a coma. After an authentication failure, the port is unauthorized and the *Held* state is entered, where the machine remains until the expiration of a timer. At the Authenticator, the purpose of the *Held* state is to discourage brute force attacks, because it discards all EAPOL frames received while in this state. At the Supplicant, the purpose is to avoid continuously trying to authenticate with an Authenticator that doesn't exist or isn't able to authenticate the Supplicant.

The permanence of the state machines is not a major problem in the network access control situation, where only one Supplicant resides in the device attempting to access the network, and the access switch or AP can be dimensioned so that the supported number of Authenticators is sufficient for the expected number of Supplicants. But in the peer-to-peer situation, each station might want to communicate along the time with any number of other stations, and for each of them an Authenticator and a Supplicant would be created in the local machine. The state machines related to the session with every peer the station has sometime communicated with, remain forever in the local station consuming resources that are no longer needed. A solution for this situation could be to replace the *Held* state by a new one, *Kill*, which would release all the resources associated to the disappearing state machine.

## 5    Proposed Modifications for Adapting IEEE 802.1X Model to Peer-to-Peer Scenarios

Taking into account the previous considerations, the solution we have adopted for security association management between Ethernet end stations is based on IEEE 802.1X and IEEE 802.11i models, with some modifications.

Although the involved stations are functionally equivalent, we have decided to continue using the two roles, Authenticator and Supplicant. The reason is that this role separation is basic in all the IEEE 802.1X operation: the EAPOL and EAP protocols are defined to work between a requestor (Authenticator) and a responder (Supplicant), and the correspondent state machines reflect this. Therefore, maintaining the Authenticator-Supplicant scheme is essential in order to reuse the existing protocols and state machines with minor modifications.

However, instead of each station of a pair having to implement both the Authenticator and Supplicant roles, one of the stations will accommodate the Authenticator and the other one the Supplicant, as shown in Fig. 3. To be more precise, the station that wishes to establish the communication will create a Supplicant PAE for the peer station. On reception of the first EAPOL message (EAPOL-Start), the targeted station will create an Authenticator PAE that will start the authentication sending EAP requests, and the Supplicant will answer to them with EAP responses. This way, if a mutually authenticating EAP method is used, a sole authentication exchange will satisfy the PAEs controlling the port at both ends.

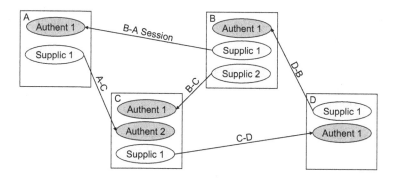

**Fig. 3.** PAEs' roles in Ethernet peer-to-peer secure sessions

The EAPOL messages exchanged between the Authenticator and Supplicant will have the standard format, but with a modified EtherType so that intermediate switches don't apply any special handling to this traffic and forward it through the switched network.

Some modifications are needed in the IEEE 802.1X state machines in order to support "tie breaking". In the case that two stations initiate authentication with each other at the same time, only the one initiated by the station with the highest MAC address will progress. Therefore, the station with the highest MAC address will ignore any EAPOL-Start message received from a station towards which it has a running Supplicant. In the Supplicant of the station with the lowest MAC address, a retry and timeout mechanism will end without success due to the absence of an answer from the peer and will cause the Supplicant's disappearance.

This possibility of killing an existing PAE is also new compared to the IEEE 802.1X state machines. A new state *–Kill–* has been defined, that kills the PAE to which that state machine belongs, releasing all the resources reserved for that PAE. The different situations where the authentication or key management procedures might fail have been considered and analyzed. In the cases where a subsequent successful exchange is not probable, and therefore there is no sense in keeping the PAE alive, the state machines have been modified to transition to the *Kill* state, killing the PAE.

Although each Ethernet station is connected to the switched network via a dedicated link, the traffic exchanged between the peers is subject to multiple attacks [9], so it has to be protected. For this reason, the EAP method used will have to allow not only mutual authentication but also the derivation of a master key. After successful authentication, the Authenticator and Supplicant will derive a temporary key from that master key by means of the 4-way handshake defined in IEEE 802.11i. As in the IEEE 802.11i case, after successful authentication and key establishment, the Authenticator and Supplicant PAEs will authorize their respective ports, allowing thereafter the traffic to and from the peer station, encrypted with the derived key.

The proposed scheme has been implemented on a Linux platform with kernel 2.6.8. We have used hostapd (v0.4.7) and wpa_client (v0.4.7), an open source implementation of an IEEE 802.1X infrastructure Authenticator and Supplicant, modified to be supported on an Ethernet driver, together with a PAE module that corrects a fault in the port authorizing capabilities of the Supplicant. We have corrected, modified and complemented those packages in order to implement the aforementioned behavior, and the implementation is operational in a controlled network of 4 stations. In particular, the features that have required modifications in the original code include, amongst others:

– Several Authenticator and Supplicant PAEs have to coexist within the same system, without mutual interference.
– Either a Supplicant or an Authenticator PAE has to be able to authorize a port.
– Authenticator and Supplicant PAE's state machines have to support "tie breaking"

- Authenticator and Supplicant PAE's state machines have to include a *Kill* state and transitions to it under different failure situations.
- The IEEE 802.11i handshakes have to be executed in an Ethernet environment.

Functional tests have already been performed to check that the achieved implementation behaves as desired in normal conditions and under failure situations. Performance tests are not finished but we don't expect big problems.

# 6   Conclusions and Future Work

We have identified some weak points in the procedure defined at IEEE 802.1X-IEEE 802.11i for the establishment of security associations when it is to be used between peer stations, as in ad-hoc networks. These limitations are also present if that model is applied to establish secure sessions between end stations of an switched Ethernet network. We have proposed some modifications to the original IEEE 802.1X model in order to easily overcome those limitations. The proposed modifications do not negatively affect the utilization of the model in the scenarios where these standards have been traditionally used.

In our current implementation, a station doesn't discover the authentication and cipher suites supported by the station it wishes to establish a session with. Instead, all the stations make use of a predefined security capability set. However, we are defining the interworking with a registering server, where every station will register its security capabilities when it attaches to the network. Any station wishing to establish a secure session with a peer will obtain from the server the security capabilities supported by the targeted station, which will allow the initiating station to select the most suitable policy and initiate authentication and key establishment procedures.

As soon as the registering server is operative and every station contacts the server when it attaches to the network, it is straightforward to assign to the server the role of broadcast key manager: it will generate, manage and distribute the broadcast key to all the stations registered in the network.

In parallel with this work, there are ongoing efforts within our research team to develop a FPGA-based Ethernet interface card with advanced encryption capabilities, which will encrypt/decrypt the traffic to/from a specific station with the encryption algorithm selected and the keys established by means of the mechanisms described in this paper.

# Acknowledgements

This ongoing work is being performed by the I2T Research Team of the University of the Basque Country (Universidad del País Vasco / Euskal Herriko Unibertsitatea) within the framework of the project "EthSec: Security in End-to-End Networks" (TIC2003-09585-C02-0), a coordinated project of the R&D&i National Plan funded by the Spanish Ministry of Science and Technology.

# References

1. IEEE-SA Standards Board, IEEE 802.1X$^{TM}$. IEEE Standard for Local and metropolitan area networks – Port-Based Network Access Control. 2004.
2. IEEE-SA Standards Board, IEEE 802.11$^{TM}$. IEEE Standards for Information Technology – Telecommunications and Information Exchange between Systems – Local and Metropolitan Area Network – Specific Requirements – Part 11: Wireless LAN Medium Access Control (MAC) and Physical Layer (PHY) Specifications. 1999.
3. IEEE-SA Standards Board, IEEE 802.11i$^{TM}$. IEEE Standard for Information Technology – Telecommunications and information exchange between systems – Local and metropolitan area networks – Specific requirements – Part 11: Wireless LAN Medium Access Control (MAC) and Physical Layer (PHY) specifications – Amendment 6: Medium Access Control (MAC) Security Enhancements. 2004.
4. Aboba, B., Blunk, L., Vollbrecht, J., Carlson, J., Levkowetz, H.: Extensible Authentication Protocol (EAP), IETF RFC 3748. 2004.
5. Chen, J., Wang, Y.: Extensible authentication protocol (EAP) and IEEE 802.1x: tutorial and empirical experience. IEEE Communications Magazine, Vol.43. No.12 (2005) 26–32.
6. Borisov, N., Goldberg, I., Wagner, D.: Intercepting Mobile Communications: The Insecurity of 802.11. MobiCom'01: Proceedings of the 7th annual international conference on Mobile computing and networking (2001) 180-189.
7. Chen, J., Jiang, M., Liu, Y.: Wireless LAN security and IEEE 802.11i. IEEE Wireless Communications, Vol.12. No.1 (2005) 27–36.
8. http://europa.eu.int/information_society/eeurope/2005/all_about/action_plan/index_en.htm
9. Dubrawsky, I.: SAFE Enterprise Layer 2 Addendum. Cisco Systems Whitepaper, 2004. http://www.cisco.com/warp/public/cc/so/cuso/epso/sqfr/sfblu_wp.pdf

# Secure Data Management in Reactive Sensor Networks

L. Chaithanya[1,*], M.P. Singh[2,**], and M.M. Gore[3,***]

[1] EMC Data Storage Systems (India) Ltd, Bangalore, India
lekkalapudi_chaithanya@emc.com
[2] Department of Computer Science and Engineering
National Institute of Technology Patna, India
writetomps@gmail.com
[3] Department of Computer Science and Engineering
Motilal Nehru National Institute of Technology, Allahabad, India
goremm@acm.org

**Abstract.** A wireless sensor network (WSN), an ad hoc network of resource constrained sensor nodes, has become an attractive option for monitoring applications. The wide use of sensor networks is due to the cheap hardware and detailed information they provide to the end user. As with every network of every computing device, security is one of the key issue of sensor networks. The resource constrained nature of sensor nodes make the security quite challenging. The sensor networks are prone to many kinds of security attack viz. report fabrication attack, denial of service attack, Sybil attack, traffic analysis attack, node replication attack, physical attack etc. The report fabrication attack is a security attack in which the adversary tries to generate bogus reports by compromising the sensor nodes. This paper proposes a security solution that makes cluster based sensor networks resilient to report fabrication attacks. The proposed solution relies on symmetric key mechanisms, appropriate for random deployment and also handles the node failures.

## 1 Introduction

Wireless sensor network is a network of resource constrained sensor nodes, where the sensor nodes organize themselves to form a sensor network. The sensor networks are now a days widely used in applications such as health monitoring, environmental monitoring, and military applications [1]. The popularity and application domain of WSN's are growing day by day, as they provide cost effective solution to most of the applications.

---

* This work was carried at Motilal Nehru National Institute of Technology, Allahabad during his stay as Masters' student.
** He is also a Ph.D. candidate at Motilal Nehru National Institute of Technology, Allahabad.
*** Partially supported by the Information Security Education and Awareness (ISEA) Project of Ministry of Communication and Information Technology, Government of India.

A. Bagchi and V. Atluri (Eds.): ICISS 2006, LNCS 4332, pp. 235–248, 2006.

The sensor networks can be broadly classified as proactive sensor networks and reactive sensor networks [2]. The proactive sensor network is the one in which the sensor nodes periodically send the sensed values to the base station.[1] The reactive sensor network is the one in which the sensor nodes react to the occurrence of particular events such as abnormal variation in temperatures, pressure, detection of enemy movement, etc and send the captured information (sensed value) to the base station.

The sensor network is prone to security attacks as any other ad hoc network. Security is an important aspect in sensor networks as:

- They are often deployed in hostile terrain in which the sensor nodes are left unattended and the sensor nodes are physically accessible by adversaries.
- They are not manufactured to be tamper proof, in order to reduce the costs of sensor nodes [3].
- They are often used in time critical applications such as monitoring leakage of hazardous gases in industries and forest fire monitoring, etc [4].

Hence, the security in sensor network is critical to any application. Without security, the use of wireless sensor network in any application domain may result in undesirable consequences [5].

The security threats in sensor networks can range from eavesdropping the communication channel to node compromises, where the adversary may be able to get hold of all the information stored in sensor nodes [3], [6].

The security threats in sensor networks can be classified as outsider attacks and insider attacks [3].

**Outsider Attacks.** The outsider attacks are the one in which the adversary tries to attack the sensor network without having the knowledge about the network. The security attacks such as eavesdropping the communication channel (where the adversary obtains the sensed values by hearing the communication channel), injecting malicious messages into the sensor network, and denial of service attack (where the adversary jams the communication channel using signals of high strength), come under the clause of outsider attacks [6].

**Insider Attacks.** When the adversary compromises a sensor node, it gets hold of the information stored in the sensor node such as the cryptographic keys, location of the sensor node etc. If an adversary tries to launch an attack on sensor network using that information, then this kind of attacks are known as insider attacks. The security attacks such as report fabrication attack (RFA), node replication, generation of bogus reports, Sybil attack [6] are the type of insider attacks.

All the above security threats can be defended using strong cryptographic mechanisms. But, the cryptographic mechanisms developed for traditional wired networks can not be used for sensor networks due to the following node specific and communication specific constraints:

---

[1] It is the end user for the wireless sensor network.

**Resource Constrained Nature.** The sensor nodes are constrained in computation, communication, and storage capabilities. For example, the MICA2 mote works on 4 MHz 8 bit AMTEL 128L processor, 128KB onboard flash memory, two AA batteries and provides a transmission range between 15 ft- 100 ft [7]. So, the security mechanisms for securing sensor networks have to be developed in such a way that they consume minimal amount of resources.

**Communication Patterns.** The communication paradigm in sensor network can be either one-one, many-one, or many-many depending on application requirements [8]. So the security mechanisms must be developed such that they not only support one-one communication but also others.

**Single Trusted Entity.** The sensor networks will be generally deployed with an assumption that base station is only the trusted entity in sensor network [3]. As it is resourceful and is assumed not to be compromised by the adversaries, the security mechanisms developed for sensor networks must be scalable such that the base station should not become the bottleneck.

**Requirements of In Network Processing.** In most of the sensor network applications, the data is aggregated and enroute to the base station to reduce the communication overhead and minimize the resource consumption. So, the security mechanisms developed for sensor networks must support in network processing [5].

Due to the above constraints, the security mechanisms basically developed for two party communications which uses public key cryptography are not viable for sensor networks. Thus new security mechanisms have to be developed or existing mechanisms have to be scaled, such that they are feasible to be used by the sensor nodes.

The remaining paper is organized as follows. Section 2 discusses about the report fabrication attack and the related work. Section 3 presents the assumptions, threat model and describes the proposed RFA management protocol in detail. Section 4 explains the handling of the node failures. Section 5 presents the security analysis. Section 6 discusses the protocol implementation and simulation results. Section 7 concludes the work and presents future work.

## 2    Report Fabrication Attacks

As discussed in section 1, report fabrication attack is an insider attack. In report fabrication attack, a single compromised node or a set of compromised nodes are used to generate forged report for a non existing event, either to misguide the system or to deplete the resources of the sensor nodes in the sensor network. The report fabrication attack is a severe security threat in reactive sensor networks. For example when used for time critical applications, a single forged report can cost much damage. So, there is a need to develop the security protocols which are resilient to report fabrication attacks. An attempt for the same is carried out in this paper.

## 2.1   Related Work and Motivation

The Report fabrication attacks is one of the most recent security attack which has been paid less attention in the wireless sensor network security literature [5], [6]. The IIHA (An Interleaved Hop-by-Hop Authentication Scheme for Filtering of Injected False Data in Sensor Networks) tries to make the cluster based sensor networks resilient to report fabrication attacks [9], but there are some drawbacks with this approach. The drawbacks are as follows:

- It assumes that all the clusters contain at least $n+1$ nodes. But when the sensor nodes are randomly deployed, the number of nodes varies from cluster to cluster [10], [11]. So, this approach is not appropriate for random deployment.
- It does not handle the unavailability of nodes either due to the physical damage or node failure [12]. If a single node fails to report, then the report generated by the cluster becomes invalid.
- It uses LEAP [13] for neighborhood discovery and shared key establishment, which itself is prone to security attacks [11].
- It is energy expensive as it requires fixed path to be maintained from the cluster head to the base station.

In [14], an attempt was made to provide effective security solution for the flat sensor network model. It uses the location dependent approach, where the sensor nodes need to be deployed with careful planning. However, according to [15] the solutions that have been designed for the flat networks are unlikely to be optimal for a cluster based networks. So, a solution needs to be tailored to the particular network organization (cluster based sensor networks) to be effective.

The existing approaches [9], [14] focus mainly on the enroute filtering framework in which the forged report will be dropped enroute from source to the base station and the node that has dropped the forged report generates alarm message about the cluster that has generated the forged report. In this approach the base station needs to trust the node which has generated the alarm message, as there is a possibility of generation of bogus alarm messages about the lower associated clusters or the cells by a compromised node enroute [3]. In the case of cluster based sensor network, where the cluster head is responsible for aggregation and generating final report, the probability of generation of false report is $1/n$ ($n$ is number of nodes in the cluster).

The strength of the approaches to defend against the report fabrication attacks mainly depends on:

- The ability of sensor network to suppress the generation of the false reports.
- The ability of the base station to differentiate between the forged report and legitimate report and take an action against the neighborhood that has generated the forged report.
- The ability of the sensor network to restrict the scope of attacks of the compromised nodes to a particular cluster in which they reside.

Due to the above reasons the enroute filtering has no role to play in cluster based sensor networks.

# 3   The Proposed RFA Management Protocol

This section describes the working of the proposed RFA (**R**eport **F**abrication **A**ttack) management protocol in detail. First, the threat model under consideration is presented. This is followed by the assumption about wireless sensor network and its components. A brief explanation on various notations is presented next. At last, algorithm is presented in detail along with explanation of its different phases so as to illustrate working of the proposed RFA management protocol.

## 3.1   Assumptions

The assumptions for the system model are as follows

- The base station is static, resourceful, and is a trusted entity.
- Sensor network once deployed will be static.
- All the sensor nodes in the sensor network have same capabilities in computation and communication.
- The data will be routed securely from the source to the base station with out dropping or modifying enroute.
- The sensor network will not be attacked during the cluster setup phase and topology discovery phase that is for the first '$t$' seconds [11], [13].
- The denial of service attack in which the sensor node is intermittently isolated from the sensor network is not addressed in this approach.

## 3.2   Threat Model

If a sensor node is compromised then

- All the information stored in sensor node will be revealed to the adversary.
- The adversary can create the clones of the sensor node and deploy them across the sensor network.
- It may illegitimately take multiple identities.

The adversary may

- Eavesdrop the communication channel in the sensor network.
- Replay the old messages.
- Inject malicious messages into the sensor network.
- Physically destroy the sensor node.

## 3.3   Notation

$E_{K_m}$: Encryption using key $K_m$.
$K_{i,j}$: Shared key between nodes i and j.
$MAC(k, s)$: **M**essage **A**uthentication **C**ode computation on message '$s$' using key '$k$'.
$RFT$: **R**eport **F**abrication **T**hreshold.

## 3.4   Working of the Proposed RFA Management Protocol

The proposed RFA management protocol has been divided into four phases namely

*(1) Initialization phase,*
*(2) Secure cluster setup phase,*
*(3) Topology discovery phase, and*
*(4) Event detection and secure reporting.*

These phases are presented in Algorithm 1.1 given below.

**Algorithm 1.1** Algorithm for Proposed RFA Management Protocol

1   **Initialization Phase:**
2   Initialize *status*=NULL
3   Every node is initialized with $Nodeid(N_i)$, $MasterKey(K_m)$, $NodeKey(K_i)$, $ClusterKey(K_i^c)$, $RFT$
4   **Secure Cluster Setup Phase:**
5   every node initializes its *holdback* value randomly
6   after every $t_c$ seconds each node decrements the *holdback* value by one
7   if ($holdback == 0$ && $status == $ NULL)
8       set $status = CLUSTER\_HEAD$
9       broadcast *cluster_hello*
10  on receiving the *cluster_hello* broadcast
11      If ($status == $ NULL)
12          set status $= CLUSTER\_MEMBER$
13          compute the shared key using secure hash function '$h$'
14          reply with *cluster_hello_reply* message to cluster head
15      else if ($status != $ NULL)
16          store the cluster head information for future use
17  cluster head on receiving *cluster_hello_reply* message
18      computes the shared key with cluster members using '$h$'
19  **Topology Discovery Phase:**
20  base station initiates the topology discovery phase by broadcasting the *base_hello* message
21  cluster head(s) on receiving first *base_hello* message
22      compute the shared key using hash function '$h$' and forward the *base_hello* to its neighbor cluster heads
23      send the *base_reply*
24  on receiving the *base_reply*
25      if (receiving node of *base_reply* $== BASE\_STATION$)
26          compute the shared key using '$h$'
27          learn about the cluster using *base_forward_reply*
28      else if (receiving node of *base_reply* $== CLUSTER\_HEAD$)
29          compute the shared key using the information in *base_reply*
30          forward the *base_forward_reply* part of it to next hop towards the base station
31  on receiving further *base_hello* messages
32      send *hello_reply* to the cluster head from which the *base_hello* has been received

33  on receiving *base_forward_reply*
34     route the *base_forward_reply* to next hop towards the base station
35  on receiving *hello_reply*
36     the cluster head(s) compute the shared key using '*h*'
37  **Event Detection and Secure Reporting Phase:**
38  if the cluster member detects an event
39     it sends *report* to its own cluster head
40  if the cluster head receives at least '*m*' reports from its members
41     it prepares the *final_report* and routes it to base station in hop-by-hop authenticated fashion
42  **End of Algorithm 1.1**

**Initialization Phase:** The initialization phase takes place before the sensor nodes are deployed. During initialization phase each and every node '*i*' is assigned unique identifier $N_i$ ranging from 0 to *n*-1 (where *n* is the number of sensor nodes in the network), and is preloaded with the keying information listed below.

**Master Key ($K_m$).** A 64 bit key that is shared among all the sensor nodes and the base station which is used during the secure cluster setup and topology discovery phases. In order to ensure the security, this key will be erased after topology discovery phase.

**Node Key ($K_i$).** This is a secret 64 bit key that each and every node shares with base station. This key will be used for authentication purpose while reporting to the base station.

**Cluster Key ($K_i^c$).** Each and every node '*i*' is loaded with unique cluster key $K_i^c$ and will be used by the nodes that will become cluster heads.

**Report Fabrication Threshold (RFT).** RFT is the parameter that determines the number of nodes that have to endorse the occurrence of an event. It is determined based on the number of nodes in the cluster as follows

$$m = \lceil RFT * no. \ of \ nodes \ in \ the \ cluster \rceil; if \ m > 2$$
$$m = 2; if \ m \leq 2 \tag{1}$$

The RFT value can be varied from 0.5 to 1.0 (which ensures that at least 50 percent of the cluster members have to report the occurrence of event). If RFT is 1 then all the nodes in the cluster have to endorse the occurrence of an event. Depending on the security requirement of the application the RFT value can be set.

Once all the nodes are preloaded with the required data the base station is informed about the node and key mappings. The sensor nodes are deployed redundantly such that each and every node has more than one cluster head in its communication range (in order to overcome the disadvantage due to single point failures).

**Secure Cluster Setup Phase:** During this phase, all the sensor nodes are organized into disjoint clusters of different sizes. In this phase, each and every sensor node is assigned a randomly generated holdback value as in [10], which determines the amount of time the sensor node has to wait before advertising its decision to become cluster head. When the holdback becomes zero the sensor node advertises its decision to become cluster head by broadcasting *cluster_hello* message.

$$cluster\_hello : \{cluster\_hello, C_{id}, K_i^c\}_{E_{K_m}} \qquad (2)$$

where $C_{id}$ is node id of the node broadcasting *cluster_hello*

The nodes which are within the communication range of sensor node that have not taken the decision to become the cluster head or have not received any cluster head advertisement, receive and decrypt the message. They respond by

- Computing the shared key with the cluster head using secure hash function 'h'

$$K_{C_{id},j} = h(\ K_i^c, C_{id}|K_m|j\ ) \qquad (3)$$

- Acknowledge the *cluster_hello* by sending *cluster_hello_reply*, so that cluster head knows the members of its cluster and computes the shared key as in equation (3).

$$cluster\_hello\_reply : \{cluster\_hello\_reply, C_{id}, j, MAC(K_{c_{id},j}, j|C_{id})\}_{E_{k_m}} \qquad (4)$$

The sensor nodes does not switch off the timers as soon as they become the member of single cluster. They wait for maximum time and collect the information about the cluster heads within its communication range, which helps in the case of single point failures.

By the end of the cluster setup phase all the sensor nodes are organized into disjoint clusters, each and every cluster member computes a shared key with the cluster head. Cluster head also does the same and computes the $'m'$ value (which determines the number of nodes within the cluster that have to endorse the occurrence of a particular event).

**Topology Discovery Phase:** Topology discovery phase is the one during which the sensor network is organized as a connected graph and the base station learns about the topology of the network. The base station initiates this phase by broadcasting *base_hello* message. Upon receiving the first *base_hello* message each and every cluster head responds to it by

- Computing the shared key with the base station or the cluster head from which it has received the *base_hello* as in equation (3).

$$base\_hello : \{base\_hello, C_{id}, hop\_count\}_{E_{K_m}} \qquad (5)$$

- Sending the *base_reply* to the sender of the *base_hello*. *base_reply* acts as an acknowledgement to the *base_hello*. It also contains the payload holding details of the cluster head and the cluster members destined to the base station.

$$base\_reply: \quad y_0 \leftarrow \{id's \, of \, the \, cluster \, members\}$$
$$y_1 \leftarrow \{y_0, MAC(K_{c_{id}}, y_0)\}_{E_{K_{c_{id}}}}$$
$$y_2 \leftarrow \{base\_forward\_reply, C_{id}, y_1\} \quad (6)$$
$$y_3 \leftarrow \{base\_reply, C_{id}, MAC(K_{c_{id},j}, j|C_{id}), y_2\}_{E_{k_m}}$$

$base\_reply$ consists of all the values calculated in $y_0, y_1$, and $y_2$ that is $y_3$ is nothing but the $base\_reply$.

– Forwarding the $base\_hello$ to the downstream cluster heads by incrementing the $hop\_count$.

For further $base\_hello's$ the cluster heads respond by sending $hello\_reply$ which acts as an acknowledgement to the $base\_hello$. The $hello\_reply$ is similar to $cluster\_hello\_reply$ but $cluster\_hello\_reply$ is intra-cluster reply and $hello\_reply$ is inter-cluster reply which helps in setting up the connected graph between clusters.

On receiving the $base\_reply$ the cluster head responds by computing the shared key as in the secure cluster setup phase as in equation (3) and forwards payload $base\_forward\_reply$ to the base station. On receiving the $hello\_reply$ the receiving cluster head responds by computing the shared key as in equation (3).

By the end of topology discovery phase the base station learns about the topology of the network.

**Event Detection and Secure Reporting:** Once the network has been setup the sensor nodes monitor the environment for the events of interest. If any event occurs, each and every node *'i'* sensing the event prepares the report as in equation (7) and report it to it's cluster head.

$$y_0 \leftarrow \{event\_info\} \quad (7)$$
$$y_1 \leftarrow \{y_0, MAC(K_i, y_0), MAC(k_{C_{id},i}, y_0)\}_{E_{k_{C_{id},i}}}$$
$$y_2 \leftarrow \{report, C_{id}, y_1\}$$

The cluster head receives at least *'m'* report from its member and takes MAC's (MCA's have been computed for the base station). Further, cluster head computes XOR of all the MAC's in order to reduce the communication overhead that is XORing all the MAC's rather than sending individually. Now, Cluster head includes its own identity in the report to prepare the final report as in equation (8). Finally, cluster head sends this final report to base station in hop-by-hop authenticated fashion.

$$y_0 \leftarrow \{event\_info, MAC_1 \oplus MAC_2 \oplus \ldots \oplus MAC_m\}$$
$$y_1 \leftarrow \{y_0, MAC(K_{C_{id}}, y_0)\}_{E_{k_{c_{id}}}}$$
$$y_2 \leftarrow \{final\_report, C_{id}, y_1\} \quad (8)$$

The base station on receiving the final report checks for the source (that is the cluster head from which the report has originated) and validates the report by computing the MAC. If the report fails the validation check, the base station discards the report, otherwise the base station initiates appropriate action.

# 4    Handling Node Failures

The sensor networks are often deployed in hostile areas unattended. There is great probability of physical damage to the sensor nodes. As the reactive sensor networks are generally used in time critical applications, the failure of single node may lead to disastrous consequences. So, there is a need to handle the node failures effectively.

## 4.1    Cluster Member Failure

In order to handle the cluster member failures, this paper assumes that the cluster head frequently pings the cluster members and keeps a track of them. If a cluster member fails to respond to the cluster heads activity, the cluster head notifies it to the base station so that the base station recomputes the '$m$' value and send it to the cluster head.

## 4.2    Cluster Head Failure

As the cluster members contain the information about the cluster heads within the communication range (the cluster member gathers this information during the cluster setup phase). If cluster head becomes unavailable, the cluster members may execute orphan adoption protocol as in [15].

# 5    Security Analysis

## 5.1    Secure Cluster Setup and Topology Discovery Phases

The security of the two phases is based on the assumptions that the sensor nodes will not be tampered for the first '$t$' seconds after the sensor network deployment, the sensor nodes will not behave undeterministically until and unless they are tampered. So, the above assumptions [11], [13] ensure that only legitimate senor nodes become part of sensor network. In order to ensure confidentiality all the messages are encrypted using master key ($K_m$), which is shared by all the nodes in the sensor network. The MAC (Messages Authentication Code), which ensures authenticity and integrity of the message is used where ever required (for multi hop messages). This work also assumes that all the nodes share a random counter value with base station as well as single hop neighbors, as it offers semantic security [8] and as well as protects against replaying of messages.

## 5.2    Event Detection and Secure Reporting

During the normal operation of network, the effect of the node compromise depends upon the type of the node compromised. The compromised node may be either the cluster head or cluster member. If a cluster member is compromised, then the adversary tries to generate the bogus reports and send it to the cluster head. But as the valid event must be endorsed by at least $m$ nodes, it is violated in such case. So if the cluster head receives less than $m$ reports then it detects the node compromise with in the cluster, and takes an action either by re-computing and distributing the new keys or issuing a refresh command so that all the nodes hash the keys [11]. From the above approach, the adversary will only be able to generate a forged report once it has compromised at least $m$ nodes in the cluster.

If the cluster head has been compromised then the adversary can generate bogus reports and route it to the base station. As the base station verifies the authenticity of each and every report, the bogus report can be easily identified by base station. The base station may respond to the bogus report by revoking the cluster from the sensor network as in [11]. The malicious cluster head may also report about the unavailability of the cluster members unnecessarily. So the base station does not isolate the node as soon as it receives such report. It handles such situation by declaring the nodes as ORPHAN by unicasting the orphan status to it. So, if the cluster member is available it may join other cluster using the orphan adoption protocol [15].

# 6   Implementation Details and Simulation Results

## 6.1   Implementation Details

The RFA management protocol is implemented in NesC programming language with the underlying operating system as TinyOS. Value of $t_c$ is 750 milliseconds that is after every 750 milliseconds holdback value of every node decreases by one. The component graph of the protocol is as shown in the Fig. 1.

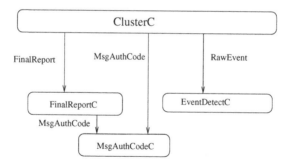

**Fig. 1.** Component graph

**CluserC.** ClusterC is the main component. It Contains the logic for initialization phase, secure cluster setup phase, and topology discovery phase.

**EventDetetionC.** This component is responsible for monitoring the environment in which the sensor network is deployed, for occurrence of events of interest.

**MsgAuthC.** This component computes MAC, and uses RC5 encryption algorithm to encrypt the messages.

**FinalReportC.** This component generates the final report and also verifies the received report during the event detection and secure reporting phase.

Due to the resource constrained nature of sensor nodes, the cryptographic algorithms are not only selected based on their strength, but also based on the on energy conserving nature. As Evaluation of security mechanisms in in wireless sensor networks [16] identifies the RC5 encryption algorithm as the right candidate for sensor motes, we chose it for our implementation. In order to save the memory the same algorithm is used for performing all cryptographic primitives as in [8] this means that the same algorithm has been used for all purposes such as encryption, key computation, and MAC computation.

### 6.2   Simulation Results

We simulated the RFA management protocol using the TOSSIM (TinyOS simulator) [17] by varying the number of sensor nodes in the sensor network. The following graph in Fig. 2. and Table 1. shows the relationship between the number of sensor nodes and simulation time for secure sensor network setup.

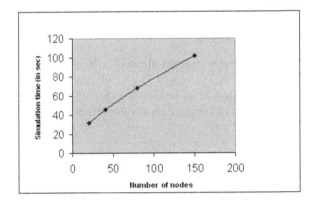

**Fig. 2.** Number of nodes Vs Simulation time

**Table 1.** Number of nodes Vs Simulation time

| Number of nodes | Simulation time (in sec) |
|---|---|
| 20 | 31.763 |
| 40 | 45.737 |
| 80 | 68.196 |
| 150 | 101.819 |

## 7   Conclusion and Future Work

The proposed RFA management protocol provides the security mechanism to report fabrication attack in cluster based sensor networks. This protocol is feasible to run on a sensor mote. The simulation results show that the proposed approach is scalable.

The current work can be extended for energy-efficient security mechanism for wireless sensor network so as to increase the life of the wireless sensor network.

**Acknowledgements.** The Authors will like to thank Mr. G. V. Krishna Rao, Mr. Girish Patnaik, Mr. Vijay Ukani, and Ms. Jaya Laxmi for their valuable comments and suggestion during the development of work [18] and during the preparation of manuscript of the first draft.

# References

1. Zia, T.A.: An overview of wireless sensor networks and their security issues. (In: Google Scholar)
2. Ibriq, J., Mahgoub, I.: Cluster-based routing in wireless sensor networks: Issues and challenges. In: proceedings of symposium on performance evaluation of computer and telecommunication systems ((SPECTS'04). (2004) 759–766
3. Shi, E., perrig, A.: Designing secure sensor networks. IEEE Wireless Communications **11**(6) (2004) 38–43
4. Brennan, S.M., Mielke, A.M., Torney, D.C., Maccabe, A.B.: Radiation detection with distributed sensor networks. IEEE Computer **37**(8) (2004) 57–59
5. Law, Y.W., Havinga, P.J.M.: How to secure a wireless sensor network. In: Proceedings of the International Conference on Intelligent Sensors, Sensor Networks and Information Processing. (2005) 89–95
6. Akyildiz, I.F., Su, W., Sankarasubramaniam, Y., Cayirci, E.: Wireless sensor networks security: A survey. In: International Journal of Computer and Telecommunications Networking. Volume 38. (2002) 393–422
7. Anastasi, G., Conti, M., Gregori, E., Falchi, A., Passarella, A.: Performance measurements of mote sensor networks. In: Proceedings of the 7th ACM international symposium on Modeling, analysis and simulation of wireless and mobile systems, Venice, Italy (2004) 174 – 181
8. Perrig, A., Szewczyk, R., Wen, V., Culler, D., Tygar, J.D.: SPINS: Security protocols for sensor networks. In: Seventh Annual International Conference on Mobile Computing and Networks (MobiCOM 2001). (2001) 189–199
9. Zhu, S., Setia, S., Jajodia, S., Ning, P.: An interleaved hop-by-hop authentication scheme for filtering of injected false data in sensor networks. In: IEEE Symposium on Security and Privacy, IEEE Computer Society (2004) 259–271
10. Singh, M.P., Gore, M.M.: A new energy-efficient clustering protocol for wireless sensor networks. In: Second International Conference on Intelligent Sensors, Sensor Networks and Information Processing (ISSNIP 2005), Melbourn, Australia (2005) 25–30
11. Dimitriou, T., Krontiris, I.: A localized, distributed protocol for secure information exchange in sensor networks. In: Proceedings of the 19th IEEE International Parallel and Distributed Processing Symposium(IPDPS), IEEE Computer Society, Washington, DC, USA, IEEE Computer Society (2005) 240.1
12. Perrig, A., Stankovic, J.A., Wagner, D.: Security in wireless sensor networks. Communication ACM **47**(6) (2004) 53–57
13. Zhu, S., Setia, S., Jajodia, S.: LEAP: efficient security mechanisms for large-scale distributed sensor networks. In: CCS '03: Proceedings of the 10th ACM conference on Computer and communications security, New York, NY, USA, ACM Press (2003) 62–72

14. Yang, H., Ye, F., Yuan, Y., Lu, S., Arbaugh, W.A.: Toward resilient security in wireless sensor networks. In: Proceedings of the 6th ACM Interational Symposium on Mobile Ad Hoc Networking and Computing, MobiHoc 2005, Urbana-Champaign, IL, USA, May 25-27, 2005, ACM (2005) 34–45

15. Oliveira, L., Wang, H.C., Loureiro, A.: LHA-SP: secure protocols for hierarchical wireless sensor networks. In: 9th IFIP/IEEE International Symposium on Integrated Network Management, Department of Computer Science, Federal University of Minas Gerais, Brazil (2005) 31–44

16. Guimarães, G., Souto, E., Sadok, D.F.H., Kelner, J.: Evaluation of security mechanisms in wireless sensor networks. In: ICW/ICHSN/ICMCS/SENET, IEEE Computer Society (2005) 428–433

17. Levis, P., Lee, N., Welsh, M., Culler, D.: TOSSIM: accurate and scalable simulation of entire tinyOS applications. In: Proceedings of the first international conference on Embedded networked sensor systems (SenSys-03), New York, ACM Press (2003) 126–137

18. Chaithanya, L.: Secure data management in reactive sensor network. Master's thesis, Department of Computer Science and Engineering, Motilal Nehru National Institute of Techology, Allahabad, Uttar Pradesh, India (2006)

# Security Ontology: Simulating Threats to Corporate Assets

Andreas Ekelhart, Stefan Fenz, Markus D. Klemen, and Edgar R. Weippl

Secure Business Austria — Security Research,
Favoritenstraße 16, A-1040 Vienna, Austria
{aekelhart,sfenz,mklemen}@securityresearch.at,
weippl@ifs.tuwien.ac.at
http://www.securityresearch.at

**Abstract.** Threat analysis and mitigation, both essential for corporate security, are time consuming, complex and demand expert knowledge. We present an approach for simulating threats to corporate assets, taking the entire infrastructure into account. Using this approach effective countermeasures and their costs can be calculated quickly without expert knowledge and a subsequent security decisions will be based on objective criteria. The ontology used for the simulation is based on Landwehr's [ALRL04] taxonomy of computer security and dependability.

**Keywords:** security ontology, threat modeling, risk analysis.

## 1 Introduction

Over the years, IT-security has become a much diversified field of research, no longer limited to the classical virus attack. Applied IT-security also has to consider physical attacks, acts of nature beyond human control, industrial espionage, etc.

Although security is crucial for every company, approaches to security, including evaluation and implementation of safeguards, vary widely. Wrong decisions are made based on insufficient knowledge about the security domain, threats, possible countermeasures and the own infrastructure. The following reasons have been identified:

First, security terminology is vaguely defined; this leads to confusion among experts as well as the people who should be counseled and served [Don03]. Without a shared terminology communication, especially in a complicated domain like security, cannot be successful. Ontologies provide a perfect solution: not only can terms be defined, but also relationships between them. Reasoning about the generated knowledge opens further possibilities. Nonetheless, at the present time, ontologies are not yet widely used in commercial applications.

Second, the development of adequate security concepts and plans requires a thorough threat analysis. Small and medium sized businesses often avoid this step due to a lack of skilled personnel and budget constraints. Various IT-standards exist: the GSHB [BSI04], for example, is a comprehensive and well

A. Bagchi and V. Atluri (Eds.): ICISS 2006, LNCS 4332, pp. 249–259, 2006.

developed approach to security. Companies can become certified if they meet a specified baseline. Drawbacks of this standard are the complexity (approximately 3,000 pages) and insufficient risk analysis support - quantitative risk evaluation is not addressed. Cobit [COB06], an IT governance framework based on best practices, is complex to use and does not address security threats and safeguards in detail. The ISO 17799 standard [ISO06] includes risk analysis and benchmarking, but the operational expense to obtain a certification is usually too high for small and medium sized businesses.

Every security decision must consider the concrete company environment. The employee responsible for security is often not aware of all relevant details of the infrastructure. To obtain the necessary information by interviewing colleagues or studying plans is time consuming and thus the risk analysis is often based on an incomplete picture.

Throughout this paper we use the following definition for the term ontology:

*'An ontology defines the basic terms and relations comprising the vocabulary of a topic area as well as the rules for combining terms and relations to define extensions to the vocabulary.'* [GPFLC04]

Furthermore, we distinguish lightweight and heavyweight ontologies. Lightweight ontologies include concepts, concept taxonomies, relationships between concepts, and properties that describe concepts [GPFLC04]. Heavyweight ontologies add axioms and constraints to lightweight ontologies [GPFLC04].

The security ontology is based on Landwehr's [ALRL04, LBMC94] taxonomy; we extended it to form a heavyweight ontology. Landwehr's security and dependability classification [ALRL04] (for further details see Section "Security Ontology") was enriched by domain specific concepts and attributes to incorporate enterprise infrastructure and role schemes.

The main goal of current research activities is to provide a security ontology that unifies existing approaches such as [BSI04], [ALRL04], [LBMC94], and [eCl06] to support small and medium sized businesses' IT-security risk analysis and mitigation. The ontology "knows" which threats endanger which assets and which countermeasures could lower the probability of occurrence, the potential loss or the speed of propagation for cascading failures. In addition, each infrastructure object in the ontology can be annotated with outage costs and each countermeasure object with acquisition and maintenance costs. These capabilities enable the company to calculate the outage costs caused by a certain disaster and the costs of different countermeasures. The costs of countermeasures can be read directly from the ontology, while the benefit is calculated in simulation runs (see 3.3).

## 2   Security Ontology

The security ontology consists of three parts. The first part is based on the security and dependability taxonomy by Landwehr [ALRL04], the second part describes concepts of the (IT) infrastructure domain, and the third part provides enterprises with the option to map their persons and role models.

The ontology is coded in OWL (Web Ontology Language [OWL04]) and the Protege Ontology Editor [Pro05] was used to edit and visualize the ontology and its corresponding instances.

The following subsections describe the parts in more detail:

## 2.1 Security and Dependability Taxonomy

Figure 1 shows the *security and dependability taxonomy's* concept structure; for further information the paper [ALRL04] provides the reader with a detailed description. As Figure 1 shows, the taxonomy is designed in a very general

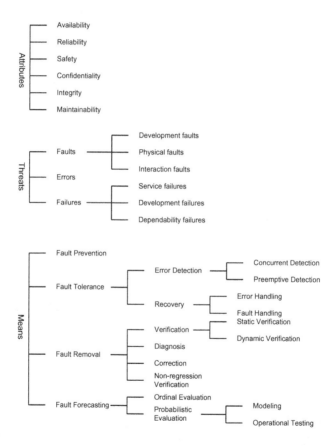

**Fig. 1.** Security and Dependability Taxonomy [ALRL04]

way, which makes it easy to extend it with additional concepts. Instances and dependencies were inserted to populate the taxonomy. Figure 2 represents the sub-tree "sec:Threat," which is part of the security ontology and was derived from Landwehr's taxonomy [ALRL04].

The sub-concept "sec:Fire" was inserted as the first real concept; it is classified as a physical fault, which belongs to the super-concept "sec:Threat." With "sec:threatened" and "sec:affects," the first dependencies were inserted; "sec:threatened" describes how every instance of any "sec:Threat" sub-concept threatens all instances of any "ent:Infrastructure" subclass. "sec:affects" shows how every instance of a "sec:Threat" subconcept affects one or more instances of the "sec:Attribute" concept. To every introduced concept in the ontology, a

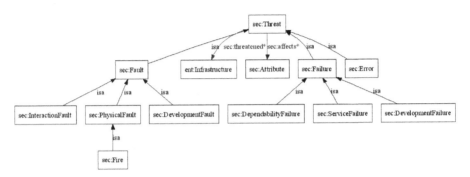

**Fig. 2.** Sub-tree 'sec:Threat'

semantic definition in natural language in form of a 'rdfs:comment' is added. To provide useful knowledge for simulating threats to corporate assets, the ontology still has to be extended with additional concepts describing the (IT) infrastructure and personnel structure.

## 2.2 Infrastructure Concepts

Figure 3 shows the security ontology's infrastructure area. The company building, with its corresponding floors and rooms, can be described using the infrastructure framework. To map the entire building plan exactly on the security ontology, each room is described by its position within the building. The ontology "knows" in which building and on which floor a certain room is located. The attributes "ent:nextToRoomHorizontal" and "ent:nextToRoomVertical" describe the exact location of each room. Each instance of "ent:ElectronicDevice" and "ent:Safguard" is located in a particular room. A room can, of course, also contain more concepts. The current ontology uses a flexible and easily extendable structure: additional concepts can be included without effort.

The concept "ent:Safeguard" is subdivided into "ent:CounterMeasure" and "ent:Detector," which are used to model detectors (fire, smoke, noise, etc.) and their corresponding countermeasures (fire extinguisher, alarm system, etc.).

Beside "ent:Infrastructure," the concepts "ent:Role" and "per:Person" ensure that both technical and personnel structures can be mapped into the current ontology.

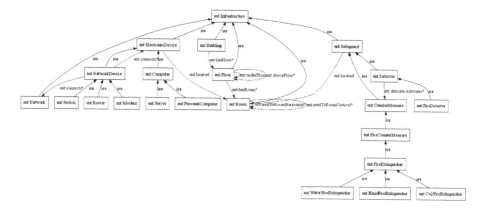

**Fig. 3.** Sub-tree 'ent:Infrastructure'

## 2.3   Person and Role Concepts

The concept "per:Person" enables the ontology to map natural persons. Figure 4 represents the role concept for assigning certain roles to natural persons. Several instances of "per:Person" were created in order to assign them with different roles. The current ontology considers only sub-concepts of "ent:Employee"; if necessary, additional roles can be added easily.

After describing the security ontology, the next section presents a practical example and makes the benefit for SME's clear.

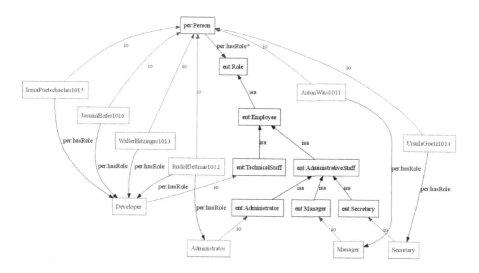

**Fig. 4.** Sub-tree 'per:Person' and 'ent:Role'

# 3 Example

In this section we provide an example of how a company would use the afore-mentioned security ontology to model an IT infrastructure.

## 3.1 The Company

The company is an SME with six employees. Their main business is software sales and custom programming to modify their standard software. The company rents two floors (first and second floor) of a five-floor building in the center of a small town. On the first floor (Figure 5), there is one office, a storage room and

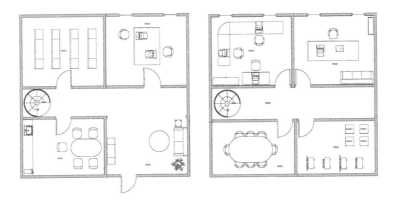

**Fig. 5.** Floor I          **Fig. 6.** Floor II

a lunchroom. The server room, a meeting room, and two more offices are located on the second floor (see Figure 6). The following listing shows the allocation of relevant (IT) infrastructure elements:

- First floor - Office room (R0103): 2 PC's
- First floor - Storage room (R0104): data media (archived)
- Second floor - Server room (R0202): 4 Servers, 1 Router, 2 Switches, 1 Modem
- Second floor - Office room (R0203): 1 PC, 1 Notebook
- Second floor - Office room (R0204): 3 PC's

The infrastructure is mapped on the sub-tree "ent:Infrastructure" (compare Figure 3). The following listing gives an example for an OWL definition describing a certain PC with its attributes:

```
<ent:PersonalComputer rdf:ID="Pc4">
 <ent:deliveryTime rdf:datatype="http://www.w3.org/2001/
 XMLSchema#int">3</ent:deliveryTime>
 <ent:assetCost rdf:datatype="http://www.w3.org/2001/
 XMLSchema#int">1500</ent:assetCost>
```

```
<ent:outageCost rdf:datatype="http://www.w3.org/2001/
XMLSchema#int">0</ent:outageCost>
<ent:antiVirus rdf:datatype="http://www.w3.org/2001/
XMLSchema#boolean">false</ent:antiVirus>
<ent:hasOs rdf:datatype="http://www.w3.org/2001/
XMLSchema#string">WinXpPro</ent:hasOs>
<ent:located rdf:resource="#R0204"/>
</ent:PersonalComputer>
```

The concept "ent:PersonalComputer" with its concrete instance "Pc4" has the attributes "ent:deliveryTime," "ent:assetCost," "ent:outageCost," "ent:antivirus," "ent:hasOs," and "ent:located." If this or any other instance is destroyed by a particular disaster, the ontology "knows" how long it will take to get a new one, how much it costs, where it is located, and the outage costs per day. Apart from "ent:antivirus" and "ent:hasOs," all attributes are inherited from the supra-concept "ent:Infrastructure."

### 3.2   The Disaster

After describing the company with its infrastructure, the current subsection defines the disaster that will hit our software company.

We chose the event of fire as a physical threat scenario. The simulation should show the amount of damage over a certain period of time and in consideration of the fire source. A certain room can be defined as the fire source; the speed of propagation without any countermeasures will be five minutes per floor and five minutes per room. Every element of the infrastructure is assigned to a certain room. In the case of fire, all infrastructure elements within a room will be completely destroyed. The outage costs per room correspond to the outage costs sum of all destroyed elements, which are located in the room. It is possible to assign countermeasures to any room. These safeguards can lower the probability of occurrence and the speed of propagation in the case of fire. The attribute "ent:damage" addresses the damage which results when the countermeasure is executed.

The following OWL code-snippet shows an example of the countermeasure element "ent:WaterFireExtinguisher":

```
<ent:WaterFireExtinguisher rdf:ID="WaterFireExtinguisher0102">
<ent:located rdf:resource="#R0102"/>
<ent:assetCost rdf:datatype="http://www.w3.org/2001/
XMLSchema#int">500</ent:assetCost>
<ent:damage rdf:datatype="http://www.w3.org/2001/
XMLSchema#float">0.7</ent:damage>
<ent:deliveryTime rdf:datatype="http://www.w3.org/2001/
XMLSchema#int">5</ent:deliveryTime>
<ent:startTime rdf:datatype="http://www.w3.org/2001/
XMLSchema#float">0.0</ent:startTime>
<ent:extinguishingTimeRoom rdf:datatype="http://
www.w3.org/2001/XMLSchema#int">1</ent:extinguishingTimeRoom>
</ent:WaterFireExtinguisher>
```

We can see that this extinguisher is located in room R0102 and will start immediately when switched on. Instance "WaterFireExtinguisher0102" will extinguish the room within one minute. The attribute "ent:startTime" is important for countermeasures that are not activated automatically (e.g. hand fire extinguisher).

## 3.3   The Simulation

The framework for our threat analysis has been explained in the preceding sections, we will now present a tool called "SecOntManger," which processes the ontology knowledge of simulated threats. This prototype handles IT costs and poses as proof of concept. Further threat effects, as well as infrastructure components, can be added easily due to the generic structure.

In our example the management wants to know the impact that fire will have on the infrastructure, what countermeasures exist and the benefits they offer. For this purpose we show two program runs, one against the unprotected company and another including safeguards:

- The first program run without countermeasures: "SecOntManager" offers an intuitive graphical user interface, shown in Figure 7. A threat and a corresponding starting point have to be chosen before a simulation can be started. We chose fire as the threat and the server room (room0202) as the origin of the fire. The program run produces a detailed log file, which shows how the fire spreads from room to room and what damage it causes. An abridgment of this file can be seen in the following listing:

```
Current Room: <http://secont.com/secont.rdf#R0203>
    http://secont.com/secont.rdf#Pc7: 0
    used by Person: http://secont.com/secont.rdf#AntonWais1011
    Salary: 3000
    Total outage costs of infrastructure component / 5min: 0.347
    Total damage costs of infrastructure component: 2000
    Recovery time and costs: 4 days: 2200
    ...
Search Detectors:
    Detector found: /
    Countermeasure activated: /
```

At the end of the simulation all occuring costs are visualized in a line chart (see Figure 7). The time axis unit is set to minutes. Four curves, reflecting different cost categories, exist: The blue curve visualizes the damage. In the example, the damage costs rise very fast due to the speed of fire - within 30 minutes every room was destroyed. By zooming in, displaying only the first 30 minutes, we can see how the damage evolves. After all rooms "burned down," no further damage could occur. Red are the outage costs, taken from assigned outage costs of infrastructure components and employee's costs. Outage costs rise constantly in the simulation until recovery. The green curve shows recovery costs: delivery times for destroyed components are taken into consideration. When components are available and paid, connected outage costs decrease, visually spoken, the red line flattens. Additional installation costs lift the recovery costs upon damage. When every component is recovered, the pre-threat state is reached and outage costs do not rise anymore. Furthermore the total of all costs is reflected by the yellow curve. Fire costs 73,605 and it takes a minimum of five days to recover from the effects.

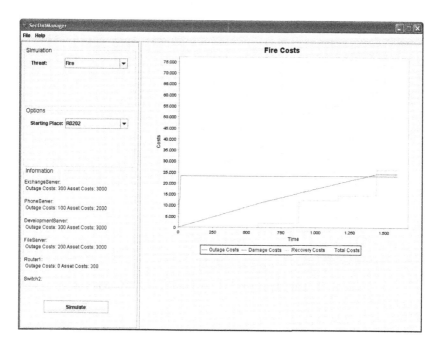

**Fig. 7.** SecOntManager: Without countermeasures

– Second program run with countermeasures enabled: We now concentrate on reducing the damage by installing safeguards. "SecOntManager" offers to install fire suppression systems in the building. We decide for pre-action pipes in the entire building. Necessary detectors and fire extinguishers are added to rooms in the OWL file. The costs amount to 7,200. Running the simulation produces the cost chart in Figure 8. As can be seen, the total damage decreases drastically to 28,329. After installing safeguards, the fire cannot spread; it is detected and extinguished shortly after breakout. Nevertheless costs and recovery times are still very high. The reason is that water extinguishers have a high damage factor concerning electronic devices and we have chosen the server room as place of fire origin. "SecOntManager" also offers $CO_2$ fire extinguishers for locations with high electronically damages. Replacing the water extinguisher by a more expensive $C0_2$ extinguisher the total costs are reduced to 10934, which are mostly outage costs of one server which caused the fire. By adding a redundant server the outage time and costs could be cut to zero.

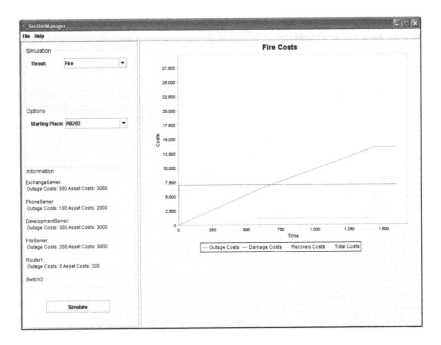

**Fig. 8.** SecOntManager: With countermeasures enabled

## 4  Conclusion

We presented an approach that eliminates the former flaws and allows us to simulate threats to corporate assets while taking the entire infrastructure into account. Increasingly, businesses require accurate security concepts and plans to protect themselves and their clients against various threats, including physical attacks, acts of nature beyond human control, industrial espionage, etc. Establishing an all-encompassing IT-security concept demands in-depth knowledge of existing threats, the company, and possible countermeasures. We propose an ontology-based approach combining security- with business-domain knowledge to model companies. The ontology guarantees shared and accurate terminology as well as portability. Knowledge of threats and corresponding countermeasures, derived from IT-security standards, are integrated into the ontology framework. Moreover, we implemented a prototype capable of simulating threats against the modeled company by processing the knowledge contained in the ontology. "SecOntManager" visualizes the damage caused by specific threats, outage costs, and the recovery time. Running the program with added safeguards shows their benefits and offers objective data for decision making, which safeguards to implement and to avoid installing countermeasures that are not cost-effective. An enhanced prototype with advanced risk analysis and broader threat support will take failure probability into account and will be developed in pilot installations with partner companies.

# Acknowledgements

This work was performed at the Research Center Secure Business Austria in association with the Vienna University of Technology.

# References

[ALRL04]    Algirdas Avizienis, Jean-Claude Laprie, Brian Randell, and Carl E. Landwehr. Basic concepts and taxonomy of dependable and secure computing. *IEEE Trans. Dependable Sec. Comput.*, 1(1):11–33, 2004.

[BSI04]     It-grundschutzhandbuch. http://www.bsi.de/gshb/deutsch/download/ GSHB2004.pdf, 2004.

[COB06]     Cobit. http://www.isaca.org/, 2006.

[Don03]     Marc Donner. Toward a security ontology. *IEEE Security and Privacy*, 1(3):6–7, May/June 2003.

[eCl06]     eclass. http://www.eclass.de/, 2006.

[GPFLC04]   Asunción Gómez-Pérez, Mariano Fernández-López, and Oscar Corcho. *Ontological Engineering*. Springer, London, first edition, 2004.

[ISO06]     Iso17799. http://www.iso.org/, 2006.

[LBMC94]    Carl E. Landwehr, Alan R. Bull, John P. McDermott, and William S. Choi. A taxonomy of computer program security flaws. *ACM Comput. Surv.*, 26(3):211–254, 1994.

[OWL04]     Owl web ontology language. http://www.w3.org/TR/owl-features/, 2004.

[Pro05]     The protege ontology editor and knowledge acquisition system. http://protege.stanford.edu/, 2005.

# Two-Stage Credit Card Fraud Detection Using Sequence Alignment

Amlan Kundu[1], Shamik Sural[1], and A.K. Majumdar[2]

[1] School of Information Technology
[2] Department of Computer Science & Engineering
Indian Institute of Technology, Kharagpur, india
{kunduamlan@sit,shamik@sit,akmj@cse}.iitkgp.ernet.in

**Abstract.** A phenomenal growth in the number of credit card transactions, especially for on-line purchases, has also led to a substantial rise in fraudulent activities. Implementation of efficient fraud detection systems has thus become imperative for all credit card companies in order to minimize their losses. In real life, fraudulent transactions could be interspersed with genuine transactions and simple pattern matching techniques are not often sufficient to detect the fraudulent transactions efficiently. In this paper, we propose a hybrid approach in which anomaly detection and misuse detection models are combined. Sequence alignment is used to determine similarity of an incoming sequence of transactions to both a genuine card holder's sequence as well as to sequences generated by a validated fraud model. The scores from these two stages are combined to determine if a transaction is genuine or not. We use stochastic models for studying the performance of the system.

## 1 Introduction

The popularity of online shopping has been growing rapidly over the last several years. According to a recently conducted ACNielsen study, one-tenth of the world's population has now started shopping online [1]. Germany and Great Britain have the largest number of online shoppers and credit card is the most popular mode of payment (59%) [1]. As the number of credit card users rises worldwide, opportunity for thieves to steal credit card details and subsequently commit fraud also increases. Credit card frauds can be broadly categorized into the following three types.

a) Physical card gets lost or stolen and is used by a fraudster.
b) Card number is stolen and used in indirect shopping.
c) Credit card skimming, where the data from a card magnetic strip is electronically copied onto another card.

The first type can lead to a huge financial loss as long as the card holder does not realize the loss of the card. Once the card holder realizes, the institution issuing the card can cancel it. In the second and the third type of fraud, the card holder normally comes to know about the fraudulent transactions after a

A. Bagchi and V. Atluri (Eds.): ICISS 2006, LNCS 4332, pp. 260–275, 2006.

long period of time, often on receipt of monthly credit card bill. The only way to detect these two types of fraud is to analyze the transaction patterns of the card holder and find out unusual transactions.

The total amount of credit card fraud in the USA itself is reported to be $2.7 billion in 2005 and estimated to be $3.0 billion in 2006 out of which $1.6 billion and $1.7 billion, respectively, are the estimates of on-line fraud [2]. The estimated fraud in the UK due to card skimming is more than £100$m$ a year. The second type of fraud is also quite common, accounting for £150.8$m$ a year in the UK alone [3].

As humans tend to exhibit specific behavioristic profiles with certain probability, a card holder's behavior can be captured by a set of sequences containing information about the typical purchase category, the time since the last purchase, the amount of money spent, etc. Credit card fraud can be reduced substantially by detecting fraud through an analysis of past spending patterns. The basic idea of our approach is that fraudsters are not familiar with the card holder's spending profile and as they try to derive maximum gain in a limited time, they show some behavioristic deviation from the normal profile.

Currently available fraud detection systems (FDS) are either misuse-based or anomaly-based. A misuse-based FDS cannot detect any new fraud pattern. On the other hand, anomaly based detection systems often raise a large number of false alarms. We use sequence alignment techniques, normally used to solve problems in the bioinformatics domain, to determine possible cases of fraudulent transactions. Our model is based on the strengths of both anomaly and misuse based detection models. This feature of our FDS helps to overcome the drawbacks of existing fraud detection systems and makes it an efficient fraud detection model.

The rest of the paper is organized as follows. Section 2 describes background work related to credit card fraud detection and sequence alignment. Section 3 presents the architecture and algorithm of our two-stage fraud detection system. In Section 4, we explain the experiments conducted and analyze the results. Finally, we conclude in Section 5 of the paper.

## 2  Background

### 2.1  Credit Card Fraud Detection

Credit card fraud detection has drawn a lot of interest and a number of techniques, with special emphasis on data mining and neural networks, have been proposed. One of the early attempts was by Ghosh and Reilly [4], who proposed credit card fraud detection with a neural network. They have built a system which is trained on a large sample of labeled credit card transactions. These transactions contain example fraud cases due to lost cards, stolen cards, application fraud, counterfeit fraud, mail-order fraud and NRI (non-received issue) fraud. Stolfo et al [5] have suggested a credit card fraud detection system using meta-learning techniques to learn models of fraudulent transactions. Meta-learning is a general strategy that provides a means for combining and integrating a number of separately learned classifiers or models. A meta-classifier is thus trained on the correlation of the predictions of the base classifiers. The meta-learning system allows financial institutions to share their models of fraudulent transactions by exchanging classifier agents. Aleskerov et al [6] have presented CARDWATCH, a database mining system used for credit card fraud detection. The system, based on a neural learning module, provides an interface to a variety of commercial databases. Fan et al [7] have suggested the application of distributed data mining in credit card fraud detection. Brause et al [8] have presented an approach involving advanced data mining techniques and neural network algorithms to obtain high fraud coverage combined with low false alarm rate. Chiu et al [9] have proposed web services and data mining techniques to establish a collaborative scheme for credit card fraud detection in the banking industry. In this scheme, participant banks share their knowledge about fraud patterns in a heterogeneous and distributed environment. To establish a smooth channel of data exchange, web services techniques such as XML, SOAP and WSDL are used. Phua et al [10] have done an extensive survey of existing data mining based fraud detection systems and published a comprehensive report. Vatsa et al [11] have recently proposed a game theoretic approach for credit card fraud detection. They have modeled the interaction between attacker and fraud detection system as a multi-stage game between two players, each trying to maximize his payoff.

Since fraud is the result of an act of intrusion where transactions are not performed by legitimate users, fraud detection systems are closely related to intrusion detection systems except for some specific requirements that they have. Recent research in the field of intrusion detection shows that algorithms commonly used in the bioinformatics domain can be applied in the field of intrusion detection as well. Takeda [12] has suggested the use of sequence alignment for network intrusion detection. Coul et al [13] have proposed pair-wise sequence alignment for intrusion detection. According to their work, simple pattern matching is not effective in a detection model where new patterns are a mix of both good and bad data. Transactions coming to a credit card processing system also form a combination of genuine and fraudulent transactions when a card has been compromised. Novel techniques, therefore, need to be developed to handle this complex situation. We feel that detection of fraudulent credit card transactions can be modeled as a string matching problem and sequence alignment algorithms can be effectively used. In the next subsection, we briefly describe the sequence alignment technique and indicate how it can be applied to the field of credit card fraud detection. To the best of our knowledge, this is the first ever attempt to develop credit card fraud detection system using sequence alignment.

## 2.2   Sequence Alignment

A sequence is an ordered list of elements. A sequence $S'$ is a subsequence of a sequence S if $S'$ can be derived from S by deleting some of the elements of S without disturbing the relative position of the other elements. Let $S_1$ and $S_2$ be two given sequences and $S'$ be a subsequence of both $S_1$ and $S_2$, then $S'$ is called a common subsequence of $S_1$ and $S_2$. Sequence alignment is a technique used to arrange two or more sequences in order to measure their similarity. It is a generalization of the longest common subsequence problem where the purpose is to find a common subsequence of greatest possible length. Figure 1 shows an example of sequence alignment. Here the sequence $S_1 = <$ GTCATGCGATAAGAGGCCTT $>$ is aligned with the sequence $S_2 =<$ GTCTGCGATGCAAGCCTT $>$. In $S_2$, a gap (-) is introduced after 'GTC' since the very next element 'A' in S1 does not match with the next element 'T' in $S_2$. Similarly, two gaps are introduced in $S_1$ and three gaps in $S_2$. The symbols that match in their current position in the two sequences are shown with a match (|) marker.

```
G T C A T G C G A T - - A A G A G G C C T T
|   |   |   |   |   |   |   |       |   |   |           |   |   |   |
G T C - T G C G A T G C A A G - - - C C T T
```

**Fig. 1.** Example of sequence alignment with gap (-) and match (|)marker

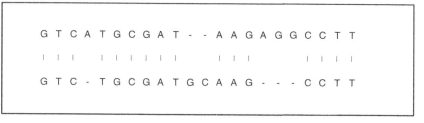

**Fig. 2.** Global alignment and local alignment

There are two main types of sequence alignment, namely, global alignment and local alignment. A global alignment is an arrangement of sequences in which all the elements in both the sequences participate in the alignment. Local alignment method finds related regions within sequences having significant similarity. Global alignment is effective when the two given sequences are almost similar in length and have homogeneity over the entire string. For sequences having different length or without homogeneity over entire string, local alignment is preferred. Figure 2 shows an example in which all the elements in both the sequences participate in the global alignment but related regions ($<$ ATGCCATGCGAT $>$,$<$ ATGCCTGCGAT $>$) within the sequences participate in local alignment. Needleman-Wunsch first proposed an efficient dynamic algorithm for global alignment [14]. The algorithm uses a matrix method of calculation. If we have to align two sequences $S_1$ and $S_2$, then each cell in the score matrix denotes a sub-alignment between the two subsequences that form a sub-matrix. At this point, there are three ways to proceed, "insert a gap in $S_1$ sequence and move down the matrix", "insert a gap in $S_2$ sequence and move to right of the matrix" or "try for a match in both $S_1$ and $S_2$ and move forward diagonally". Smith-Waterman proposed a local alignment algorithm [15], which is only a slight modification of the Needleman-Wunsch's global alignment algorithm. The algorithm sets all negative Needleman-Wunsch's scoring matrix cells to zero and starts back-tracing from the highest scoring matrix cell and proceeds until a cell with score zero is encountered. The time complexity of both Needleman-Wunsch's algorithm and Smith-Waterman's algorithm are $O(mn)$ for two given sequences of length $m$ and $n$. Some heuristics can change the performance of these algorithms drastically. The Basic Local Alignment Search Tool (BLAST) and a FAST-All (FASTA) are the two most popular heuristic approaches for sequence alignment [16]. Both BLAST and FASTA search for local sequence similarity but BLAST is extremely fast. The BLAST program achieves much of its speed by avoiding the calculation of optimal alignment scores for a handful of unrelated sequences. Credit card transactions also demand on-line response time. A fraud detection system embedded in credit card transaction processing should not adversely affect the response time. At the same time, the FDS should also be effective. Any attempt to align credit card transaction sequences without using heuristics is bound to slow down the speed of processing. Hence, we use BLAST as the sequence alignment tool.

BLAST comprises of three steps. In the first step, it compiles a list of high-scoring words (neighboring word) of length W from a given query sequence. In the second step, each of the neighboring words is compared with database sequences. If the neighboring word is identical to a word (sequence fragment) of database, a hit is recorded. Basically, a neighboring word is smaller compared to a database sequence so that it can be matched with a fragment of a database sequence and not with the whole sequence. In the third step, every hit-sequence is extended without gap in both directions and the extension is stopped as soon as the score is less than a threshold value. In the second step only one neighboring word may hit a database sequence but finally in the third step, since the hit region is extended in both directions, local alignment is achieved with respect to the query sequence. All the extended segment pairs whose scores are equal to or better than the threshold are retained. These segment pairs are called HSP (High-scoring Segment Pair) and the best one is called MSP (Maximal Segment Pair).

# 3    Two-Stage Fraud Detection System

In credit card processing system, every card has a certain credit limit and any transaction within the available credit limit is a theoretically valid transaction. A fraudster can guess the credit limit of a card and impersonate as the genuine card holder. So, credit limit itself is not sufficient to prevent fraud in credit cards. Credit card users normally do transactions of value much lower than the credit limit of the card. They also follow some typical spending behaviors. For example, on a given card, at the beginning of the billing period, usually high value transactions are carried out, then medium value transactions, and at the end of the period, low value transactions occur. The card holder's spending behavior also depends on his income. Even the probability of a number of successive high value transactions for a genuine card holder can be quite low. In most of the cases, each card holder's spending behavior is somewhat different from the others. Since a fraudster is not expected to be familiar with a card holder's behavior and as he tries to have maximum possible gain in a limited time, there can be significant behavioristic deviation in his actions. The card holder's spending behavior can be captured by quantizing the transaction amount up to credit limit into a number of ranges. Weekly or monthly behavior of the card holder can then be represented using a sequence of these quantized amounts.

In our model, we quantize the transaction amount into three ranges, namely, low, medium and high. Based on the past history of fraudulent transactions, a credit card issuing bank can build a set of sequences potentially followed by credit card thieves. For example, repeating high value transactions three times in succession could be a possible sequence of actions of a thief, while repeating low value transactions may not be a valid signature. In such cases, a potential fraud sequence of length three would be High, High, High and not Low, Low, Low. It should be noted at this stage that, our system is not limited by any assumption about a fixed fraud model. Any fraud model developed and refined by the issuing bank and its corresponding sequence of fraudulent transactions can be used seamlessly in this approach. This is one of the biggest advantages of our work. Good sequences, on the other hand, are card holder specific, and can be easily developed based on the transaction history of the card holder. The detailed working principle and the architecture are explained later in this section.

## 3.1   Problem Formulation

**Definition 1.** *GD-sequence and BD-sequence*: Let DS= $\{S_1, S_2, S_3, \cdots, S_N\}$ be the set of good or genuine transaction sequences for a credit card $C_k$. Then each sequence $S_i \epsilon$ DS is called a *GD-sequence* for the credit card $C_k$. *BD-sequences* are the sequences of bad or fraudulent transactions that have already been identified by the credit card issuing bank using a validated fraud model.

**Definition 2.** *Q-sequence*: A transaction sequence yet to be verified by the FDS is called a *Q-sequence*. A *Q-sequence* with N elements can be divided into a number of small consecutive subsequences (words) of size $N'$ where $N' \leq N$. This window size $N'$ is called QW-size (query window size)and each word is called a Q-word (Query word).

**Definition 3.** *High-scoring Segment Pair*: A *High-scoring Segment Pair* (HSP) is a pair of two sequence fragments of arbitrary but equal length whose alignment is locally maximal and for which the alignment score exceeds a given threshold.

When a transaction is carried out on a given credit card, the current value of transaction amount is quantized to generate an element of a sequence. The current element along with the last $N-1$ number of elements forms a sequence of elements of length N. If this sequence contains only elements from genuine transactions, then the sequence is expected to align well with the GD-sequence for this particular card holder. On the other hand, if all the elements are from fraudulent transactions, then the sequence would align well with a BD-sequence generated from a validated fraud model. In the event of a credit card having been compromised with the card holder unaware of the theft, the sequence of elements is expected to contain a mix of both genuine and fraudulent transactions. This sequence of good and bad transactions represented by their amounts forms a Q-word. In the first stage, the Q-word is aligned with the GD-sequence. Had the fraudulent transactions not been there, the Q-words would have aligned well with the GD-sequences. However, due to the presence of transactions deviating from the GD-sequence, mismatches will be observed when the Q-words are aligned with the GD-sequences. If the mismatches are indeed caused by fraudulent transactions, the sequence of elements in the Q-words not aligned with GD-sequence, would now align well with the BD-sequence. In a second stage, we, therefore, perform alignment of non-matched elements from the first stage to the BD-sequence. A good score (G-score) is assigned according to the similarity between Q-word and GD-sequence obtained in the first stage. A bad score (B-score) is assigned according to the similarity between deviated transactions in Q-word and BD-sequence in the second stage. The FDS finally raises an alarm if the total score (G-score − B-score) is below the alarm threshold (A-threshold).

It may be argued that one-stage sequence alignment is itself sufficient for anomaly-based fraud detection as indicated in [6]. However, the problem with one stage alignment is that even due to occasional variations in the spending pattern of the card holder, a large number of false alarms would be raised a typical situation in anomaly-based FDSs. Using the second stage, in which the deviations observed in the first stage are matched with learnt fraud signatures, we eventually combine a misuse model with anomaly model - a unique approach proposed by us. If the fraud model and hence, the BD-sequence is not available, the approach reduces to an anomaly based fraud detection system.

## 3.2   Implementation Details

The architecture of the proposed system is shown in Figure 3. As new transactions come to the credit card processing system, a Q-sequence is formed by taking the last N number of transactions. A list of Q-words is generated from the Q-sequence in the first stage. Since a Q-word may not match completely with GD-sequences due to the presence of potentially bad transactions, some transactions from the Q-word can be removed to get a significant match with a GD-sequence. The ordered list of removed transactions is called an R-sequence (removed sequence), which is next checked to see if it has a high similarity with BD-sequence.

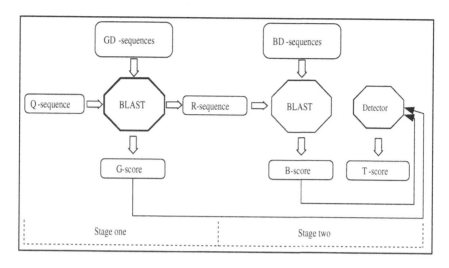

**Fig. 3.** Architecture of the proposed two-stage fraud detection system

A unit match score $\partial$ is assigned to each matched element in the aligned sequence and a unit mismatch score $\partial'$ is assigned to each mismatched element in that aligned sequence. Let L be the length of a Q-word and N be the number of matches with aligned GD-sequence, then

$$G\text{-}score = N \times \partial - (L - N) \times \partial'. \tag{1}$$

The R-sequence of length L-N is next aligned with BD-sequence. Let M be the number of matches with aligned BD-scquence and R-sequence, then

$$B\text{-}score = M \times \partial - ((L - N) - M) \times \partial'. \tag{2}$$

A set of R-sequences is formed for each combination of GD-sequence and Q-word where G-score is above a certain threshold value. Each R-Sequence taken from the set of R-Sequences is aligned with BD-Sequences to obtain the B-score for maximal segment pair. The total score (T-score) is computed by the detector as follows.

$$T\text{-}score = G\text{-}score - B\text{-}score. \tag{3}$$

Figure 3 shows that the first stage of our fraud detection system evaluates G-score in the alignment process with Q-sequence and GD-sequence. The second stage evaluates B-score in the alignment process with R-sequence and BD-sequence. Both the first stage and the second stage use BLAST for sequence alignment. Figure 4 shows the complete algorithm of the two-stage fraud detection system. A set of HSPs is obtained from a Q-word and for each HSP an R-sequence is obtained. G-score and B-score are evaluated by the alignment process and alarm is raised when $T\text{-}score \leq A\text{-}threshold$.

```
Algorithm: Two_stage fraud_detection
Begin
    Input: Q-sequence, QW-size, A-threshold
    Output: T-score

    For each Q-word in Q-sequence do
    Begin
      HSP_set = Blast_GD_alignment(Q-word)
        For each HSP in HSP_set do
        Begin
            G-score = Get_score(HSP, Q-word)
            R-sequence = Get_rsequence(HSP, Q-word)
            MSP = Blast_DB_alignment(R-sequence)
            B-score = Get_score(MSP, R-sequence);
            T-score = G-score - B-score
            If (T-score ≤ A-threshold) then
                Raise_alarm()/* Raise alarm to notify fraud */
        End
    End
End

Algorithm: Blast_GD_alignment
/* Returns all high scoring segment pairs for a given
   Q-word */

Algorithm: Get_score
 /* Returns good score or bad score for a given segment pair
    (HSP or MSP) along with Q-word or R-sequence*/

Algorithm: Get_rsequence
/* Returns the ordered mismatch symbols from Q-word of
   given HSP and Q-word */

Algorithm: Blast_DB_alignment
/* Returns maximal segment pair by comparing a given
   sequence with DB-sequences */
```

Fig. 4. Algorithm of the proposed two-stage fraud detection system

## 4   Results and Discussions

Performance analysis of the proposed system can be done meaningfully only
when a sufficient number of genuine and fraudulent transactions are available. To
achieve this, we have built a simulator that generates transactions with various
distributions. Card holders are broadly classified into three categories, namely,
low, medium and high spending groups. A large percentage of transactions of

the high spending group card holders contain high priced items. Medium and low spending groups are defined similarly. The thieves are also classified into three categories, namely, low, medium and high risk-loving groups. Thieves in the high risk-loving group carry out frequent high-value transactions. Medium and low risk-loving groups are defined similarly.

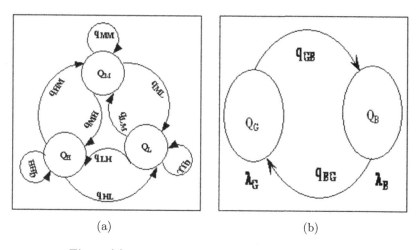

(a)                                         (b)

**Fig. 5.** (a)Transaction generator (b)Two-state MMPP

The simulator (transaction generator) can generate transactions for a group of card holders or a group of fraudsters using three different states $Q_H$, $Q_M$ and $Q_L$ with their associated state transition rates $q_{ij}$ where $i\epsilon\{H, M, L\}$ and $j\epsilon\{H, M, L\}$. Figure 5(a) shows a three-state transaction generator where high-value transactions are generated in the $Q_H$ state, medium-value transactions in $Q_M$ and low-value transactions in $Q_L$. As mentioned before, fraudulent transactions are interspersed with genuine transactions. The two types of transactions are generated by two different parties, namely, genuine card holders and fraudsters. Hence, these are independent events with separate arrival rates. This real life scenario is captured using a Markov Modulated Poisson Process (MMPP). It is a doubly stochastic Poisson process where the arrival rate is determined by the state of the underlying Markov Chain. Since the Markov Chain has a finite number of states, the Poisson arrival rate takes discrete values corresponding to each state. A two-state MMPP is shown in Figure 5(b). The model has two states $Q_G$ (Good state) and $Q_B$ (Bad state). In the $Q_G$ state, Poisson arrival rate is $\lambda_G$ while in $Q_B$, arrival rate is $\lambda_B$. $q_{GB}$ is the probability of transition from $Q_G$ to $Q_B$. $q_{BG}$ is defined similarly. In $Q_G$, good transactions are generated by the transaction generator of Figure 5(a) according to a specified card holder's group. Bad transactions are generated in the $Q_B$ state using the same transaction generator of Figure 5(a) according to a specified fraudster's group. It should be kept in mind that two instances of the transaction generator in Figure 5 are running, one in each state of Figure 5(b).

We use standard performance metrics to analyze the different test cases. True Positive (TP) is the percentage of fraudulent transactions identified as fraudulent, True Negative (TN) is the percentage of genuine transactions identified as genuine, False Positives (FP) is the percentage of genuine transactions identified as fraudulent, and False Negative (FN) is the percentage of fraudulent transactions identified as genuine. FN and TN can be represented in terms of TP and FP, respectively as $FN = 100 - TP$ and $TN = 100 - FP$. It is important to achieve high TP and low FP in a fraud detection system. However, design constraints are such that any attempt to improve TP, results in higher FP as well. So, we empirically determine the design parameters of the system and then simulate with input variations.

Different possible cases were considered over a large number of transactions generated by the simulator. The results observed were plotted for groups of thieves and for groups of users. The effectiveness of the fraud detection system is dependent on the Q-word length (W) and the alarm threshold (T). In Figures 6– 8 , we study the percentage of TP/FP for different values of T and W under three combinations of thief profiles for a given card holder's profile. We set user profile to be high and vary thief profile as low, medium and high.

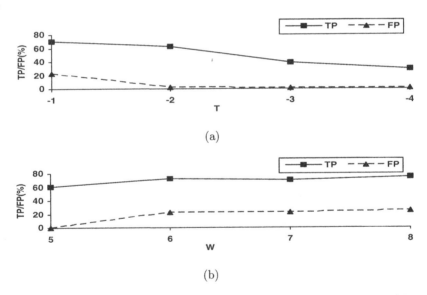

(a)

(b)

**Fig. 6.** Variation of TP/FP for High spending user and Low risk-loving thief (a) Variation with T keeping W fixed at 7 and (b) Variation with W keeping T fixed at -1

In the first set of each figure, namely, Figures 6(a), 7(a) and 8(a), we vary T keeping W fixed at 7. In the second set of results, we vary W keeping T fixed at -1. From Figures 6(a), 7(a) and 8(a), it is clear that TP and FP decrease with increasing value of T. A genuine sequence is treated as fraudulent if it has alignment score below T. As the value of T decreases, FP also decreases. The same explanation holds for TP also. Figures 6(b), 7(b) and 8(b) show the

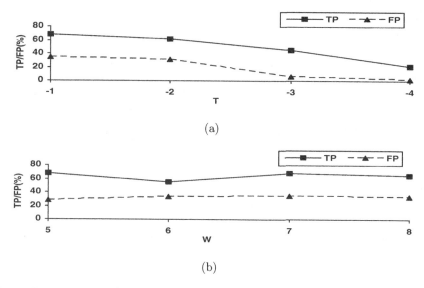

**Fig. 7.** Variation of TP/FP for High spending user and Medium risk-loving thief (a) Variation with T keeping W fixed at 7 and (b) Variation with W keeping T fixed at -1

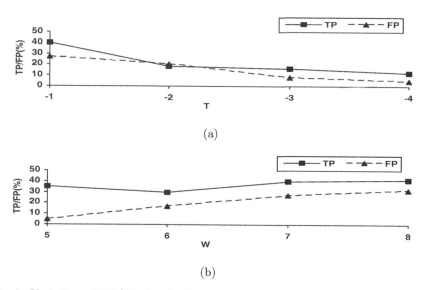

**Fig. 8.** Variation of TP/FP for High spending user and High risk-loving thief (a) Variation with T keeping W fixed at 7 and (b) Variation with W keeping T fixed at -1

variation on TP/FP with W for a fixed value of T. It is seen that both TP and FP increase with increasing value of W. The reason is that as W increases, the Q-words become less similar with GD-Sequences due to the probabilistic behavior of the card holder, causing FP to increase. A fraudulent sequence is detected as fraudulent (TP) if it has a score below T. As W increases, the Q-word becomes less similar to GD-Sequences, which makes the score fall below T. Based on the above observations, we set W=7 and T= -1 in our FDS design.

From the above figures, it is also observed that the effectiveness of the FDS depends on the combination of the category of the thief and that of the user. The FDS works more effectively for "High spending user and Low risk-loving thief" combination compared to "High spending user and High risk-loving thief" combination. This is expected since higher the deviation of the thief's behavioristic pattern, higher is the probability of detecting a fraudulent transaction.

The probability of fraud detection also increases if there are successive fraudulent transactions in the Q-word. While simulating, the number of successive occurrences of fraudulent transactions can be increased by increasing the Poisson arrival rate ($\lambda_B$) in the Bad state of Figure 5(b). The results are shown in Figure 9. It is observed that as $\lambda_B$ increases, the number of successive bad transactions within a given window size also increases, causing TP to rise.

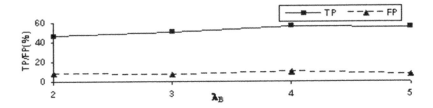

**Fig. 9.** Variation of TP/FP with rate of generation of fraudulent transactions

The fraud detection probability improves when the number of fraudulent transactions increases in a Q-word. Lower probability of transition $q_{GB}$ with constant $q_{BG}$ implies less number of fraudulent transactions in a Q-word. In this situation, FP increases as shown in Figure 10(a). Lower of transition probability $q_{BG}$ with constant $q_{GB}$ results in an opposite effect as shown in Figure 10(b).

Finally, in Figures 11(a) – 11(b) we show the effect of adding the second stage in the fraud detection process. In these figures, TP1 and FP1 denote true positives and false positives in one-stage FDS i.e., an FDS in which only deviations from genuine card holder's behavior is measured. TP2 and FP2 denote the same in a two-stage FDS as proposed here. Results are shown with variation in W and T, respectively. It is observed that the percentage of true positives is much higher in the two-stage approach as proposed in this paper. The number of false positives is also comparable in the two approaches.

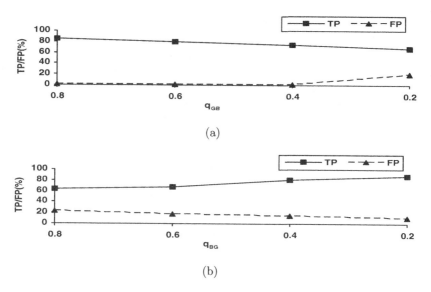

**Fig. 10.** Variation of TP/FP with (a) qGB and (b) qBG

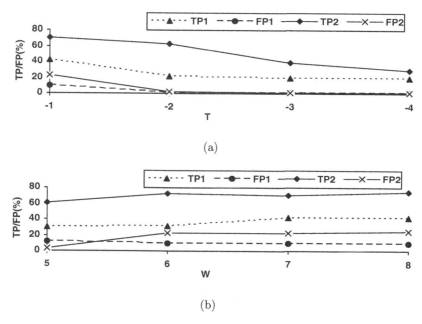

**Fig. 11.** Comparative study of TP/FP for a one-stage FDS and a Two-stage FDS (a) Variation with T keeping W=7 (b) Variation with W keeping T= -1

## 5   Conclusions

We have proposed a novel two-stage fraud detection model which is based on the strengths of both anomaly and misuse based detection techniques. In the first stage, a genuine card holder's profile is used to find any behavioristic deviation of a transaction. The second stage is based on misuse detection in which signatures of fraudulent transactions, which have previously been caught by the credit card company, are used as a fraud model. The deviated transactions from the first stage are passed to the second stage to check for any behavioristic similarity with a fraudster's profile. A simple scoring system is used to compute both good score and bad score, which are combined to determine if there is any cause for alarm.

**Acknowledgments.** This work is partially supported by a research grant from the Department of Information Technology, Ministry of Communication and Information Technology, Government of India, under Grant No. 12(34)/04-IRSD dated 07/12/2004.

## References

1. http://www2.acnielsen.com/reports/documents/2005_cc_onlineshopping.pdf, Global Consumer Attitude Towards Online Shopping, 28 Apr 2006.
2. http://www.epaynews.com/statistics/fraud.html, Statistics for General and Online Card Fraud, 22 Apr 2006.
3. http://news.bbc.co.uk/2/hi/business/3256799.stm Business news on Preventing card fraud BBC NEWS, 8 Mar 2005.
4. S. Ghosh, D.L. Reilly, Credit Card Fraud Detection with a Neural-Network, Proceedings of the Annual International Conference on System Science, Pages 621-630, 1994.
5. S. J. Stolfo, D.W. Fan, W. Lee, A.L. Prodromidis, Credit Card Fraud Detection Using Meta-Learning: Issues and Initial Results, Proceedings of the Workshop on AI Methods in Fraud and Risk Management, 1997.
6. E. Aleskerov, B. Freisleben, B. Rao, CARDWATCH: A Neural Network Based Database Mining System for Credit Card Fraud Detection, Proceedings of the IEEE/IAFE, Pages 220-226, 1997.
7. W. Fan, A.L. Prodromidis, S.J. Stolfo, Distributed Data Mining in Credit Card Fraud Detection, Proceedings of IEEE Intelligent Systems, Pages 67-74, 1999.
8. R. Brause, T. Langsdorf, M. Hepp, Neural Data Mining for Credit Card Fraud Detection, International Conference on Tools with Artical Intelligence, Pages 103-106, 1999.
9. C. Chiu, C. Tsai, A Web Services-Based Collaborative Scheme for Credit Card Fraud Detection, Proceedings of the IEEE International Conference on e-Technology, e-Commerce and e-Service, Pages 177-181, 2004.
10. C. Phua, V. Lee, K. Smith, R. Gayler, A Comprehensive Survey of Data Mining-based Fraud Detection Research, Proceedings of the Artical Intelligence, 2005.
11. V. Vatsa, S. Sural, A.K. Majumdar, A Game- Theoretic Approach to Credit Card Fraud Detection, Lecture Notes in Computer Science, Springer Verlag, Proceedings of International Conference on Information Systems Security, Pages 263-276, 2005.

12. K. Takeda, The application of bioinformatics to network intrusion detection, Security Technology, 39th Annual International Conference (CCST) IEEE, Pages 130-132, 2005.
13. S. Coul, J.Branch, B. Szymanski, E. Breimer, Intrusion Detection: A Bioinformatics Approach, Proceedings of the 19th Annual Computer Security Applications Conference (ACSAC) IEEE, Pages 24-33, 2003.
14. S.B. Needleman, C.D. Wunsch, A general method applicable to the search for similarities in the amino acid sequence of two proteins. Journal of Molecular Biology, Pages 443-453, 1970.
15. T. F. Smith, M.S. Waterman, Identification of common molecular subsequences. Journal of Molecular Biology, Pages 195-197, 1981.
16. S. F. Altschul, W. Gish, W. Miller, W. Myers, J. Lipman, Basic Local Alignment Search Tool, Journal of Molecular Biology, Pages 403-410, 1990.

# New Malicious Code Detection Using Variable Length $n$-grams

D. Krishna Sandeep Reddy, Subrat Kumar Dash, and Arun K. Pujari

Artificial Intelligence Lab, University of Hyderabad
Hyderabad - 500 046, India
krishnasandeep.reddy@yahoo.co.in, subrat.dash@gmail.com,
akpcs@uohyd.ernet.in

**Abstract.** Most of the commercial antivirus software fail to detect unknown and new malicious code. In order to handle this problem generic virus detection is a viable option. Generic virus detector needs features that are common to viruses. Recently Kolter et al. [16] propose an efficient generic virus detector using $n$-grams as features. The fixed length $n$-grams used there suffer from the drawback that they cannot capture meaningful sequences of different lengths. In this paper we propose a new method of variable-length $n$-grams extraction based on the concept of episodes and demonstrate that they outperform fixed length $n$-grams in malicious code detection. The proposed algorithm requires only two scans over the whole data set whereas most of the classical algorithms require scans proportional to the maximum length of $n$-grams.

**Keywords:** Malicious code detection, $n$-grams, Data Mining, Episodes.

## 1 Introduction

Malicious code is any code added, changed, or removed from a software system to intentionally cause harm or subvert the system's intended function [19]. Any computer system is vulnerable to malicious code whether or not it is attached to other systems. Examples of malicious code include viruses, Trojan horses, worms, back doors, spyware, Java attack applets, dangerous ActiveX and attack scripts. Combining two or more of these categories can lead to fatal attack tools. Recent *Gartner* report [12] ranked viruses and worms as top security threats and hence detecting malicious code has become one of the prime research interests in the field of information security. In this paper, we concentrate on computer viruses. These are self-replicating software entities that attach themselves to other programs. There are two approaches that are poles apart in virus detection. One approach is too generic which includes Activity monitors and Integrity management systems. The other approach, *Signature based virus detection*, is too specific and also popular. Almost all the commercial antivirus products rely on this approach. In this, a database of virus signatures is maintained and a program is detected as a virus program based on the presence of these virus signatures. There are two main disadvantages in this technique [19].

A. Bagchi and V. Atluri (Eds.): ICISS 2006, LNCS 4332, pp. 276–288, 2006.

- Unknown and new viruses will easily escape the detection by simple defenses, like code obfuscation, as their signatures are not present in the database [6].
- This technique is not scalable. As the number of known viruses increases, the size of the signature database increases and also the time of checking a file for virus signatures increases.

Generation of virus signature is a cumbersome process and is prone to generating false positives on benign programs. Unlike signature based detection, generic virus detector uses features that are common to most of the viruses and that characterize only the virus programs. The assumption here is that viruses have certain typical characteristics in common and these characteristics are not present in benign programs. For instance, most of the virus writers use virus generating toolkits [25], for example PS-MPC (Phalcon-Skism Mass-Produced Code Generator), to write and compile their code. It is believed that more than 15,000 variants of viruses were generated using this kit alone and there are more than 130 such kits available. The viruses generated using a toolkit have certain features that are specific to the toolkit, the compiler and also the programming environment [3].

It is clear from the foregoing discussion that a generic virus detector is though desirable is very difficult to accomplish in its true form. A practical approach is to develop a machine learning based detector where the detection process learns the generic characteristics from a set of known examples but avoids identifying any specific signatures. Recently there have been several such attempts for detection of malicious code.

Kephart et al. [15] propose the use of Neural Networks to detect boot sector malicious binaries. Using a Neural Network classifier with all bytes from the boot sector malicious executables as input, it is shown that unknown boot sector malicious executables can be successfully identified with low false positive rate. Later, Arnold et al. [2] apply the same techniques to Win32 binaries. Motivated by the success of data mining techniques in host based and network intrusion system, Schultz et al. [23] propose several data mining techniques to detect different types of malicious executables. In a companion paper [24] the authors develop a UNIX mail filter that detects malicious Windows executables based on the above work. Byte sequences are used as the set of features as machine codes are most informative to represent executables. The RIPPER algorithm of rule discovery and Naive Bayes classifiers are used for classification in this study. Abou-Assaleh et al. [3] observe that $n$-grams extracted from byte sequences can be used as an effective feature. They use Common $n$-gram (CNG) as the features and propose a k-NN classification for detecting computer virus. Kolter et al. [16] independently realise that $n$-grams can possibly be used as a set of features. However, as the set of all $n$-grams is very large, it is proposed to use few of them selected based on their information gain. Kolter et al. [16] also investigate several classification techniques, which are implemented in WEKA [27] and boosted J48 algorithm reportedly gave good results. Static analysis, where analysis of program is done without executing it, is attempted in [6,17]. Dynamic analysis which combines testing and debugging to detect malicious activities by running a program includes wrappers [4], sandboxing [1] etc. Behavior blocker is a method used in Bloodhound technology (Symantec) and ScriptTrap technique (Trend Inc.).

It is also interesting to note that many of these techniques use byte $n$-grams as the basic features to detect malicious codes. Byte $n$-grams are overlapping continuous substrings, collected in a sliding-window fashion where the windows of fixed size $n$ slides one byte at a time. N-grams have the ability to capture implicit features of the input that are difficult to detect explicitly. Byte $n$-grams can be viewed as features in the present context when an executable program is viewed as a sequence of bytes. Importance of byte $n$-gram in detecting computer virus has been realised more than once in the computer virology research. In 1994, a byte $n$-gram-based method is used for automatic extraction of virus signatures [15]. The major difficulty in considering byte $n$-grams as a feature is that the set of all byte $n$-grams obtained from the set of byte strings of virus as well as of the benign programs is very large. There are several feature selection techniques proposed in [28] and the important ones are *document frequency* and *information gain*. Recently, it is shown in [22] that class-wise relevant n-grams can be a better feature selection technique.

The main disadvantage of fixed-length $n$-grams is that they cannot capture meaningful $n$-gram sequences [9] of different lengths. Though variable length $n$-grams are previously used in intrusion detection [8,9,14,18] and text categorization [5,11], no attempts have been made to use them in malicious code detection. Recently, we have [8] demonstrated that episodes as variable length $n$-grams can be used for IDS. In this paper we propose a very elegant and novel method of detection of malicious codes by extracting the common features of virus programs as variable length $n$-grams, based on the concept of episodes [7]. The proposed detection technique works as follows.

We use an efficient method of extracting variable length $n$-grams (*episodes*) and select class-wise relevant $n$-grams. We take $m$ relevant $n$-grams from each of the two classes virus and benign to get $M$ features which are used in vector space model representation. We use supervised classification techniques such as Ada Boost, J48 and demonstrate that variable length $n$-gram method of detection is better than fixed length approach.

The rest of the paper is organized as follows. In section 2, we propose an episode discovery algorithm that is used for a set of sequences. The episode discovery algorithm proposed in [8] is only for one sequence at a time. But in the present case, it is necessary to find episodes for a set of sequences. In section 3 we describe the concept of relevant episodes. Section 4 describes the experimental results of the proposed method and comparative study with earlier methods. Conclusion follows in section 5.

## 2    Episode Discovery Algorithm

Episodes are meaningful subsequences of a continuous sequence. Any method of finding episodes in a large sequence is essentially finding the break points in the sequence and hence can be viewed as sequence segmentation method [13]. There are many proposals of segmenting sequence in general and specifically segmenting time series in the fields of telecommunications, speech processing, signal processing, text processing etc. The objective of sequence segmentation can be different in different contexts [10]. In the present context, we are interested in segmenting categorical sequence into meaningful subsequences. Cohen et al. [7] proposed an efficient method of sequence segmentation based on voting experts approach. We adopt this algorithm for the present context and extend the same to handle multiple sequences.

The main idea of Cohen et al. [7] algorithm is that it has two experts who vote their inference for break points. The frequency expert measures the likelyhood of a subsequence to be an episode based on its frequency of occurrence. The higher the frequency of subsequences, the lower is the chance that it contains a break point. Similarly the entropy expert measures the entropy at a point. If an element associates (precedes) itself with several other elements then it has higher probability of being a break point compared to an element which precedes only few elements. This phenomenon is captured by computing the entropy of the association. The original algorithm combines the frequency and entropy scores at each location of the sequence and identifies the possible location of break points. The subsequence between two consecutive break points is an episode. In order to efficiently handle the computation of entropy and frequency along different locations in a sequence, it is proposed [7] to represent this information in a trie structure.

In order to build the trie for a sequence, a user specified parameter $d$, the depth of the trie is needed. The sequence is read one symbol at a time and its preceding $d - 1$ symbols are also taken. Each of the $d$ subsequences are inserted into the trie with frequency value set to 1 if, the subsequence is not yet present in the trie. Else, the frequency of the subsequence is incremented by 1. The complete algorithm for construction of trie is given in [8].

**Definition 1.** *Entropy of a node ($e(x)$) refers to the entropy of the sequence from the root node to the concerned node ($x$). Let $f(x)$ be the frequency of the node $x$ and $x_1$, $x_2$, ..., $x_\ell$ be its child nodes. The probability of the subsequence represented at node $x_1$, denoted as $p(x_1)$, is given by*

$$P(x_1) = \frac{f(x_1)}{f(x)}$$

*The entropy of $x$ is given by*

$$e(x) = -\sum_{i=1}^{\ell} p(x_i) \log p(x_i)$$

It can be noted that the entropy for the leaf nodes is zero. Now, each of the nodes in the trie has two parameters, frequency ($f$) and entropy ($e$). We standardize these parameters [7] for each of the level in the trie taking means ($\overline{f}$, $\overline{e}$) and standard deviations ($\sigma_{\overline{f}}$, $\sigma_{\overline{e}}$). Both the parameters contribute equally in finding the break points by assigning scores to the probable positions.

In the present context, we extend the algorithm to determine episodes from a set of sequences. The simple extension would mean that we construct one trie for each sequence. But we propose to store the information of all sequences in a single trie structure. Thus we can capture the frequency and entropy of any element over all the sequences together. The method of construction of trie for multiple sequences is illustrated in Example 1.

**Example 1:** Let us consider the following set of four sequences.
$S_1 = $ (bf 0e 3a bf d8 3a 3a bf)
$S_2 = $ (3a bf bf 0e 3a 3a bf bf d8 3a)
$S_3 = $ (bf d8 3a bf 0e 3a bf 0e 3a 0e 3a)
$S_4 = $ (0e 3a bf d8 3a 3a bf 3a bf 0e 3a)

The trie structure for $S_1$ can be obtained by using algorithm in [8] with $d = 4$ as shown in Figure 1. From the trie structure we note that (bf) appears 3 times in $S_1$, (3a bf) appears twice and (3a 3a) appears once. The structure captures the frequency of $n$-grams of different lengths (at most $d-1$). We embed $S_2$ on this structure to get the trie representing $S_1$ and $S_2$ (Figure 2). The final trie structure after considering all the sequences is shown in Figure 3. The algorithm for finding episodes from each of the sequences, using the above obtained combined trie structure ($T_k$), is given in Figure 4.     □

For each of the sequence $S_t$ we take a sliding window of length $k(= d - 1)$. Let $x_1, x_2, \ldots, x_k$ be the elements falling in the window at one instance. For each of the $k$ possible break points in the window, we examine the frequency and entropy as follows.

The entropy at location $i$ (between $x_i, x_{i+1}$) is the entropy of the node $x_i$ at level $i$ of the trie along path $x_1$, $x_2$, ..., $x_i$. For example, for $S_1$, with $k$=3 we get a window (bf|0e|3a|) with 3 positions for break points. The entropy at the first location is entropy of the node labelled (bf) at the first level of the trie. Similarly entropy at the second location is the entropy of the node labelled (0e) at level 2

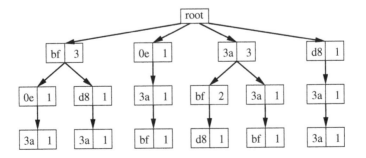

**Fig. 1.** Trie for $S_1$ in Example 1 with depth=4

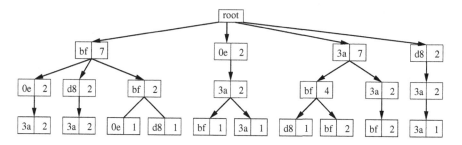

**Fig. 2.** Trie after $S_1$ and $S_2$ given in Example 1 with depth=4

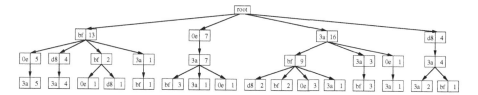

**Fig. 3.** Combined trie for all the four sequences in Example 1 with depth=4

with (3a) as the parent at level 1 in the trie. The location corresponding to the highest entropy in the window is identified and its score is incremented by 1.

The frequency at location $i$ is calculated by the sum of the frequencies of subsequences $(x_1 \ldots x_i)$ and $(x_{i+1} \ldots x_k)$. For example, the frequency at the first location of the window (bf|0e|3a|) is $f(\text{bf}) + f(\text{0e 3a})$, where $f(\text{bf})$ refers to frequency of the node labelled (bf) at the first level of the trie and $f(\text{0e 3a})$ refers to frequency of the node labelled (3a) at the second level of the trie whose parent node is (0e) at level 1. The score at the location with highest frequency is incremented by 1. In this case, our goal is to maximize the sum of the frequencies of the left and right subsequences of the probable break point.

After sliding the window across the sequence, we end up with scores for each location in the sequence. In a stream of $|S_t|$ 1-grams, there are $|S_t| - 1$ positions within the sequence. If a position is repeatedly voted for break point by different windows then it is likely to accrue a locally-maximum score. We choose the positions with local maximum of the score as break points of the episode.

**Example 1 (Contd.):** Continuing Example 1, we can find the list of episodes from each of the four sequences using the algorithm given in Figure 4. These are as follows.

$E_1 = ((\text{bf 0e 3a}), (\text{bf d8 3a}), (\text{3a bf}))$
$E_2 = ((\text{3a bf}), (\text{bf 0e 3a}), (\text{3a bf}), (\text{bf d8 3a}))$
$E_3 = ((\text{bf d8 3a}), (\text{bf 0e 3a}), (\text{bf 0e 3a}), (\text{0e 3a}))$
$E_4 = ((\text{0e 3a}), (\text{bf d8 3a}), (\text{3a bf}), (\text{3a bf 0e 3a}))$

□

Algorithm: to find episodes for a set of sequences $S$
Input: $T_d$ (trie of depth $d$) and $S$

do for each of the node $x \in T_d$
  calculate entropy $e(x)$
enddo
do for each level $L_i$ of $T_d$
  find mean frequency $(\overline{f})$ and mean entropy $(\overline{e})$
  find standard deviations $(\sigma_{\overline{f}}$ and $\sigma_{\overline{e}})$ taking $\overline{f}$ and $\overline{e}$ respectively
  $f(x) = \frac{f(x)-(\overline{f})}{\sigma_{\overline{f}}}$ for $x \in L_i$
  $e(x) = \frac{e(x)-(\overline{e})}{\sigma_{\overline{e}}}$ for $x \in L_i$
enddo
do for each sequence $S_t(s_1, s_2, \ldots, s_{|S_t|}) \in S$
  Episodes $E_t = \phi$
  initialize $score(i) = 0$, for $1 \le i \le |S_t|$
  do for $i = 1$ to $(|S_t| - k + 1)$
    take a window of length $k$ starting at position $i$ in $S$
    do for each of the $k$ possible boundary positions in the window
      find $Max_j\{f(s_i, \ldots, s_{i+j}) + f(s_{i+j+1}, \ldots, s_{i+k-1})\}, 0 \le j < k$
      increment $score(i + j)$
      find $Max_j\{e(s_i, \ldots, s_{i+j})\}, 0 \le j < k$
      increment $score(i + j)$
    enddo
  enddo
  $start = 1$
  do for $i = 2$ to $(|S_t| - 1)$
    if $(score(i) > score(i - 1))$ and $(score(i) > score(i + 1))$
      $end = i$
      add $(s_{start}, \ldots, s_{end})$ to $E_t$
      $start = end$
    endif
  enddo
  add $(s_{start}, \ldots, s_{|S_t|})$ to $E_t$
enddo

**Fig. 4.** Episode discovery algorithm for a set of sequences using a combined trie

Observing the above episodes, it is clear that episode discovery algorithm gives meaningful sequences. If we consider fixed length $n$-grams, say n = 2, then obviously we lose valuable information by missing 3-grams.

## 3   Relevant Episodes

We observe that there can be large number of episodes for a single program and when we consider all the programs in the training set the set of distinct episodes becomes very large. We introduce here two novel concepts- *relevant episodes* for a class and a new feature selection measure, namely *class-wise episode frequency*.

The main aim of feature selection is to identify a smaller set of features that are representative of the virus and benign classes.

Let the set of virus programs be $V$ and the set of benign programs be $B$.

**Definition 2.** *The class-wise episode frequency of an episode with respect to a class $V$ (or, $B$) is the number of times it occurs in the class $V$ (or, $B$).*

While the term frequency is a kind of global measure, the class-wise episode frequency is a local measure with respect to a class. The main advantage of class-wise episode frequency is that we can analyze each class independently. This saves memory requirement as we handle only episodes of one class at a time.

For each executable program $t$ in a class $T$ of programs, let $E_t$ be the set of all episodes. The set of all episodes for T, $E(T)$ is $\cup_{t \in T} E_t$. We assume that the elements of $E(T)$ are arranged in the non-increasing order of class-wise episode frequency.

**Definition 3.** *We define $E^k(T)$ as the relevant episodes for $T$ which is a subset of $E(T)$ containing only first $k$ elements.*

Thus the relevant episodes for classes $V$ and $B$ are $E^k(V)$ and $E^k(B)$, respectively. We get the set of relevant episodes for the whole training data as $E^k(V) \bigcup E^k(B)$.

With the set of relevant episodes for the data set, we build the vector space model which is a concept derived from information retrieval. An executable program is represented as a vector of $t_1, t_2, \ldots, t_M$, where $t_i (1 \leq i \leq M)$ is a binary (0-1) value denoting the occurrence of the $i^{th}$ relevant episode. The value 1 represents the occurrence of an episode and its absence is represented by 0. Thus each unique relevant episode corresponds to a dimension. Our training set consists of a set of labeled vectors – the vector representation of the set of programs together with the respective class label (virus or benign).

As we observed, the detection problem reduces essentially to supervised classification problem. Several algorithms exist [20] for supervised classification like support vector machine, decision tree, neural networks etc. We use the metaclassifier Ada Boost with J48 as base classifier available in WEKA [27]. The reason for choosing this particular classifier is that the authors of previous work [16] in this area claimed that they got the best results for this classifier.

# 4   Experimental Setup and Results

No standard data set is available for the detection of malicious executables unlike intrusion detection. Data sets (i.e. viruses) collected from the website VX Heavens [26] were used by [3,16]. The benign executables were collected from their respective laboratories. We collected 250 viruses from [26] and 250 benign executables from our lab. For viruses, we used only the loader programs; we did not use the infected programs in our analysis. At present, we only concentrate on viruses. Each executable in the dataset is converted to hexadecimal codes in an ASCII format.

The set of programs for each class $V$ and $B$ are used to build the trie with $d=4$ and from the tries, the set of episodes for each individual executables are extracted. The top $m$ episodes in order of class-wise frequency are selected for each class. These are combined to get a set of relevant episodes of size $M$ with duplicates removed.

We experimented with $M$ values as 100 and 500. The classification is done with the metaclassifier Ada Boost M1 with J48 as base classifier. These algorithms are implemented in WEKA [27], which is a collection of machine learning algorithms for solving data mining problems implemented in Java and open sourced under the GPL. For the classifiers we use the default values given by WEKA and to evaluate our approach, we used stratified ten-fold cross-validation.

We compared our method with that of the method proposed by Kolter et al. [16] for two reasons. First, the method in [16] is so far the best method of generic virus detection using $n$-grams. The other reason is that this method takes fixed length $n$-grams as features and information gain as the measure for feature selection. We use the same dataset for both the methods for comparison. We experimented with $n$ as 2, 3 and 4, whereas $M$ is taken as 100 and 500. We give the results as ROC curves in Figures 5-8.

In Data Mining, ROC (Receiver Operating Characteristics) curves are used to compare classification capability of different algorithms. The more the area under the ROC curve of an algorithm, the more robust and better it is in classification.

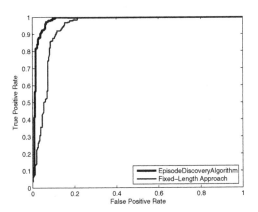

**Fig. 5.** Fixed vs Variable length $n$-grams: Profile length $= 100$, $n = 2$ for fixed length $n$-grams

Figure 5 shows the ROC curves of the proposed method and the fixed-length $n$-gram approach (with $n = 2$) with profile length as 100. It is evident from the graph that the proposed method gives a 100% detection rate with a false positive rate of 0.11 whereas the fixed-length method attains it with a false positive rate of 0.216. Even for fixed-length of $n=3$ and 4, proposed method gives consistantly better results in comparison to fixed-length $n$-gram approach as can be seen from figures 6 and 7.

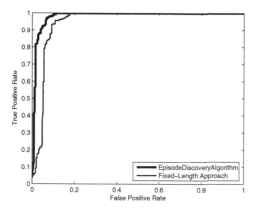

**Fig. 6.** Fixed vs Variable length $n$-grams: Profile length $= 100$, $n = 3$ for fixed length $n$-grams

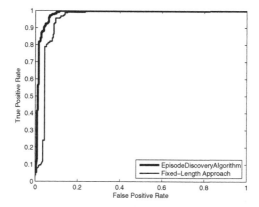

**Fig. 7.** Fixed vs Variable length $n$-grams: Profile length $= 100$, $n = 4$ for fixed length $n$-grams

For profile length of 500, as given in Figure 8, the accuracy of our method is more pronounced than the fixed-length approach. The proposed method achieved a detection rate of 70.8% with zero false positive, and 100% detection with 2.6% false positive rate. For the same profile length fixed-length $n$-gram method, for $n=4$, shows the lowest detection rate of 15% with 1.5% false positive rate and attains 100% detection rate with 20% false positive rate.

Taking area under ROC curve as performance criteria, from the visual inspection of the ROC curves it is clear that our proposed method outperforms the method in [16] in all cases. Based on the experimentation we infer the following. The variable-length $n$-grams approach is better than fixed length $n$-grams approach as the fixed-length $n$-grams do not capture the long meaningful sequences while keeping the size and number of $n$-grams manageable. Moreover it is also

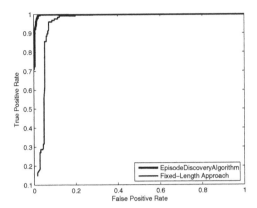

**Fig. 8.** Fixed vs Variable length $n$-grams: Profile length $= 500$, $n = 4$ for fixed length $n$-grams

observed that possibly class-wise episode frequency is a better measure for feature selection than the information gain. This is also demonstrated in detail in the context of fixed length $n$-grams in [22].

When it comes to advanced computer viruses like polymorphic viruses, static analysis methods do not work. To tackle these viruses, static analysis methods should be combined with dynamic analysis methods for efficient detection. For example, polymorphic virus consists of three components – decryption routine, mutation engine and virus body. Since the mutation engine and the virus body are encrypted and decryption routine is different in each replication, it is not possible to directly apply any static analysis method (including our method) to detect this virus. Instead we can use a dynamic analysis technique (like sandboxing) that trick a polymorphic virus into decrypting and revealing itself [21]. On this decrypted virus we can use the static analysis method. Here we assume that a polymorphic virus must decrypt before it can execute normally.

## 5   Conclusion

The main objective of the present work is to establish that proper feature extraction and selection technique can help in efficiently detecting virus programs. We showed here that episodes as variable length $n$-grams are better than usual fixed length $n$-grams. We also showed that selecting frequent episodes in terms of class-wise relevance is a better feature selection technique. We demonstrate that a supervised classification by the proposed feature selection method gives better accuracy and less false positive in comparison to earlier proposed methods.

In $n$-gram approach attaching semantic meaning for the relevant $n$-grams (episodes) is not yet explored by us. Our future work will be to develop a semantic aware method and include different kinds of malicious and benign executables in our training data.

# Acknowledgment

This research is supported by Ministry of Communications and IT, Govt of India under the grant no. 12(22)/04-IRSD dated: 04.02.2004.

# References

1. Anagnostakis, K. G., Sidiroglou, S., Akritidis, P., Xinidis, K., Markatos, E., Keromytis, A. D.: Detecting targeted attacks using shadow honeypots. In: Proceedings of the $14^{th}$ USENIX Security Symposium (2005)
2. Arnold, W., Tesauro, G.: Automatically generated Win32 heuristic virus detection. In Proceedings of the 2000 International Virus Bulletin Conference (2000)
3. Assaleh, T. A., Cercone, N., Keselj, V., Sweidan R.: Detection of new malicious code using N-grams signatures. In: Proceedings of the Second Annual Conference on Privacy, Security and Trust (2004) 193–196
4. Balzer, R., Goldman, N.: Mediating Connectors. In: Proceedings of the $19^{th}$ IEEE International Conference on Distributed Computing Systems Workshop, Austin, TX, (1999) 73–77
5. Cavnar, W., Trenkle, J.: N-gram based text categorization. In: Proceedings of SDAIR-94, 3rd Annual Symposium on Document Analysis and Information Retrieval (1994) 161–175
6. Christodorescu, M., Jha, S.: Static analysis of executables to detect malicious patterns. In: Proceedings of the 12th USENIX Security Symp, Washington, DC, August (2003) 169–186
7. Cohen, P., Heeringa, B., Adams, N. M.: An unsupervised algorithm for segmenting categorical timeseries into episodes. In: Proceedings of the ESF Exploratory Workshop on Pattern Detection and Discovery, London, UK. September (2002) 49-62
8. Dash, S. K., Reddy, K. S., Pujari, A. K.: Episode Based Masquerade Detection. In: Proceedings of 1st International Conference on Information Systems Security, Kolkata, Dec (2005), LNCS Vol. 3803, pp. 251-262
9. Debar, H., Dacier, M., Nassehi, M., Wespi, A.: Fixed vs. variable-length patterns for detecting suspicious process behavior. Journal of Computer Security, $8(2/3)$ (2000)
10. Firoiu, L.: Segmenting Time Series with a Hybrid Neural Networks – Hidden Markov Model. citeseer.ist.psu.edu/firoiu02segmenting.html (2002)
11. Furnkranz, J.: A study using $n$-gram features for text categorization. Technical Report OEFAI-TR-9830, Austrian Research Institute for Artificial Intelligence (1998)
12. Gartner Inc.: $www.gartner.com/press\_releases/asset\_129199\_11.html$ (2005)
13. Gionis, A., Mannila, H.: Segmentation Algorithms for Time Series and Sequence Data. SIAM International Conference on Data Mining, Newport Beach, CA. (2005)
14. Jiang, G., Chen, H., Ungureanu, C., Yoshihira, K.: Multi-resolution abnormal trace detection using varied-length N-grams and automata. In: Proceedings of the Second International Conference on Autonomic Computing (2005)
15. Kephart, J. O., Sorkin, G. B., Arnold, W. C., Chess, D. M., Tesauro, G. J., White, S. R.: Biologically inspired defenses against computer viruses. In: Proceedings of IJCAI '95, Montreal, August (1995) 985–996
16. Kolter, J. K., Maloof, M. A.: Learning to detect malicious executables in the wild. In: Proceedings of the Tenth ACM SIGKDD International Conference on Knowledge Discovery and Data Mining (2004)

17. Lo, R. W., Levitt, K. N., Olsson, R. A.: MCF: A malicious code filter. Computers & Society, **14**(6) (1995) 541–566
18. Marceau, C.: Characterizing the behavior of a program using multiple-length N-grams. In :Proceedings of the 2000 Workshop on New security paradigms (2000)
19. McGraw, G., Morrisett, G.: Attacking Malicious Code: A Report to the Infosec Research Council. IEEE Software, September/October (2000)
20. Mitchell, T.: Machine Learning. McGraw-Hill, New York, NY (1997)
21. Nachenberg, C.: Understanding and managing polymorphic viruses. The Symantec Exterprise Papers, Vol XXX.
22. Reddy, D. K. S., Pujari, A. K.: N-gram Analysis for New Computer Virus Detection. *Communicated* to the Journal in Computer Virology.
23. Schultz, M. G., Eskin, E., Zadok, E., Stolfo, S., J.: Data mining methods for detection of new malicious executables. In: Proceedings of IEEE Symposium on Security and Privacy (2001)
24. Schultz, M. G., Eskin, E., Zadok, E., Bhattacharyya, M., Stolfo, S. J.: MEF: Malicious Email Filter, A UNIX mail filter that detects malicious windows executables. In: Proceedings of USENIX Annual Technical Conference (2001)
25. Szor, P.: The Art of Computer Virus Research and Defense. Addison Wesley, 2005
26. VX Heavens: *http : //vx.netlux.org*
27. Witten, I., Frank, E.: Data mining: Practical machine learning tools and techniques with Java implementations. Morgan Kaufmann, San Francisco, CA (2000)
28. Yang, Y., Pedersen, J. O.: A comparative study on feature selection in text categorization. In: Proceedings of 14th International Conference on Machine Learning (1997) 412–420

# A Dead-Lock Free Self-healing Algorithm for Distributed Transactional Processes

Wanyu Zang and Meng Yu

Monmouth University, NJ 07724, USA
myu@monmouth.edu

**Abstract.** Even though self-healing techniques for transactional processes have attracted enough attention in recent years, several critical issues regarding the distributed systems have not been addressed. For example, if we do the recovery under sustained attacks, in which condition the recovery can terminate? Is a synchronized clock necessary for distributed recovery? In this paper, we proposed a dead-lock free algorithm for coordinated recovery and answered related questions. We also proved that under specific situations, we have to freeze the recovery scheme to guarantee that the recovery can make progress.

**Keywords:** Attack recovery, self-healing, distributed systems, transactional processes.

## 1  Introduction

Distributed transactional processing systems (e.g., distributed database systems and workflow systems) are important in most critical infrastructures such as financial services. These services rely on the correctness, availability, and reliability of the processing systems. Each transactional process consists of a set of transactions (or tasks[1]) that are related to each other in terms of the semantics of a business process. Each transaction represents a specific unit of work that the business needs to do (e.g., a specific application program, a database transaction). A consistent and reliable execution of distributed transactional processes is crucial for all organizations.

However, it is well known that system vulnerabilities cannot be totally eliminated, and such vulnerabilities can be exploited by attackers who penetrate the system. We believe in that at least four aspects should be considered while building defense mechanisms for a secure, reliable system: **protection, detection, response**, and **restore**. Current research pays more attention to the research of protection, detection, and response, e.g., access control of a secure system, intrusion detection of both systems or network, congestion control of network, than to the research of restore that recovers a system to normal service level.

---

[1] A workflow transaction is also called a "task". We do not distinguish them in our paper.

A. Bagchi and V. Atluri (Eds.): ICISS 2006, LNCS 4332, pp. 289–302, 2006.

The attack recovery is important because no defense, or detection system is perfect in the real world. Therefore, after the attacker successfully breaks into the system, we need to bring the system back to its original integrity level. Our work focuses on the recovery from successful attacks.

In this work, we focus on those intrusions that inject malicious transactions into a distributed transaction processing system instead of the attacks that only crash the system. These intrusions can happen in many situations, for example, when attackers access a system with stolen (guessed, cracked, etc.) passwords or when some defense mechanisms, such as access control, are broken by the attackers. Under such intrusions, transactions and data may be forged or corrupted. For one example, an attacker may forge bank transactions to steal money from accounts of others, thereby generating malicious transactions. For another example, the attacker may schedule a travel with forged credit card information that carries incorrect data in transactions.

If these malicious transactions were not recovered in time, they would sooner or later spread misleading information or damage to a lot of legitimate transactions and other hosts, generating more trash data in the distributed system. To correct the situation, the malicious transactions must be removed from the system, and all affected transactions must be repaired.

However, the solution is not trivial. For example, the damage can spread not only among transactional processes, but also across hosts. The local view to the system is not enough for correct and complete recovery. The global knowledge of the distributed system is necessary to trace damage spreading and repair damage.

Existing techniques cannot solve above problems. For example, intrusion detection (ID) techniques, which have received much attention, are very limited in tracing the damage spreading. The damage directly caused by the attacker may be spread by the execution of normal, legitimate transactions without being detected by an IDS. Furthermore, the IDS could have a delay especially if the IDS depends on the system log [14]. If a transaction appears in the system log, the transaction has already been successfully executed and committed. It cannot be handled by any workflow fault handling mechanism [6,3,37] because it does not appear as a fault to the system. It is a successful intrusion of corrupting data and appears as a normal transaction to the system. In fact, an immediately detected and stopped attack is not a successful attack. It is not harmful to the system and it is out of the scope of this paper.

Previous work [1,23,24,27,22,26,28], especially [38,39], has built fundamental theories and a simple prototype system for attack recovery. Based on the dependency relations among the transactions, which can be obtained through the analysis of the system log or the applications, our system finds out all the damage and generates recovery transactions to repair the damage. However, some theoretical issues regarding the distributed system have not been addressed. For example, the termination and dead-lock of recovery. We will address these problems in this paper.

## 2   Preliminaries

We have proposed two attack recovery models for transactional processes in previous work [40,39]. However, these models ignored some important features in distributed systems for the theoretical simplicity.

### 2.1   Unrecoverable Transactions

In a distributed system, we need to consider both inside operations and interactions with the outside world. The formal models in our previous work failed to formalize interactions with the outside world. Since interactions with the outside world are not recoverable, we use an $OWS$ (outside world site) to model the outside world. All transactions happened on an $OWS$ are *unrecoverable*. We consider all inputs obtained from users and all outputs to the users happen on a user site $S_u$ which is a $OWS$. All user's transactions are called $OWT$s (outside world transactions). For example, a transaction that a user withdraws money from a ATM cannot be recovered. It is an $OWT$ and the ATM is an $OWS$.

### 2.2   Notation of Distributed Transactions

Existing attack recovery models also failed to describe site bindings and process qualifiers that will be defined in the following example. Therefore, they are unable to describe distributed transactional processes accurately. By introducing new notations through an example, we will build a dependency relation based model to describe all theoretical results in a formal way.

Figure 1 demonstrates several typical damage spreading modes. In the figure,

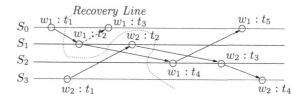

**Fig. 1.** Two transactional processes with forward domino effects

each node (circle) is a transaction. Every transaction belongs to a transactional process, e.g., $w_1 : t_1$ belongs to process $w_1$ and $w_2 : t_1$ belongs to process $w_2$, where $w_2$ is a *process qualifier*. When the location where a transaction executes matters, we use a pair $(w_i : t_j, s_k)$, which is called a *site binding*, to represent transaction $w_1 : t_j$ executing on site $s_k$, e.g., $(w_1 : t_1, s_0)$ and $(w_2 : t_3, s_2)$ in the figure.

### 2.3   Dependency Relations

We define dependency relations in the following since damage spreads through dependency relations and executing orders of recovery transactions are determined by dependency relations. In Figure 1, the start node of an arrow will be executed right before the end node, which defines a *precedence* relation. For example, $w_1 : t_1$ *precedes* $w_1 : t_2$, which is denoted by $w_1 : t_1 \prec w_1 : t_2$. There are two execution paths in $w_1$. One is $w_1 : t_1t_2t_4t_5$. The other one is $w_1 : t_1t_2t_3$. $w_1 : t_2$ makes decision on which execution path will be selected. The selection between $w_1 : t_2$'s successor $w_1 : t_3$ or $w_1 : t_4$ is called *control dependence*, which is denoted by $w_1 : t_2 \to_c w_1 : t_3$ and $w_1 : t_2 \to_c w_1 : t_4$. In the figure, execution path $w_1 : t_1t_2t_4t_5$ was selected.

Assume $\prec$ is a relation on set $\mathcal{S}$ then we define minimal$(\mathcal{S}, \prec) = x$ where $x \in \mathcal{S} \wedge \nexists x' \in \mathcal{S}, x' \prec x$. Note there may be more than one result qualified by the definition of minimal$(\mathcal{S}, \prec)$. For example, $\mathcal{S} = \{t_i, t_j, t_k\}$, $t_i \prec t_k$ and $t_j \prec t_k$, then both $t_i$ and $t_j$ are qualified results for minimal$(\mathcal{S}, \prec)$. In cases like this, we randomly select one qualified result as the value of minimal$(\mathcal{S}, \prec)$. The task scheduler is supposed to choose minimal$(\mathcal{S}, \prec)$ to execute.

Once $w_1 : t_2$ is identified as a transaction compromised by the attacker, and the selection of execution path $w_1 : t_1t_2t_4t_5$ was wrong, the execution of $w_1 : t_4$ and $w_1 : t_5$ need to be recovered. Furthermore, if $w_2 : t_3$ reads information generated by $w_1 : t_4$, which is *flow data dependence* denoted by $w_1 : t_4 \to_f w_2 : t_3$, the damage will be spread to $w_2 : t_3$. Note that even though no message has been sent from $w_1 : t_4$ to $w_2 : t_3$, they may still have data dependencies since they may share data objects on the same site. Similarly, if we have $w_2 : t_3 \to_f w_2 : t_4$ then $w_2 : t_4$ will be damaged as well.

In the above example, damage is spread through dependency relations. We can similarly define the other two types of data dependence. If $t_j$ modifies data objects after $t_i$ reads them, then $t_j$ is *anti-flow dependent* on $t_i$, which is denoted by $t_i \to_a t_j$. If $t_i \prec t_j$, and they have common data objects to modify, then $t_j$ is *output dependent* on $t_i$, which is denoted by $t_i \to_o t_j$.

All the relations $\to_f$, $\to_a$ and $\to_o$ are data dependency relations and are not transitive. From the well known results of concurrency and parallel computing, if $t_j$ is data dependent on $t_i$, then they cannot run in parallel or concurrently, and $t_i \prec t_j$ must be satisfied. Otherwise, we will get wrong results.

## 2.4  Concurrency Restrictions in Recovery

We use a simple example to explain that there do exist such restrictions on executing orders of transactions in dependency relation based recovery.

Since the process qualifier and site binding do not change the results of the following discussion, we remove them in notations for the simplicity. Consider transactions $t_1 : a = 1, t_2 : b = 2$, and $t_3 : y = a + b$, which are executed in the sequence of $t_1 \prec t_2 \prec t_3$. We have $t_1 \to_f t_3 \wedge t_2 \to_f t_3$. Assume that $t_2$ has been identified as compromised by an IDS, so the value of $b$ is corrupted. Therefore, $t_3$ is also corrupted since it reads a incorrect $b$. To recover, $t_2$ needs to be undone followed by redone. $t_3$ needs to be redone. We must satisfy the sequence of undo$(t_2) \prec$ redo$(t_2) \prec$ redo$(t_3)$ in the recovery. Any other execution will get wrong results. The precedence relations introduced by dependency relations is called *concurrency restrictions*.

The concurrency restriction for transactions without process qualifiers and site bindings has been studied and formally described in [39,40]. The concurrency restriction is also caused by dependency relations. However, we can break anti-flow dependency relations by introducing multi-version data, as described in [40].

## 2.5   Transactional Processes

With above notations, transactional processes can be modeled as $(T, S, \prec, \rightarrow_f, \rightarrow_a, \rightarrow_o, \rightarrow_c)$, where $T$ is a set of transactions with process qualifiers, $S$ is a set of sites that are corresponding to a host or a processor in the distributed system, $S_u \in S$ is an $OWS$, and all dependency relations among transactions. With the model, we can trace damage spreading in the distributed system, work out concurrency restrictions, and solve other important problems addressed in the rest of the paper.

# 3   The Integrated Recovery Algorithm

Our algorithm includes recovery analysis as the first part and damage repair as the second part.

We assume that the recovery components of the system, and all related information and communication are trustable. For example, we assume that all information is authenticated.

The following algorithm runs on each site for the attack recovery.

1. Wait $\sigma$ seconds, where $\sigma < \alpha$ ($\alpha$ will be explained in Section 4), for the set of damaged transactions $B_i$ reported by an IDS or the set $B_s$ reported by other sites
2. Local recovery analysis generates $\langle R, \prec \rangle$ based on $B_s \cap B_i$;
3. Send all $s_j|w_k|t_l \in R$ as set $B$, where $j \neq i$, and $\prec$ to site $s_j$;
4. If $minimal(R \cap T, \prec)$ has been changed in $\alpha$ seconds, then go to step 1;
5. do the repair according to $G\langle R, \prec \rangle$
6. go to step 1;

In the algorithm, $T$ contains all transactions submitted by users. We assume that recovery transactions in $R$ consist of undo transactions and redo transactions. $R \cap T$ includes damaged transactions that need to be redone.

We assume that dependency relations are carried by transactional processes. There are two kinds of information being transferred among different sites during the recovery: 1) identified damage transactions, and 2) recovery transactions and executing orders.

In the algorithm, step 1 to step 4 are for recovery analysis, which generates recovery a recovery scheme denoted by $G\langle R, \prec \rangle$. Step 5 repairs the damage.

Our recovery algorithm does not need a global synchronized clock because the recovery, including the recovery analysis and the repair, depends only on the precedence relations among transactions. The precedence relations usually are integrated in the specification of transactional processes.

The rationale and termination of the algorithm will be discussed in the following sections.

# 4   Recovery Analysis

Recovery analysis consists of damage tracing and recovery scheme generation. Damage is spread through dependency relations, including both data dependencies and control dependencies. The damage can be spread intra-transactional processes, or inter-transactional processes. Damage tracing identifies all damaged transactions through dependency relations.

We consider $G\langle T, \rightarrow \rangle$ as a dependency graph. Since transactional processes can be modeled as a dependency graph, the procedure of damage tracing can be described as a procedure of chasing the dependency graph. Rules proposed in [39] describes how to chase the graph to identify all damaged transactions. A sink node which has 0 out degree will not affect any other nodes even if it is damaged.

Recovery scheme generation generates recovery transactions and execution orders according to the results of damage tracing. The recovery scheme can be modeled as $G\langle R, \prec \rangle$, where $R$ is the set of recovery transactions, and $\prec$ is the precedence relations. The recovery scheme generation constructs the recovery graph increasingly.

## 4.1   Overlaps of Undetermined Segments

In a distributed system, message may arrive the destination not in the same order as they were sent. An IDS may identify damage not in the same order as the damage happened. These situations affect the progress of recovery analysis.

**Definition 1.** *If an IDS reports an incidents sequence $i_1 i_2 \cdots i_n$, where for any $i_j$ and $i_k$, $1 \leq j < k \leq n$, $i_j \prec i_k$ then the IDS reports incidents in the temporal order.*

It is possible that IDSs do not report incidents according to the temporal order, then the situation in Figure 2 needs to be considered.

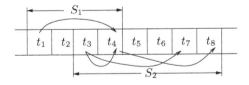

**Fig. 2.** Overlap of Two Segments

In the figure, the IDS, or a message from other sites, firstly reports $t_3$ as a damaged transaction, which leads to $t_4, t_7$, and $t_8$ identified as damaged transactions. All these transactions are in segment $S_2$. Transaction $t_1$ may be reported as damaged after the incident reporting $t_3$. According to the dependency relations denoted by curve arrows in the figure, segment $S_1$ will be re-scanned. There will be a overlap between $S_1$ and $S_2$, where $S_1 \cap S_2 \neq \phi$.

In the figure, since $t_4$ has been identified as damaged in $S_1$, it is not necessary to re-scan all transactions in $S_1$. We found the following truth regarding the local recovery analysis.

**Theorem 1.** *A Local recovery analysis can terminate for a finite sequence of incidents no matter if the segment of incidents are reported in temporal orders or not.*

PROOF: For each incident, the length of the system log is limit since the number of transactions committed is limit. Therefore the scan of the system log can terminate. For a finite sequence of incidents, the scan of the system log can terminate because the possible overlaps do not affect the total number of committed transactions. $\square$

## 4.2   Termination of Recovery Analysis for Temporal Reports

If damage is reported in temporal order, we have the following results for the global recovery analysis.

**Lemma 1.** *If all IDSs report incidents in the temporal order, the global recovery analysis of $minimal(T, \prec)$ is acyclic, and the transaction is identified by the IDS.*

PROOF: By contradiction. Assume that in the recovery analysis, $t \in minimal$ $(T, \prec)$ in the distributed system has been visited twice. In other words, $t$ is in a circle in the recovery analysis. Since the IDS reports incidents in the temporal order, the IDS will not report the incident including $t$ twice. Therefore, the second visit to the transaction should be caused by damage spreading, say, the transaction is dependent on other transactions happened earlier, e.g., $t' \prec t$ which is contradictory to our assumption that $t \in minimal(T, \prec)$.

According to our discussion, since $t$ is not affected by other transactions, $t$ should be reported by the IDS.                                        $\square$

**Theorem 2.** *If all IDSs report incidents in the temporal order, the global recovery analysis can make progress.*

PROOF: Since all IDSs report incidents in the temporal order, according to Lemma 1, the recovery analysis of $t \in minimal(T, \prec)$ will not be cyclic. Therefore, $t$ can be recovered anyway. We can always choose $minimal(T, \prec)$ in the rest transactions.                                        $\square$

**Theorem 3.** *If all IDSs report incidents in the temporal order and there is no further incidents reported or the damage is contained, the global recovery analysis will terminate.*

PROOF: This can be concluded from Theorem 2 directly.                  $\square$

## 4.3   Termination of Recovery Analysis for Temporally Segmented Reports

It is difficult to require an IDS to report all incidences according to the temporal order strictly. We have the following theorem to weaken the requirement to the IDS.

**Definition 2.** *If an incidence sequence reported by the IDS can be segmented into several segments, $S_1, S_2, \cdots, S_n$, for any $i_j \in S_j$ and $i_k \in S_k$, $1 \leq j < k \leq n$, $i_j \prec i_k$, then the incidents reported by the IDS can be* temporally segmented. *The time span that a segment $S_i$ covers is called the* cycle $\alpha_i$ *of $S_i$. The cycle of an incidence sequence is defined as $\alpha = \max(S_1, S_2, \ldots, S_n)$.*

Note that $\alpha$ appears in the algorithm.

**Lemma 2.** *If all incident sequence generated by IDSs can be temporally segmented, the global recovery analysis of $minimal(T, \prec)$ is acyclic.*

PROOF: Since all incident sequence generated by IDSs can be temporally segmented, each of them can be denoted by $S_1, S_2, \cdots, S_n$, for any $i_j \in S_j$ and $i_k \in S_k$, $1 \leq j < k \leq n$, $i_j \prec i_k$. Assume that $e_k = minimal(T, \prec)$ and $e_k \in S_k$, then for any $e_j \in S_j$ and $e_k \in S_k$, $1 \leq j < k \leq n$, $e_j \prec e_k$.

According to the discussion of the overlap of undetermined segments, the recovery will not be pull back further than $e_k = minimal(T, \prec)$ in each segment.

$minimal(T, \prec)$ in the global recovery analysis will not be visited twice for the same reason in Lemma 1. □

**Theorem 4.** *If all incident sequence generated by IDSs can be temporally segmented, the global recovery analysis can make progress.*

PROOF: According to Lemma 2, the recovery analysis of $minimal(T, \prec)$ is acyclic, so its recovery analysis can be done. We can always choose $minimal(T, \prec)$ from the rest transactions. Therefore, the global recovery analysis can make progress. □

**Definition 3.** *For task $t$, if there does not exist $t'$, such that $t' \to t$, we say the recovery of $t$ is* independent.

**Theorem 5.** *For any damage spreading graph $G'\langle T', \prec \rangle$ containing $t$, $t \in minimal(T', \prec)$ if and only if $t$ is independent.*

PROOF: This can be proved according to Definition 3. □

As long as the damage chasing speed is faster than the spreading speed, the recovery analysis can terminate.

**Theorem 6.** *If 1)all incident sequence generated by IDSs can be temporally segmented, , 2)there is no further incidents reported, and 3)the damage is contained, then the global recovery analysis will terminate.*

PROOF: According to Theorem 4, the recovery analysis can always make progress, which reduces the total number of incidents to be analyzed. Since incidents reported has limit number and damage is contained, which means the total number of damaged transactions will not increase. Therefore, the global recovery analysis will terminate. □

Assume there are $n$ sites in the system and $M_i = minimal(T_i, \prec)$ for the $i$th site, then $M = M_1 \cap M_2 \cap \ldots \cap M_n$ is the *recovery line*. For any transaction $t \prec t'$, $t' \in M$, $t$ does need recover. The recovery line indicates the "left" boundary of recovery. Any transactions on the left of the recovery line, in other words, happened earlier then the recovery line, does not need to be recovered.

# 5   Damage Containment and Repair

**Definition 4.** *A recovery graph is a directed graph containing all recovery tasks as vertices and precedence relations as edges.*

The procedure of repair is the traversal of the recovery graph.

If referring to the data in the recovery graph is not allowed, we say the damage is *contained*. If no further revision is allowed on the recovery graph, we say the recovery graph is *frozen*. Damage contain requires that all data items generated by damaged transactions not to be referred until these transactions are recovered.

When the damage chasing is done, the recovery graph can be frozen. The condition to freeze a recovery graph can be determined by several times longer then the length of IDS report segments. By this way, even though overlaps between recoveries may occur, we can guarantee the progress of recovery.

**Theorem 7.** *If a transactional process is acyclic, then the repair procedure is dead-lock free.*

PROOF: Figure 3 shows the recovery graph (the right one) constructed from

**Fig. 3.** The construction of a recovery graph

$a \prec b \wedge a \prec c$ (the left one). In the figure, $a', b', c'$ are undo transactions of $a, b$, and $c$. The recovery graph is acyclic.

According to our previous conclusions [39,40] (theorems to generate precedence relations), all possible precedence relations between undo and redo transactions are displayed in the figure. Since the original transactional process is acyclic, the recovery graph will also be acyclic. Therefore, the repair procedure will be dead lock free.     □

**Theorem 8.** *The repair procedure can make progress and terminate if 1)the damage is contained, 2)the recovery graph is frozen, and 3) all transactional processes are acyclic.*

PROOF: According to the definition of containment and freezing of the recovery graph, damage will not be spread by referring the recovery graph and the recovery line has been identified. Since we can choose to recover any transaction in the recovery line, the recovery line will move forward. In other words, the recovery can make progress. Since the recovery graph has been frozen. The number of recovery transactions is limit. Furthermore, the recovery is dead-lock free according to Theorem 7 since all transactional processes are acyclic. Therefore, the recovery can terminate.     □

## 6    Related Work

**Intrusion Detection.** One critical step towards intrusion-tolerant systems is intrusion detection (ID), which has attracted much attention over the past years [5,29,11,9,31,32,30,15,17]. The existing methodology of ID can be roughly classed as anomaly detection, which is based on profiles of normal behaviors [12,33,16,34], and misuse detection, which is based on known patterns of attacks, called signatures [10,8,35]. However, existing anomaly detection techniques focuses on identifying attacks on OS and computer networks, which cannot be directly used to detect malicious transactions. Although there are some works on database ID [4,36], these methods are neither application aware nor at transaction-level, which are the two major design requirements of the ID component of the attack recovery system.

An Intrusion Detection System (IDS) [18] can detect some intrusions. But, in a distributed computing system, the damage directly caused by the attacker may be spread by executing normal transactions without being detected by the IDS. The IDS is unable to trace damage spreading and cannot locate all damage to the system.

**Fault Tolerance.** The failure handling of workflow has been discussed in recent work [6,3,37]. Failure handling is different from attack recovery in two aspects. On one hand, they have different goals. Failure handling tries to guarantee the atomic of workflows. When failure happens, their work find out which transactions should be aborted. If all transactions are successfully executed, failure handling does nothing for the workflow. Attack recovery has different goals, which need to do nothing for failure transactions even if they are malicious because failure malicious transactions have no effects on the workflow system. Attack recovery focuses on malicious transactions that are successfully executed. It tries to remove all effects of such transactions. On the other hand, these two systems active at different times. Failure handling occurs when the workflows are in progress. When the IDS reports attacks, the malicious transactions usually have been successfully executed. Failure handling can do nothing because no failure occurred. Attack recovery is supposed to remove the effects of malicious transactions after they are committed.

The checkpoint techniques [19,20] also do not work for efficient attack recovery. A checkpoint rolls back the whole system to a specific time. All work, including both malicious transactions and normal transactions, after the specific time will be lost, especially when the delay of the IDS is very long. In addition, checkpoints introduce extra storage cost.

**Distributed Computing Systems.** De-centralized distributed computing is becoming more and more popular. In distributed computing models, transactions specifications cannot be accessed in a center node. They are carried by workflow itself or stored in a distributed style. In either case, our theories are still practical. We need to process the specifications of distributed transactional processes in a distributed style.

In some work such as [2], security and privacy is important, and the whole specification of workflows avoids being exposed to all processing nodes to protect

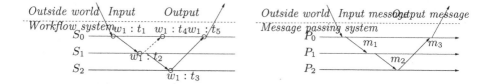

**Fig. 4.** A transactional process moving through sites

**Fig. 5.** Message passing system

privacy. Our theories are based on the dependence relations among transactions. The specification can be best protected by exposing only dependent relations to the recovery system.

**Rollback Recovery.** Rollback recovery, e.g. [13,21], is surveyed in [7]. Rollback recovery focuses on the relationship of message passing and considers temporal sequences based on message passing. In contrast, we focus on data and control dependence relations inside transactions. In fact, message passing is a kind of data dependence relation but not vice versa (e.g., a data dependence relation caused by more than one message passing steps or by sharing data). We also observed that in attack recovery an execution path may change due to control dependence, causing different patterns of message passing. In addition, our methods exploit more detail in dependence relations than the methods that are message passing based; therefore our method is more effective and efficient for attack recovery. Our method also better matches the workflow model.

In our work, we deal with transactional processes. Although rollback recovery is a good analogy to transactional processes, it is simply not a dual of the latter and its results cannot be simply applied to transactional processes. A comparison between transactional processes and the message passing model is shown in Figure 4, Figure 5, and Table 1.

**Table 1.** A Comparison between the Dependency Relation based Model and the Message passing Model

| | Dependency Relation based Model | Message Passing Model |
|---|---|---|
| Where to execute a process | on multiple sites | on a single site |
| Where failures happen | in the middle of a transactional process | at the end of a computing process |
| Domino effects | forwards | backward |
| Recovery | through compensate transactions | through check pointing |
| Damage caused | is not strictly time related while strictly dependence related | is strictly time related while not strictly dependence related |
| Consequences | orphan transactions and orphan processes | orphan messages and orphan processes |

**Self-Healing Database Systems.** In [1,23], When intrusions have been detected by the IDS, the database system isolates and confines the impaired data. Then, the system carries out recovery for malicious transactions. ITDB has actually implemented the on-the-fly damage assessment and repair algorithm proposed in [1]. In [25], the authors have proposed a general isolation algorithm. However, this algorithm cannot be directly implemented on top of an off-the-shelf DBMS. ITDB has developed a novel SQL rewriting approach to implement the algorithm. Finally, the design and implementation of almost every key ITDB component have been described in detail in previous publications [24,27,22,26,28,1], Recent work considering more detailed dependency relations has been published in [40,39].

However, this work is the first work on fundamental theories regarding the feasibility of self-healing distributed transactional processes.

# 7   Conclusions

In this paper, we proposed a dead-lock free self-healing algorithm for distributed transactional processes. We discussed dead-lock, progress, and terminating problems regarding the distributed algorithm by introducing a serial theorems. Our results can serve as guidelines to design other dead-lock free and effective distributed recovery algorithms.

# References

1. P. Ammann, S. Jajodia, and P. Liu. Recovery from malicious transactions. *IEEE Transaction on Knowledge and Data Engineering*, 14(5):1167–1185, 2002.
2. Vijayalakshmi Atluri, Soon Ae Chun, and Pietro Mazzoleni. A chinese wall security model for decentralized workflow systems. In *Proceedings of the 8th ACM conference on Computer and Communications Security*, pages 48–57. ACM Press, 2001.
3. Qiming Chen and Umeshwar Dayal. Failure handling for transaction hierarchies. In Alex Gray and Per-Åke Larson, editors, *Proceedings of the Thirteenth International Conference on Data Engineering, April 7-11, 1997 Birmingham U.K*, pages 245–254. IEEE Computer Society, 1997.
4. C. Y. Chung, M. Gertz, and K. Levitt. Demids: A misuse detection system for database systems. In *14th IFIP WG11.3 Working Conference on Database and Application Security*, 2000.
5. D. E. Denning. An intrusion-detection model. *IEEE Trans. on Software Engineering*, SE-13:222–232, Feb. 1987.
6. Johann Eder and Walter Liebhart. Workflow recovery. In *Conference on Cooperative Information Systems*, pages 124–134, 1996.
7. E. N. (Mootaz) Elnozahy, Lorenzo Alvisi, Yi min Wang, and David B. Johnson. A survey of rollback-recovery protocols in message-passing systems. *ACM Computing Surveys*, 34(3):375–408, September 2002.
8. T.D. Garvey and T.F. Lunt. Model-based intrusion detection. In *the 14th National Computer Security Conference*, Baltimore, MD, October 1991.

9. P. Helman and G. Liepins. Statistical foundations of audit trail analysis for the detection of computer misuse. *IEEE Trans. on Software Engineering*, 19(9):886–901, 1993.
10. K. Ilgun. Ustat: A real-time intrusion detection system for unix. In *the IEEE Symposium on Security and Privacy*, Oakland, CA, May 1993.
11. R. Jagannathan and T. Lunt. System design document: Next generation intrusion detection expert system (nides). Technical report, SRI International, Menlo Park, California, 1993.
12. H. S. Javitz and A. Valdes. The sri ides statistical anomaly detector. In *Proceedings IEEE Computer Society Symposium on Security and Privacy*, Oakland, CA, May 1991.
13. David R. Jefferson. Virtual time. *ACM Transaction on Programming Languages and Systems*, 7(3):404–425, July 1985.
14. Christopher Kruegel and Giovanni Vigna. Anomaly detection of web-based attacks. In *CCS'03*, pages 251–261, Washington, DC, USA, October 27-31 2003.
15. T. Lane and C.E. Brodley. Temporal sequence learning and data reduction for anomaly detection. In *5th ACM Conference on Computer and Communications Security*, San Francisco, CA, Nov 1998.
16. W. Lee and D. Xiang. Information-theoretic measures for anomaly detection. In *2001 IEEE Symposium on Security and Privacy*, Oakland, CA, May 2001.
17. Wenke Lee, Sal Stolfo, and Kui Mok. A data mining framework for building intrusion detection models. In *1999 IEEE Symposium on Security and Privacy*, Oakland, CA, May 1999.
18. Wenke Lee and Salvatore J. Stolfo. A framework for constructing features and models for intrusion detection systems. *ACM Transactions on Information and System Security*, 3(4):227–261, 2000.
19. Jun-Lin Lin and Margaret H. Dunham. A survey of distributed database checkpointing. *Distributed and Parallel Databases*, 5(3):289–319, 1997.
20. Jun-Lin Lin and Margaret H. Dunham. A low-cost checkpointing technique for distributed databases. *Distributed and Parallel Databases*, 10(3):241–268, 2001.
21. Yi-bing Lin and Edward D. Lazowska. A study of time warp rollback machanisms. *ACM Transactions on Modeling and Computer Simulations*, 1(1):51–72, January 1991.
22. P. Liu. Dais: A real-time data attack isolation system for commercial database applications. In *the 17th Annual Computer Security Applications Conference*, 2001.
23. P. Liu, P. Ammann, and S. Jajodia. Rewriting histories: Recovery from malicious transactions. *Distributed and Parallel Databases*, 8(1):7–40, 2000.
24. P. Liu and S. Jajodia. Multi-phase damage confinement in database systems for intrusion tolerance. In *Proc. 14th IEEE Computer Security Foundations Workshop*, pages 191–205, Nova Scotia, Canada, June 2001.
25. P. Liu, S. Jajodia, and C.D. McCollum. Intrusion confinement by isolation in information systems. *Journal of Computer Security*, 8(4):243–279, 2000.
26. Peng Liu and Ying Wang. The design and implementation of a multiphase database damage confinement system. In *the 2002 IFIP WG 11.3 Working Conference on Data and Application Security*, 2002.
27. P. Luenam and P. Liu. Odar: An on-the-fly damage assessment and repair system for commercial database applications. In *the 2001 IFIP WG 11.3 Working Conference on Database and Application Security*, 2001.
28. P. Luenam and P. Liu. The design of an adaptive intrusion tolerant database system. In *IEEE Workshop on Intrusion Tolerant Systems*, 2002.

29. T. Lunt, A. Tamaru, F. Gilham, R. Jagannathan, C. Jalali, H. S. Javitz, A. Valdes, P. G. Neumann, and T. D. Garvey. A real time intrusion detection expert system (ides). Technical report, SRI International, Menlo Park, California, 1992.

30. Teresa Lunt and Catherine McCollum. Intrusion detection and response research at DARPA. Technical report, The MITRE Corporation, McLean, VA, 1998.

31. T.F. Lunt. A survey of intrusion detection techniques. *Computers & Security*, 12(4):405–418, Jun. 1993.

32. B. Mukherjee, L. T. Heberlein, and K.N. Levitt. Network intrusion detection. *IEEE Network*, pages 26–41, Jun. 1994.

33. D. Samfat and R. Molva. Idamn: An intrusion detection architecture for mobile networks. *IEEE J. of Selected Areas in Communications*, 15(7):1373–1380, 1997.

34. S. Sekar, M. Bendre, and P. Bollineni. A fast automaton-based method for detecting anomalous program behaviors. In *2001 IEEE Symposium on Security and Privacy*, Oakland, CA, May 2001.

35. S.-P. Shieh and V.D. Gligor. On a pattern-oriented model for intrusion detection. *IEEE Trans. on Knowledge and Data Engineering*, 9(4):661–667, 1997.

36. S. Stolfo, D. Fan, and W. Lee. Credit card fraud detection using meta-learning: Issues and initial results. In *AAAI Workshop on AI Approaches to Fraud Detection and Risk Management*, 1997.

37. Jian Tang and San-Yih Hwang. A scheme to specify and implement ad-hoc recovery in workflow systems. *Lecture Notes in Computer Science*, 1377:484–498, 1998.

38. Meng Yu, Peng Liu, and Wanyu Zang. Intrusion masking for distributed atomic operations. In *The 18th IFIP International Information Security Conference*, pages 229–240, Athens Chamber of Commerce and Industry, Greece, 26-28 May 2003. IFIP Technical Committee 11, Kluwer Academic Publishers.

39. Meng Yu, Peng Liu, and Wanyu Zang. Self-healing workflow systems under attacks. In *The 24th International Conference on Distributed Computing Systems(ICDCS'04)*, pages 418–425, 2004.

40. Meng Yu, Peng Liu, and Wanyu Zang. Multi-version based attack recovery of workflow. In *The 19th Annual Computer Security Applications Conference*, pages 142–151, Dec. 2003.

# An Efficient Public Key Cryptosystem Secure Against Chosen Ciphertext Attack

Hossein Ghodosi

School of Mathematics, Physics, and Information Technology,
James Cook University, Townsville, Qld 4811, Australia
hossein@cs.jcu.edu.au

**Abstract.** Devising public key cryptosystems that are secure against chosen ciphertext attacks has been the subject of investigation by many researchers. However, there are actually very few secure and efficient systems in the literature.

In this paper, we introduce a secure and efficient public key cryptosystem. The main advantage of our schemes is that we employ a problem *equivalent to the well-studied RSA problem*, and thus our schemes do not rely on conjectures or unproven claims. Therefore, the resulting schemes are as secure as the RSA system.

**Keywords:** RSA Cryptosystem, Semantic Security, Chosen Ciphertext Attack, Equivalent-RSA Problem.

## 1 Introduction

Public key cryptosystems, in the sense of Diffy-Hellman [7], provide public access to the encryption key while the decryption key is kept secret by the recipient of the cryptogram. The algebraic structure of public key cryptosystems provides a considerably strong tool to the cryptanalyst. This is why very few secure public key cryptosystems have been discovered since the invention of its concept in 1976. Even the classical version of the most popular public key cryptosystem, i.e. the RSA [17] system, does not satisfy some security criterion (e.g., it is neither semantically secure nor secure against adaptive chosen ciphertext attack).

**Semantic Security:** This notion of security simply means that a cryptogram should not reveal any useful information about the plaintext. That is, in a semantically secure encryption system, a cryptogram is indistinguishable from a random string. The *indistinguishability of encryptions*, was first introduced by Goldwasser and Micali [11]. Under this notion of security, a semantically secure encryption system is said to be broken if the cryptanalyst can find two messages $m_0$ and $m_1$, such that it can distinguish between their cryptograms. Assessment of a public key cryptosystem against this attack can be made in the following scenario. Let the encryption system be an oracle that accepts the plaintext and outputs the cryptogram. The cryptanalyst can choose polynomially many plaintexts, and obtain their relevant cryptograms. Then it chooses two messages $m_0$,

A. Bagchi and V. Atluri (Eds.): ICISS 2006, LNCS 4332, pp. 303–314, 2006.

$m_1$ and submits them to the encryption oracle. At this stage, we assume that the oracle chooses a random bit $b \in \{0, 1\}$ and outputs the encryption of $m_b$. The semantical security of the encryption system is broken if the cryptanalyst can distinguish (with more than 50% probability) whether the output is the cryptogram of $m_0$ or $m_1$.

Semantic security is of paramount importance where the message space is small (e.g., in electronic auction, where a bidding value must be chosen from a predetermined list). It is hard to believe that a deterministic public key cryptosystem can be semantically secure, since one can compute the encryption of all possible messages, and compare them with the target cryptogram. That is, semantic security requires probabilistic encryption[1]. Note that the classical RSA system is not secure against this attack, but OAEP [1] and the ElGamal [9] encryption systems are semantically secure [19].

**Chosen Ciphertext Security:** To assist the security of a public key cryptosystem against the Chosen Ciphertext Attack (CCA), the assumption is that the cryptanalyst also has access to the decryption oracle. The cryptanalyst can select any cryptogram, and observe the corresponding plaintext. The cryptanalyst aims to find out the secret key or encrypt a "target" cryptogram. A cryptosystem is said to be secure against CCA if the cryptanalyst fails in this attack.

A restricted scenario for the cryptanalyst is that the cryptanalyst has not seen the "target" cryptogram before having access to the decryption oracle. This scenario, also called the "lunch-time" or "midnight" attack, was first introduced by Naor and Yung [13]. The most powerful attack to a cryptosystem is, however, the *adaptive chosen ciphertext attack*, which is defined by Rackoff and Simon [16]. In this scenario, the adversary has seen the "target" cryptogram before having access to the decryption oracle. The adversary is not allowed to ask the decryption of the "target" cryptogram, but can obtain the decryption of any relevant cryptogram (even modified ones based on the target cryptogram). A cryptosystem is said to be secure against the Adaptive Chosen Ciphertext Attack (ACCA) if the cryptanalyst fails to obtain any partial information about the plaintext relevant to the "target" cryptogram. Note that classical public key cryptosystems, i.e., the original RSA and ElGamal public key cryptosystems, are not secure against this attack. For example, in an RSA system with public parameters $(n, e)$, let the target cryptogram be $c$, where $c = m^e \pmod{n}$. The cryptanalyst can ask for decryption of the cryptogram $c'$, where $c' = cr^e$, for some random $r$. After receiving the result $m' = (c')^d = (m^e r^e)^d = mr$, the original message $m$ can be computed, using $m = m'/r$. A similar attack is applied to the ElGamal cryptosystem[2].

---

[1] Although randomness is necessary, it is not sufficient. In section 3 we introduce a scheme, which is probabilistic, but not semantically secure.

[2] An alternative security notion is the *non-malleability* [8]. A cryptosystem is said to be non-malleable if, given a cryptogram, it is hard to generate another cryptogram such that there is a known relationship between the plaintexts relevant to the original and the generated cryptogram. According to this definition, the non-malleability is equivalent to the security against ACCA.

One way of immunizing a cryptosystem against ACCA is that the encryption algorithm should destroy the mathematical relationship between the plaintext and its cryptogram. Moreover, the decryption algorithm must be designed in a way such that it does not output the result, if the result does not satisfy a predetermined structure. In this way, not every cryptogram is a good/acceptable input to the decryption oracle. In other words, finding an acceptable cryptogram implies that the message is known to the adversary (this is known as the *Plaintext-Awareness* [1]). However, if the adversary knows the message, he learns nothing from deciphering the cryptogram (i.e., the chosen ciphertext attack makes no sense).

**Our Contribution:** We present a new public key cryptosystem, which is secure against ACCA. Compared to Pointcheval's work [15], which is claimed to be very efficient, our scheme is about two times faster. In addition, the proposed cryptosystem has the following advantages:

1. We utilize a mathematical problem, which is proven to be *equivalent to the well-studied RSA problem.*
2. Consequently, the security of resulting schemes do not rely on any conjecture and/or unproven claims.
3. Its efficiency is the same as the classical RSA system, while it is secure from the viewpoint of semantic and CCA/ACCA criteria.

The organization of this paper is as follows. In section 2, we first give a brief review of previous works. We then review the results achieved by Pointcheval [15], since the proposed scheme follows a similar structure. In section 3, we introduce an equivalent-RSA (ERSA) problem. We also introduce a basic scheme built over the ERSA problem. In section 4, we show how to construct secure systems according to our basic scheme. We also discuss the security of the proposed systems. In section 5, we discuss the efficiency of the proposed schemes.

## 2    Previous Work

Naor and Yung [13] have shown how to construct a public key cryptosystem secure against CCA. Later Dolev, Dwork and Naor [8], and Rackoff and Simon [16] have shown how to construct cryptosystems secure against ACCA. Although these schemes are provably secure, they are very inefficient and therefore completely impractical.

The first attempt to design an efficient public-key cryptosystem secure against CCA was made by Damgård [6]. In this work two constructions, one based on any deterministic public key system and the other based on the ElGamal public key system, have been presented. However, there is no proof of security in this system (in fact, the work ends with an open problem; asking the reader to prove or disprove the assumption made in the paper). This scheme is secure against the "lunch-time" attack, but is not secure against ACCA [20,19].

Zheng and Seberry [20] presented three methods for immunizing public key cryptosystems against ACCA. In [12], Lim and Lee have shown that, in some cryptosystems, Zheng-Seberry's method fails under known plaintext attacks. They then presented two schemes that are claimed to be secure against ACCA. However, both schemes were subsequently broken by Frankel and Yung [10].

Bellare and Rogaway [1] presented the OAEP concept, which is heuristically secure under the random oracle model (a hash function plays the role of random oracle).

Cramer and Shoup [5] have pointed out that, although the security under the random oracle model is valuable, it is not reliable. They also presented a new public key cryptosystem, which is secure against ACCA under standard intractability assumptions. Their work was possibly the best achievement to date in the design of public key cryptosystems secure against ACCA.

Pointcheval [15] argued that Cramer and Shoup's scheme [5] requires more than four exponentiations for an encryption, and presented a new scheme based on the *dependent-RSA* problem. Informally, the dependent-RSA problem of [15] states that "given $m^e$ in an RSA system, find $(m+1)^e$." Their *conjecture* is that, this problem is hard. In order to achieve semantic security, they have defined another problem called the *Decisional Dependent-RSA* problem. This problem states that, for a randomly chosen r, two pairs $(m^e, r)$ and $(m^e, (m+1)^e)$ are indistinguishable. Their *conjecture* is that this problem is intractable when $e$ is greater than $2^{60}$. Based on these conjectures, they have then presented the following schemes:

**The DRSA Encryption Scheme:** This scheme is an RSA-version of the El-Gamal encryption. That is, in order to encrypt a message $m$ for the RSA system with public parameters $(n, e)$, the sender chooses $k \in_R Z_n^*$ and computes the cryptogram $C = (A, B)$, where

$$A = k^e \pmod{n} \quad \text{and} \quad B = m \times (k+1)^e \pmod{n}.$$

The recipient of the cryptogram retrieves the message by first computing $k = A^d$ (mod $n$), and then $m = B/(k+1)^e \pmod{n}$. This scheme is shown to be semantically secure (due to the indistinguishability of $k^e$ and $(k+1)^e \bmod n$).

**The DRSA-1 Encryption Scheme:** This is a strengthened version of the DRSA encryption scheme for attaining security against ACCA. Let $\ell$ be a security parameter, and $h : Z_n \times Z_n \to \{0, 1\}^\ell$ be a hash function. The ciphertext of a message $m$ is a triple $(A, B, H)$, such that:

$$A = k^e, \quad B = m \times (k+1)^e, \quad \text{and} \quad H = h(m, k).$$

Here, $k$ is a random value. To decrypt the cryptogram, the receiver computes:

$$k = A^d \pmod{n}, \quad \text{and} \quad m = B/(k+1)^e \pmod{n},$$

and then checks for equality $H \stackrel{?}{=} h(m, k)$. If the equality is satisfied, then $m$ is accepted to be the message; otherwise, the cryptogram is rejected. This scheme is shown to be secure against ACCA, since the probability of generating an acceptable cryptogram, without knowing the message, is negligible.

**The DRSA-2 Encryption Scheme:** This is similar to DRSA-1, but the resulting scheme is equivalent to the computational problem rather than to the decisional one. Let $k_1$ be the size of the plaintext, $k_2$ a security parameter, let $h_1 : Z_n \rightarrow \{0,1\}^{k_1}$ and $h_2 : \{0,1\}^{k_1} \times Z_n \rightarrow \{0,1\}^{k_2}$ be two hash functions. The cryptogram of a message $m$ is a triple $(A, B, H)$, such that:

$$A = k^e, \quad B = m \oplus h_1\left((k+1)^e \bmod n\right), \quad \text{and} \quad H = h_2(m, k).$$

To decrypt the cryptogram, the receiver computes:

$$k = A^d \pmod n \quad \text{and} \quad m = B \oplus h_1\left((k+1)^e \bmod n\right),$$

and then checks for equality $H \overset{?}{=} h_2(m, k)$. They have shown that this scheme is also non-malleable, and thus secure against ACCA.

## 3  Definitions

In the RSA cryptosystem, the modulus $n$ is the product of two large (and preferably safe) primes, i.e., $n = pq$, where $p = 2p' + 1$ and $q = 2q' + 1$. The public-key is an integer $e$, which is co-prime with $\phi(n)$, where $\phi(n) = (p-1)(q-1)$. The decryption key $d$, is the inverse of $e$ modulo $\phi(n)$, i.e., $d \times e \equiv 1 \bmod \phi(n)$. The public parameters of the system are $(n, e)$, while the prime numbers are discarded and $d$ is kept secret.

Encryption[3] of a message $m$, is $c$, where $c = m^e \pmod n$. The recipient, who knows the secret key, $d$, can retrieve the message $m$, using $c^d = (m^e)^d = m$. Anyone else, who has no knowledge about the secret key, $d$, is faced with the following problem, which is known as the RSA problem.

Name:    The RSA Problem
Instance: Given RSA public parameters $(n, e)$ and a cryptogram $c = m^e$
Question: Find $m$

This problem is believed to be intractable for proper construction of the underlying RSA system.

In this section we introduce a new problem, derived from the RSA problem. We will show that the problem is equivalent to the RSA problem.

Name:    The Equivalent RSA Problem (ERSA)
Instance: Given RSA public parameters $(n, e)$ and a cryptogram $c = m^e$
Question: Find $m^{e+1} \pmod n$

**Theorem 1.** *The RSA and ERSA problems are equivalent.*

---

[3] The standard practice for encrypting a message with RSA is to first encode the message and then raise the encoded value to the public exponent $e$ [4].

*Proof.* Let there be an algorithm $\mathcal{A}$ that solves the RSA problem, i.e., it can retrieve $m$ from $m^e$ mod $n$. We apply algorithm $\mathcal{A}$ to the ERSA problem. First we obtain $m$ from $m^e$, and then compute $m^{e+1}$  (mod $n$) (with just one multiplication, i.e., $m \times m^e$).

On the other hand, let there be an algorithm $\mathcal{B}$ that can solve the ERSA problem. That is, given $m^e$ mod $n$, it can compute $m^{e+1}$ mod $n$. We apply algorithm $\mathcal{B}$ on the RSA problem. First we obtain $m^{e+1}$ from $m^e$, and then compute $m$, using $(m^{e+1})/(m^e)$ mod $n$.

### 3.1  Basic Scheme

Utilizing the ERSA problem we construct a probabilistic encryption scheme, which is as secure as the RSA system.

**Initialization:** Consider an RSA setting with public parameters $(n, e)$, and the secret key $d$, where $d = 1/e$ mod $\phi(n)$.

**Encryption:** To encrypt a message $0 \leq m < n$, the sender chooses $k \in_R Z_n^*$, and computes:

$$a = k^e \quad (\text{mod } n), \quad \text{and} \quad b = m \times k^{e+1} \quad (\text{mod } n).$$

The cryptogram is $(a, b)$.

**Decryption:** The recipient of the cryptogram $(a, b)$ can retrieve the message $m$, using:

$$k = a^d \quad (\text{mod } n) \quad \text{and} \quad m = b/(a \times k).$$

**Theorem 2.** *The basic scheme (presented above) is as secure as the RSA system.*

*Proof.* Let there be an algorithm $\mathcal{A}$ that can break the RSA system. i.e., given a cryptogram $m^e$ mod $n$, it can retrieve $m$. We apply this algorithm to our basic scheme, where the cryptogram is $(a, b)$. From the first entry of this pair, the algorithm can retrieve $k$. Then, the message $m$ can be computed using $m = b/(a \times k)$.

On the other hand, assume that there exists an algorithm $\mathcal{B}$ that can break our basic scheme, i.e., given a cryptogram $(k^e, m \times k^{e+1})$, it can retrieve $m$. We show that the algorithm $\mathcal{B}$ can be used in order to break the RSA system. Given a cryptogram $c = m^e$ in an RSA system $(n, e)$, we choose $r \in_R Z_n$, and set the pair $(c, r) = (m^e, k \times m^{e+1})$ as a cryptogram for our proposed scheme[4]. That is, we have a cryptogram $(m^e, k \times m^{e+1})$, which is a cryptogram for our basic

---

[4] Although we do not know $m$ , and thus $m^{e+1}$, there exists a random $k$ that satisfies the equation $r = k \times m^{e+1}$ mod $n$ —that is, $k = r/(m^{e+1})$ mod $n$ (note that the inverse of $m^{e+1}$ mod $n$ always exists, otherwise $m$ must have a common factor with $n$, which enables the sender to break the RSA system.)

scheme (here, $k$ plays the role of a message and $m$ plays the role of a random value). Now, by applying the algorithm $\mathcal{B}$ on pair $(m^e, k \times m^{e+1})$, we first retrieve $k$ and then compute $m$, using $r/(k \times c)$. That is, we retrieve the message from the cryptogram of a classical RSA system.

**Theorem 3.** *The presented probabilistic encryption scheme is not semantically secure.*

*Proof.* Given a cryptogram $(k^e, r)$, where $r = m_b \times k^{e+1}$, and two messages $m_0, m_1$, one can easily find the relevant plaintext. It works as follows; compute $u = r/(m_0 \times k^e)$. If $u^e = k^e$, then $(k^e, r)$ is a cryptogram for the message $m_0$, otherwise it is a cryptogram for the message $m_1$.

That is, given two pairs $(a_1, b_1)$ and $(a_2, b_2)$, where one pair is a genuine cryptogram for a message $m$ and the other is chosen randomly, one can distinguish these two pairs. This is because, if $(a_i, b_i) = (k^e, m \times k^{e+1})$, for an index $i$, $i \in \{1, 2\}$, then

$$\left( \frac{b_i}{m \times a_i} \right)^e = a_i \pmod{n}.$$

While for a randomly chosen pair probability of satisfying this equality is negligible.

# 4    Schemes Secure Against CCA and ACCA

In order to achieve indistinguishability of a cryptogram with a random pair, we employ a proper hash function (i.e., with collision resistance a and randomness property) to hide $k^{e+1}$.

## 4.1    ERSA Encryption Scheme

This scheme is similar to our basic scheme, but it utilizes a hash function. The scheme works as follows:

**Initialization:** An RSA system with public parameters $(n, e)$, where $n$ is the RSA modulus and $e$ is the encryption key. Let $d$ be the decryption key and $h$ be a proper hash function.

**Encryption:** To encrypt a message $0 \le m < n$, select $k \in_R Z_n^*$, and compute:

$$a = k^e \pmod{n}, \quad \text{and} \quad b = h(k^{e+1}) \times m \pmod{n}$$

The cryptogram is $(a, b)$.

**Decryption:** The recipient of the cryptogram $(a, b)$ first computes $k = a^d$, and then retrieves the message, using

$$m = \frac{b}{h(k^{e+1})} \pmod{n}.$$

**Theorem 4.** *The ERSA encryption scheme is semantically secure against CCA.*

*Proof.* See [15].

It is not difficult to show that a cryptogram in ERSA system looks like a randomly chosen pair, since the first entry is a cryptogram of a random value in the original RSA and thus is indistinguishable from a random value. The second entry is the multiplication of the message, $m$, in the output of a hash function, and therefore is random. Note that in a random pair, one cannot find any logical relationship between two entries. While in ERSA system, there is a strong relationship between two entries of a cryptogram. This relationship, however, cannot be utilized in order to distinguish a cryptogram from a random pair, except one can solve the RSA problem. That is, we proved the following theorem.

**Theorem 5.** *If RSA problem is intractable, then a cryptogram in the ERSA system is indistinguishable from a random pair.*

In spite of randomness characteristic of cryptograms in the ERSA system, the scheme is not non-malleable.

**Theorem 6.** *The ERSA scheme is not secure against ACCA.*

*Proof.* Let $(a, b)$ be a cryptogram for a message $m$, i.e., $a = k^e$ and $b = h(k^{e+1} \times m)$, for some random value $k$. One can ask for decryption of an innocent looking cryptogram $(a, r)$, where $r = u \times b = u \times m \times k^{e+1}$, for some random value $u$. As it can be seen, the modified cryptogram is a correct cryptogram for the message $m' = u \times m$. Hence, after receiving $m'$, the original message $m = m'/u$ will be retrieved.

### 4.2  ERSA-1 Encryption Scheme

In order to achieve security against ACCA, a common technique is to attach a tag to the cryptogram.

**Initialization:** Consider an RSA system with public parameters $(n, e)$ and the secret key $d$. Let $h$ be a proper hash function.

**Encryption:** To encrypt a message $0 \leq m < n$, select $k \in_R Z_n^*$, and compute,

$$a = k^e, \quad b = h(k^{e+1}) \times m, \quad \text{and} \quad c = h(m||k).$$

where $m||k$ denotes the concatenation of $m$ and $k$. The cryptogram is $(a, b, c)$.

**Decryption:** For this scheme we assume that the encryption algorithm is an oracle that works in the following way.

1. It computes $k = a^d \pmod{n}$, and then retrieves the message, $m$, using $b/h(k^{e+1})$.

2. It outputs the message $m$ if $c = h(m\|k)$, otherwise it returns '?', denoting that the cryptogram is not genuine.

As can be seen, any modification to the second entry of the cryptogram implies some modification of the third entry, otherwise the encryption oracle will detect the modification. However, the third entry is a hash function. Because of the one-wayness property of the underlying hash function, it is intractable to know the output without knowledge of the input. But the input to this hash function is a concatenation of $m$ and $k$. Hence, generating a good/acceptable cryptogram implies knowledge of the message. That is, the plaintext awareness property, which is equivalent to non-malleability is achieved.

**Theorem 7.** *The ERSA-1 encryption scheme is semantically secure against ACCA.*

Note that in some systems, prior to the decryption process the cryptogram may be examined to verify whether or not it satisfies any predetermined conditions. This property is very useful, especially when the scheme is used by a group instead of an individual (i.e., in society-oriented cryptographic applications – see [18]).

### 4.3   ERSA-2 Encryption Scheme

**Initialization:** Consider an RSA system with public parameters $(n, e)$. Let $\ell$ be the size of the plaintext and $h_1(.), h_2(.)$ be two hash functions, such that $h_1 : Z_n \rightarrow \{0,1\}^\ell$.

**Encryption:** To encrypt a message $0 \leq m < n$, the sender chooses $k \in_R Z_n^*$ and computes:

$$a = k^e \pmod{n}, \quad b = m \oplus h_1(k^{e+1} \bmod n), \quad \text{and} \quad c = h_2(m\|k).$$

The cryptogram then is a triple $(a, b, c)$.

**Decryption:** The recipient of the cryptogram first computes;

$$k = a^d \pmod{n}, \quad \text{and} \quad m = b \oplus h_1(k^{e+1} \bmod n).$$

If $c = h_2(m\|k)$, then it outputs the message $m$; otherwise, it outputs '?'.

**Theorem 8.** *The ERSA-2 encryption scheme is semantically secure against adaptive chosen ciphertext attack.*

*Proof.* See [15].

## 4.4  Security

Security of ERSA, ERSA-1, and ERSA-2 encryption schemes (from the point of view of semantical security and security against chosen ciphertext attacks) can be demonstrated in the way of Pointcheval's work, since these schemes are similar to DRSA, DRSA-1, and DRSA-2 (we refer interested readers to [15]). The substantial difference in the security of these two schemes, however, is that our schemes are constructed over a problem that is proven to be equivalent to the RSA problem, and we have not utilized any conjecture an/or any unproven claim. That is, the security of our schemes is equivalent to the security of the classical RSA system.

Note that in our basic scheme, the cryptogram $(k^e, m \times k^{e+1})$ does not help an opponent to learn any useful information about the message. That is, dividing the second entry by the first entry and/or computing the greatest common divisors of these two items gives absolutely no useful information to the opponent (indeed, we have shown that the security of our basic scheme is equivalent to the security of classical RSA system —see Theorem 2).

## 5  Efficiency

In [15], it has been claimed that their scheme is the most efficient scheme to date in this field. Here, we compare the efficiency of our schemes with their work. Both schemes have similar structures and it is straightforward to compare their efficiency. In [15], the sender and the receiver each needs to perform two exponentiations. This is because calculation of $k^e$ and $(k+1)^e$ must be done by both the sender and the receiver. In our scheme, although the sender and the receiver must compute $k^e$ and $k^{e+1}$, the calculation of $k^{e+1}$ needs just one multiplication (i.e., $k^{e+1} = k^e \times k$).

Another efficiency factor in our schemes is that our schemes do not require any constraint on the size of the public-key, $e$. However, in order to achieve reasonable level of security in [15], it has been conjectured that the chosen $e$ must be larger than $2^{60}$.

Altogether, the efficiency of our scheme is comparable to the classical RSA system. The sender needs to perform one exponentiation (to the size of the public key), and the receiver also needs to perform one exponentiation (to the size of the secret key) –with one or two extra multiplications and/or computing hash functions.

**Remark:** Okamoto and Pointcheval [14] have presented the RSA-REACT, which works as follows:

**Initialization:** Consider an RSA system with public parameters $(n, e)$ and the secret key $d$. Let $h$ be a proper hash function, $g$ be a random generator, and Sym be a secure symmetric cryptosystem.

**Encryption:** To encrypt a message $m$, select $k \in_R Z_n^*$, and compute,

$$a = k^e, \quad u = g(k), \quad b = SymE_u(m), \quad \text{and} \quad c = h(k||m||a||b).$$

The cryptogram is $(a, b, c)$.

**Decryption:** They assume that the encryption algorithm is an oracle that works in the following way.

1. It computes $k = a^d \pmod{n}$, and then retrieves $u$, using the generator $g$, as $u = g(k)$.
2. It uses the computed $u$ as a decryption key for the predetermind symmetric system Sym, in order to retrieve the message $m$, using $m = SymD_u(b)$.
3. It outputs the message $m$ if $c = h(k||m||a||b)$, otherwise it returns '?', denoting that the cryptogram is not genuine.

Our observation is that, if $m$ is a long message then (the RSA system is used for key exchanging in a symmetric cryptosystem environment) the efficiency of this scheme is comparable to the efficiency of our schemes (in our schemes, $m$ will plays the role of the key for symmteric scheme which is passed to the other party, and then can be used to encrypt/decrypt a message/cryptogram). Howevere, in case of short messages (i.e., $0 < m \leq n$ this scheme is less efficient than our proposed schemes (set aside the assumption of having a secure random generator and a secure symmetric cryptosystem).

# References

1. M. Bellare and P. Rogaway, "Optimal Asymmetric Encryption –How to Encrypt with RSA," in *Advances in Cryptology - Proceedings of EUROCRYPT '94* (A. Santis, ed.), vol. 950 of *Lecture Notes in Computer Science*, pp. 92–111, Springer-Verlag, 1994.
2. D. Bleichenbacher, "Chosen Ciphertext Attacks Against Protocols Based on the RSA Encryption Standard PKCS#1," in *Advances in Cryptology - Proceedings of CRYPTO '98* (H. Krawczyk, ed.), vol. 1462 of *Lecture Notes in Computer Science*, pp. 1–12, Springer-Verlag, 1998.
3. R. Canetti, O. Goldreich, and S. Halevi, "The Random Oracle Model, Revisited," in *30th Symposium on the Theory of Computing (STOC)*, 1998.
4. J. Coron, D. Naccache, Y. Desmedt, A. Odlyzko, and J.P. Stern, "Index Calculation Attacks on RSA Signature and Encryption," *Designe, Codes and Cryptography*, vol. 38, pp. 41–53, 2006.
5. R. Cramer and V. Shoup, "A Practical Public Key Cryptosystem Provably Secure against Adaptive Chosen Ciphertext Attack," in *Advances in Cryptology - Proceedings of CRYPTO '98* (H. Krawczyk, ed.), vol. 1462 of *Lecture Notes in Computer Science*, pp. 13–25, Springer-Verlag, 1998.
6. I. Damgård, "Towards Practical Public Key Systems Secure Against Chosen Ciphertext attacks," in *Advances in Cryptology - Proceedings of CRYPTO '91* (J. Feigenbaum, ed.), vol. 576 of *Lecture Notes in Computer Science*, pp. 445–456, Springer-Verlag, 1992.

7. W. Diffie and M. Hellman, "New Directions in Cryptography," *IEEE Trans. on Inform. Theory*, vol. IT-22, pp. 644–654, Nov 1976.

8. D. Dolev, C. Dwork, and M. Naor, "Non-Malleable Cryptography," in *23rd Annual Symposium on the Theory of Computing (STOC)*, pp. 542–552, 1991.

9. T. ElGamal, "A Public Key Cryptosystem and a Signature Scheme Based on Discrete Logarithms," *IEEE Trans. on Inform. Theory*, vol. IT-31, pp. 469–472, July 1985.

10. Y. Frankel and M. Yung, "Cryptanalysis of the Immunized LL Public Key Systems," in *Advances in Cryptology - Proceedings of CRYPTO '95* (D. Coppersmith, ed.), vol. 963 of *Lecture Notes in Computer Science*, pp. 287–296, Springer-Verlag, 1995.

11. S. Goldwasser and S. Micali, "Probabilistic Encryption," *Journal of Computer and System Sciences*, vol. 28, pp. 270–299, 1984.

12. C. Lim and P. Lee, "Another Method for Attaining Security Against Adaptively Chosen Ciphertext Attacks," in *Advances in Cryptology - Proceedings of CRYPTO '93* (D. Stinson, ed.), vol. 773 of *Lecture Notes in Computer Science*, pp. 420–434, Springer-Verlag, 1994.

13. M. Naor and M. Yung, "Public-key Cryptosystems Provably Secure against Chosen Ciphertext Attacks," in *22nd Annual ACM Symp. on Theory of Computing*, pp. 427–437, 1990.

14. T. Okamoto and D. Pointcheval, "RSA-REACT: An Alternative to RSA-OAEP," in *Proceedings of Second NESSIE Workshop*, Egham, UK, 2001.

15. D. Pointcheval, "New Public Key Cryptosystems Based on the Dependent-RSA Problem," in *Advances in Cryptology - Proceedings of EUROCRYPT '99* (J. Stern, ed.), vol. 1592 of *Lecture Notes in Computer Science*, pp. 239–254, Springer-Verlag, 1999.

16. C. Rackoff and D. Simon, "Noninteractive Zero-knowledge Proof of Knowledge and Chosen Ciphertext Attack," in *Advances in Cryptology - Proceedings of CRYPTO '91* (J. Feigenbaum, ed.), vol. 576 of *Lecture Notes in Computer Science*, pp. 433–444, Springer-Verlag, 1992.

17. R. Rivest, A. Shamir, and L. Adleman, "A Method for Obtaining Digital Signatures and Public-Key Cryptosystems," *Communications of the ACM*, vol. 21, pp. 120–126, Feb 1978.

18. V. Shoup and R. Gennaro, "Securing Threshold Cryptosystems against Chosen Ciphertext Attack," in *Advances in Cryptology - Proceedings of EUROCRYPT '98* (K. Nyberg, ed.), vol. 1403 of *Lecture Notes in Computer Science*, pp. 1–16, Springer-Verlag, 1998.

19. Y. Tsiounis and M. Yung, "On the Security of ElGamal based Encryption," in *Proceedings of the First International Workshop on Practice and Theory in Public Key cryptography (PKC '98)*, vol. 1431 of *Lecture Notes in Computer Science*, pp. 117–134, Springer-Verlag, 1998.

20. Y. Zheng and J. Seberry, "Practical Approaches to Attaining Security against Adaptive Chosen Ciphertext Attacks," in *Advances in Cryptology - Proceedings of CRYPTO '92* (E. Brickell, ed.), vol. 740 of *Lecture Notes in Computer Science*, pp. 292–304, Springer-Verlag, 1993.

# A Partial Image Encryption Method
# with Pseudo Random Sequences

Y.V. Subba Rao, Abhijit Mitra, and S.R. Mahadeva Prasanna

Department of Electronics and Communication Engineering,
Indian Institute of Technology Guwahati, North Guwahati 781039, India
{subba,a.mitra,prasanna}@iitg.ernet.in

**Abstract.** We propose an effective approach for partial image encryption with pseudo random sequences (PRS). It is known that an image can be considered as a combination of correlated and uncorrelated data as well as most of the perceptual information are present in the correlated data rather than the uncorrelated data. Hence, the amount of residual intelligence present in an encrypted image depends on the correlated data. It is, therefore, sufficient to encrypt the correlated data instead of encrypting the entire image in order to speed up the entire operation. From the perception point of view, the most significant bit (MSB) planes have high adjacent correlation between the pixels whereas the least significant bit (LSB) planes contain comparatively more uncorrelated data. PRS with simple hardware like $m$-sequences and Gold sequences have less correlation between the adjacent bits. These can therefore serve as a good alternative for partially encrypting the MSB planes with low complexity to provide security against casual listeners. It is observed from the results that the new approach is able to reduce the residual intelligence as would have been obtained by encrypting the entire image.

**Keywords:** Partial encryption, Residual intelligence, Pseudo random sequence.

## 1 Introduction

In the present era, it is important to protect the information when it is passed through an insecure channel. One way to provide such protection is to convert the intelligible data into the unintelligible ones prior to transmission and such a process of conversion with a key is called encryption [1]-[5]. Decryption is a reverse process of the encryption. To protect the information from unauthorized users, the key must be kept secret. Private and public key encryptions are two kinds in cryptography. In symmetric or private key encryption [3]-[4], the encryption and decryption processes are performed with the same key. But in asymmetric or public key encryption [2], these operations are performed with different keys. The entire security of the encryption technique depends on the key. Further, the security needed may be against two types of attackers, namely, casual listeners/observers or professional unauthorized recipients, termed as cryptanalysts. In the former case, the security is needed only in terms of hours while

A. Bagchi and V. Atluri (Eds.): ICISS 2006, LNCS 4332, pp. 315–325, 2006.
© Springer-Verlag Berlin Heidelberg 2006

in the later it may be in terms of years. The duration roughly indicates the amount of time that is needed to analyze the information available in unintelligible form in the insecure channel without the knowledge of keys to derive the underlying information. The scenario where security is needed against casual listener/observer, the cryptographic structure should be as simple as possible in order to reduce the cost.

Our proposed scheme is mainly concentrated towards the private key encryption. Both symmetric and asymmetric key encryption provides nearly same amount of security. Depending on the application either of the technique is preferred. In real time applications, where security needs to be provided against casual listeners, the encryption of the entire image with classical techniques [6]-[8] like advanced encryption standard (AES), or, international data encryption algorithm (IDEA) are not always advantageous due to high computational complexity. Further, in multimedia applications classical techniques consume enough computational time for encryption due to its bulk size. Partial encryption approach therefore outperforms the conventional ones when speed is the main criteria. In partial encryption techniques usually the significant information have to be encrypted and insignificant information remain non-encrypted. Considerable amount of recent research papers have focused towards different kinds of partial encryption techniques in image processing. Such partial encryption techniques, reported in the literature [9]-[12], can be categorized into three broad classes with the first one being encrypting only the AC-coefficients in discrete cosine transform (DCT) domain. This technique, however, does not provide sufficient security due to the perceptual information present in DC-coefficients [9]. The next method is to encrypt the first few significant coefficients or few subbands in wavelet domain which becomes complex in selection of significant coefficients, and, the last one is the encryption of selective bitplanes in the image with classical algorithms with high computational complexity. We focus on a partial encryption technique with pseudo random sequences which is less computationally complex yet effective. To the best of our knowledge, no work has been reported in the literature using the same technique till now.

Pseudo random sequences (PRS) [13]-[15] are simple to generate yet offer reasonably considerable security and can be produced with linear feedback shift registers in high speed. The PRS are widely used in communications due to their randomness based on the properties of low cross correlations. Images usually have high correlation between the neighborhood pixels, demanding the need of sequences which would possess low adjacent correlation properties to provide sufficient security. PRS with simple hardware like $m$-sequences and Gold sequences therefore emerge as a good alternative for partially encrypting the MSB planes. It can also be observed from the results that the new approach provides is able to reduce the residual intelligence as would have been obtained by encrypting the entire image.

The paper is organized as follows. In Section 2, we deal with the PRS, and in particular, $m$-sequences and Gold sequences. Section 3 provides the main idea behind the partial encryption techniques at length. The proposed scheme of

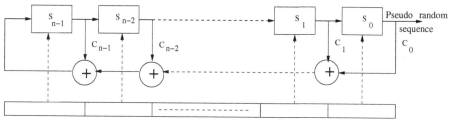

(INITIAL SEED ( which is transmitted through secured channel )

**Fig. 1.** Block diagram of a $m$-sequence generator

partial encryption with PRS is introduced in Section 4. Section 5 presents the results and also briefs about the effectiveness of the proposed scheme. The paper is concluded by summarizing the present work along with the scope of future work in Section 6.

## 2   Pseudo Random Sequences (PRS)

PRS are periodic sequences that contain the following noise like properties: (i) balance property, (ii) single peak auto correlation function property, and, (iii) run property. These three properties make PRS efficient for encryption. However, due to the second property, adjacent bits' correlation becomes considerably less, thereby making the PRS more effective for image encryption when compared with data encryption due to high adjacent correlation present in the images.

### 2.1   Maximal Length Sequences

The $m$-sequence generator is usually constructed with linear feedback shift registers (LFSR). The general structure of such a $m$-sequence generator is shown in Fig. 1. The $m$-sequences are, by definition, the largest codes that can be generated by a given shift register or a delay element of given length. A $m$-sequence generator contains $n$ shift registers and is initiated with a starting seed, which is usually transmitted through a secured channel for intended users only. The outputs of the shift registers are multiplied with the coefficients ($C_{n-1}, C_{n-2}, \ldots, C_1, C_0$) of a primitive polynomial with respect to mod-2 operation. The resultant output obtained by the modulo operation is then fed back to the first shift register. The resultant output is called as $m$-sequence. Note that the periodicity of a $m$-sequence generator is $2^{n-1}$, which, in turn, means the length of the sequence depends on the length of the LFSR. The primitive polynomial can be also be found from the $2n$ length sequence. M-sequences contains the following two autocorrelation values: 1 and $-\frac{1}{N}$. M-sequences produce the autocorrelation value $-\frac{1}{N}$ with even one bit delay, making the adjacent correlation value very low.

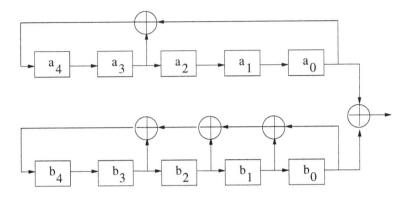

**Fig. 2.** A typical Gold sequence generator

## 2.2    Gold Sequences

As shown in Fig. 2 the Gold sequences can be generated by the xor operation of the two $m$-sequences. Note that with only a few chosen pairs of $m$-sequences we can produce the Gold sequences which are called preferred pairs. The length of the Gold sequences is also same as the individual $m$-sequence's length. But it provides more security compared to $m$-sequences. Gold sequences are very simple to generate. Using two preferred $m$-sequence generators of degree n, with a fixed non-zero seed in the first generator, $2^n$ Gold codes are obtained by changing the seed of the second generator from 0 to $2^n - 1$. Another Gold sequence can be obtained by setting all zero to the first generator, which is the second $m$-sequence itself. In total, $2^n + 1$ Gold codes are available. Consider an $m$-sequence represented by a binary vector $a$ of length N, and a second sequence $a'$ obtained by sampling every $q^{th}$ symbol of $a$. In other words, $a' = a[q]$, where $q$ is odd and either $q = 2^k + 1$ or $q = 2^{2k} - 2^k + 1$. Two $m$-sequences $a$ and $a'$ are called the preferred pair if

$$n \neq 0 \quad (\text{mod } 4) \tag{1}$$

i.e., $n$ is odd or $n = 2$ (mod 4). The relation between $n$ and $k$ in such Gold sequences follows the below stated property.

$$gcd(n, k) = \begin{cases} 1 \text{ for } n \text{ odd} \\ 2 \text{ for } n = 2 \quad (\text{mod } 4) \end{cases} \tag{2}$$

Gold sequence autocorrelation $R_{xx}(k)$ and cross correlation functions $R_{xy}(k)$ can be defined as

$$R_{xx}(k) = \begin{cases} 1 & k = 0 \\ \{-\frac{t(n)}{N}, -\frac{1}{N}, \frac{t(n)+2}{N}\} & k \neq 0 \end{cases} \tag{3}$$

$$R_{xy}(k) = \{-\frac{t(n)}{N}, -\frac{1}{N}, \frac{t(n)+2}{N}\} \tag{4}$$

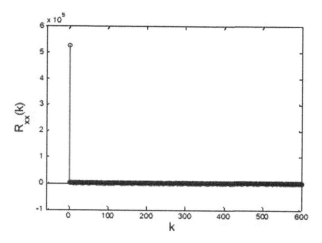

**Fig. 3.** Autocorrelation function of a Gold sequence

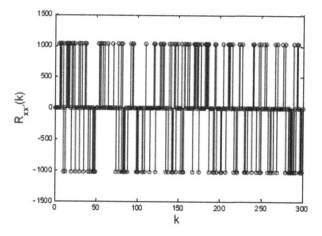

**Fig. 4.** Crosscorrelation function of Gold sequences

where

$$t(n) = \begin{cases} 1 + 2^{0.5(n+1)} & \text{for } n \text{ odd} \\ 1 + 2^{0.5(n+2)} & \text{for } n \text{ even} \end{cases}$$

The auto and cross correlations for one/multiple typical Gold sequence(s) of period $2^{19} - 1$ are shown in Fig. 3 and Fig. 4.

## 3   Partial Encryption Techniques

In these schemes the significant and insignificant information is separated from the image. The significant part of the image is to be encrypted and insignificant

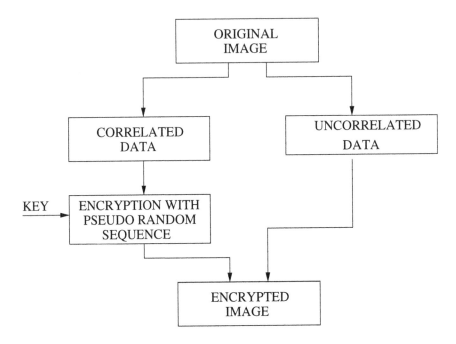

**Fig. 5.** Block diagram of partial encryption technique

part remains non-encrypted. After the encryption the significant and insignificant parts are combined before transmission. This encrypted image is transmitted through an insecure channel to the receiver. At the receiver the encrypted image is again decomposed into significant and insignificant components, the decryption operation is performed only on significant part and then combined to get original image. If the significant information is very less the public key encryption techniques will be preferred or otherwise the private key techniques are often used.

## 4   The Proposed Scheme

In the proposed scheme, the image is initially separated into correlated and uncorrelated data by dividing it into first four MSB planes and last four LSB planes. The correlated data (first four MB planes) are encrypted with the highly uncorrelated PRS while keeping the uncorrelated data as unencrypted ones. After the encryption of correlated data, it is combined with the remaining data to form the final encrypted image. The block diagram of the proposed scheme is shown in Fig. 5. In the present work we consider the first four MSB planes as correlated data as it is seen that for reducing the residual intelligence as could be obtained by encrypting the entire image, we need to encrypt a minimum of these four bit planes. Here first we encrypt the MSB planes of the image with the $m$-sequence generated by the pseudo random generator as shown in Fig. 1.

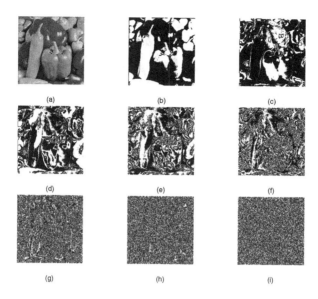

**Fig. 6.** Decomposition of image. (a) Original image. (b)-(i) The bitplanes starting from the MSB to LSB planes respectively.

### 4.1 Partial Encryption with Gold Sequences

M-sequences can be estimated if some part of the sequence is known. To overcome this disadvantage, the length of LFSR should be large. Therefore, encryption with $m$-sequence trades off security against the length of the shift register. One good alternative to overcome this problem is to use Gold sequences. With four different auto correlation values, sometimes Gold sequences produce adjacent correlation less than the $m$-sequence. Due to less adjacent correlation Gold sequence offers more security and removes the redundancy better than $m$-sequences. The adjacent correlation will be very high in first four MSB planes compared to the remaining bitplanes. After the encryption, the correlation decreases very significantly and achieves nearly equal to the LSB planes.

## 5 Results and Discussions

The proposed scheme has been implemented in the *Matlab* with several test images. Below are some results applied on the standard *Peppers* gray scale image. The Fig. 6 shows the bit planes in the Peppers image. The most significant bitplanes have high adjacent correlation between the bits and least significant bitplanes have very less correlation. So they appear as noisy bitplanes.

### 5.1 Partial Encryption with M-Sequences

We can observe that the adjacent correlation is present in the first four bitplanes in Fig. 6. Fig. 7 shows the partial encryption of image. The bit planes

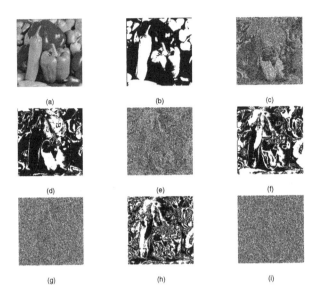

**Fig. 7.** Partial encryption with $m$-sequences. (a) Original image. (b, d, f, h) Bit planes to be encrypted from the MSB plane. (c, e, g, i) Encrypted images using the combination of encrypted and remaining bit planes.

to be encrypted and encrypted images after combining the encrypted and unencrypted bit planes are shown in Fig. 7. After the encryption of the first two MSB planes the encrypted image appears as the noisy image. However, it is also necessary to encrypt the third and fourth MSB planes because these planes have some perceptual information. The resultant image doesn't have the significant information after the encryption of four MSB plane. Fig. 8 shows the decryption process of the partial encryption. If the correlation is measured among the pixels in the encrypted images, it will be found that, compared to original image, the correlation decreases significantly. But the correlation among the pixels in the image after the encryption of first four bitplanes is nearly same as that of the encryption of all bitplanes.

## 5.2   Partial Encryption with Gold Sequences

Fig. 9 shows the original image, the bit planes to be encrypted and the encrypted images after combining the encrypted and unencrypted bit planes. The encrypted image after encryption of first four bit planes has no perceptual information. The redundancy reduces in the encrypted bitplanes and the encrypted image appeared as a random noisy image. The decryption process of the partial encryption with Gold sequences is shown in Fig. 10. The adjacent correlation of the encrypted bitplanes and encrypted images contains very less value compared to the images encrypted with $m$-sequences.

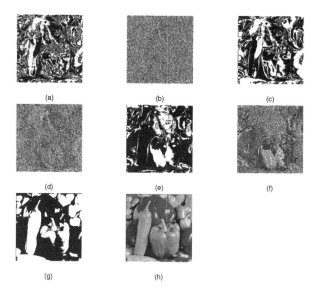

**Fig. 8.** Decryption of partial encryption with $m$-sequences. (a, c, e, g) Decrypted bit planes from the MSB plane. (b, d, f, h) Decrypted images using the combination of decrypted and the remaining bitplanes.

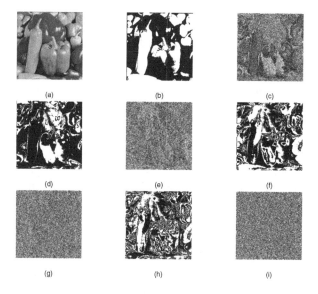

**Fig. 9.** Partial encryption with Gold sequences. (a) Original image. (b, d, f, h) Bit planes to be encrypted from the MSB plane. (c, e, g, i) Encrypted images using the combination of encrypted and remaining bitplanes.

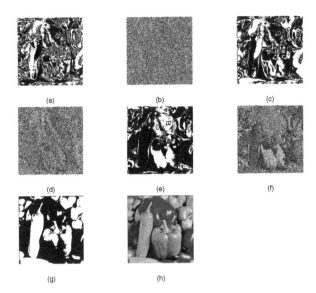

**Fig. 10.** Decryption of partial encryption with Gold sequences. (a, c, e, g) Decrypted bit planes from the MSB bitplane. (b, d, f, h) Decrypted images using the combination of decrypted and the remaining bitplanes.

## 6    Conclusions

A simple yet effective technique for partial image encryption is proposed. The main idea stems from the fact that the most information in an image is present in the correlated data. This information is converted into unintelligible form by encrypting with the uncorrelated sequences. This paper has presented an approach for the partial encryption of image using pseudo random sequences with simple hardware. From the results, it is observed that partial encryption method achieves the same security with the improvement in processing speed. The performance of the method mainly depends on the differentiation of correlated and uncorrelated information in the image. Here we have treated the MSB planes as correlated information. However, even in MSB planes sometimes uncorrelated data are present. A better approach might reduce the computational time further if proper importance is given for separating the correlated data in the image considering the above point.

## References

1. Feng, Y., Li, L., Huang, F.: A Symmetric Image Encryption Approach based on Line Maps. in Proc. Int. Symp. Sys. and Cont. Aeros. Astro. (2006) 1362–1367
2. Diffie, W., Hellman, M. E.: New Directions in Cryptography. IEEE Trans. Info. Theory **22** (1976) 644–654
3. Stallings, W.: Cryptography and Network Security. Englewood Cliffs, NJ: Prentice Hall (2003)

4. Elbirt, A. J., Paar, C.: An Instruction-Level Distributed Processor for Symmetric-Key Cryptography. IEEE Trans. Parallel and Distributed Systems **16** (2005) 468–480
5. Yang, S., Lu, Z., Han, S.: An Asymmetric Image Encryption Based on Matrix Transformation. in Proc. IEEE Int. Symp. Comm. and Info. Tech. (ISCIT) **1** (2004) 66–69
6. Dang, P. P., Chau, P. M.: Image Encryption for Secure Internet Multimedia Applications. IEEE Trans. Consumer Electronics **46** (2000) 395–403
7. Hou, Q., Wang, Y.: Security Traffic Image Transmission Based on EZW and AES. in Proc. IEEE Intelligent Transportation Sys. **1** (2003) 86–89
8. Ziedan, I. E., Fouad, M. M., Salem, D. H.: Application of Data Encryption Standard to bitmap and JPEG Images. in Proc. IEEE National Radio Science Conf. (NRSC) (2003) 1–8
9. Droogenbroeck, M. V., Benedett, R.: Techniques for a Selective Encryption of Uncompressed and Compressed Images. in Proc. Advanced Concepts for Intelligent Vision Systems (ACIVS) (2002) 90–96
10. Chaeng, H., Li, X.: Partial Encryption of Compressed Images and Videos. IEEE Trans. Signal Processing **48** (2000) 2439–2451
11. Podesser, M., Schmidt, H. P., Uhl, A.: Selective Bitplane Encryption for Secure Transmission of Image Data in Mobile Environments. in Proc. 5th IEEE Nordic Signal Processing symp.(NORSIG) (2002)
12. Pommer, A., Uhl, A.: Selective Encryption of Wavelet Packet Subband Structures for Obscured Transmission of Visual Data. in Proc. IEEE Benelux Signal Processing symp (2002) 25–28
13. Wang, L. T., McCluskey, E. J.: Linear Feedback Shift Register Design Using Cyclic Codes. IEEE Trans. Computers **37** (1988) 1302–1306
14. Fuster, A., Garcia, L. J.: An efficient algorithm to generate binary sequences for cryptographic purposes. Theoretical Computer Science **259** (2001) 679–688
15. Golomb, S. W.: Shift Register Sequences. Alegan park press (1982)
16. Sudharsanan, S.: Shared Key Encryption of JPEG Color Images. IEEE Trans. Consumer Electronics **51** (2005) 1204–1211

# High Capacity Lossless Data Hiding

Hyeran Lee[1] and Kyunghyune Rhee[2]

[1] Department of Computer Science, Pukyong National University,
599-1, Daeyeon3-Dong, Nam-Gu, Busan 608-737, Republic of Korea
hrlee@pknu.ac.kr
[2] Division of Electronic, Computer and Telecommunication Engineering,
Pukyong National University
khrhee@pknu.ac.kr

**Abstract.** Most data embedding techniques proposed so far lead to distortions in the original image. These distortions create problems in some areas such as medical, astronomical, and military imagery. Lossless data hiding is an exact restoration approach for recovering the original image from the stego image. In this paper, we present a lossless data embedding technique with a higher embedding capacity. We propose two lossless data embedding methods; first, a part of the unusable groups U are changed into the usable groups. Secondly, a discrimination function f is modified to improve the embedding capacity. We provide experimental results to demonstrate the effectiveness of our proposed algorithm.

**Keywords:** Lossless Data Hiding, High Capacity, Authentication, Restoration, Watermarking.

## 1 Introduction

Digital rights management (DRM) systems are built from several components that allow setting efficient electronic commerce of intangible goods [1]. Watermarking is the core technology and it is most closely associated with DRM [2]. The digital image has to be provided at the end point in digital form. It is always possible to make illegal copies of digital images. In general, robust watermarks are embedded in the host image such that owner of image is protected by his copyright [3]. A copyright owner distributes his digital image with his invisible watermark embedded in it. Watermarking systems can be classified according to many different criteria. One of them is classified into visible and invisible ones. Visible watermarks cause noticeable changes in the original image when they are embedded, whereas invisible watermarks do not create any perceptible artifacts. Invisible watermarks are divided into robust, fragile, and semi-fragile watermarks. The objective of robust watermarks is to control access and to prevent illegal copying of copyrighted image. It is an important application, especially for digital image, because digital copies can be easily made, they are perfect reproductions of the original, and they can easily and inexpensively be distributed over the Internet with no quality degradation. In contrast, fragile watermarks can be used to confirm authenticity of a digital content [4]. They can also be

A. Bagchi and V. Atluri (Eds.): ICISS 2006, LNCS 4332, pp. 326–336, 2006.

used in applications where it is important to figure out how the digital content was modified or which portion of it has been tampered with. Semi-fragile watermarks [5]. are designed to survive standard transformations, such as lossy compression, but they well become invalid if a major change has taken place [6] In a point of view of data hiding, in most cases, the cover image will experience some permanent distortion due to data hiding and cannot be inverted back to the original image. In some application such as law enforcement and medical image systems, it is desired to reverse the marked image back to the original image after the hidden data are retrieved. We employ the lossless data hiding to satisfy this requirement. In this paper, we present the authentication and the restoration of image using lossless data embedding. We focus on high capacity lossless data embedding. Fridrich et al. [7] and Honsinger et al. [9] used the spread spectrum approach to add the information payload with the host signal. The methods are robust to a wide range of distortions, but due to use of modulo arithmetic, salt-and-pepper noise are introduced and the embedding capacity is low. Goljan et al. [8] divided the image into disjoint groups (Regular, Singular, and Unusable). The whole image is scanned and Regular-Singular groups are checked whether there is a need to apply the flip operation while embedding information. Though this method involves low and invertible distortions, the capacity is not very high. Our proposed algorithm is modify the above scheme [8] to improve embedding capacity. The rest of the paper is structured as follows. In the next Section, we introduce the general principle of lossless data hiding and the problem of overflow and underflow and Section 3 presents the proposed high capacity lossless data hiding method. In Section 4, simulation results are shown and lastly, conclusions are given in Section 5.

## 2    The General Principle of Lossless Data Hiding and the Problem of Overflow and Underflow

### 2.1    The General Principle of Lossless Data Hiding

Watermarking for valuable and sensitive images such as military and medical image presents a major challenge to most of watermarking algorithms. Reversible data embedding embeds invisible data into a digital image in a reversible fashion. As a basic requirement, the quality degradation on the digital image after data embedding should be low. Intriguing feature of reversible data embedding is the reversibility, that is, when the digital image has been authenticated, one can remove the embedded data to restore the original image. The motivation of reversible data embedding is providing a distortion-free data embedding [10]. In sensitive images such as military and medical image, every bit of information is important. Reversible data embedding will provide the original image when the digital image is authenticated. In scientific research, military, and some other fields, the original media are very difficult and expensive to obtain. Therefore, it is also desired to have the original media inverted back after the hidden data are extracted. The marking techniques satisfying this requirement are referred to as reversible, lossless, distortion-free, or invertible data hiding techniques. We prefer to use the term "lossless data hiding." Celik et al. [5] classified the lossless watermarking techniques in two types. In the first type of algorithms a spread spectrum signal corresponding to the information payload is superimposed on the host signal during encoding. During decoding process, the payload is removed from the watermarked image in the restoration step. The advantage of these algorithms is the use of spread spectrum signal as payload and the increase of the robustness. But the disadvantages are they create salt-and-pepper artifacts in watermarked image due to modulo arithmetic, and offer very limited capacity. In the second type of algorithms some features of the original image are replaced or overwritten with the watermark payload. The original portions of the image that will be replaced by watermark payload are compressed and passed as a part of the embedded payload during embedding. During the decoding process this compressed payload-part is extracted and decompressed. Thus the original image is recovered by replacing the modified portions with these decompressed original features. The advantage of second type of algorithms is they do not suffer from salt-and-pepper artifacts. The disadvantages are they are not as robust as the first type of algorithms, and the capacity, though higher than the first type of algorithms, is still not good enough. However, algorithms of the second type are better than the first type for content authentication where fragility is more important than robustness. Our proposed algorithm belongs to the second type, and we try to solve the problem that capacity is not enough. In [11], lossless data hiding algorithms are classified into the three categories: Those for fragile authentication, those for high embedding capacity, and those for semifragile authentication. The first several lossless data hiding algorithms developed at the early stage belong to the first category. In fact, the fragile authentication does not need much data to be embedded in a cover image, so the embedding capacity is relatively small, namely, the amount of embedding data is rather limited. The second category of high embedding capacity needs much larger capacity that those of the first category, however, the visual quality will be deteriorated. Semifragile authentication allows some incidental modification, say, compression within a reasonable extent. For the purpose of semifragile authentication, lossless data hiding algorithms have to be robust to compression. Our proposed algorithm belongs to the second one among the three categories.

### 2.2 The Problem of Overflow and Underflow

For a given image, after the embedding in image, it is possible to cause overflow and underflow problem, which means the grayscale values of some pixels in the embedded image may exceed the upper bound or the lower bound. In [9], using modulo 256 addition can avoid overflow and underflow. For instance, for an 8-bit gray image, its gray scale ranges from 0 to 255. The overflow refers to the gray scale exceeding 255, whereas the underflow refers to below 0. It is clear that either case will destroy losslessness. In [12], histogram modification is used to prevent the overflow and underflow resulting in the perturbation of the bitplanes of the integer wavelet transform (IWT) coefficients in data embedding. In [10], to avoid overflow and underflow, the algorithm only embeds data into the pixel pairs that will not lead to overflow and underflow, so a two-dimensional binary bookkeeping image is losslessly compressed and embedded as overhead. In general, lossless data embedding algorithms are necessary an additional overhead to avoid overflow and underflow. However, our proposed lossless data embedding algorithm is not necessary any overheads, since embedding process of our algorithm makes a change of pixel value within ranges from 0 to 255 for an 8-bit gray scale.

## 3   High Capacity Lossless Data Hiding Algorithm

In this section, a high capacity lossless data hiding method is proposed. We modify the conventional lossless data embedding method[8] to improve the embedding capacity. In our proposed algorithm, we describe two lossless data embedding techniques. In the first technique, a part of the unusable groups U is changed into the usable groups. In the second method, discrimination function $f$ is modified to improve the embedding capacity.

### 3.1   Method 1

Let us assume that the original image is a grayscale image with $M \times N$ pixels and with pixel values from the set $P$. For example, for an 8-bit grayscale image, $P = 0, , 255$. First, we divide the image into disjoint block of $n$ adjacent pixels $G = (x_1, ..., x_n)$, $G' = (x_3, x_1, x_4, x_2, ..., x_{n-1}, x_n, x_{n-3}, x_{n-2})$. In the $G'$, for example of $n = 4$, all pixels are divided by block of 4 pixels and are permutated with adjacent two pixels such like $(x_3, x_4, x_1, x_2), (x_7, x_8, x_5, x_6), ..., (x_{n-1}, x_n, x_{n-3}, x_{n-2})$. We define so called discrimination function $f$ that assigns a real number $f(x_1, ..., x_n)$, to each pixel block $G = (x_1, ..., x_n)$ such like equation (1). The purpose of this function is to capture the smoothness or "regularity" of the block of pixels $G$.

$$f(x_1, x_2, ..., x_n) = \sum_{i=1}^{n-1} |x_{i+1} - x_i| \tag{1}$$

We use the discrimination function to classify the type of block. The type of block is classified into three different categories; Regular, Singular, and Unusable block. Finally, we define an invertible operation called "flipping" $F$. Flipping is a permutation of gray levels that entirely consists of two-cycles. Thus, $F$ will have the property that $F(F(x)) = x$. An example of the invertible operation $F$ can be the permutation between 0 and 1, 2 and 3, 4 and 5, and so on. Another example is the permutation between 0 and 2, 1 and 3, 4 and 6, and so on. The amplitude of the latter flipping is stronger than the former. The amplitude $A$ of the flipping permutation $F$ is defined as the average change of $x$ under the application of $F$:

$$A = \frac{1}{|P|} \sum_{x \in P} |x - F(x)| \tag{2}$$

We use the discrimination function f and the flipping operation $F$ to define three types of pixel blocks:

$$\text{Regular blocks:} \quad G \in R \Leftrightarrow f(F(G)) > f(G)$$

$$\text{Singular blocks:} \quad G \in S \Leftrightarrow f(F(G)) < f(G)$$

$$\text{Unusable blocks:} \quad G \in U \Leftrightarrow f(F(G)) = f(G)$$

For the unusable blocks U, we reclassify U blocks into Regular blocks and Singular blocks again to improve the embedding capacity

$$\text{Regular blocks:} \quad G' \in R \Leftrightarrow f(F(G')) > f(G')$$

$$\text{Singular blocks:} \quad G' \in S \Leftrightarrow f(F(G')) < f(G')$$

$$\text{Unusable blocks:} \quad G' \in U \Leftrightarrow f(F(G')) = f(G')$$

The $R$ and $S$ groups are flipped into each other under the flipping operation $F$, while the unusable groups $U$ do not change their status, $F(R) = S, F(S) = R, and F(U) = U$. As a data embedding method, by assigning binary 1 and 0 to $R$ and $S$ blocks respectively, 1 bit can be embedded into each $R$ or $S$ block. The $U$ block is skipped. The algorithm losslessly compresses the RS-vector $C$ as an overhead for bookkeeping usage in reconstruction of the original image late. If the bit to be embedded does not match the type of block under consideration, the flipping operation $F$ is applied to the block to obtain a match. We take the compressed RS-vector $C$, append the message bits to it, and embed the resulting bit-stream in the image. We use a theoretical estimate $Cap'$ for the real capacity [8].

$$Cap' = N_R + N_S + N_R \log \left( \frac{N_R}{N_R + N_S} \right) + N_s \log \left( \frac{N_S}{N_R + N_S} \right)$$

For data extraction, the algorithm scans the marked image in the same manner as in the data embedding. From the resultant RS-vector, the embedded data can be extracted. The overhead portion well be used to reconstruct the original image, the remaining portion is the payload. Figure 1 shows embedding process of method 1.

## 3.2   Method 2

We only describe the difference from the method 1. The discrimination function f is used to capture the smoothness or "regularity" of the block. In the method 2, we changed a discrimination function to be used in the method 2 as shown in equation (3).

$$f'(x_1, x_2, ..., x_{M \times N}) = \sum_{k=0}^{M \times N/64-1} \sum_{j=0}^{64/n-1} \sum_{i=1}^{n-1} |x_{64k+4j+i+1} - x_{64k+4j+i}| \quad (3)$$

As shown in (3) discrimination function $f'$ accumulates the value from the next 64 blocks. In general, the numbers of $R$ and $S$ type are larger than those of $U$

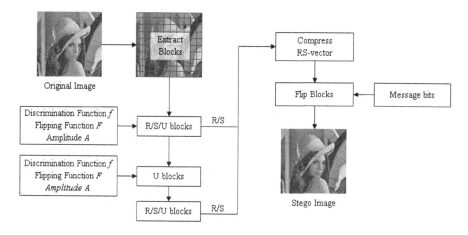

**Fig. 1.** Embedding process of method 1

type in regular image. Similarly the number of $R$ type is larger than that of $S$ type. The $U$ type of block can change the $R$ and $S$ type using (3). Because the number of $R$ and $S$ type of block are larger than those of $U$ type in generally, in order to continue this condition, we use accumulating of value of blocks. The increasing of $R$ and $S$ type can improve the capacity. In the method 1, the blocks are classified into three categories $R$, $S$, and $U$. Then the $U$ blocks are reclassified into three categories $R$, $S$, and $U$ again to improve the embedding capacity. But in the method 2, the $U$ blocks are not classified again. We used original three block types. The remaining is same as method 1. Figure 2 shows embedding process of method 2.

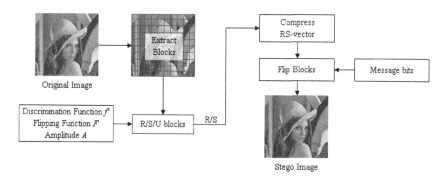

**Fig. 2.** Embedding process of method 2

## 4  Experimental Result and Discussions

In this section, we present the experimental results of the proposed algorithm and then compare the results with other algorithms. We apply the proposed

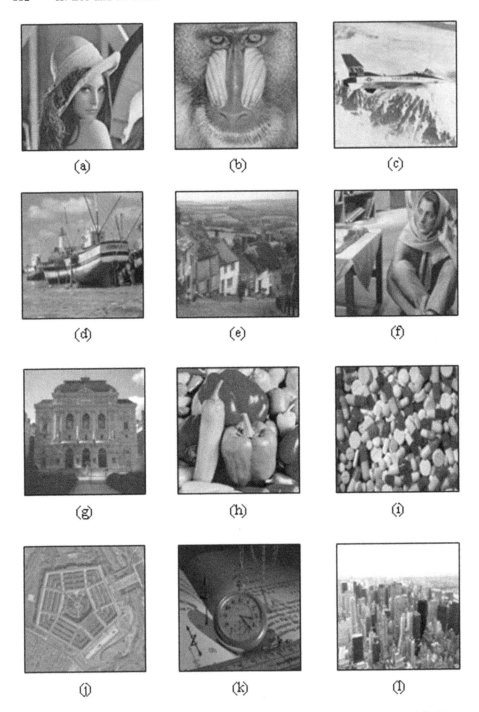

**Fig. 3.** Fig. 3. Test images (256256) (a) Lena, (b) Baboon, (c) Airplane, (d) Fishingboat, (e) Goldhill, (f) Barbara, (g) Opera, (h) Peppers, (i) Pills, (j) Pentagon, (k) Watch, (l) Newyork

method to various standard grayscale test images, including "Lena", "Pepper", "Baboon", "Airplane", "Fishingboat", "Goldhill", "Barbara", "Opera", "Peppers", "Pills", "Pentagon", "Watch", and "Newyork" as shown in Fig. 3. We use grayscale $256 \times 256$ pixel images with 8-bit grayscale levels per pixel. We have used JBIG for compression.

**Table 1.** Estimated capacity $Cap'$ for test images (Method 1)

| Test image name | Estimated capacity $Cap'$ for amplitude $a=1,...,7$ | | | | | | |
|---|---|---|---|---|---|---|---|
| (256× 256) | 1 | 2 | 3 | 4 | 5 | 6 | 7 |
| Lena | 1211 | 4068 | 5870 | 7408 | 8099 | 9272 | 4869 |
| Baboon | 120 | 337 | 701 | 985 | 1322 | 1822 | 2276 |
| Airplane | 1032 | 2501 | 3540 | 3875 | 4102 | 4107 | 4172 |
| Fishingboat | 494 | 1306 | 2076 | 2738 | 3325 | 3799 | 4060 |
| Goldhill | 203 | 690 | 1370 | 1993 | 2694 | 3339 | 3828 |
| Barbara | 189 | 667 | 1062 | 1618 | 1894 | 2392 | 2493 |
| Opera | 690 | 1828 | 2912 | 3570 | 3934 | 4308 | 4731 |
| Pepper | 666 | 2142 | 3322 | 4251 | 5181 | 5418 | 5852 |
| Pills | 223 | 830 | 1533 | 2237 | 2997 | 3412 | 3908 |
| Pentagon | 189 | 634 | 1355 | 2003 | 2512 | 3136 | 3812 |
| Watch | 1000 | 1764 | 2193 | 2507 | 2759 | 2729 | 2936 |
| Newyork | 52 | 199 | 358 | 624 | 754 | 1067 | 1355 |
| Average $Cap'$/MxN | 1.71% | 3.14% | 4.36% | 5.32% | 6.05% | 6.71% | 6.62% |
| Average PSNR(dB) | 52.95 | 46.46 | 42.66 | 39.98 | 37.9 | 36.23 | 34.92 |

**Table 2.** Estimated capacity $Cap'$ for test images (Method 2)

| Test image name | Estimated capacity $Cap'$ for amplitude $a=1,...,7$ | | | | | | |
|---|---|---|---|---|---|---|---|
| (256× 256) | 1 | 2 | 3 | 4 | 5 | 6 | 7 |
| Lena | 3944 | 7670 | 9618 | 11266 | 11938 | 12380 | 12086 |
| Baboon | 989 | 2004 | 3776 | 5032 | 6150 | 7161 | 8374 |
| Airplane | 4519 | 7197 | 8755 | 9731 | 10663 | 11142 | 11158 |
| Fishingboat | 2340 | 5343 | 7080 | 9427 | 10642 | 11190 | 11609 |
| Goldhill | 1197 | 3491 | 5411 | 7050 | 8612 | 10150 | 11374 |
| Barbara | 1008 | 3268 | 4405 | 5901 | 6357 | 7375 | 7895 |
| Opera | 3459 | 6746 | 9331 | 10607 | 11751 | 11812 | 11796 |
| Pepper | 4342 | 8543 | 10852 | 12081 | 12994 | 13400 | 13470 |
| Pills | 2265 | 5193 | 7800 | 9699 | 11304 | 11671 | 12304 |
| Pentagon | 1377 | 3980 | 6811 | 8286 | 9988 | 10609 | 11681 |
| Watch | 4516 | 6531 | 8402 | 9464 | 9681 | 9704 | 10290 |
| Newyork | 274 | 905 | 1618 | 2839 | 3362 | 4384 | 5095 |
| Average $Cap'$/MxN | 3.84% | 7.74% | 10.66% | 12.89% | 14.42% | 15.38% | 16.17% |
| Average PSNR(dB) | 49.51 | 43.63 | 40.19 | 37.72 | 35.79 | 34.19 | 32.91 |

## 4.1  Experimental Results

Table 1 and Table 2 show the experimental results we have obtained in the proposed method 1 and method 2 respectively. These results show that the proposed algorithm offers lossless data hiding with higher capacity and imperceptible artifacts.

**Table 3.** Estimated capacity $Cap'$ for test images ([8])

| Test image name | Estimated capacity $Cap'$ for amplitude $a=1,...,7$ | | | | | | |
|---|---|---|---|---|---|---|---|
| (256× 256) | 1 | 2 | 3 | 4 | 5 | 6 | 7 |
| Lena | 865 | 2480 | 3414 | 4144 | 4497 | 5085 | 5342 |
| Baboon | 157 | 390 | 850 | 1084 | 1472 | 2011 | 2485 |
| Airplane | 1257 | 2913 | 3915 | 4280 | 4436 | 4419 | 4464 |
| Fishingboat | 584 | 1494 | 2320 | 3027 | 3639 | 4012 | 4327 |
| Goldhill | 237 | 776 | 1501 | 2152 | 2918 | 3574 | 4069 |
| Barbara | 227 | 795 | 1226 | 1795 | 2092 | 2594 | 2703 |
| Opera | 842 | 2070 | 3235 | 3897 | 4246 | 4596 | 4960 |
| Pepper | 1430 | 2688 | 3972 | 4955 | 5822 | 5989 | 6404 |
| Pills | 349 | 1070 | 1932 | 2677 | 3503 | 3945 | 4464 |
| Pentagon | 239 | 754 | 1567 | 2251 | 2834 | 3479 | 4174 |
| Watch | 1171 | 1951 | 2405 | 2774 | 3004 | 2989 | 3109 |
| Newyork | 62 | 234 | 391 | 697 | 823 | 1144 | 1486 |
| Average $Cap'$/MxN | 0.94% | 2.24% | 3.39% | 4.28% | 4.99% | 5.57% | 6.10% |
| Average PSNR(dB) | 49.46 | 43.54 | 39.99 | 37.51 | 35.6 | 34.03 | 32.66 |

**Table 4.** Comparing capacity and PSNR offered by [8] and the proposed algorithm (a=1,2)

| Test image name | Estimated capacity $Cap'$ for amplitude $a=1,2$ | | | | | |
|---|---|---|---|---|---|---|
| (256× 256) | $a=1$ | | | $a=2$ | | |
| | [8] | Method 1 | Method 2 | [8] | Method 1 | Method 2 |
| Lena | 865 | 1211 | 3944 | 2480 | 4068 | 7670 |
| Baboon | 157 | 120 | 989 | 390 | 337 | 2004 |
| Airplane | 1257 | 1023 | 4519 | 2913 | 2501 | 7197 |
| Fishingboat | 584 | 494 | 2340 | 1494 | 1306 | 5343 |
| Goldhill | 237 | 203 | 1197 | 776 | 690 | 3491 |
| Barbara | 227 | 189 | 1008 | 795 | 667 | 3268 |
| Opera | 842 | 690 | 3459 | 2070 | 1828 | 6746 |
| Pepper | 1430 | 666 | 4342 | 2688 | 2142 | 8543 |
| Pills | 349 | 223 | 2265 | 1070 | 830 | 5193 |
| Pentagon | 239 | 189 | 1377 | 754 | 634 | 3980 |
| Watch | 1171 | 1000 | 4516 | 1951 | 1764 | 6531 |
| Newyork | 62 | 52 | 274 | 234 | 199 | 905 |
| Average $Cap'$/MxN | 0.94% | 1.71% | 3.84% | 2.24% | 3.14% | 7.74% |
| Average PSNR(dB) | 49.46 | 52.95 | 49.51 | 43.54 | 46.46 | 43.63 |

## 4.2   Comparison with Other Algorithms

Table 3 shows the experimental results of [8]. Table 4, 5, and 6 are comparing capacity and PSNR offered by [8] and the proposed algorithm. The method [8] divides pixels into $R$, $S$, and $U$ blocks. $U$ blocks are not use. On the other

**Table 5.** Comparing capacity and PSNR offered by [8] and the proposed algorithm (a=3,4)

| Test image name (256× 256) | Estimated capacity $Cap'$ for amplitude a=3,4 | | | | | |
|---|---|---|---|---|---|---|
| | a=3 | | | a=4 | | |
| | [8] | Method 1 | Method 2 | [8] | Method 1 | Method 2 |
| Lena | 3414 | 5870 | 9618 | 4144 | 7408 | 11266 |
| Baboon | 850 | 701 | 3776 | 1084 | 985 | 5032 |
| Airplane | 3915 | 3540 | 8755 | 4280 | 3875 | 9731 |
| Fishingboat | 2320 | 2076 | 7080 | 3027 | 2738 | 9427 |
| Goldhill | 1501 | 1370 | 5411 | 2152 | 1993 | 7050 |
| Barbara | 1226 | 1062 | 4405 | 1795 | 1618 | 5901 |
| Opera | 3235 | 2912 | 9331 | 3897 | 3570 | 10607 |
| Pepper | 3972 | 3322 | 10582 | 4955 | 4251 | 12081 |
| Pills | 1932 | 1533 | 7800 | 2677 | 2237 | 9699 |
| Pentagon | 1567 | 1355 | 6811 | 2251 | 2003 | 8286 |
| Watch | 2405 | 2193 | 8402 | 2774 | 2507 | 9464 |
| Newyork | 391 | 358 | 1618 | 697 | 624 | 2839 |
| Average $Cap'$/MxN | 3.39% | 4.36% | 10.66% | 4.28% | 5.32% | 12.89% |
| Average PSNR(dB) | 39.99 | 42.66 | 40.19 | 37.51 | 39.98 | 37.72 |

**Table 6.** Comparing capacity and PSNR offered by [8] and the proposed algorithm (a=5,6)

| Test image name (256× 256) | Estimated capacity $Cap'$ for amplitude a=5,6 | | | | | |
|---|---|---|---|---|---|---|
| | a=5 | | | a=6 | | |
| | [8] | Method 1 | Method 2 | [8] | Method 1 | Method 2 |
| Lena | 4497 | 8099 | 11938 | 5085 | 9272 | 12380 |
| Baboon | 1472 | 1322 | 6150 | 2011 | 1828 | 7161 |
| Airplane | 4436 | 4102 | 10663 | 4419 | 4107 | 11142 |
| Fishingboat | 3639 | 3325 | 10642 | 4012 | 3799 | 11190 |
| Goldhill | 2918 | 2694 | 8612 | 3574 | 3339 | 10150 |
| Barbara | 2092 | 1894 | 6357 | 2594 | 2392 | 7375 |
| Opera | 4246 | 3934 | 11751 | 4596 | 4308 | 11812 |
| Pepper | 5822 | 5181 | 12994 | 5989 | 5418 | 13400 |
| Pills | 3503 | 2997 | 11304 | 3945 | 3412 | 11671 |
| Pentagon | 2834 | 2512 | 9988 | 3479 | 3136 | 10609 |
| Watch | 3004 | 2759 | 9681 | 2989 | 2729 | 9704 |
| Newyork | 823 | 754 | 3362 | 1144 | 1067 | 4384 |
| Average $Cap'$/MxN | 4.99% | 6.05% | 14.42% | 5.57% | 6.71% | 15.38% |
| Average PSNR(dB) | 35.6 | 37.9 | 35.79 | 34.03 | 36.23 | 34.19 |

hand, our proposed method uses the part of $U$ blocks to embed the data. Hence, the experimental results prove that our proposed algorithm is better, since it gives higher capacity for almost all images and fair PSNR value is good. The capacity of both proposed methods is more improve than [8]. Method 2 using accumulating value of blocks is more improve than Method 1.

## Acknowledgement

This work was supported by grant No. R01-2006-000-10260-0 from the Basic Research Program of the Korea Science & Engineering Foundation.

## References

1. W. Rosenblatt, W. Trippe, and S. Mooney, : Digital Rights Management, *New York*, 2002.
2. E. T. Lin, A. M. Eskicioglu, and R. L. Lagendijk, "Advances in Digital Video Content Protection," *Proceedings of the IEEE*, vol. 93, issue 1 pp. 171-183, January 2005.
3. I. J. Cox, J. Kilian, F. T. Leighton, and T. Shamoon, "Secure spread spectrum watermarking for multimedia," *IEEE Transaction Image Processing*, vol. 6, pp.1673-1687, December 1997.
4. P. W. Wong, "A watermark for image integrity and ownership verification," *Proceedings of IEEE International Conference Image Processing*, pp.455-459, 1998.
5. M. U. Celik, G. Sharma, E. Saber, and A. M. Tekalp, "Hierarchical watermarking for secure image authentication with localization," *IEEE Transaction Image Processing*, vol. 11, No. 6, pp. 585-595, 2002.
6. Cox, I. J., Miller, M. L., and Bloom, J.A.: Digital Watermarking *Kaufmann*, San Francisco, 2001.
7. J. Fridrich, m. Goljan, R. Du, "Invertible Authentication," *in proceedings of SPIE Photonics West, Security and Watermarking of Multimedia Contents* , vol. 3971. San jose, California, USA, January 2001.
8. M. Goljan, J. Fridrich, and R. Du, "Distortion-free data embedding for images," *in 4th Information Hiding Workshop*, pp. 27-41, April 2001.
9. C. W. Honsinger, P. W. jones, M. Rabbani, and J. C. Stoffel, "Lossless recovery of an original image containing embedded data," *United States patent*, 6,278,791, 2001.
10. J. Tian, "Reversible watermarking by difference expansion," *in Proceedings of Multimedia and Security Workshop at ACM Multimedia*, December 2002.
11. B. Furht, D. Kirovski : Multimedia Security Handbook *CRC Press*, New York, 2005.
12. G. Xuan, Y.Q. Shi, Z.C. Ni, J. Chen, l Yang, Y. Zhen, and J. Zhen, " High Capacity lossless Data Hiding Based on Integer Wavelet Transform," *Proceeding of IEEE international Symposium on Circuits and Systems*, Vancouver, Canada, 2004.

# An Implementation and Evaluation of Online Disk Encryption for Windows Systems

Vartika Singh, D.R. Lakshminarasimhaiah, Yogesh Mishra,
Chitra Viswanathan, and G. Athithan

Center for Artificial Intelligence and Robotics, C.V. Raman Nagar,
Bangalore 560093, India
{vartikas,dr.lnarasim,findyogesh2000,chitravishy,athithan.g}@gmail.com

**Abstract.** The threat of loss of privacy of data due to the theft of hard disks requires that the data in hard disks is protected by means of encryption. In this paper we propose an implementation of a disk-driver-based sector level encryption for windows platforms. The implementation provides for strong security to the data at the sector-level, independent of the mounted file-system. The encryption of data is done at the granularity of partitions, leaving aside the boot partition, thus not affecting system boot-up process. Adapting a scheme proposed in the literature, the initialization vector is kept different for different sectors and is changed every time the sector is written into. The complete implementation is tested and evaluated using standard benchmark suites. The paper ends with a discussion on the usability of the implementation and future directions of its development.

**Keywords:** Storage security, Disk encryption, Initialization vector, Storage data encryption/decryption, and Sector-level encryption.

## 1 Introduction

This paper addresses the threat of loss of privacy due to theft or capture of computer hard disks, and of a solution for securing the hard disk data at rest by means of on-line encryption on a Windows system. Perhaps the typical method to provide encryption of the contents in the hard disk is to use a solution presented in [1], which allows users to select the files or directories for encryption. This solution however, is quite inconvenient for the users, as it requires them to encrypt and decrypt the files manually and often periodically [2]. Again, more user interactions mean more exposure of the data and files meant to be secure may be left plain in the hard disk while the user is working on it.

Another option is encrypting at the file system level, as is done for example by Cryptographic File System (CFS) [3] and Transparent Cryptographic File System (TCFS) [4] in Linux, and Encrypting File System (EFS) [5] in Windows platforms. The choice of directory/file to be protected is with the user as also is the management of encryption keys. The granularity is as good as in the manual encryption system. The only drawback of this approach is the complexity

A. Bagchi and V. Atluri (Eds.): ICISS 2006, LNCS 4332, pp. 337–348, 2006.
© Springer-Verlag Berlin Heidelberg 2006

involved in its implementation. File systems have a complex programming interface to the operating system, quite often causing compatibility and version skew issues [9]. Also this approach would require addressing memory management and the cache management as the New Technology File System (NTFS) is tightly integrated with the above two. Migration of the solution from one version of the O/S and its kernel to other versions would be difficult and time consuming.

Another approach is to employ StegFS [6], which along with steganography uses encryption. Although StegFS achieves plausible deniability of data's existence, the performance degradation is a factor of 6 to 196, making it impractical for most applications [7].

A disk driver-based approach helps in avoiding the problems of the above approaches. It addresses the problem at the level of raw partitions. It is certainly safer than the user level encryption approach. It also provides mandatory security, while avoiding the complexity of the file system-based approach. The development of the driver for encryption is not only simple but the approach is also quite elegant and all encompassing. This simplicity and elegance is possible because in a windows system the drivers are layered in a form of stack, each functioning in a modular way. In case of systems having just a single user account such as personal desktops, full disk encryption is considered to be safer than file level encryption.

There are several implementations of disk encryptions for Linux systems. Some of the commonly used ones are [8], [9], [10]. Our endeavour has been to develop a solution for Windows systems. When the development work started, there were no commercial or open source solutions. Therefore, we chose to develop and evaluate an independent solution based on the disk driver approach. Though there is a recent commercial product for hard disk security of Windows systems [11], technical details regarding implementation and evaluation are, of course, not available. The approach reported here balances ease of usage, security and performance for a typical windows systems user. In particular, the implementation is suited for a situation, where only a subset of the hard disk data, categorized as sensitive, needs protection. It is a standard guideline to change the initialization vector for every sector as frequently as possible. This guideline is followed in the implementation reported here with the help of a scheme proposed in the literature. In the following sections, this paper explains the standard approach for disk level encryption, fills in the operational requirements, and reports about an implementation and its evaluation.

## 2   Disk Driver-Based Approach

The disk driver-based encryption scheme targets the raw partitions. To explain it briefly, the driver for the file system takes control from the application, does the required processing, such as parsing the filename, finding the physical location of file on the hard disk and creating the necessary buffers. It then passes the file to the drivers below it in the stack. The request is parsed and processed through a chain of drivers, until it reaches the driver at the bottom of the stack.

The read and write requests passing between the file system driver and the disk driver can be intercepted by inserting another driver written for the purpose of encryption, in between these two drivers. This driver for encryption, having gotten the control of the data passing between these two levels can do the encryption and decryption on-the-fly.

Since file systems access the hard disk at the granularity of the sector, i.e. 512 bytes, each sector is read and written independently of the other sectors. This approach not only hides the file system names, their sizes, directory structure, and modification dates, but also provides flexibility with regard to the type of file system being used, and the way the file system stores data on the disk. Encryption of the data is done irrespective of the disk compression and caching schemes being used. The enciphering transform here acts on 512 bytes of data under the control of a secret key and a known tweak or initialization value. It also acts on the data of the sector for bringing variability in the cipher text across time [12]. It can be implemented as a mode of operation for any block cipher encryption scheme e.g. Advanced Encryption Standard, AES algorithm. The cipher text has the same length as the plain text.

Encrypting the entire hard disk entails a lot of time in the decryption of the system files during the boot up phase. Further, in a typical system, most of the data may not be categorized as secret or sensitive. In these cases encrypting the complete hard disk is unwarranted. Unless required otherwise, the best option for a windows/Linux system is to have a single encrypted partition and to keep all sensitive data in that partition. In the following three sub-sections, we discuss the implementation details, key management issues and the cryptographic implementation of the disk driver-based approach of disk data security.

## 2.1  Details of Implementation

The scheme proposed here is to insert a filter crypto disk driver between the file system driver and the disk driver of that partition. This allows the user to carry on with his work in other (plain) partitions without the added overhead of ciphering. Any request coming from the user space to the encrypted partition will now have to pass through the crypto filter driver. The driver will then have access to the data being read or written. Thus, the data being read, while coming up will be decrypted by the driver, and the data being written, while going to the hard disk, will be encrypted by it. Since the data being read is decrypted only before coming into the application space, the sensitive data is always in encrypted form in the hard disk.

The only requirement for the data residing in the encrypted partition alias drive to be read properly is for the key to be provided beforehand. Failing to do so will render the drive unreadable and unrecognizable by the Windows file system. A diagrammatic representation of the working of the system is shown in Fig. 1

As shown in the Fig. 1, the data going to the other drives (partitions) in the system will reside on the hard disk in plain form.

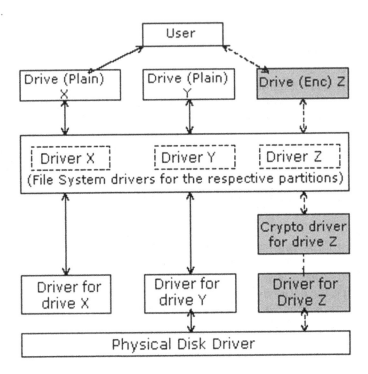

**Fig. 1.** Schematic flow of encrypted and plain data. The filled boxes and the dashed lines show the path of encrypted data.

## 2.2   Encryption and Decryption Processes

As the smallest unit of data storage on the hard disk is of size 512 bytes, i.e. one sector, the encryption has to be done per sector, independent of the other sectors. This has the advantage of preventing corruption of any sector from influencing the sectors lying adjacent to it.

Since, its possible for data in two different sectors to be the same sometimes, using the same key will lead to same cipher texts. In order to bring in variability between two sectors having the same content, we use a known tweak value as pre-encryption whitening. The data in the plain text is first XORed with the tweak, i.e. the sector address in the hard disk, and then encrypted with the key in order to thwart position-based attacks.

The fixed size of sectors in hard disks makes adding extra data difficult, which in turn prevents traditional integrity checking using standard message authentication codes (MACs). Thus, Cipher Block Chaining (CBC) will have to be used as the encryption mode. Since CBC creates interdependence between blocks, we can use this to ensure that none of the plaintext bits that were input into the encryption have been changed, thus providing indirect means of integrity checking. However, sectors encrypted in this way are said to be malleable. An attacker can indirectly control unencrypted data by altering the cipher text.

These two issues, i.e. of position-based attacks and malleability of data have been tackled partially, by using parallelizable enciphering mode [13], tweakable block ciphers [14] and the draft proposal on tweakable wide-block encryption given by Shai Halevi [12]. Our implementation is based on the ideas of these three papers. Thus, the approach reported here, keeping in mind the sector-address dependent encryption and CBC, is to divide a sector into 32 blocks of 16 bytes each.

$$P = (P_1, P_2.., P_{32})  \qquad (1)$$

$$C = (C_1, C_2.., C_{32})  \qquad (2)$$

Here, $P$ and $C$ denote the plaintext and the cipher text blocks respectively. The sector address or the logical block address, also called tweak, is denoted as $T$. Let the key be denoted by $K$, the block-encryption procedure by $E_K$, and the block-decryption procedure by $D_K$. To encrypt a sector, get the sector address $T$ and XOR it with all but first plain text blocks of the sector. We get the initialization vector (IV) for the first block using Eq. 3.

$$IV = T \bigoplus P_2 \bigoplus P_3 \bigoplus \cdots \bigoplus P_{32}  \qquad (3)$$

Now, $IV$ is XORed with $P_1$ and then encrypted with a block encryption algorithm such as the AES. Next, $P_2$ is XORed with $C_1$ and the result is encrypted to obtain $C_2$ and so on. Fig. 2(below) illustrates the procedure.

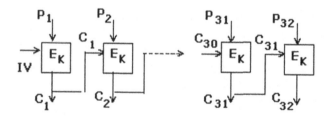

**Fig. 2.** The above figure illustrates the encryption procedure for a sector of 512 bytes each. The $IV$ as calculated in eq.3 is used as the tweak for the first block, then $C_1$ is used as the tweak for the next block, and so on. $E_K$ denotes the block encryption routine.

For decrypting the cipher text of the sector, divide the cipher text sector into 32 blocks of 16 bytes each (eq. 2). We start from the last block, using $C_{n-1}$ as the tweak value for it. After decrypting the last block, that is, $C_n$, we XOR the resulting value with the tweak, $C_{n-1}$ to obtain $P_n$ . Proceeding in a similar manner until we have done with the last but one block, the final tweak value is taken as $IV$ (eq.3) and the same procedure is repeated. The Fig. 3 below explains the decryption procedure.

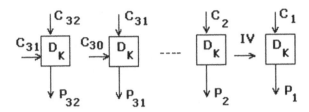

**Fig. 3.** The figure illustrates the decryption procedure for a sector of 512 bytes each. The decryption is done in a manner exactly in reverse to the encryption procedure. $C_{32}$ is decrypted with the block algorithm and the result is XORed with $C_{31}$ to obtain $P_{32}$. The procedure is same for all the blocks except that $IV$ is used for XORing for the first block.

### 2.3   Key Management Issues

In encrypted communications, the well-known key management process involves creating, using and then destroying a key. If a key is lost or compromised, the solution is to create or agree on a new key and continue operations. Since the old key was for the previous but completed communications, this isn't a serious issue. The old keys need not be stored for more than a small window of time. With storage, however, one has to retain the encryption keys for longer durations. This is due to the fact that the time of next access of an encrypted piece of data cannot be predicted easily.

One approach for key management is to divide a partition into several zones and have a separate key for each zone. Thus, if a key is lost, then the loss of data is limited to that particular zone. But then the storage, access and administration of the keys become a big problem. Also, the performance overheads for searching the relevant key for the zone might add up increasing the disk I/O.

Using a single key for the whole disk or a partition of a disk and deriving different keys for different zones/sectors is an unsolved problem and is an open area for research [15]. Some work is being done in the field to standardize the key back up format, but it still is in draft form [16]. The implementation reported here uses a single key that is common for all sectors of the partition, and changes it after a suitable interval of time, selectable by the user. The storage of key involves another problem. Storing it on the hard disk itself means increasing the chances of it being stolen easily along with the data. The better option is to store the key in an external token like a smart card or a thumb-drive. This token can be used once to load the key into the system memory, and then be removed from the system and be physically secured.

Since the encryption engine is a driver that comes up at the system boot up time, the key has to be loaded into the memory before the driver gets loaded. This entails making the token bootable, so that the key can be loaded into the memory before the driver comes up. The driver will read the key into its own process space, and lock it. Since, the key should not be at any period of time written onto the hard disk, it is locked by the driver in the non-pageable area of the memory. So there is no possibility of the key being written to the disk even temporarily, since the page containing it will never be swapped out.

The key is loaded into the memory with the help of the boot image file. The file is inside an external token such as thumb-drive or a smart card. The system should be booted with this device. If the token contains the correct image file, the correct key will be loaded into the system, and the metadata of the partition will be decrypted correctly. But if the file is incorrect, the key loaded will be incorrect; the metadata will be decrypted incorrectly, and the partition will not be accessible at all.

Authenticating a key requires comparing the entered key, or passphrase, or its MAC, against some authentic data, which is again to be stored somewhere on the hard disk or on the token. Since the operating system files are not being encrypted, we can let the user enter the passphrase to decrypt the contents of the token. If the passphrase is incorrect, the key will fail to load. And if the pass phrase is correct but an incorrect token device is being used, the 'key' will be loaded, but the file system will fail to mount on the partition. Thus, during the key load phase, the requirement to access the data in the partition is to know the pass phrase and to have the key token.

For changing the key, the token containing the new key is inserted into the slot, and the partition is read in blocks of integral number of sectors with the old key (amounts to decryption) and written with the new key (amounts to encryption). To have a better performance, the number of sectors in a single read could be increased, but this could lead to slowing of other processes running in the system.

## 3   Performance Evaluation

The performance of the driver varies widely with the type of usage it is being subjected to. It works with almost imperceptible change in the rate of data flow with the personal desktop stations being used for usual development, multimedia and word processing sort of tasks. It works well with database and client server environment too, given that the database and server applications are not installed in the encrypted drive. As long as the drive contains only the data to be accessed, the system as a whole gives acceptable working performance.

Since the windows file system is tightly coupled with several modules, like memory manager, cache manager, I/O manager and several others, the working of the driver also depends on the amount of memory available to the system. As the driver resides almost at the bottom layer of the driver stack, the read/write requests reaching it are almost always at the dispatch level [17]. This brings in the need for providing critical section environment for the code executing in these routines in the form of spin-locks. Putting the read/write (decryption/encryption) code inside the critical region ensures that while the enciphering is going on, no other thread of execution will interfere with the data being processed by it. The data, which the driver is working upon for ciphering, is locked in the non-pageable area of the driver during the course of the encryption.

The above two aspects of implementation put the other processes, trying to access the driver on hold until the spin-lock becomes free. Also a portion of the nonpageable memory, which is a critical resource, is tied down. This, in turn increases the number of page faults and swapping, which further leads to more I/O seeks.

The cipher algorithm used for the performance evaluation is AES with 128 bit keys. The AES runs fastest with the key size of 128 bits [18]; therefore, the driver was not tested with other key sizes. The system used for testing was Microsoft Windows Server 2000 5.00.2195 SP3, running on Intel Pentium 4 CPU 2.66 GHz. The system RAM was of size 1 GB. The hard disk size was 40 GB with ATA interface.

### 3.1   Nbench

This tool is a benchmarking program for measuring CPU speed for both, integer and floating point operations, main memory speed and disk read and write speeds in MB/sec [19]. The tests were run for 20 threads of execution.

The tool is used here for disk read and write speeds, i.e. the I/O throughput for a file written and read sequentially, from the beginning to the end. The disk seek and rotation times are not being measured. The file is created with the attribute FILE_NO_BUFFERING, so that the OS will not cache the file, and all I/O will go directly between the application buffer and the disk. Thus, there should be no misleading speedup from OS caching, even if the file is quite small.

As seen in Fig. 4 (below), for both the runs, the amount of data read for the encrypted drive is on the average 3.014% less then for read requests and 4.89% less for the write requests.

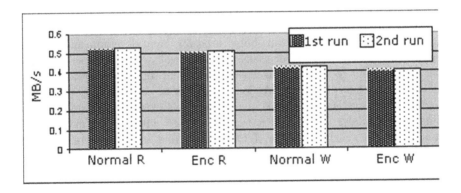

**Fig. 4.** Results of the benchmark Nbench. The results are depicted in four pairs of bars. Each pair showing the outcome of two runs, the first and second. The first two pairs compare the outcome of running the tests on plain and encrypted drive for disk reads, and the second two pairs compare the results for disk writes. Clearly the overheads are marginal.

## 3.2   Postmark

This tool tests the workstations mainly as file-servers, where the sizes of the files are quite small but the number of files is large [20]. At any given time files are being rapidly created, read, written or deleted all over the disk drives. This tool is designed to create a large pool of continually changing files and to measure the transaction rates. The tool was configured to run for four different settings, namely, 500 transactions on 500 files, 50000 transactions on 1000 files and 20000 files, and 100000 transactions on 20000 files. The file sizes range between 500 bytes to 9.766 Kilobytes. Unix file buffered I/O is used with block size being read at a time being equivalent to a sector size, i.e. 512 bytes.

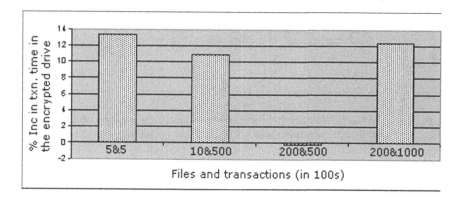

**Fig. 5.** Results of the benchmark Postmark. The bars show the percentage excess time taken by the encrypted drive as compared to the plain drive.

As seen in the Fig. 5 (above), the encrypted disk takes 13.31% more for a small number of transactions (500) on a small number of files. But as we increase the number of files the difference gradually decreases and finally starts increasing again.

We can easily conclude that the driver performs optimally for a certain range, below and above which, it starts taking more time as compared to normal reads and writes.

## 3.3   IOMeter

IOMeter is a Disk IO benchmark available from Intel [21]. It measures the data transfer rates under a controlled environment. This test was run with completely random requests each for block size of 2 KB, 8 KB and 16 KB. The request sizes are distributed as 67% read and 33% write. The test load ran for 1-256 outstanding I/O requests.

The tool has a ramp-up period of 30 seconds in order to avoid transient effects.The test was run for duration of fifteen minutes, and was repeated three times.

Fig. 6 (below) shows, the difference between the system performance working on the encrypted and plain driver in terms of data transfer rates (MB/s), number of transactions (IO/s) and the CPU utilization. We can see that as block-size is increased, the encrypted partition deteriorates in performance. However, the CPU utilization increases significantly with the increase in data block.

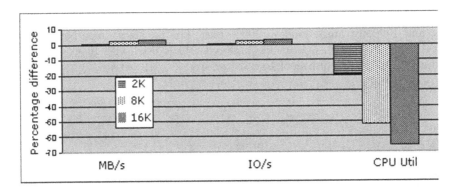

**Fig. 6.** Results of the benchmark IOMeter. The test shows the excess amounts in terms of data transferred, IO operations and CPU Utilizations for the encrypted partition case.

## 4   Discussion on Usability

Having too rigorous an implementation of security often forces a user to circumvent or ignore it entirely. Too simple a system may not provide any good security at all [2]. A very good and strong crypto implementation, bug-free code, rigorously proven protocols do not often guarantee security if the user forgets to click on the encrypt button. This is a drawback, which comes with the user-space implementations. Relying on the user to use the protocol correctly becomes an added burden of maintaining security. The problem of remembering the keys, choosing the new keys might make the user forego the whole procedure altogether.

Storing the keys on an external media after encryption using a passpharase, reading the keys once at the boot time giving the passphrase, removing the key media and then physically securing the key token removes a lot of burden from the user while he is using the system. In a server class system the administrator can handle these boot time responsibilities leaving the user to his/her own specific tasks.

Another issue in encrypted storage is that most of the storage security implementations require an empty partition to be created first and then some formatting. After this the user can move his data to that particular partition. There should be a provision for keeping the older data intact in place and still encrypt the drive. Also the older data should not be anywhere else temporarily, unless that area is cleanly wiped out after the data has been moved back. The proposed approach of encrypting the complete windows partition requires no shifting of older data.

Usually application installation in windows is quite an easy job. A simple click on an EXE file and then following step-by-step instructions are quite enough for a quick installation. So, the installation is not an issue in a windows system other than formatting the drive, for which two options are given to the user. If the drive is empty, then a quick Windows format can be done. Else a complete encryption of the partition has to be done, which will consume some time depending on the size of the partition.

## 5 Conclusion

For single application type of workloads such as a server, I/O is the limiting factor, but the encryption operations lie along a critical path in the I/O subsystem. Since I/O operations cannot complete until the encryption/decryption is done, encryption negatively impacts performance in some cases.

Secondly caches greatly impact the workload by significantly changing the amount of data to be decrypted.

The disk-based encryption is a better method to provide storage security as compared to file system-based security if no other features corresponding to the file-system are to be provided. This method not only demands an easier developmental effort, but also is more stable in terms of different versions of Windows. Also, this approach covers the issue of raw partitions as well.

The present implementation is based on a simple approach to key management. It leaves out the case of data retrieval in case of key loss and having different keys for different sectors/zones without a great impact on performance. The integrity checking of data is left to the NTFS.

The implementation is independent of the underlying hardware interface. Hence, though tested on ATA hard disks, this solution would work for SCSI hard disks as well. However, its compatibility with USB enabled disks remains to be examined. Adapting this solution for a network server [22], and transmitting the encrypted disk data securely over the wire is another task for the future.

**Acknowledgement.** The authors thank Director, CAIR for providing them with an environment for the development of the secure storage implementation reported in this paper. They also thank the reviewers for their critical comments that helped in improving the quality of the paper.

## References

1. Garfinkel, S.: PGP: Pretty Good Privacy. O'Reilly and Associates, First Edition (1994)
2. Whitten A., Tygar, J.D.: Why Johnny Can't Encrypt: A Usability Evaluation of PGP 5.0. USENIX Security Symposium (1999)

3. Blaze, M.: A cryptographic file system for Unix. In Proceedings of 1st ACM conference on Communications and Computing Security. ACM Press New York, NY, USA, (1993) 9-16
4. Cattaneo, G., Persiano, G., Del Sorbo, A., Cozzolino, A., Mauriello, E., Pisapia, R.: Design and implementation of a transparent cryptographic file system for UNIX. Technical Report, University of Salerno (1997)
5. Microsoft Corporation: Encrypting File System for Windows 2000. Technical report,,www.microsoft.com/windows2000/techinfo/howitworks/security/encrypt.asp (1999)
6. McDonald, A.D., Kuhn, M.G.: StegFS: A Steganographic File System for Linux. Information Hiding (1999) 462-477
7. Wright, C.P., Dave, J., Zadok, E.: Cryptographic File Systems Performance: What You Don't Know Can Hurt You. In Proceedings of Second IEEE Security In Storage Workshop (2003) 47
8. Dowdeswell, R., Ioannidis, J.: The Cryptographic Disc Driver. In Proceedings of the Annual USENIX Technical Conference, FREENIX Track (2003)
9. Kamp, P.: GBDE - GEOM-based disk encryption, In Proceddings of BSDCON03 http://phk/freebsd.dk/pubs/bsdcon-03.gbde.paper.pdf (2003)
10. Latham, A.: ppdd - practical privacy disk driver documentation, http://linux01.gwgd.de/ alatham/ppdd.html (2002)
11. Hard disk encryption with SafeGuardEasy. http://americas.utimaco.com/
12. Draft Standard for Tweakable Wide-block Encryption. IEEE Computer Society Security in Storage Working Group (SISWG) (2005)
13. Halevi, S., Rogaway., P.: A Parallelizable Enciphering mode. In Proceedings of the CT-RSA, San Francisco, CA, USA, (2004) 292-304
14. Liskov, M., Rivest, R.L., Wagner, D.: A Tweakable block ciphers, CRYPTO - 2002, Santa Barbara, California, USA (2002)
15. Hughes, J.: IEEE Standard for Encrypted Storage. IEEE Computer, Vol. 37, no. 11 (2004) 110-112
16. Naor, D.: Draft proposal for Key Backup Format for Wide block encryption. IEEE Computer Society Security in Storage Working Group (SISWG) http://siswg.org/docs/index.html (2004)
17. Oney, W.: Chapter 4: Synchronization. Programming the Microsoft Windows Driver Model. Microsoft Press (2002)
18. AES Algorithm Efficiency. http://fp.gladman.plus.com/cryptography_technology/aesr1/
19. Nbench. http://www.acnc.com/04_02_02.html
20. Katcher, J.: Postmark: A New Filesystem Benchmark. Technical Report TR3022, Network Appliance. http://www.acnc.com/04_02_01.html
21. IOMeter. http://iometer.sourceforge.net (2004)
22. Gibson, G.A., Meter, R.V.: Network attached storage architecture. Communications of the ACM, Vol 43, No 11, (2000) 37-45

# Disclosure Risk in Dynamic Two-Dimensional Contingency Tables (Extended Abstract)[*]

Haibing Lu[1], Yingjiu Li[1], and Xintao Wu[2]

[1] Singapore Management University, 80 Stamford Road, Singapore 178902
[2] University of North Carolina at Charlotte, 9201 Univ. Blvd, Charlotte, NC 28223

## 1 Introduction

Two-dimensional contingency tables are central products of many information organizations such as statistical agencies, census bureaus, and health insurance information agencies. In a contingency table, any sensitive information about individuals must be protected, while some aggregated information can be released. The disclosure risk is that the aggregated information can be used to infer some sensitive information about individuals. Since the disclosure of sensitive information may compromise privacy, confidentiality, and national interests, one needs to carefully assess the latent risk of disclosure and take effective methods to protect the data.

The problem of protecting data from disclosure risk has long been a focus in statistical database research [1,5,3]. While previous study has been primarily focused in the area of static tables, we investigate how to evaluate and limit the risk of disclosure for dynamic tables. In particular, we define two types of information disclosure based on the concern that the aggregated information released before and after each update may help a snooper to deduce certain cell values being increased or decreased. We study the relationship between dynamic disclosure and static disclosure. We also investigate the distribution of the cells that are subject to dynamic disclosure. Based on the distribution pattern, we propose an effective method to eliminate the risk of dynamic disclosure. More details about this paper is at http://www.mysmu.edu/faculty/yjli/ICISS_full.pdf.

## 2 Two-Dimensional Contingency Tables

In this section, we briefly review our previous results on two-dimensional contingency tables [4]. We consider a two-dimensional contingency table with $m$ rows and $n$ columns: $\{a_{ij} \mid 1 \leq i \leq m, 1 \leq j \leq n\}$, where each cell $a_{ij}$ is nonnegative (e.g., counts). Let $a_{+j} = \sum_{i=1}^{m} a_{ij}$ and $a_{i+} = \sum_{j=1}^{n} a_{ij}$, which we call *one-dimensional marginal totals*. It is easy to verify $\sum_{j=1}^{n} a_{+j} = \sum_{i=1}^{m} a_{i+}$, indicating that the one-dimensional marginal totals are *consistent*. We call this

---

[*] Work of Lu and Li was supported in part by SMU Research Office. Work of Wu was supported in part by USA National Science Foundation Grant IIS-0546027.

A. Bagchi and V. Atluri (Eds.): ICISS 2006, LNCS 4332, pp. 349–352, 2006.

equation the *consistency condition*. The *inference problem* asks whether the private information of cell values (i.e., $a_{ij}$) can be inferred from the public information of aggregations (i.e., $a_{i+}$ and $a_{+j}$ which satisfy the consistency condition). To solve this problem, one needs to know what the exact bounds that a data snooper can obtain for a cell value from the released marginal totals.

A value $\underline{a}_{ij}$ is said to be a *lower bound* of $a_{ij}$ if for any possible solution $\{a'_{ij}\}$ to the feasibility problem, the inequality $\underline{a}_{ij} \le a'_{ij}$ always holds. A value $\underline{a}_{ij}$ is said to be the exact lower bound of $a_{ij}$ if (i) it is a lower bound, and (ii) there exists a solution $\{a'_{ij}\}$ to the feasibility problem such that $a'_{ij} = \underline{a}_{ij}$. An upper bound or exact upper bound $\overline{a}_{ij}$ can be defined similarly.

It is known that the Fréchet bounds $[\max\{0, a_{i+} + a_{+j} - a_{++}\}, \min\{a_{i+}, a_{+j}\}]$ are the exact bounds that a snooper can obtain for each cell value $a_{ij}$ given the marginal totals in a two-dimensional contingency table [2].

Based on the exact bounds, a snooper can infer sensitive information about internal cells from different perspectives. Four types of information disclosure can be defined: (i) *Existence disclosure*: The lower bound of an internal cell is positive. (ii) *Threshold upward disclosure*: The lower bound of an internal cell is greater than a positive threshold. (iii) *Threshold downward disclosure*: The upper bound of an internal cell is less than a positive threshold. (iv) *Approximation disclosure*: The difference between the lower bound and the upper bound of an internal cell is less than a positive threshold. In [4], we studied the distribution of the cells that are subject to different types of disclosure. The following result regarding existence disclosure and threshold upward disclosure will be used in this paper.

**Theorem 1.** *Consider existence disclosure or threshold upward disclosure in a two-dimensional contingency table. The cells subject to disclosure must be in the same row or column, but not both.*

# 3   Dynamic Two-Dimensional Contingency Tables

The previous study on the four types of disclosure is targeted on *static* tables, in which the update of information is not considered. In practice, however, many organizations have been providing services for *dynamic* tables, in which the cell values and marginal totals can be updated over time. One example is that the national statistical offices have been moving from periodic releases of static tabulations to online services that provide a large number of users with dynamically-updated data sets. To limit the disclosure in such dynamic tables, one needs to evaluate not only the four types of static disclosure as reported above, but also the two types of dynamic disclosure as addressed below.

**Definition 1.** Increasing disclosure: *It is known that an internal cell value increases in update.*

Let $\{a_{ij} \mid 1 \le i \le m, 1 \le j \le n\}$ denote the table before update and $\{\tilde{a}_{ij} \mid 1 \le i \le m, 1 \le j \le n\}$ the table after update. The Fréchet bounds for $a_{ij}$ (before update) and for $\tilde{a}_{ij}$ (after update) are $[max\{0, a_{i+} + a_{+j} - a_{++}\}, min\{a_{i+}, a_{+j}\}]$ and $[max\{0, \tilde{a}_{i+} + \tilde{a}_{+j} - \tilde{a}_{++}\}, min\{\tilde{a}_{i+}, \tilde{a}_{+j}\}]$, respectively. From a snooper's point of view, $a_{ij}$ increases in update if and only if $max\{0, \tilde{a}_{i+} + \tilde{a}_{+j} - \tilde{a}_{++}\} > min\{a_{i+}, a_{+j}\}$.

**Definition 2.** Decreasing disclosure: *It is known that an internal cell value decreases in update.*

From a snooper's point of view, $a_{ij}$ decreases in update if and only if $min\{\tilde{a}_{i+}, \tilde{a}_{+j}\} < max\{0, a_{i+} + a_{+j} - a++\}$. Since increasing disclosure and decreasing disclosure are defined for dynamic tables, they are called dynamic disclosure in general. The four types of disclosure defined in the previous section are called static disclosure in contrary. Given a table's marginal totals before and after update, the dynamic disclosure can be easily evaluated by comparing the Fréchet bounds before and after update.

Dynamic disclosure is loosely related to static disclosure. There is no deterministic relationship between dynamic disclosure and static disclosure except for some special cases. These special cases are summarized into the following two statements: (i) If an updated cell is subject to increasing disclosure, it is also subject to existence disclosure. (ii) No updated cell is subject to both decreasing disclosure and threshold-upward/existence disclosure.

## 4    Disclosure Limitation

In this section, we study the distribution of the cells that are subject to dynamic disclosure. Based on the distribution pattern, we propose a disclosure limitation method.

**Theorem 2.** The updated cells subject to increasing disclosure or decreasing disclosure must be in the same row or column, but not both.

To eliminate the risk of dynamic disclosure, we propose to combine the row or column in which some cells are subject to disclosure with another row or column. First, consider the increasing disclosure. From Theorem 2, we know that at most one row or column is subject to increasing disclosure. Without loss of generality, we assume that one row is subject to disclosure. Our limitation method combines this row with *any* of the other rows. After combination, the lower bounds of any cells which are previously subject to increasing disclosure become zero. Therefore, the threat of increasing disclosure is eliminated.

Next, let us consider the decreasing disclosure. Because this disclosure is due to relatively small upper bound after update, we need to increase this upper bound such that it is no longer smaller than the corresponding lower bound before update. From Theorem 2, we know that at most one row or column is subject to decreasing disclosure. In general, however, one cannot eliminate the risk of decreasing disclosure by simply combining this row or column with any of the other rows or columns, as one can do for eliminating the risk of increasing disclosure. The reason is that the upper bound of a cell is determined by both row marginal and column marginal. To increase the upper bound, both rows and columns are to be combined.

To limit the risk of decreasing disclosure for a single cell $a_{ij}$, our method is to combine row $i$ and column $j$ with *some* of the other rows and columns. If the sum of the combined rows and the sum of the combined columns are both greater than or equal to the lower bound of the cell before update, the risk of decreasing disclosure for this cell is eliminated. In order to maximize information released, we combine as few rows and columns as possible. To achieve this goal, we combine row $i$/column $j$ with those rows/columns whose marginal totals are among the largest.

Now consider how to eliminate the risk of decreasing disclosure for the entire table. Without loss of generality, we assume that all of the cells that are subject to decreasing disclosure are in the same row $i$. Let $L$ be the largest lower bound of these cells before update. To eliminate the risk of decreasing disclosure for the entire table, our method is to combine as few rows and columns as possible such that after combination the exact upper bound of any cell is greater than or equal to $L$. To achieve this goal, we combine row $i$ with some of the other rows whose marginal totals are among the largest until the sum of the combined rows is greater than or equal to $L$. We also combine those columns in which those cells subject to decreasing disclosure reside. If the sum of the combined columns is smaller than $L$, we put more columns whose marginal totals are among the largest into the combination until the sum is greater than or equal to $L$; otherwise we may partition those columns into multiple groups and combine the columns in each group such that the sum of the combined columns in each group is greater than or equal to the largest lower bound of the "problem cells" in this group before update[1]. Note that if the sum of all rows or all columns is still less than $L$, the risk of decreasing disclosure cannot be eliminated anyway. In this extreme case, releasing the grand total $a_{++}$ itself will incur decreasing disclosure.

# References

1. N. R. Adam and J. C. Wortmann. Security-control methods for statistical databases: a comparative study. *ACM Computing Surveys*, 21(4):515–556, 1989.
2. L. H. Cox. On properties of multi-dimensional statistical tables. *Journal of Statistical Planning and Inference*, 117(2):251–273, 2003.
3. Josep Domingo-Ferrer. Advances in inference control in statistical databases: An overview. In *Inference Control in Statistical Databases*, pages 1–7, 2002.
4. H. Lu, Y. Li, and X. Wu. Disclosure analysis for two-way contingency tables. In *Privacy in Statistical Protection (PSD 2006)*, 2006.
5. L. Willenborg and T. de Walal. *Statistical Disclosure Control in Practice*. Springer Verlag, 1996.

---

[1] There is an optimization problem on how to partition the columns so that the released information is maximal. This problem can be considered as a dual problem of the Bin Packing problem.

# A Survey of Control-Flow Obfuscations

Anirban Majumdar, Clark Thomborson, and Stephen Drape

Secure Systems Group
Department of Computer Science, The University of Auckland,
Auckland, New Zealand, Private Bag 92019
{anirban,cthombor,stephen}@cs.auckland.ac.nz

**Abstract.** In this short survey, we provide an overview of obfuscation and then shift our focus to outlining various non-trivial control-flow obfuscation techniques. Along the way, we highlight two transforms having provable security properties: the dispatcher model and opaque predicates. We comment on the strength and weaknesses of these transforms and outline difficulties associated in generating generalised classes of these.

## 1 Introduction

The motivation for research in obfuscation stems from the problem of software piracy. An obfuscating transform attempts to manipulate code in such a way that it becomes unintelligible to automated program analysis tools used by malicious reverse engineers. It works by performing semantic preserving transformations which aim to increase the difficulty of automatically extracting computational logic out of the code. Depending on the size of software and the complexity of transforms, a human adversary may also find the obfuscated code difficult to comprehend; however, this is not a mandatory requirement.

The first formal definition of obfuscation was given by Collberg et al. [1,2]. They defined an obfuscator in terms of a semantic-preserving transformation function $\mathcal{T}$ which maps a program $\mathcal{P}$ to a program $\mathcal{P}'$ such that if $\mathcal{P}$ fails to terminate or terminates with an error, then $\mathcal{P}'$ may or may not terminate. Otherwise, $\mathcal{P}'$ must terminate and produce the same output as $\mathcal{P}$. Collberg et al. classified obfuscating transforms into three useful categories:

- **Layout obfuscation:** Changes or removes useful information from the intermediate language code or source code, e.g. removing debugging information, comments, and scrambling/renaming identifiers.
- **Data obfuscation:** Targets data and data structures contained in the program, e.g. changing data encoding, variable and array splitting and merging.
- **Control-flow obfuscation:** Alters the flow of control within the code, e.g. reordering statements, methods, loops and hiding the actual control flow behind irrelevant conditional statements.

This paper focuses on the latter category since the first two have been extensively investigated before [1,3].

A. Bagchi and V. Atluri (Eds.): ICISS 2006, LNCS 4332, pp. 353–356, 2006.

## 2    The Dynamic Dispatcher Model

Wang et al. [4] and Chow et al. [5] made the first commendable attempt to lay theoretical foundations for control-flow obfuscations of sequential programs. The theoretical basis in Wang et al.'s technique is the `NP-complete` argument of determining precise indirect branch target addresses of dispatchers in the presence of aliased pointers. Chow et al., on the other hand, uses `PSPACE-complete` argument of determining the reachability of a flattened program dispatcher. Control-flow flattening makes all basic blocks appear to have the same set of predecessors and successors. The actual control-flow during execution is determined dynamically by a dispatcher. Thus, the dispatcher module is the most important component in the flattened (obfuscated) program. In Wang's technique, each flattened basic block while exiting, changes the dispatcher variable through complicated pointer manipulation on some global data structure. Chow et al.'s technique, on the other hand, views the dispatcher as a deterministic finite automaton that determines the overall control-flow of the obfuscated flattened program from a state space of given transitions. However, if the state space is rather small, it will not be difficult to deobfuscate the dispatcher. For this reason, its authors expand the state space by incorporating numerous dummy states.

Since we do not have an average-case hard instance generator for either `NP-complete` or `PSPACE-complete` problems, these theoretical foundations are still incomplete. However even in their current state, these models provide some "fuzzy" confidence in the security of the real-world obfuscation systems they describe. Eventually we would hope to prove security results for some models of obfuscation. Then the only real-world attacks would be to subvert the assumptions of these models, analogous to how a provably-secure cryptographic system can never be "cracked", but may still be subverted e.g. by "social engineering" methods of password discovery.

## 3    Opaque Predicates

An opaque predicate is a conditional expression whose value is known to the obfuscator, but is difficult for an adversary to deduce statically. A predicate $\Phi$ is defined to be *opaque* at a certain program point $p$ if its outcome is only known at obfuscation time. Following Collberg et al. [2], we write $\Phi_p^F (\Phi_p^T)$ if predicate $\Phi$ always evaluates to False (True) at program point $p$ for all runs of the same program. We call such predicates *Opaquely True (False)* at program point $p$. The opaqueness property is necessary for guaranteeing the resilience of control-flow transformations.

*Algebraic predicates* have invariants that are based on well-known mathematical axioms [6]. A predicate of this class is $\Phi : [(x(x + 1)\%2 == 0]$, which is opaquely true for all integers. To an adversary having previous knowledge about the embedding of algebraic predicates in the program, static analysis attack over the obfuscated code will simply be reduced to code pattern matching. *Opaquely non-deterministic predicates* are based on some function parameter selected at random [6]. The stealthiness of these predicates will be increased greatly if their random integers are drawn from a probability distribution which resembles the values of integer constants typically observed in programs.

Collberg et al. [1] used the intractability property of pointer aliasing to construct *aliased opaque predicates*. Their construction is based on the fact that it is impossible for approximate and imprecise static analysers to detect all aliases all of the time [7]. The basic idea is to construct a dynamic data structure and maintain a set of pointers on this structure. Opaque predicates can then be designed using these pointers and their outcome can be statically determined only if precise inter-procedural alias analysis can be performed on this complicated data structure. Collberg et al.'s definition of the resilience of an opaque predicate does not take into account dynamic analysis attacks. If an attacker can monitor the heap, registers, etc. during execution, then it may be revealed that a given predicate always evaluates to true or false.

Palsberg et al. [8] observed that in order to protect against a dynamic debugging attack, the obfuscator needs to avoid a predicate from evaluating to the same result. They proposed using *dynamically opaque predicates*, which are a family of correlated predicates which all evaluate to the same result in any given run, but in different runs they may evaluate to different results. It is an open problem to construct correlated dynamic opaque predicates and will be part of our future research. These predicates could have the following structure:

$$\texttt{if } (\varPhi_1) \ S_1 \ ;$$
$$\texttt{if } (\neg\varPhi_2) \ S_1' \ ;$$

where $S_1$ and $S_1'$ are variant versions of the same code block which are difficult to merge. A possible attack for this transformation is to prove that $S_1 \equiv S_1'$ and $\varPhi_1 \Leftrightarrow \varPhi_2$. If this is the case, then this obfuscated structure may be replaced by $S_1$ under certain conditions (such as $S_1$ does not change the value of $\neg\varPhi_2$).

In [9], Majumdar and Thomborson suggested creating *temporally unstable opaque predicates* in a distributed environment of concurrently executing mobile agents from respective copies of aliased data structure values. A temporally unstable opaque predicate can be evaluated at multiple times at different program points during a single program execution such that the values observed to be taken by this predicate are not identical. There are a couple of advantages of making opaque predicates temporally unstable. The first one concerns its reusability; one predicate can be reused multiple times to obfuscate different control flows. Secondly, they are also resilient against static analysis attacks since their values depend on dynamically changing message communication patterns between participating agents. In addition to their resilience against static analysis attacks, temporally unstable opaque predicates are also difficult to attack by dynamic monitoring. For mounting a dynamic attack, the authors assumed an adversary capable of monitoring local states of individual agents through some malicious sniffer agent. Even in this adversarial model, it was argued, using the results of Chase and Garg [10], that constructing a global state from these partially observed agent local states is a computationally intractable problem.

# 4    Discussion and Future Work

In this brief survey, we highlighted the dispatcher model and opaque predicates for control-flow obfuscation. We also noted that obfuscatory strength cannot be guaranteed, in part because it is not known how to arbitrarily generate hard problem instances. Furthermore, the techniques which use hard complexity results as their theoretical basis are "wrong-way" reductions, from a complexity-theoretic perspective. These reductions explain why we should not expect to have exact static analysis tools that will work on all programs, however they do not prove the hardness of deobfuscating any specific output of any specific obfuscation system. Even so, an obfuscation system will have great practical importance if it resists all known attacks for at least as long as it would take to replace an obfuscated program by a differently-obfuscated program.

# References

1.  Collberg, C., Thomborson, C., and Low, D.: A Taxonomy of Obfuscating Transformations. Technical Report#148. 36 pp. Department of Computer Science, The University of Auckland, New Zealand. 1997.
2.  Collberg, C., Thomborson, C., and Low, D.: Manufacturing Cheap, Resilient, and Stealthy Opaque Constructs. In Proceedings of 1998 ACM SIGPLAN-SIGACT Symposium on Principles of Programming Languages (POPL'98). Pages 184-196. 1998.
3.  Drape, S.: Obfuscation of Abstract Data Types. DPhil thesis. Computing Laboratory. Oxford University. England. 2004.
4.  Wang, C., Hill, J., Knight, J.C., and Davidson, J.W.: Protection of software-based survivability mechanisms. In Proceedings of the 2001 conference on Dependable Systems and Networks. IEEE Computer Society. Pages 193-202. 2001.
5.  Chow, S., Gu, Y., Johnson, H., and Zakharov, V.A.: An Approach to the Obfuscation of Control-Flow of Sequential Computer Programs. In the proceedings of $4^{th}$ International Conference on Information Security, LNCS Volume 2200. Pages 144-155. Springer-Verlag. Malaga, Spain. 2001.
6.  Venkatraj, A.: Program Obfuscation. MS Thesis. Department of Computer Science, University of Arizona. 2003.
7.  Horwitz, S.: Precise Flow-insensitive may-alias in NP-hard. In ACM Transactions on Programming Languages and Systems (TOPLAS), Vol. 19 No. 1. Pages 1-6. 1997.
8.  Palsberg, J., Krishnaswamy, S., Kwon, M., Ma, D., Shao, Q., and Zhang, Y.: Experience with software watermarking. In Proceedings of $16^{th}$ IEEE Annual Computer Security Applications Conference (ACSAC'00). IEEE Press. p308. New Orleans, LA, USA. 2000.
9.  Majumdar, A. and Thomborson, C.: Manufacturing Opaque Predicates in Distributed Systems for Code Obfuscation. In Proceedings of the $29^{th}$ Australasian Computer Science Conference (ACSC'06). Pages 187-196. ACM Digital Library. Hobart, Australia. 2006.
10. Chase, C. and Garg, V.K.: Detection of global predicates: Techniques and their limitations. In the Journal of Distributed Computing, Volume 11, Issue 4. Pages 191-201. Springer-Verlag. 1995.

# Filtering Out Unfair Recommendations for Trust Model in Ubiquitous Environments

Weiwei Yuan[1], Donghai Guan[1], Sungyoung Lee[1], Young-Koo Lee[1,*],
and Heejo Lee[2]

[1] Department of Computer Engineering, Kyung Hee University, Korea
[2] Department of Computer Science and Engineering, Korea University

**Abstract.** This paper presents a novel context-based approach to filter
out unfair recommendations for trust model in ubiquitous environments.
Context is used in our approach to analyze the user's activity, state and
intention. Incremental learning based neural network is used to dispose
the context in order to find doubtful recommendations. This approach
has distinct advantages when dealing with randomly given irresponsible
recommendations, individual unfair recommendations as well as unfair
recommendations flooding.

## 1 Introduction

The basis for the trust model to make decision on unfamiliar service requesters
are the recommendations given by recommenders who have past interaction
history with the requesters. However, in the large-scale, open, dynamic and
distributed ubiquitous environments, there may possibly exist numerous self-
interested recommenders who give unfair recommendations to maximize their
own gains (perhaps at the cost of others). Therefore, finding ways to avoid or reduce the influence of unfair recommendations from self-interested recommenders
is a fundamental problem for trust model in ubiquitous environments.

The possible scenarios for unfair recommendations are: (1) Individual Unfair
Recommendation: honest recommender gives inaccurate recommendation due to
incorrect observation, or the recommender maliciously gives unfair recommendation (the recommender may be a malicious node or a node which acted honest
but suddenly gives unfair recommendation due to his own benefits (called Inside Job)). (2) Unfair Recommendations Flooding: a number of recommenders
collude to give unfair recommendations (more than 50% of total recommendations), which causes the flooding of unfair recommendations. The flooding
may be caused by malicious nodes or those who acted honest (called Inside
Job Flooding). (3) Randomly Given Recommendation: the recommender gives
random recommendation due to the lack of responsibility.

There are mainly three methods had been proposed for filtering out unfair
recommendations in previous works. One is to use polling method, e.g. in [1],
the authors used basic polling as well as enhanced polling. The enhanced polling

---

* Corresponding author.

A. Bagchi and V. Atluri (Eds.): ICISS 2006, LNCS 4332, pp. 357–360, 2006.

differs from basic polling by requesting voters to provide their servent_id to prevent a single malicious user to create multiple recommendations. Another method is to give weighted value to each recommender (also called reputation based method) [2], [3]. This method regards recommendations given by low reputation recommenders as malicious. The third method is to use the combination of filters [4]. It suggests that cluster filtering is suitable to reduce the effect of unfairly high recommendations and frequency filtering can guarantee the calculation of trust not be influenced by the unfair recommendations flooding. However, these methods take at least one of the following assumptions, which makes them disable to deal all the unfair recommendations scenarios: (1) recommendations provided by different recommenders on a service requester will follow more or less the same probability distribution, (2) the higher rank the recommender has, the more authority his recommendation will have. E.g., it is impossible to filter out Inside Job and Inside Job Flooding using reputation based method since it takes assumption (2).

This paper introduces a novel context-based approach using incremental learning algorithm to deal with the possible unfair recommendation scenarios. Instead of taking the assumptions of previous works, context is used in our approach to analyze the user's activity, state and intention. The learning of context is incrementally increased by a Cascade-Correlation architecture neural network.

## 2   The Proposed Approach

Trust is subjective since it is based on each user's own understanding. Hence it is relatively easy for the malicious recommender to pretend honest and for the honest recommender to be misunderstood as malicious because of the different understandings, which makes it difficult to differentiate between the unfair and fair recommendations. Our key idea for the solution is that: recommenders may give different recommendations due to their different understandings, however, one recommender will follow the rule of himself, i.e., one recommender usually gives similar recommendations in similar context. In case one recommender gives exceptional recommendations compared with his own previous ones in similar context, the reason lies in two aspects. One is that this recommendation is a mischievous one. The other is that the recommender's rule on recommendation giving has changed, e.g. the recommender now only gives positive recommendation to requesters whose past interaction with him is more than 80% successful in stead of 60%.

We use incremental learning based neural network, the Cascade-Correlation architecture in particular, to learn each recommender's rule on recommendation giving since the acquisition of a representative training data for the rule is time consuming and the rule is also possible to dynamically change from time to time. Cascade-Correlation is useful for incremental learning, in which new information is added to an already-trained network. It begins with minimal network, then automatically trains and adds new hidden units one by one, creating a multilayer structure [5]. Fig. 1 gives the process of training Cascade-Correlation. In

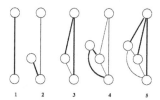

**Fig. 1.** Training of Cascade-Correlation Architecture

1, we train weights from input to output. In 2, we add a candidate unit and train its weights to maximize the correlation with the error. In 3, we retrain the output layer. We train the input weights for another hidden unit in 4. Output layer is retrained in 5, etc. The usage of Cascade-Correlation architecture has several advantages: it learns quickly; the network determines its own size and topology; it retains the structures it has built even if the training set changes.

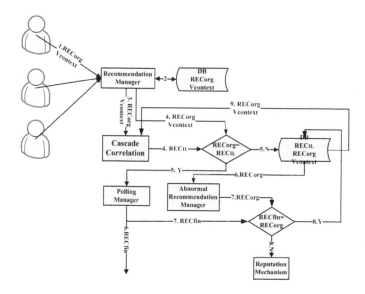

**Fig. 2.** Architecture for Filtering out Unfair Recommendations

We use the architecture shown in Fig. 2 to filter out the unfair recommendations. Recommendation Manager first collects recommendations ($REC_{org}$) from all recommenders, along with the context value $V_{context}$ under which recommendations were given. For each recommender, the input of Cascade-Correlation architecture is $V_{context}$ and the output is $REC_{IL}$, which is the recommendation that one recommender will give due to his past behavior when given $V_{context}$. If $REC_{org}=REC_{IL}$, it means that the recommender gives the same recommendation as previous behavior. In this case, we regard $REC_{com}$ as a reliable recommendation and use basic voting mechanism to calculate the final recommendation $REC_{fin}$. Otherwise if $REC_{org} \neq REC_{IL}$, $REC_{org}$ is regarded as a doubtful recommendation. In this case, if $REC_{org} \neq REC_{fin}$, we regard $REC_{org}$ as mischievous or incorrect. Otherwise, if $REC_{org} = REC_{fin}$, the possible situations are: (1) the recommender's rule on recommendation giving has changed, (2) the currently neural network is not enough to reflect the recommender's rule on recommendation giving since the Cascade-Correlation architecture begins with a minimal network and the knowledge on the recommender's rule is incrementally increased. In this case, $V_{context}$ as well as $REC_{org}$ will be given back as retrain data to the Cascade-Correlation architecture.

## 3    Conclusions

In this paper we propose a robust trust model for ubiquitous environments, in which a context-based approach is used to filter out unfair recommendations. The learning of the context is based on incremental learning neural network. The filtered out recommendations may be the intended unfair recommendations as well as the mis-observation by the recommenders. Since our approach concentrates on the doubtful behaviors of each entity, it has special advantages when dealing with inside job, which is lack of considerations in previous works. In the future work, we plan to simulate our proposed method based on CAMUS [6] middleware. We also plan to add risk analysis in our context-based trust model. We believe that to filter out unfair recommendations by using context-based trust model presents a promising path for the future research.

**Acknowledgements.** This research is supported by the Ubiquitous Computing and Network (UCN) Project, the Ministry of Information and Communication (MIC) 21st Century Frontier R&D Program in Korea.

## References

1. F. Cornelli, E. Damiani, S.D.C.D. Vimercati: Choosing Reputable Servants in a P2P Networks. ACM WWW2002, USA.
2. BP. Xu, J. Gao, H. Guo: Rating Reputation: a necessary consideration in reputation mechanism. Proceedings of 2005 International Conference on Machine Learning and Cybernetics.
3. W. Song, V. V. Phoha, X. Xu: An adaptive recommendation trust model in multi-agent system. IEEE/WIC/ACM IAT'04.
4. C. Dellarocas: Building trust online: the design of robust reputation reporting mechanisms for online trading communities. A combined perspective on digital era, Idea Book Publishing (2004).
5. S.E. Fahlman, C. Lebiere: The Cascade-Correlation Learning Architecture. ATechnical Report CMU-CS-90-100, School of Computer Science, Carnegie Mellon University.
6. H.Q. Ngo, A. Shehzad, S.L. Kiani, M. Riaz, K. A. Ngoc, S.Y. Lee: Developing Context-aware Ubiquitous Computing Systems with a Unified Middleware Frame-Work. EUC2004.

# Secure Itineraries Framework for Mobile Agent Systems

Rajwinder Singh, Navdeep Kaur, and A.K. Sarje

Department of Electronics and Computer Engineering,
Indian Institute of Technology Roorkee, Roorkee, India
{rwsingh,nrwsingh}@yahoo.com

**Abstract.** Mobile agent system raises significant security concerns and requires a thorough security framework, with a wide range of strategies and mechanisms, for the protection of both agents and agent hosts, against possibly malicious behavior. Researchers have identi?ed several security attacks. In general, the behavior of mobile agents is often prescribed by the set of tasks represented in an itinerary. The design and implementation of an itinerary can be a complex, time intensive task. A mobile agent running on a host may attacks, if the host is malicious. The attacks may be on the agent's static data, its collected information (dynamic data) and its itinerary. Hence itineraries must be made secure, in order to get secure agent behavior. In this paper, we propose the development of protocols, which provide security and robustness to different kinds of agent itineraries and present a comparison of the performance of these protocols with some existing ones.

**Keywords:** Itineraries, mobile agent security, serial itinerary, parallel itinerary.

## 1 Introduction

Itineraries [1] may be viewed as a specification of agent movement. Itineraries typically consist of a list of tasks to be executed sequentially and the locations where the tasks are to be performed. Most mobile agent systems do not talk of securing agent itineraries. Systems which discuss itinerary-based security are given in [2,3]. However, it is not clear how an agent behaves if an intended host is unreachable and how the output of a clone agent is made secure when it is received back at the launcher host. In this paper, we focus on the issue of efficiently dispatching mobile agents, while protecting their itineraries. We present a model which supports different itinerary architectures and is built on Secure Mobile Agent Platform System (SMAPS). The model allows efficient dispatching of a large number of mobile agents in parallel. It is also robust in the sense that an agent can be dispatched to any of the listed hosts, without time-consuming repeated tries to temporarily unreachable hosts. The rest of the paper is organized as follows. Section 2 presents concept of agent mobility; section 3 gives our security model and presents the proposed security protocols.

A. Bagchi and V. Atluri (Eds.): ICISS 2006, LNCS 4332, pp. 361–364, 2006.

Section 4 discusses practical experiments carried out in order to compare their performance with some existing protocols. Conclusion is given in section 5.

## 2    Agent Mobility

In SMAPS, the following itineraries are possible: (a) Serial Itinerary: - A multi-hop agent travels from node to node on the network and the result is sent back to the agent launcher by the last host in the itinerary. (b) Virtual Serial Itinerary: - In this model, an agent host works like a master host and user authentication is required only at this host. The master host deputes a master agent to create clones of the received agent to work as worker agents and dispatches these worker agents, one after another, to remote hosts in the itinerary. The result obtained after completion from each host, are recorded separately and sent to the master agent. The agent in this case is a 2-hop agent. (c) Parallel Itinerary: - In this model, the master host dispatches all of them (worker agents) to remote hosts together, in parallel. After dispatching all the worker agents, the master agent is ready to receive results from remote hosts.

## 3    Proposed Security Model

An itinerary is composed of different kinds of itinerary elements. The basic form of an itinerary element is

$$I_i = (H_0, H_{i-2}, H_{i-2}, H_i, H_{i+1}, H_{1+2}, O_i, C_i, t) \tag{1}$$

Where $H_i$ is the IP address of the agent launcher, $H_{i-2}$ and $H_{i-1}$ are the IP addresses of the previous host, $H_1$ is host being visited, $O_i$ represents the designated object for host, $C_i$ represents classes, which are used for executing the method and $t$ is timestamp to identify the agent's journey and prevent replay attack.

### 3.1    Protocol for Increasing Robustness of a Simple Serial Itinerary

In the model given at [3] nested encryption has been used to protect serial itineraries. We have modified this by improving on robustness by the following sequence of statements shown in (1). Once the protocol has been employed over the complete itinerary, a protected itinerary $I_0$ is obtained where

$$I_0 = \begin{bmatrix} E_{PH_1}(S_O(H_0, -, H_0, H_1, H_2, H_3, C_1, O_1, t)) \\ E_{PH_2}(S_O(H_0, H_0, H_1, H_2, H_3, H_4, O_2, C_2, t)) \\ E_{PH_3}(S_O(H_0, H_1, H_2, H_3, H_4, H_5, O_3, C_3, t)) \\ E_{PH_3}(S_O(H_0, H_{n-2}, H_{n-1}, H_n, -, O_n, C_n, t)) \end{bmatrix} \tag{2}$$

In our model, the agent's methods and host addresses are sealed together.

## 3.2 Protocol for Incorporating Both Security and Robustness in a Simple Serial Itinerary

Unfortunately, Equation (2) is only secure if the hosts involved do not compete against one another. This problem can be overcome by using one trusted host. This trusted host executes a small code for re-injecting the agent in the predefined itinerary, when an unreachable host is found. In this model an itinerary element can be defined as

$$I_i = (H_0, H_{i-1}, H_i, H_{i+1}, H_{RH}, Oi, C_i, t) \tag{3}$$

Where $H_{RH}$ represents the IP address of the trusted host.

The following are the steps of the protocol that has been developed for sealing an n-element itinerary of an agent shown in (3).

1. ForI=1,n, repeat thru (a) - (b) a. The agent owner signs the itinerary element. (b) The owner encrypts the signed itinerary element with the public key of the host.

2. The agent owner signed and sealed by public key of the trusted host and re-injects the agent in the itinerary. Once the protocol has been employed over the itinerary, a protected itinerary $I_0$ is obtained, as follows:

$$I_0 = \begin{bmatrix} E_{P_{RH}}(S_O((H_0, H_1, O_{RH}, C_{RH}, t)) \\ E_{PH_1}(S_O(H_0, H_0, H_1, H_2, H_{RH}, O_1, C_1, t)) \\ E_{PH_2}(S_O(H_0, H_1, H_2, H_3, H_{RH}, O_2, C_2, t)) \\ E_{PH_n}(S_O(H_0, H_{n-1}, H_{RH}, H_{RH}, O_n, C_n, t)) \end{bmatrix} \tag{4}$$

Compared to the first protocol, we have used just one additional method and one trusted host to provide a more robust itinerary.

## 3.3 Protocol for Secure and Robust Complex Serial Itinerary

This protocol takes care of the security of sub-itinerary elements in an itinerary. The serial itinerary element with sub itinerary elements can be defined by

$$I_i = (H_0, H_{i-1}, H_i, H_{i+1}, H_{RH}, Oi, C_i, SI_{im}, t) \tag{5}$$

Where $SI_{im}$ represents the set of m sub- itinerary elements, m $>= 0$. The itinerary elements $I_i$ will be executed in serial, but their sub-itinerary elements can be executed in either virtual serial or parallel manner.

1. For I=1,n repeat thru (3)
2. Get the number of elements m in the sub-itinerary element $I_i$.(a) For j = I, m . (i) The agent owner signs the sub itinerary element. (j) The agent owner encrypts the signed element in (i) with the public key of the host $h_j$.(b) Go to (a)
3. On applying the protocol in section (2a)-2(b) on the elements of the sub itinerary, we get a protected sub itinerary $ES_s$.
4. The agent owner signs itinerary element $I_i$ with its signed and sealed sub itinerary elements and then agent owner encrypts the signed itinerary element

with the public key of the host $H_i$. A protected itinerary $I_0$ is obtained after employed the protocol, where

$$
I_0 = \begin{bmatrix} E_{P_{RH}}(S_O((H_0, H_L, O_{RH}, C_{RH}, t)) \\ E_{PH_1}(S_O(H_0, H_0, H_1, H_2, H_{RH}, O_1, C_1, ES_1, t)) \\ E_{PH_n}(S_O(H_0, H_{n-1}, H_{RH}, H_{RH}, O_n, C_n, ES_1, t)) \end{bmatrix} \tag{6}
$$

## 4  Performance Analyses and Comparison

We have physically compared both models to generate secure itineraries for different agent code and itinerary sizes. Due to space limitation, we only present the summary of results. The following observations can be drawn from the results:

1. The Mir model runs out of memory for very small itinerary sizes in each case.
2. The time taken to encrypt the itinerary, in each case, is non-linear for the Joan Mir model and approximately linear for ours.
3. The amount of time taken by the Joan Mir model is up to 40 times more than ours.
4. The amount of memory required is also about 4 times more for the Joan Mir model.

## 5  Conclusion

In this paper we have introduced three protocols to protect agents roaming on the network. The first approach is not robust when hosts are unreachable. We have modified it to improve its performance and robustness. This is the first protocol. Unfortunately, this introduces security problems when hosts collude and is useful only when there is no competition between them. Hence we introduced a second protocol, which provides both security and robustness. The third protocol is provided for complex serial itineraries and their sub-itinerary with parallel/virtual serial itinerary elements. It improves the performance of the system by executing the agent's methods in parallel. The protocols presented in this paper are likely to have wide applications in commerce and business systems e.g., in an e-banking application.

## References

1. Borrell, J., Robles, S., Serra, J., Riera, A.: Securing the Itinerary of Mobile Agents through a Non-Repudiation Protocol. IEEE International Carnahan Conference on Security Technology (1999) 461-464
2. Westhoff, D., Schneider, M., Unger, C., Kenderali, F.: "Methods for Protecting a Mobile Agent's Route. 2nd International Information Security Workshop. LNCS, Vol.1729, Springer-Verlag, Berlin Heidelberg New York (1999) 57-71
3. Mir, J., Borrell, J.: Protecting General Flexible Itineraries of Mobile Agents. Information Security and Cryptography. LNCS, Vol.2288, Springer Verlag (2002)

# Malafide Intension Based Detection of Privacy Violation in Information System

Shyam K. Gupta[1], Vikram Goyal[1], and Anand Gupta[2]

[1] Department of Computer Science and Engineering, IIT Delhi
Hauz Khas, New Delhi-16
{skg,vkgoyal}@cse.iitd.ernet.in
[2] Dept. of Comp. Sci. and Engg. N.S.I.T. Delhi, Sector-3, Dwarka,
New Delhi
anand@coe.nsit.ac.in

**Abstract.** In the past few years there has been an increased focus on privacy issues for Information Systems. This has resulted in concerted systematic work focused on regulations, tools and enforcement. Despite this, privacy violations still do take place. Therefore there is an increased need to develop efficient methods to detect privacy violations. After a privacy violation has taken place, the post-event diagnostics should make use of any post-event information which might be available. This information (malafide intention) might play a decisive role in determining violations. In this paper we propose one such framework which makes use of malafide intentions. The framework is based on the hypothesis that any intrusion/unauthorized access has a malafide intention always associated with it and is available in a post-event scenario. We hereby propose that by analyzing the privacy policies and the available malafide intention, it is possible to detect probable privacy violations.

## 1 Introduction

Privacy is of paramount importance in e-commerce, banking and plethora of web services. Many authors have proposed privacy policies[1,2,3]. Such policies include Purpose amongst many other parameters. Any access to the information system requires a bonafide purpose. For example, address might be requested for the purpose of delivery to a Courier agency. In-spite of lot being done towards providing robust privacy[2,3,4], there has been a steady rise in breach of privacy. These intrusions vary in sophistication which depends on factors like (1) number of users involved in the intrusion (single user/multiple users), (2) queries used (single query/multiple queries) and (3) the nature of information retrieved (inferred/explicit).

Therefore there is requirement of a framework which can identify probable privacy violations. The framework will help (a) to narrow down upon possible perpetrators, (b) to take actions against them if their complicity in intrusion is confirmed and (c) to locate the loop-holes in the privacy or access control policy which resulted in the breach.

We propose a framework of MalDViP (**Mal**afide Intention based **D**etection of **Viol**ation in **P**rivacy) system which can detect the malafide accesses for a given Malafide Intention and attack configuration. The framework is based on the hypothesis which states "A malafide intention is always associated with a privacy violation attack and

A. Bagchi and V. Atluri (Eds.): ICISS 2006, LNCS 4332, pp. 365–368, 2006.

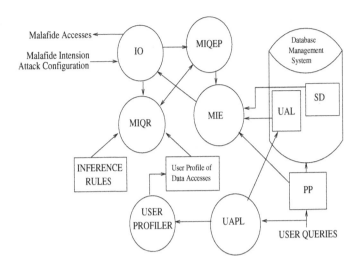

**Fig. 1.** Abstract Design of MalDViP system

it is available for post-event forensics" [4]. In this paper we consider a "single user, multiple queries and explicit access" attack configuration.

### 1.1 Assumptions

The following assumptions have been made in this paper:

1. A privacy policy is being enforced. Consequently, privacy violations occur either through misuse of privileges by a valid/authorized user or leakage of information due to hacking of the system by an unauthorized person masquerading as an authorized user. (This assumption is needed to limit the scope of the problem of detection of privacy violation).
2. The system does not deal with detection of privacy violation either by revealing of information through deduction method as discussed in statistical database literature [5] or by covert channel.
3. The mode of attack is "single user-identity, multiple queries, and explicit access".

### 1.2 Paper Layout

The rest of the paper is organized as follows: Section 2 describes the overview of MalD-ViP system (architecture, structures and modules). Section 3 provides algorithm for probable privacy violating accesses. Conclusion of the paper is described in section 4.

## 2 MalDViP System Modules and Structures

Figure 1 illustrates the MalDViP framework which tries to achieve such characteristics. The administrator/auditor of the MalDViP system is the only person who can interact with the Input-Output module of MalDViP system. The administrator specifies the

*Malafide Intention* and *Attack Configuration* and provides them as input to the Input-Output (IO) module. The IO module acts as the fronted to the MalDViP system. It parses the MI and provides it to MIQR (Malafide Intention Query Rewriter)[4]. The MIQR then rewrites the queries based on IR (inference rules) and User Profile. The rewritten query is then passed on to MIQEP (Malafide Intention Queries Execution Planner). The MIQEP schedules the queries for execution and passes the queries to the MIE (Malafide Intention Executor). MIE gets the query executed and returns the result to IO. For the execution of query MIE uses other modules like UAL (User Access Log), SD (Snapshot Database), PP (Privacy Policy), and UAPL (User Accesses Parser and Logger). The UAL stores all the information logged by UAPL. The structure for log table is also discussed in [2,3]. The SD provides the snapshot of database at any particular instant and outputs the actual contents accessed by the user query. It is similar to the backlog database discussed in [2]. Every access made to the information system is filtered through PP (Privacy Policy). The UALP collects the authorized user accesses from the application layer along with the purpose of each access, user-id and role-id of each access. It then parses the queries to attributes, tables names and conditional expression and logs them all with a time-stamp into UAL. The output of the system is a set of accesses (malafide accesses) set for each user.

## 3   MalDViP Algorithm

The MIE module determines the malafide accesses from the UAL structure. The input to this module is MI's global clauses, block queries, an Attack Configuration, and a SD. The output of this module is the set of users with their malafide accesses. Mathematically this module can be written as a function

$$f(Malafide\ Information, UAL, SD, PP) = U \times 2^{Q_i}$$

where $U$ is set of users and $Q_i$ is the set of accesses of respective user and the Malafide Information is a structure which has as its members (i) the global clauses and (ii) target data specification of MI [4].

An user query in UAL has two data values (i) actual data accessed by the query (which is a set of tuples) (ii) the query itself in the form of a character string (we

---

**Algorithm 1.** Generate-Malafide-Accesses

Input: PP $Pl$, Malafide Information $M$, SD $BD$, UAL $QL$

Output: A list of malafide users with their set of malafide accesses set

1: Generation of Indexing keys i.e. Role-Purpose pairs by analysis of Malafide Information $M$ specification and Privacy Policy $Pl$. Apply these keys to $QL$ to get user accesses which are used in next step.

2: $Candidate - Accesses \leftarrow$ Test for data attributes overlapping and condition overlapping between target data specified in $M$ and User Accesses in $QL$.

3: Perform dynamic test over the $Candidate - Accesses$ of each user individually which checks for actual data(obtained from $BD$) overlapping with the target data and finds out users who have taken the threshold amount of target data specified in $M$. Output the accesses passing this test as malafide accesses.

---

term it as query expression). The proposed algorithm 1 can be viewed as composed of two phases i.e. static analysis followed by dynamic analysis. In static analysis various string matching operations are performed over the query expression to eliminate non-suspicious queries. In the dynamic analysis the query result is analyzed. The dynamic analysis is extremely expensive therefore must be avoided on non-suspicious accesses.

First two steps of the algorithm 1 perform static analysis since it does not use data accessed by a query. The third step is dynamic testing and uses the actual data accessed by the user.

## 4   Conclusion

In this paper we have proposed a framework called MalDViP which detects probable privacy violations using malafide intentions. The framework is based on the hypothesis that there is always a malafide intention associated with a privacy violation and is available in post-event scenario. Our framework uses a syntax very similar to SQL for malafide intention and is rich enough to incorporate additional information. The focus of the paper is presentation of the framework. Further optimizations will follow later. The algorithm proposed by us uses privacy policies for malafide accesses determination. Though the algorithm deals with "single user identity, multiple queries and explicit accesses" scenario, the framework supports other attack configurations too.

## Acknowledgments

We thank Department of Information Technology, Govt. of India for funding the project "Design and Development of Malafide Intention based Privacy Violation Detection".

## References

1. Agrawal, R., Kiernan, J., Srikant, R., Xu, Y.: Hippocratic databases. In: Proceedings of the 28th VLDB Conference, Hong Kong, China (2002)
2. Agrawal, R., Bayardo, R., Faloutsos, C., Kiernan, J., Rantzau, R., Srikant, R.: Auditing Compliance with a Hippocratic Database. In: Proceedings of the 30th VLDB Conference, Toronto, Canada (2004)
3. LeFevre, K., Agrawal, R., Ercegovac, V., Ramakrishnan, R., Xu, Y., DeWitt, D.: Limiting disclosure in Hippocratic databases. In: 30th Internaltional Conference on Very Large Data Bases, Toronto, Canada (2004)
4. Goyal, V., Gupta, S.K., Saxena, S., Chawala, S., Gupta, A.: Query Rewriting for Detection of Privacy Violation through Inferencing. In: International Conference on Privacy, Security and Trust, Oct30-Nov1, 2006. (2006)
5. Adam, N., Wortman, J.: Security-control methods for statistical databases. ACM Computing Surveys **21(4)** (Dec 1989) 515–556

# Design and Development of Malafide Intension Based Privacy Violation Detection System (An Ongoing Research Report)

Shyam K. Gupta[1], Vikram Goyal[1], Bholi Patra[1], Sankalp Dubey[1], and Anand Gupta[2]

[1] Department of Computer Science and Engineering, IIT Delhi
Hauz Khas, New Delhi-16
{skg,vkgoyal}@cse.iitd.ernet.in, bholi.patra@yahoo.com,
csy030006@cse.iitd.ernet.in
[2] Dept. of Comp. Sci. and Engg. N.S.I.T. Delhi, Sector-3, Dwarka,
New Delhi
anand@coe.nsit.ac.in

**Abstract.** In the past few years there has been an increased focus on privacy issues for Information Systems which has resulted in concerted systematic work focused on regulations, tools and enforcement. Despite this, privacy violations still do take place. Therefore there is an increased need to develop efficient methods to detect privacy violations. We propose one such framework which uses malafide intensions (post-event information) and privacy policy to detect probable privacy violations. The framework is based on the hypothesis that every privacy violation has a malafide intension associated with it which is available in a post-event scenario.

## 1 Introduction

Various privacy policies[1,2] have been proposed to take care of privacy issues. These policies authorize access to the information system on the basis of some bonafide purpose. For example, address might be requested for the purpose of delivery to a Courier agency. In-spite of lot being done towards providing robust privacy[3,4,1,2], there has been a steady rise in breach of privacy[5,6,7]. These intrusions vary in sophistication depending on (1) number of users, (2) queries used and (3) the retrieval method. Therefore we need a framework that can identify probable privacy violations and helps in (a) reducing possible perpetrators, (b) taking action against them and (c) locating loop-holes in the privacy or access control policy which resulted in the breach.

We have developed a framework of MalDViP (**Mal**afide Intension based **D**etection of **Vi**olation in **P**rivacy) system which can detect the probable privacy violations (malafide accesses) for a given Malafide Intension and Attack Configuration (specifies sophistication level parameters). The framework's hypothesis is: "A malafide intension is always associated with a privacy violation attack and it can be used for post-event forensics".

A. Bagchi and V. Atluri (Eds.): ICISS 2006, LNCS 4332, pp. 369–372, 2006.

## 2   Architecture

We have identified the following characteristics for an ideal privacy violation detection system:

1. **Interactive.** The system should be interactive enough so that the administrator can retrieve the data of his interest.
2. **Fast and Precise.** The system should output the correct result in acceptable time.
3. **Non-Disruptive.** The system should not disturb the normal working of the information system.
4. **Fine Granularity.** The user of the system should be able to audit for the smallest unit of data i.e. even for a single cell.
5. **Usability.** The system should provide the interface to the user to provide the specification of malafide intension easily and precisely.

The framework makes the following assumptions:

1. A privacy policy is being enforced. Privacy violations occur either through misuse of privilege or masquerading as an authorized user.
2. The system does not deal with detection of privacy violation by covert channel[8].

Malafide Intension is central to the MalDViP system. Malafide Intension is essentially the intension of the intruder. Since our research limits itself to information leakage, the Malafide Intension here is the target data sought by the intruder. In our framework, malafide intension is used for privacy violation detection in a post event scenario. Therefore we can associate other information like bonafide purpose of the usage, duration, query patterns etc. Therefore we have given a syntax for specification of malafide intension which can capture all the above information. The semantics is simple, precise, unambiguous and flexible.

Figure 1 illustrates the MalDViP framework which tries to achieve such characteristics. The administrator/auditor of the MalDViP system is the only person who can

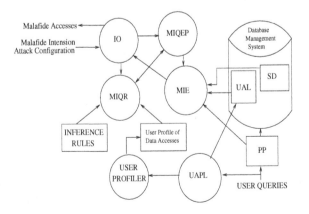

**Fig. 1.** Abstract Design of MalDViP system

interact with the Input-Output module of MalDViP system. The administrator specifies the *Malafide Intension* and *Attack Configuration* and provides them as input to the Input-Output (IO) module. The IO module acts as the frontend to the MalDViP system. It parses the MI and provides it to MIQR (Malafide Intension Query Rewrote). The MIQR then rewrites the queries based on IR (inference rules) and User Profile. The rewritten query is then passed on to MIQEP (Malafide Intension Queries Execution Planner). The MIQEP schedules the queries for execution and passes the queries to the MIE (Malafide Intension Executor). MIE gets the query executed and returns the result to IO. For the execution of query MIE uses other modules like UAL (User Access Log), SD (Snapshot Database), PP (Privacy Policy), and UAPL (User Accesses Parser and Logger). The UAL stores all the information logged by UAPL. The structure for log table is also discussed in [9,10,11]. The SD provides the snapshot of database at any particular instant and outputs the actual contents accessed by the user query. It is similar to the backlog database discussed in [9]. Every access made to the information system is filtered through PP (Privacy Policy). The UALP collects the authorized user accesses from the application layer along with the purpose of each access, user-id and role-id of each access. It then parses the queries to attributes, tables names and conditional expression and logs them all with a time-stamp into UAL.

The output of the system is a set of accesses (malafide accesses) set for each user.

## 3   Our Contribution

We have given a framework (MalDViP) which when given a Malafide Intension specification as an input, can determine the past accesses of individuals who have accessed the specific information (data specified in the Malafide Intension) during a particular duration (time-interval specified in Malafide Intension).

As a part of building of framework, we have identified the information which can aid in determining privacy violations i.e. duration, bonafide purposes, query pattern, volume of information etc. We have given a syntax for describing the Malafide Intension. The syntax is simple, unambiguous and flexible.

We have also developed algorithms for the following intrusion sophistications:

1. Single User, Multiple Queries without inferencing.
2. Single User, Multiple Queries with inferencing.

We have developed a testbed for testing our MalDViP system.

## 4   Conclusion and Future Work

In this paper we have proposed a framework called MalDViP which detects probable privacy violations using malafide intensions. The framework is based on the hypothesis that there is always a malafide intension associated with a privacy violation and is available in post-event scenario. Our framework uses a syntax very similar to SQL and is rich enough to incorporate additional information.

The algorithm proposed by us uses privacy policies for malafide accesses determination. Though the algorithm deals with "single user identity, multiple queries and explicit accesses" scenario, the framework supports other attack configurations too.

Future work includes incorporation of statistical and data-mining techniques to further refine the identification of suspicious accesses. The algorithms can be optimized to provide efficiency in detecting malafide accesses. Further we expect to extend this work for real time environment.

## Acknowledgement

We thank Department of Information Technology, Govt. of India for funding the project "Design and Development of Malafide Intension based Privacy Violation Detection".

## References

1. Ashley, P., Hada, S., Karjoth, G., Powers, C., Schunter, M.: Enterprise Privacy Authorization Language (EPAL 1.1) (2003) , IBM Research Report, 3485.
2. Godik, S., Moses, T.: OASIS, eXtensible Access Control Markup Language (XACML). OASIS (07 August 2003)
3. Bhattacharya, J., Gupta, S.K.: Privacy Broker for Enforcing Privacy Policies in Databases. In: KBCS. (2004)
4. IBM: IBM Tivoli Privacy Manager for e-business. http://www-306.ibm.com/software/info/ecatalog/en_TH/products/ K106003J38182X80.html (2003)
5. Bruno, J.B.: Security Breach Could Expose 40M to Fraud. Associated Press (June 18, 2005)
6. Barse, E.L.: Logging For Intrusion And Fraud Detection. Thesis For The Degree of Doctor of Philosophy, ISBN 91-7291-484-X Technical Report no.28D ISSN 1651-4971, School of Computer Science and Engineering, Chalmers University of Technology (2004)
7. Teasley, B.: Does Your Privacy Policy Mean Anything? http://www.clickz.com/experts/crm/analyze_data/article.php (2005)
8. Castano, S., Fugini, M., Martella, G., Samarati, P.: Database Security. Addison Wesley (1995)
9. Agrawal, R., Bayardo, R., Faloutsos, C., Kiernan, J., Rantzau, R., Srikant, R.: Auditing Compliance with a Hippocratic Database. In: Proceedings of the 30th VLDB Conference, Toronto, Canada (2004)
10. LeFevre, K., Agrawal, R., Ercegovac, V., Ramakrishnan, R., Xu, Y., DeWitt, D.: Limiting disclosure in Hippocratic databases. In: 30th Internaltional Conference on Very Large Data Bases, Toronto, Canada, (August, 2004)
11. Nanda, A., Burleson, D.K.: Oracle Privacy Security Auditing. Rampant (2003)

# Towards a Formal Specification Method for Enterprise Information System Security

Anirban Sengupta[1] and Mridul Sankar Barik[2]

[1] Centre for Distributed Computing, Jadavpur University, Kolkata 700032, India
anirban.sg@gmail.com
[2] Dept. of Comp. Sc. & Engg., Jadavpur University, Kolkata 700032, India
mridulsankar@gmail.com

**Abstract.** As information infrastructure is becoming more and more complex, and connected, the security properties like confidentiality, integrity and availability are becoming more and more difficult to protect. The international community is adopting security standards such as ISO 17799 for best practices in security management and Common Criteria for security certification of IT products. It has been recognized that the security of enterprises has to be tackled from the point of view of a management structure than from a purely technological angle, and to achieve this, the primary need is to have a comprehensive security policy. A security model is a formal way of capturing such security policies. Most existing security models cannot support a wide range of security policies. The need is to develop a formal security model that combines the intricacies of the entire gamut of existing security models and supports security policies for a wide range of enterprises.

## 1   Introduction

As information infrastructure is becoming more and more complex, and connected, the security properties like confidentiality, integrity and availability are becoming more and more difficult to protect. The adoption of Information Technology Act in different countries provides the legal validity to electronic documents in business and governance, while providing legal framework to deter the wrong-doers. Also, the international community is adopting Standards such as ISO 17799 [6] for best practices in security management and Common Criteria [7] for security certification of products. It has been recognized that the security of enterprises has to be tackled from the point of view of a management structure than from a purely technological angle.

We define an "enterprise" as an organization (Industry/Govt./Academic) created for business ventures. From the Information Security point of view, an enterprise is characterized by its Information Assets, Software Assets, Hardware Assets and People. *Information assets* pertain to input, processed, output and stored data. *Software Assets* comprise of procedures (automated and manual) that process information. *Hardware Assets* consist of Computing Systems (including technology), Communication Links (Network connections and backbone

A. Bagchi and V. Atluri (Eds.): ICISS 2006, LNCS 4332, pp. 373–376, 2006.

technologies) and IT sites (sites in which IT systems are installed or which are used for IT operations). *People* are the personnel required to plan, organize, acquire, implement, deliver, support, monitor and evaluate the information systems and services. They may be internal (employed), outsourced or contracted as required.

To manage Enterprise Information System Security effectively, the primary need is to have a comprehensive security policy. An enterprise security policy is a high-level statement of enterprise security beliefs, goals, and objectives and the general means for their attainment. It consists of a clearly defined, precise set of rules, for determining authorization on objects (resources) by subjects (users). An Enterprise Information security model is a formal way of capturing such security policies. Security model is an important concept in the design of an enterprise information system. Most existing security models cannot support a wide range of security policies, particularly enterprise level security policies. This research (funded by the Dept. of IT, Ministry of communications & IT, Govt. of India) proposes to develop a formal security model for the Enterprise wide Information Systems that combines the intricacies of the entire gamut of existing security models.

## 2  Security Models and Their Classification

There are several formal security models; they are diverse in several ways: they have been developed at different times, they treat the problem from different perspectives, and they provide different levels of detail in their specifications.

The first classification of security models is based on **system views**. The *finite-state machine model* for computation views a computer system as a finite set of states, together with a transition function to determine what the next state will be, based on the current state and the current value of the input. The *lattice model* [1] [2] [5] for security levels is widely used to describe the structure of multilevel security. The *access matrix model* [9] deals with users' access to information without regard to the semantics of the information in question. *Information-flow models* [5] require that all information transfers obey the flow relation among the security classes.

The second categorization is based on **security attributes**. *Confidentiality* models deal with the requirement that private or confidential information not be disclosed to unauthorized individuals [9] [1] [5]. *Integrity* models cater to the property that data has not been altered in an unauthorized manner while in storage, during processing, or while in transit [2] [4] [3]. *Availability* models ensure that systems work promptly and service is not denied to authorized users [13].

Finally, security models can also be classified based on **access-control techniques**. In *Discretionary Access Control* (DAC) models [9], all the subjects and objects in a system are enumerated and the access authorization rules for each subject and object in the system are specified. In a *Mandatory Access Control* (MAC) model [5] [10], all subjects and objects are classified based on predefined sensitivity levels and information flow is controlled in order to ensure confidentiality and integrity of the information. *Role-based access controls* (RBAC) [11] support arbitrary, organization-specific security policies. *Task-Based Authorization Control* (TBAC) [12] provides the abstractions and mechanisms for the "active" runtime management of security as tasks (activities) progress to completion.

# 3 A Formal Unified Security Model

The available formal models address separate facets of Information Security. Some of them describe Access Control, some of them cryptographic protocols and yet others describe Risks. But for an enterprise going for a comprehensive security program, the need is of a single model, which will cover all these aspects and will help in taking investment decisions and make operational and maintenance management of security infrastructure easier and cost-effective. This further stems from the fact that the five security objectives, viz., Confidentiality, Integrity, Availability, Accountability, and Assurance, are interdependent. Achieving one objective without consideration of the others is seldom possible.

In this backdrop, the proposal is to develop a formal unified model of Enterprise Information System Security Specification. Theory around the proposed unified model will answer questions like: 1)whether the security requirement specification model developed under the proposal is sound and complete, and 2) to what extent the enterprise security policy really maps the security requirement specifications and identifies conflicts.

The first step towards developing a unified model is to specify the Enterprise IT architecture. To obtain a clear understanding of the Enterprise IT architecture, it is necessary to draw up an Enterprise IT Resource Plan. This will consist of 4 parts:

- Network Plan [8] - A graphical representation of the components used in the IT and communications area under consideration and of the manner in which they are networked together. The plan should represent Computing Systems, Communication Links, IT Sites and Software Assets.
- Repository of Stand-alone systems - A graphical representation of the stand-alone systems containing Computing Systems, IT Sites and Software Assets.
- Information Assets - This comprises all input, processed, output and stored data.
- People - The personnel required to handle all other IT resources, like information, hardware, and software assets, for various purposes.

After all the resources have been identified and their properties have been listed, the relationships among them have to be drawn up. The Enterprise IT architecture illustrates how the various entities interact, and how information flows within the enterprise. This leads to a mathematical representation of the enterprise. The security requirements of all the entities can then be identified and aggregated accordingly to specify a unified security model for the enterprise.

# 4    Stage of the Research

The entities of an enterprise have been identified. They are as follows: 1)Information criteria (confidentiality, integrity, availability, authenticity, non-repudiation, compliance) 2)Information asset 3)Software asset (automated and manual procedures) 4)technology 5)computers (client computer, server computer) 6)network components (router, switch) 7)system (computers, network components) 8)link (connection) 9)IT site 10)User 11)Privileges (administrator, power user, guest, etc.) 12)Access permissions (read, delete, append, modify, write, execute)

We are now in the process of defining the relationships among, and functions of, these entities. After that is complete, theorems will be formulated which, in turn, will lead to the unified enterprise information security model.

# References

1. Bell, D.E, and LaPadula, L.J. "Secure Computer Systems: Unified Exposition and Multics Interpretation" ESD-TR-75-306, MTR 2997 Rev. 1, The MITRE Corporation, March 1976.
2. Biba, K. J., "Integrity Considerations for Secure Computer systems," Mitre TR-3153, Mitre Corporation, Bedford, MA, April 1977.
3. Brewer, David F. C. and Michael J. Nash. 1989. "The Chinese Wall Security Policy." In Proceedings of the 1989 IEEE Computer Society Symposium on Security and Privacy, May 1-3, 1989, Oakland, California, 206-214. Washington, D.C.: IEEE Computer Society Press. Oakland, CA.
4. Clark, David D. and David R. Wilson. "Evolution of a Model for Computer Integrity." In Report of the Invitational Workshop on Data Integrity, January 25-27, 1989, Gaithersburg, Maryland. NIST Special Publication 500-168.
5. Denning, D.E. "A Lattice Model of Secure Information Flow". Communications of ACM 19(5): 236-243 (1976).
6. "Information Technology - Code of practice for information security management", ISO/IEC 17799:2005(E), 2005.
7. "Information technology - Security techniques - Evaluation criteria for IT security", ISO/IEC 15408-1:1999(E), 1999.
8. "IT Baseline Protection Manual", BSI, 2004.
9. Lampson, B. W., "Protection", Proc. Fifth Princeton Symposium on Information Sciences and Systems, Princeton University, March 1971, pp. 437-443.
10. Sandhu, R.S., "Lattice-based access control models". IEEE Computer, 26(11):9-19, 1993.
11. Sandhu, R.S., et al. "Role-Based Access Control Models", IEEE Computer 29(2): 38-47, IEEE Press, 1996.
12. Thomas, Roshan K., and Sandhu, R.S., "Task-Based Authorization Controls (TBAC): A Family of Models for Active and Enterprise-Oriented Authorization Management", Proceedings of the IFIP TC11 WG11.3 Eleventh International Conference on Database Security XI: Status and Prospects, p.166-181, August 10-13, 1997.
13. Yu, C-F., and Gligor, V.D., "A Specification and Verification Method for Preventing Denial of Service," IEEE Trans. on Software Engineering, Vol. 16, No. 6, June 1990, 581-592.

# Recent Research on Privacy Preserving Data Mining

Alex Gurevich and Ehud Gudes

Department of Computer Science, Ben-Gurion University, Beer-Sheva, Israel
gurevich@cs.bgu.ac.il, ehud@cs.bgu.ac.il

**Abstract.** We review our recent work on privacy preserving data mining and present a new algorithm for association rules mining in vertically partitioned databases that doesnt use perturbation or secure computation.

## 1  Introduction

In our era Knowledge is not "just" information anymore, it is an asset. Data mining can be used to extract important knowledge from large databases. These days, it is often the case that such databases are distributed among several organizations who would like to cooperate in order to extract global knowledge, but at the same time, privacy concerns may prevent the parties from directly sharing the data among them. The first approach that was taken toward privacy protection in data mining was to perturb the input before the mining [1]. This approach has the benefit of simplicity. At the same time, it takes advantage of the statistical nature of data mining and directly protects the privacy of the data. The drawback of the perturbation approach is that it lacks a formal framework for proving how much privacy is guaranteed. Despite the existence of several models [1,2,4] for studying the privacy attainable through perturbation, there is no formal way to model and quantify the privacy threat from mining of perturbed data, and recently there has been some evidence that for some data, and some kinds of noise, perturbation provides almost no privacy at all [6,7]. A second approach for privacy preserving data mining uses cryptographic techniques, most often the secure computation technique is used [3,5,8,9]. This approach became very popular for two reasons: first, cryptography offers a well defined model for privacy, which includes methodologies for proving and quantifying it. Second, there exists a vast toolset of cryptographic algorithms and constructs which can be used for implementing privacy-preserving data mining algorithms.

While Secure computation (SC) has an advantage over perturbation in that it provides accurate results and not approximation, it is a much slower method and requires considerable computation and communication overhead for each SC step Naturally we would like to develop algorithms which include the advantages of the two approaches and do not include their disadvantages.

Privacy-preserving association rules mining is also an active area of research. Specifically, when data is distributed across multiple sites, and the sites have to mine it cooperatively, the privacy issue is most important. Kantarcioglu and

A. Bagchi and V. Atluri (Eds.): ICISS 2006, LNCS 4332, pp. 377–380, 2006.

Clifton [10] investigated the problem of privacy-preserving distributed mining of association rules on Horizontally partitioned data. The algorithm uses three basic ideas, randomization of the first result, encryption of results at each local site and a final step of secure computation. Vaidya and Clifton (VDC) [9] developed algorithms for privacy preserving association rule mining in Vertically partitioned data. In such databases, item-set in one database is represented as a Boolean membership vector, and the main technique, which uses the Apriori algorithm as its base, computes securely the scalar product of two or more membership vectors and checks whether the result is larger than the threshold. Again, quite complex cryptographic and randomization processes are used.

As mentioned above, the VDC algorithms involve considerable computation overhead, and also have the disadvantage that the relevant parties know exactly the item-set which is currently being computed. Another problem of the VDC algorithms is the fact that all parties know the exact support of each item-set. This fact can cause considerable exposure of the real data as was demonstrated in [11]. That motivated Rozenberg and Gudes (GB) to propose another way to solve the problem using the fake transactions method [11,12]. For example, let us describe the two-party algorithm in more detail. The $n > 2$ case is very similar. Both algorithms follow the basic collaborative Apriori algorithm of *VDC*. However, before applying the algorithm, there is a pre-processing step that populates the individual databases with fake transactions Since the fake transactions do not change real data, but only add fake information, all items with real high support will be found and we only need to eliminate the false positive results. In the first phase one site is designated as a Master, which initiates the protocol and will get the results, and the other site as a Slave. The Master is looking for all large itemsets according to its own real transactions, and check whether the found itemsets are present in the Slave real transactions. This is done with the help of a third untrusted party (this party is not trusted with the database, but it is trusted with computations) or using secure computation. The parties change roles at the end of the phase. The GB algorithms also have some problems. They expose some real data to the parties (even though the parties don't know which data is real and which is fake). Also, they are sensitive to the probing attack, although in [11] there is a method called the e-approximation method which considerably reduces the risk of a probing attack.

The above motivated us to look for a new paradigm to perform privacy-preserving distributed data mining without using the above The main idea is in the architecture which separates the entity which computes the results and the entity which finally gets the results and know what they mean. We demonstrate the idea using the vertically partitioned association rules mining

## 2    The New Architecture and Algorithm

The new architecture is depicted in Figure 1. It is composed of the participating databases, a Miner which decides what computation to be done, and the Calculator which computes without really knowing what itemset it computes.

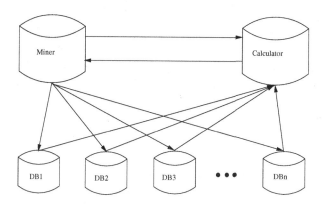

**Fig. 1.** The Architecture

Based on this basic architecture we develop three different models and algorithms. The first model supports vertically partitioned association rules mining, the second model supports horizontally partitioned association rules mining, and the third model is general and supports any data mining task. The first algorithm for vertically partitioned databases is depicted below.

---

**Algorithm 1.** First Algorithm

---

1: The miner sets the variable $i$ (the size of the itemset being checked now) to 1.
2: **repeat**
3:     The miner chooses random permutation of itemsets of i elements
4:     **for** each itemset from step 2 **do**
5:         **if** all the subsets of current itemset are frequent (apriori principle) **then**
6:             The miner orders all participants to encrypt the Transaction-ids of the transactions using the same key.
7:             The miner asks every participant about frequency of current itemset .
8:             The participants send the encrypted numbers of all relevant transactions to the "calculator".
9:                 The "calculator" finds the intersection of the encrypted transactions-ids.
10:                 The "calculator" informs the miner if the current set is frequent.
11:             **end if**
12:     **end for**
13:     The value of i is incremented by 1
14: **until** $i \geq$ the number of database attributes
15: The miner sends the results to the participants.

---

Although this algorithm is somewhat similar to the VDC algorithm in [10], it is different in two respects: the calculator doesn't know which itemset is being checked, and the exact support value is not disclosed. Furthermore, only one level of encryption is used (only transaction-ids are encrypted. )

In terms of *Privacy*, the participants and the "miner" learn nothing but the results as in secure computation. The "calculator" learns the support of the itemsets but without the possibility of knowing which itemset is being tested. No probing attack is possible, since the miner does not hold any part of the database!

In terms of *Communication cost*, in VDC, for every itemset frequency computation, it was necessary to perform secure scalar product computation which takes for every tested set at least three times sending the N values between the parties. In our algorithm, in the worst case, every side sends once, N values to the calculator, which is much less communication overhead. Comparing to GB we save all the preprocessing stage of sending the database with faked transactions.

# References

1. R. Agrawal and R. Srikant. Privacy-preserving data mining. In Proc. of the ACM SIGMOD'00, pages 439-450, Dallas, Texas, USA, May 2000.
2. I. Dinur and K. Nissim. Revealing information while preserving privacy. In Proc. of PODS'03, pages 202 - 210, June 2003.
3. W. Du and M. J. Atallah. Secure multi-party computation problems and their applications: A review and open problems. In Proceedings of the 2001 New Security Paradigms Workshop, Cloudcroft, New Mexico, Sept. 11-13 2001
4. A. Evfimievski, R. Srikant, R. Agrawal, and J. Gehrke. Privacy preserving mining of association rules. In Proc. of ACM SIGKDD'02, pages 217-228, Canada, July 2002.
5. O. Goldreich, S. Micali, and A. Wigderson. How to play any mental game - a completeness theorem for protocols with honest majority. In 19th ACM Symposium on the Theory of Computing, 1987.
6. Z.Huang, W. Du, and B. Chen. Deriving private information from randomized data. In Proc. of ACM SIGMOD'05, 2005.
7. H. Kargupta, S. Datta, Q.Wang, and K. Sivakumar. On the privacy preserving properties of random data perturbation techniques. In Proc. of ICDM'03, page 99, Washington, DC, USA, 2003.
8. Jaideep Vaidya, Chris Clifton: Secure set intersection cardinality with application to association rule mining. Journal of Computer Security 13(4): 593-622 (2005)
9. J.Vaidya, C.Clifton. Privacy Preserving Association Rule Mining in Vertically Partitioned Data. In Proceedings of SIGKDD 2002, Edmonton, Alberta, Canada.
10. J. Vaidya C. Clifton, M. Kantarcioglu, and, "Defining privacy for data mining," in National Science Foundation Workshop on Next Generation Data Mining, H. Kargupta, A. Joshi, and K. Sivakumar, Eds., Baltimore, MD, Nov. 1-3 2002.
11. B. Rozenberg, E. Gudes, Privacy Preserving Data Mining in Vertically Partitioned Databases, 7th Annual IFIP WG 11.3 Working Conference on Database and Applications Security, Estes Park, Colorado, 2003.
12. B. Rozenberg, E. Gudes, "Analysis of Two Approaches for Association Rules Mining in Vertically Partitioned Databases", Proceedings of ICDM workshop on security and privacy, Brighton, UK, 2004.

# Author Index

# Lecture Notes in Computer Science

For information about Vols. 1–4254

please contact your bookseller or Springer